zoom español

Teacher Book

Kirsty Thathapudi

With additional material by:
Abigail Hardwick
Isabel Alonso de Sudea
Maria Isabel Isern Vivancos

OXFORD
UNIVERSITY PRESS

Great Clarendon Street, Oxford OX2 6DP

Oxford University Press is a department of the University of Oxford.
It furthers the University's objective of excellence in research,
scholarship, and education by publishing worldwide in

Oxford   New York

Auckland   Cape Town   Dar es Salaam   Hong Kong   Karachi
Kuala Lumpur   Madrid   Melbourne   Mexico City   Nairobi
New Delhi   Shanghai   Taipei   Toronto

With offices in

Argentina   Austria   Brazil   Chile   Czech Republic   France   Greece
Guatemala   Hungary   Italy   Japan   Poland   Portugal   Singapore
South Korea   Switzerland   Thailand   Turkey   Ukraine   Vietnam

Oxford is a registered trade mark of Oxford University Press
in the UK and in certain other countries

© Copyright holder 2011

The moral rights of the author have been asserted

Database right Oxford University Press (maker)

First published 2011

All rights reserved. No part of this publication may be reproduced,
stored in a retrieval system, or transmitted, in any form or by any means,
without the prior permission in writing of Oxford University Press, or as
expressly permitted by law, or under terms agreed with the appropriate
reprographics rights organization. Enquiries concerning reproduction
outside the scope of the above should be sent to the Rights Department,
Oxford University Press, at the address above

You must not circulate this book in any other binding or cover
and you must impose this same condition on any acquirer

British Library Cataloguing in Publication Data

Data available

ISBN-13: 978-0-19-912758-0

10 9 8 7 6 5 4 3 2 1

Printed in Great Britain by Bell & Bain Ltd, Glasgow

Paper used in the production of this book is a natural, recyclable product
made from wood grown in sustainable forests. The manufacturing process
conforms to the environmental regulations of the country of origin.

Acknowledgements
The authors and publishers would like to thank the following people for
their help and advice: Pippa Mayfield

 **Mixed Sources**
Product group from well-managed
forests and other controlled sources
www.fsc.org   Cert no. TT-COC-002769
© 1996 Forest Stewardship Council

Contents

Summary of Unit Contents	4
Long Term Plan	6
Introduction	7
The components of *Zoom Español 1*	7
Student Book	7
Teacher Book	7
Audio CDs and MP3 files	7
Copymasters	8
Workbooks	8
Oxbox and CD–ROMS	8
Video	9
Course progression	9
The Renewed MFL Framework	10
PLTS in *Zoom Español 1*	10

Teaching notes for *Zoom Español 1*	
Starter Unit ¡Vamos!	11
Unit 0 Me presento	18
Unit 1A Me describo	41
Unit 1B El insti	65
Unit 2A Mi semana	89
Unit 2B Donde vivo yo	111
Unit 3A Me gusta comer…	132
Unit 3B Las vacaciones	155
Unit 4A ¿Lo pasaste bien?	180
Unit 4B La vida tecno	202

Symbols used in this Teacher Book:

 a pairwork activity

 a groupwork activity

 a video activity

 a listening activity – audio on accompanying CD

AT X.X reference to a National Curriculum Attainment Level

PLTS an activity has been selected as an example of particular Personal Learning and Thinking Skills

 core activities are highlighted in pale grey (see Course Progression page 9)

Summary of Unit Contents

	Contexts/Objectives	Grammar	Language learning	Cultural focus	Renewed Framework References
Starter Unit	**Introduction to *Zoom Español 1*** • Learning about Spain and Latin America • Greeting people • Understanding classroom instructions	• Four ways to say 'you' in Spanish	• Learning to pronounce vowels	• An introduction to Spain and Latin America	1.1, 1.4, 3.1, 3.2, 4.1, 4.2, 5.3, 5.4, 5.5, 5.7
Unit 0	**Talking about yourself** • Learning about Spanish-speaking people and culture • Recognising and using greetings • Talking about things you like, using the alphabet • Learning numbers 1–100 • Talking about family members • Spelling names	• Definite and indefinite articles • The verbs *tener* and *ser* • Nouns, gender and verbs	• Recording vocabulary accurately • Learning how to be an independent learner • Memory games	• Spanish people and culture	1.1, 1.4, 1.5, 2.1, 2.4, 2.5, 3.1, 4.1, 4.2, 4.3, 4.4, 5.1, 5.2, 5.3, 5.4, 5.6, 5.8
Unit 1A	**Describing yourself** • Saying dates and birthdays • Describing pets • Giving your nationality and saying what languages you speak • Describing yourself and others	• Possessive adjectives • Adjectival agreement • Working out grammar rules • Present tense of regular verbs	• When not to use capital letters • Pronouncing the Spanish 'c' • Using quantifiers • Extending sentences using simple connectives • Working out grammar rules from a pattern	• Spanish festivals	1.1, 1.4, 1.5, 2.1, 2.4, 2.5, 3.1, 3.2, 4.1, 4.2, 4.3, 4.4, 4.5, 5.1, 5.3, 5.4, 5.6, 5.8
Unit 1B	**School** • Talking about school subjects and your opinions of them • Saying what the time is and when your lessons are • Talking about what there is in your school • Talking about your school uniform and your opinion of it • Comparison of schools in different countries	• Verbs and adjectival agreement • The verbs *tener* and *ser* with telling the time • Verbs in the present tense • The use of subject pronouns in Spanish • *–ar* verbs	• Working out meanings from cognates • Learning vocabulary • *desde...hasta* • Where to put the emphasis in spoken Spanish	• School in Spain	1.1, 1.4, 1.5, 2.1, 2.4, 2.5, 3.1, 3.2, 4.1, 4.2, 4.3, 4.4, 4.5, 5.1, 5.2, 5.3, 5.4, 5.5, 5.8
Unit 2A	**Sport and leisure activities** • Talking about the weather • Talking about free time • Saying what you do in the morning • Talking about what you do after school • Talking about weekend activities	• The radical-changing verb *jugar (ue)* • *gustar* + verb • Patterns in radical-changing verbs • Reflexive verbs • The full verb *ir* – to go	• Recognising and using idioms with the verb *hacer* • Using sequencing to add interest and cohesion to what you write and say	• Spanish sports and sports people	1.1, 1.2, 1.4, 2.1, 2.2, 2.4, 3.1, 4.1, 4.2, 4.3, 4.4, 4.5, 5.1, 5.8

Summary of Unit Contents

Unit	Topic	Grammar	Skills	Culture	References
Unit 2B	**Where you live** • Saying where you live • Giving and understanding directions • Rooms of the house • Describing your bedroom • Giving your opinion of the region where you live	• Differentiating between *ser* and *estar* • Simple imperatives • Prepositions	• Pronouncing cognates correctly • Extending sentences using frequency adverbs • Improving speaking and writing with adjectives • Working out gender of new words	• Living in Spain	1.1, 1.4, 2.1, 2.4, 2.5, 3.1, 3.2, 4.1, 4.2, 4.3, 4.4, 4.5, 5.1, 5.3, 5.4, 5.5, 5.8
Unit 3A	**Eating and drinking** • Saying what you eat at different mealtimes • Talking about food you like and dislike; saying what is healthy • Asking for food in a café • Going out, ordering food, complaining • Saying who you are on the telephone • Different types of food	• Nouns and verbs (to talk about mealtimes) • *más que* and *menos que* • *tengo hambre* and *tengo sed* • Using *tú* and *usted* • Using *ir a* • Adjectives and *se come mucho*	• Giving a short presentation in Spanish • How to remember words	• The difference between mealtimes in Spain and Britain • Food in different cultures	1.1, 1.3, 1.4, 1.5, 2.1, 2.4, 2.5, 3.1, 3.2, 4.2, 4.3, 4.4, 4.5, 5.1, 5.2, 5.3, 5.4, 5.5
Unit 3B	**Holidays** • Talking about means of transport • Discussing accommodation and facilities • Making a reservation • Talking about holiday activities	• The immediate future tense • Comparisons • Formal and informal language (*tú* and *usted*) • Forming and using adverbs • Using a dictionary effectively	• Creating a dialogue from a model • Working out and comparing detail • Recreating own formal and informal dialogues	• Spanish tourist attractions • Cultural differences in the Spanish-speaking world	1.1, 1.2, 1.4, 1.5, 2.1, 2.2, 2.4, 2.5, 3.1, 3.2, 4.1, 4.2, 4.3, 4.4, 4.5, 4.6, 5.1, 5.3, 5.4, 5.5, 5.8
Unit 4A	**Talking about the past** • Saying what can/can't be done in your region and why • Saying what the weather was like • Talking about free time activities in the past tense • Giving your views in a past holiday	• The expression *(no) se puede* • The verb *ir* in the preterite • The preterite of regular verbs • Opinions in the preterite tense	• Avoiding repetition of common vocabulary • Linking sentences to avoid repetition • Writing about someone else • Improving spoken and written work	• Spanish regions	1.1, 1.2, 1.4, 1.5, 2.1, 2.2, 2.4, 2.5, 3.1, 3.2, 4.1, 4.2, 4.3, 4.4, 4.5, 4.6, 5.1, 5.3, 5.4, 5.6, 5.8
Unit 4B	**The media** • Talking about different media-based activities – saying what you like to watch on TV and why • Talking about the type of films you like and why • Describing what a film is about • Describing advantages and disadvantages of different types of media	• Words of frequency • Using *gustar* to say what other people like • The preterite tense • Asking and answering questions • *lo bueno* and *lo malo*	• Pairwork • Carrying out a survey • Looking up verbs in a dictionary • Independent learning • Presenting and defending a point of view	• Spanish media	1.1, 1.2, 1.4, 1.5, 2.1, 2.2, 2.4, 2.5, 3.1, 3.2, 4.1, 4.2, 4.3, 4.4, 4.5, 4.6, 5.1, 5.2, 5.3, 5.4, 5.5, 5.8

Long Term Plan

	Zoom Español 1 Long Term Plan									
		Year 7 objectives						Year 8 objectives*		
	¡Vamos!	Unit 0	Unit 1A	Unit 1B	Unit 2A	Unit 2B	Unit 3A	Unit 3B	Unit 4A	Unit 4B
Strand 1: Listening and speaking (L&S)										
L&S 1.1: Understanding and responding to the spoken word	•	•	•	•	•	•	•	•	•	•
L&S 1.2: Developing capability and confidence in listening								•	•	•
L&S 1.3: Being sensitive to the spoken word							•			
L&S 1.4: Talking together	•	•	•	•	•	•	•	•	•	•
L&S 1.5: Presenting and narrating		•	•	•	•	•	•	•	•	•
Strand 2: Reading and writing (R&W)										
R&W 2.1: Understanding and responding to the written word		•	•	•	•	•	•	•	•	•
R&W 2.2: Developing capability and confidence in reading								•	•	•
R&W 2.3: Being sensitive to the written word										
R&W 2.4: Adapting and building text		•	•	•	•	•	•	•	•	•
R&W 2.5: Writing to create meaning		•	•	•	•	•	•	•	•	•
Strand 3: Intercultural understanding (IU)										
IU 3.1: Appreciating cultural diversity	•	•	•	•	•	•	•	•	•	•
IU 3.2: Recognising different ways of seeing the world	•	•	•	•	•	•	•	•	•	•
Strand 4: Knowledge about language (KAL)										
KAL 4.1: Letters and sounds	•	•	•	•	•	•	•	•	•	•
KAL 4.2: Words	•	•	•	•	•	•	•	•	•	•
KAL 4.3: Gender, number and other inflections		•	•	•	•	•	•	•	•	•
KAL 4.4: Sentence structure		•	•	•	•	•	•	•	•	•
KAL 4.5: Verbs and tenses			•	•	•	•	•	•	•	•
KAL 4.6: Questions and negatives								•	•	•
Strand 5: Language learning strategies (LLS)										
LLS 5.1: Identifying patterns in the target language		•	•	•	•	•	•	•	•	•
LLS 5.2: Memorising		•		•			•			
LLS 5.3: Using knowledge of English or another language	•	•	•	•	•	•	•	•	•	•
LLS 5.4: Working out meaning		•								
LLS 5.5: Using reference materials	•				•	•	•	•	•	•
LLS 5.6: Reading aloud		•	•			•			•	
LLS 5.7: Planning and preparing	•									
LLS 5.8: Evaluating and improving		•	•	•	•	•	•	•	•	•

* Year 8 objectives continue in Zoom Español 2

Introduction

The course

Welcome to *Zoom Español 1*.

Zoom Español 1
- is a broad-ability Spanish course for 11–14 year olds with a fully-integrated video drama
- is fully flexible for all abilities with opportunities for reinforcement and extension throughout
- delivers the revised Key Stage 3 Programme of Study, PLTS and the Renewed Framework for Languages.

The components of Zoom Español 1

Student Book
The 176-page Student Book consists of nine main units, plus two introductory spreads (*¡Vamos!*). Two clear routes through the book are suggested, one for students following a two-year course, and one for students following a three-year course. Depending on the route followed, one unit represents either four or six weeks' work.

The Student Book contains the following sections:

¡Vamos!
This four-page starter unit raises students' awareness of the Spanish language and introduces them to some basic Spanish phrases and greetings, as well as to aspects of the Spanish-speaking world. Page 6 of the ¡Vamos! section introduces some key classroom language.

Unidades 0–4B
There are nine 16-page units set in different contexts. Each unit has been planned to be interesting and motivating, as well as to provide a coherent and systematic approach to language development in terms of grammar, pronunciation and study skills. An outline of the content of each unit is given on pages 4–5 of this book.

Each unit is divided into:
- four core spreads each of which includes activities in all four skills, language learning tips and grammar explanations
- a fifth spread , offering more in-depth coverage of the topic areas specifically intended for students following a three-year Key Stage 3
- a grammar and skills spread (*Labolengua*) which is divided into three sections:
  Grammar (focusing on the key grammar points from the core spreads);
  Skills (promoting language learning strategies);
  Pronunciation
- two pages of reinforcement and extension material, one for lower- and one for higher-ability students (*Extra Star and Extra Plus*), which are ideal for independent work – these can be used in class by students who finish other activities quickly or as alternative homework material
- a test page (*Prueba*), which revises the language and structures of the unit, and can also be used as a quick formative test of all four skills
- a vocabulary list and checklist
- a page of extra reading and homework material (*Leer*).

Leer
Zoom Español 1 has a nine-page reading section for students to attempt once they are confident with the core language of the unit. These pages are designed to encourage independent reading and help students develop reading strategies. There is one reading page per unit, providing activities suitable for students of all abilities. The material can be used in class by students who finish other activities quickly or for homework.

Gramática
The key grammar points taught in each unit are consolidated in a detailed grammar reference section at the back of the Student Book. This section also provides extra practice activities focusing on selected grammar points, with answers at the end of the grammar section for self-checking. Further grammar practice is provided in the Copymasters and Workbooks, and on the *Interactive OxBox CD-ROM*.

Glosario
A Spanish–English glossary contains the words in the Student Book for students' reference.

Teacher Book
Each unit contains the following detailed teaching notes:
- a Unit Overview Grid, providing a summary of the unit: contexts and objectives, language learning, grammar, key language, renewed Framework objectives and NC levels for each spread
- a Week-by-Week overview, providing details of the two- and three-year routes through each unit
- a Planner section for each core teaching spread for ease of lesson planning, providing cross-references to other course components and including suggestions for starter, plenary and homework activities
- ideas for presenting and practising new language
- detailed notes on all the Student Book material, including answers to all activities
- suggestions for further activities to reinforce and extend the content of the Student Book
- transcripts for all listening material and video clips
- answers and transcripts for the Workbook activities.

Audio CDs and MP3 files
The CDs provide the listening material to accompany the Student Book and Workbooks. The listening material was recorded by native Spanish speakers. Sound files for the Student Book and Copymasters are also available in MP3 format on the *Interactive OxBox CD-ROM*.

Introduction

Copymasters
The Copymasters provide opportunities for further practice and extension of the language of the Student Book units. All the Copymasters, together with answers and transcripts, are provided on the *Interactive OxBox CD-ROM*. Each unit has the following Copymasters:
- *Vocabulario*: a list of key vocabulary from the unit, which students can use as a reference or as an aid to learning
- *Ya sé...*: a checklist of the core language of the unit, providing an opportunity for students to review their progress and reflect on areas for improvement
- *Empezar y terminar*: starter and plenary activities
- *Escucha Star and Plus*: one page of listening activities suitable for lower-ability students and one page for higher-ability students
- *Habla*: speaking activities
- *Lee y escribe Star and Plus*: two pages of reading and writing activities, one page suitable for lower-ability students and one page for higher-ability students
- *Gramática*: consolidation and practice of key grammar points
- *¿Cómo se hace?*: language learning strategies
- *Extra Star and Plus*: extra material for students covering **Zoom Español** in three years.

Workbooks
Reinforcement and extension activities are provided in the **Zoom Español 1** Foundation and Higher Workbooks. There is one page to accompany spreads 1–5 of each unit of the Student Book, followed by:
- *Labolengua*: extra grammar practice
- *Técnica*: skills practice and language learning strategies
- *Vocabulario*: a list of key vocabulary from the unit
- *Checklist*: a checklist of the core language of the unit

The Workbooks are designed for students to write in, so are ideal for setting homework. Rubrics are provided in English throughout so that students can work independently.

OxBox CD-ROMs
The **Zoom Español** course is accompanied by two CD-ROMs: the **Zoom Español 1** *Interactive OxBox* and the **Zoom Español 1** *Assessment OxBox*.
- *The Interactive OxBox* is a CD-ROM of teacher and student-oriented resources which parallel the topic coverage of **Zoom Español 1** Student Book.
- The *Assessment OxBox* offers a suite of interactive and paper-based tests to accompany the Student Book.

OxBox also contains a "User Management" folder, into which you can import class registers and create user accounts for your students. OxBox provides two separate environments, one for teachers and one for students. Teachers have access to all of the resources; students can complete interactive activities and take tests that you have assigned to them.

OxBox is compatible with all standard Microsoft Office programs so, as well as being able to create new plans and assessments using the OxBox interface, you can also import your own Word or Excel-based lesson plans and materials into OxBox and file them in one centralised location. Many of the resources included in OxBox are themselves fully editable Word and PowerPoint files, permitting you to adapt them to the needs of a particular class or combine them with your own materials as you see fit.

The **Zoom Español 1** *Interactive OxBox* contains:
Lesson planning:
- Course overviews
- Lesson plans offering ideas and strategies for delivering the *Zoom Español* course, and suggestions on how you can combine the different resources available in the *Zoom Español* Student Book and on OxBox
- The lesson planner provides a simple template in which you can write additional lesson plans which link to resources in OxBox. Using the lesson planner, you can also customise existing plans, tailoring them to different classes by changing the materials used in the lesson.

Teaching materials:
- The video clips that are used throughout the **Zoom Español 1** Student Book
- Audio clips: the audio for the **Zoom Español 1** Student Book and Copymasters
- Copymasters together with answers and transcripts
- An interactive activity accompanying each unit of the **Zoom Español 1** Student Book. These consist of a foundation screen (NC levels 1–4) and a higher screen (NC levels 2–5/6) and practise listening, reading and writing. Interactive activities include the following activity types:
  - drag and drop
  - fill the gap
  - linking lines
  - ordering
  - multiple choice
  - sorting (putting things into categories)
- A record and playback activity and a pronunciation activity to practise speaking
- Pelmanism games
- Grammar presentations which are PowerPoint adaptations of the Labolengua spread
- An eBook of the **Zoom Español 1** Student Book.

The **Zoom Español 1** *Assessment OxBox* contains:
- A diagnostic test to help assess students' level of language awareness and prior knowledge of Spanish going into Year 7 or 8.
- Formative tests, designed to be completed by students as they progress through the course, helping them to master what they have learned and improve any areas of weakness. There are four formative tests for each unit of the course, one for each skill, each consisting of two questions (one at foundation level, and one at higher level). Question types for the listening, reading and writing are as for the interactive activities above.

Introduction

Speaking tests are in the form of record and playback activities. Students have two chances to answer each question, after which they can see a full breakdown of which bits they got right and which wrong.
- Summative tests intended to help you assess students' progress and provide them with a snapshot of the level they have reached at the end of each unit. There are four summative tests for each unit of the course, one for each skill. These are supplied in interactive form and as Word documents that can be printed out if you don't have access to the ICT suite. In a summative assessment, students may only attempt each question once and will not receive any feedback until they see their final result at the end of the test. Once all the members of a class have sat a summative test, the results are aggregated automatically enabling you to identify areas of strength and weaknesses.
- Summative end-of-term and end-of-year tests customised according to the route you are taking (two-year or three-year). These end-of-term and end-of-year tests will be made up of summative test questions for each skill for each unit. Depending on the route you are following, one suggestion of how to use the questions is as follows:

	Test	2-year pathway	3-year pathway
1st year	End of term 1	Book 1 Units 0–1B	Book 1 Units 0–1A
	End of term 2	Book 1 Units 2A–3A	Book 1 Units 1B–2A
	End of term 3	Book 1 Units 3B–4B	Book 1 Units 2B–3A
2nd year	End of term 1	Book 2 Units 0–1B	Book 1 Units 3B–4A
	End of term 2	Book 2 Units 2A–3A	Book 1 Unit 4B
	End of term 3	Book 2 Units 3B–4B	Book 2 Units 0–1B
3rd year	End of term 1		Book 2 Units 2A–2B
	End of term 2		Book 2 Units 3A–3B
	End of term 3		Book 2 Units 4A–4B

- Summative assessment guidance notes including answers, the marks available for each question and a breakdown of the National Curriculum levels that particular overall percentage scores equate to.

Video

A key feature of *Zoom Español 1* is a video drama focusing on four teenagers. It is available as part of the *Interactive OxBox* package. The function of the video is threefold:
- it serves to provide an authentic view of life in a Spanish-speaking country
- it introduces four aspirational Spanish-speaking characters, providing students with added motivation for learning Spanish
- it provides examples of key language in use, translating language learning from theory into practice.

There are two video clips per unit:
- an episode of the video drama featuring four teenagers, which ties in with activities on one or more of the four core spreads
- a video blog, in which one of the four teenagers talks about the unit topic from his or her personal perspective.

Each video drama can be used in its entirety to set the scene for the corresponding unit. Later in the unit, excerpts from the video drama will be used again to focus on specific language points. The level of language in the video drama is challenging but is made accessible for all via the activities and support provided in the Student Book and suggested in the teaching notes. This approach enables students of all abilities to experience authentic material at a higher level.

Course progression

Zoom Español is a two-part course, consisting of two Student Books of nine units each. It caters both for schools following a two-year Key Stage 3 and for those following a three-year Key Stage 3 by offering different 'routes' through each unit.

- For the three-year Key Stage 3, we suggest that you cover each unit in its entirety, including core spreads 1–4, the optional spread 5 (which provides more in-depth coverage of the unit themes) and spread 6 (grammar and skills), selecting additional material from the Extra and Leer pages as appropriate. This provides sufficient material for a half-term's teaching per unit. Following this route, two units are covered per term.
- For the two-year Key Stage 3, we suggest that your main focus should be core spreads 1–4 and spread 6 (grammar and skills), but that you may wish to use additional material selectively if time permits. On the core spreads themselves, certain activities are optional, so you may wish to use these selectively too. In the teaching notes, we have used pale grey highlighting to identify core activities on the core spreads, so that it is easy to see what is optional and what is essential. Following this 'accelerated' route, three units are covered per term.

The Week-by-Week overviews, which can be found at the beginning of each unit's teaching notes in this book, give a detailed breakdown of which activities and spreads to cover each week according to the route you are following. Essential activities in each spread are also highlighted.

Introduction

PLTS in Zoom Español 1

A key aim of *Zoom Español 1* is that students should be able to learn in a meaningful way, thinking flexibly, analysing language, problem solving, justifying answers and making predictions based on previous knowledge. The activities types included in *Zoom Español 1* help to promote thinking skills and creativity. The Planner section at the beginning of each spread lists some of the activities that promote any one of the six personal learning and thinking skills. As a guide, the following features and types of activity in *Zoom Español 1* help to promote the six PLTS:

- **Independent enquirers**
  - Video drama, video blog, *Leer section*: provide stimulus material prompting students to explore aspects of Spanish lifestyle and culture and to consider different attitudes and perspectives.
- **Creative thinkers**
  - *Think* boxes throughout, *Labolengua*: encourage students to think creatively about language, e.g. by identifying and explaining language patterns, working out meaning and developing language learning strategies.
  - *Challenge* (on spreads 1–5 of each unit) and other open-ended activities: provide opportunities for students to give a creative or personal response to the unit themes.
- **Reflective learners**
  - Spread objectives: clearly state the focus of each spread, so that students know what they are about to learn and can review their progress afterwards.
  - NC levels shown for key activities in the Student Book: this helps students to evaluate their progress and set goals. Some of the *Think* boxes encourage sharing of assessment criteria with students, so that they understand what needs to be done in order to achieve a particular NC level.
  - *Prueba* and "I can …" checklist (end of each unit): opportunity for students to review what they've learned and reflect on areas for improvement.
- **Team workers**
  - Opportunities throughout for students to work together in pairs and groups.
- **Self-managers**
  - *Think* boxes, *Labolengua*: encourage students to take responsibility for their own learning.
  - *Glosario* (end-of-unit, end-of-book), *Gramática* (end-of-book): encourage independent use of reference materials.
  - *Prueba* and "I can …" checklist: opportunity for students to review what they've learned and set their own goals for improvement.
  - *Extra Star, Extra Plus, Leer section*: ideal for independent work.
  - Workbooks: designed for self-study.
- **Effective participators**
  - Opportunities throughout for students to engage with issues of interest to young people and to consider different attitudes and perspectives.

The Renewed MFL Framework

Zoom Español has been carefully planned to ensure that all Framework objectives are covered in familiar contexts.

- **The Long Term Plan** on page 6 of this book provides an overview of the objectives to be covered in *Zoom Español 1*. The Year 8 objectives continue into *Zoom Español 2*.
- **The Summary of Unit Contents** grid on page 4 shows the objectives covered in each unit of *Zoom Español 1*.
- **The Unit Overview grids** which can be found at the beginning of the teaching notes for each unit in this book show which objectives are covered in each spread of each unit.
- The **Planner** section at the beginning of each spread includes a list of the objectives covered in that spread.

Zoom Español reflects the focus of the Renewed MFL Framework on key areas of teaching and learning. These include:

- Starters – suggestions for starter activities for each core spread are given in the Planner sections in this Teacher Book and are given in the lesson plans on the OxBox Interactive CD-ROM. Additional starter activities are provided on the *Empezar y terminar Copymasters*.
- Setting lesson objectives – The Planner sections provide a clear list of objectives for each spread.
- Modelling – *Zoom Español* provides clear examples for all activities where appropriate.
- Questioning
- Practice
- Plenaries – suggestions for plenary activities for each core spread are given in the Planner sections in this Teacher Book and are given in the lesson plans on the OxBox Interactive CD-ROM. Additional plenary activities are provided on the *Empezar y terminar Copymasters*.

¡Vamos!

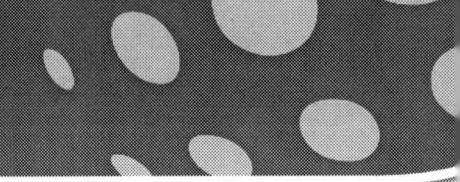

Unit Objectives

Contexts and cultural focus: An introduction to Spain and Latin America
Grammar: Four ways to say 'you' in Spanish
Language learning: Learning to pronounce vowels

¡Hola! páginas 4–5

Planner

Objectives
- listen to some greetings
- practise the five vowel sounds
- find out what you already know about Spain and Latin America

Resources
Students' Book, pages 4–5
CD 1, tracks 2–3
Foundation Workbook, pages 4–5
Higher Workbook, pages 4–5
Foundation Workbook audio, tracks 2–8
Higher Workbook audio, tracks 2–8

Key language
¡Hola!; ¿Qué tal?; Saludos; Adiós; Me llamo...

PLTS
Activity 3: Independent enquirers
Challenge: Team workers, Self-managers, Independent enquirers

Renewed Framework references
1.1, 1.4, 3.1, 3.2, 4.1, 4.2

Starters
- Ask students to look at the map of Spain as a class. Look at the statistics in the box. How do these compare with other European countries such as the UK, France and Germany? (UK population = 62,041708; France population = 65,447374; Germany population = 81,757600)
- Have a class brainstorming session. What do students already know about Spain? Who has visited Spain/Latin America?

Plenaries
- Have a class quiz on the topic of Spain and Latin America. Split the class into two teams. Each team makes up questions to ask the other team (you decide how many questions there should be). The team who answers the most correctly wins.
- Display some Spanish words on the topic of the spread that contain vowel sounds. Go round the class asking students to say one of the words, ensuring that they pronounce the vowel sound correctly.

Homework/Self-study
- Activity 3: Students find out as much as they can about Spain or one of the Spanish-speaking countries mentioned. If any of the students have visited one of these countries, invite them to share photos or to talk about their stay there.
Challenge: Students present their findings to the class.

 1 Escucha y repite.
Students listen and repeat what they hear.

🎧 **CD 1, track 2** página 4, actividad 1
- ¡Hola! ¿Qué tal? Soy Eva Hernández López de Barcelona.
- Adiós por ahora de Khalid.
- Me llamo José María Martín. ¡Hasta luego!
- Saludos de Marisa García de Buenos Aires

Pronunciation
Students listen and repeat the sounds.

🎧 **CD 1, track 3** página 4, pronunciation
a – e – i – o – u

 2 Pregunta y contesta.
Look at the map of Latin America as a class. Point out the various countries and their capital cities. Then ask questions to check understanding, e.g. ¿Cómo se llama la capital de…? Explain to students

¡Vamos!

what this question means and how to answer it, i.e. *Se llama…*. Students now work with a partner. They take it in turns to ask and answer questions about the map of Latin America, using the phrases, *¿Cómo se llama la capital de…?* and *Se llama….*

PLTS **3 ¿Cuánto sabes ya?**
Students try to answer the questions to see how much they already know about Spain and Spanish-speaking countries. They then consider how these countries compare with each other and with other European countries. Can they suggest ways of learning statistics and names of countries and capitals? They could use mnemonics to remember lists or facts.

PLTS **Challenge**
Write down at least five things you know about Spain or Latin America. Pool your ideas with the rest of the class and make up a quiz. Find out more about one of the countries of Latin America.

More able classes could produce simple brochures about the country of Latin America of their choice.

Durante la clase   páginas 6–7

Planner

Objectives
- understand classroom instructions

Resources
Students' Book, pages 6–7
CD 1, tracks 4–6
Foundation Workbook, pages 6–7
Higher Workbook, pages 6–7
Foundation Workbook audio, CD 3 tracks 28–40
Higher Workbook audio, CD 4 tracks 9–15

Key language
repite; habla; lee; escribe; contesta; indica; pregunta; mira; empareja; escucha
¿Qué página es? ¿Qué número es? ¿Cómo se dice … en español? ¿Cómo se escribe? ¿Qué quiere decir … en español? No entiendo. No lo sé. ¿Puedo ir al baño?/¿Me permite ir al baño? No tengo bolígrafo/lápiz. ¿Me prestas un bolígrafo? Por favor. Gracias.

Grammar
- Four ways to say 'you' in Spanish

Renewed Framework references
1.1, 1.4, 4.1, 5.3, 5.4, 5.5, 5.7

PLTS
Activity 5: Creative thinkers
Challenge: Creative thinkers, Self-managers, Team workers

Starters
- Display a list of class instructions in Spanish in one column and a jumbled list of the same instructions in English in a second column. Give students a time limit to match the Spanish to the English. Check answers as a class.

Plenaries
- Play a version of 'Simon Says' using classroom instructions. Decide on actions for each of the instructions first, e.g. for *escucha*, students could cup their ear as if listening to something, etc.
- Display a list of people, e.g. policeman, best friend, shop assistant, etc. and ask students to decide how they would say 'you' in Spanish for each one.

Homework/Self-study
Students write down as many instructions in Spanish as they can ready for the Challenge Activity.

AT 1.1 **1 Escucha y repite.**
Students listen and repeat what they hear.

AT 1.1 **2 Escucha e indica.**
Students listen again and this time point to the correct illustration.

 CD 1, track 4   página 6, actividad 1
escucha, repite, habla, lee, escribe, pregunta, indica, contesta, mira, empareja.

 CD 1, track 5   página 6, actividad 2
habla, escucha, contesta, empareja, escribe

¡Vamos!

Answers:
habla – c speak; escucha – a listen; contesta – h answer; empareja – j pair up; escribe – e write

AT 2.1   **3** **¡Te toca a ti! Por turnos con tu compañero.**
Students work with a partner. Partner A gives an instruction; partner B points to the relevant illustration. They then swap roles.

AT 2.1   **4** **¿Verdad o mentira? True or false?**
Students work with a partner. They give an instruction and an English meaning. Their partner says if it is true or false. They then swap roles.

Gramática
Explain to students that in Spanish there are four different ways of saying 'you'. Using the illustrations and bullet points in the Students' Book, tell students what these are and when they should be used. Ask students to work out which 'you' you would use when speaking to: a friend's grandparents, a teacher, the head teacher, and the young brother of a friend. Finally, point out that the classroom instructions at the top of the page are for one person.

Answers:
***friend's grandparents:** ustedes; **a teacher:** usted; **the head teacher:** usted; **the young brother of a friend:** tú*

AT 1.2   **5 Escucha y lee.**
PLTS   Students listen to and read the cartoon strip. They note down and words or phrases they can guess the meaning of.

 CD 1, track 6   página 7, actividad 5
1 ¿Qué página es?
2 ¿Qué número es?
3 ¿Cómo se dice… en español?
4 ¿Cómo se escribe?
5 ¿Qué quiere decir… en español?
6 No entiendo.
7 No lo sé.
8 ¿Puedo ir al baño? / ¿Me permite ir al baño?
9 No tengo bolígrafo / lápiz.
10 ¿Me prestas un bolígrafo?
11 Por favor.
12 Gracias.

AT 3.2   **6 Empareja.**
Students match the English phrases to the appropriate Spanish phrases from Activity 5.

Answers:
a 3; b 4; c 7; d 6; e 9; f 10; g 8; h 11; i 12; j 5; k 2; l 1

AT 4.2   **Challenge**
PLTS   **Think of five more instructions or classroom phrases then look them up in a dictionary or ask your teacher for the Spanish. Put all your ideas together and make a poster for the classroom.**
Encourage students to try and write the instructions in Spanish themselves before checking that they are all correct.

Foundation Workbook

Página 4 Pronunciation, vowels
- Use with Students' Book, pages 4–5

AT 1.1   **1 Listen and practise the vowels with the actions.**
The actions will help students who are visual learners.

 CD 3, track 28   página 4, actividad 1
We are going to practise saying the Spanish vowel sounds. I want you to do actions to go with each vowel, to really fix it in your mind. Let's start with 'a'. Open your mouth wide and make a big wide sound. As you say it, draw a big wide letter a in the air: a, a, a
'e' is another nice big sound. Draw a big letter e as you say it: e, e, e
And the same for 'o'. Open your mouth wide and draw a big letter o: o, o, o
Now all three: a, e, o

Next the sound 'i'. I want you to do the dot of the i as you say it. It's quite a short sharp sound: i, i, i
And the sound 'u'. You'll have to have your mouth quite closed for this, and even stick your lips out, 'u'. So I want you to draw a little u shaped mouth and concentrate on the 'u' sound: u, u, u
Let's put them all together, with the actions:
big letters: a, e, o; dot: i; mouth: u; a, e, o, i, u; a, e, o, i, u

AT 2.1   **2 Practise saying the names of these Spanish football clubs. Listen and check.**

 CD 3, track 29   página 4, actividad 2
Gran Canaria, Salamanca, La Palma, Osasuna

13

¡Vamos!

AT 2.1	**3 Try these combinations of vowels. Say them separately, then together, then in a word. Listen and check.** Further practice of sounding Spanish vowels correctly.

> **CD 3, track 30** — página 4, actividad 3
>
> u; a; ua; cuatro
> e; i; ei; seis
> i; e; ie; siete
> u; e; ue; nueve

AT 2.1	**4 Now try saying these Spanish football clubs.** Practice of using the combinations of vowels.

AT 2.1	**5 Remember to pronounce all the vowels. Say these words.** Volunteers could say these words in front of the class. Do they sound Spanish?

AT 2.1	**6 Say these Spanish football clubs.** Further practice of pronouncing vowels within words.

Página 5 Pronunciation, soft and hard consonants

- Use with Students' Book, pages 34–35

AT 1.1	**1 Listen and repeat these words. Underline the soft c (pronounced like a 'th').** Students practise pronouncing consonants. Remind them of the rule for pronouncing the 'c' sound in Spanish.

> **CD 3, track 31** — página 5, actividad 1
>
> casa, cinco, cocina

Answers: as in audioscript

AT 1.1	**2 Listen and repeat these words. Underline the soft g/j (pronounced like 'ch' in 'loch').** Allow students to listen and repeat as many times as necessary.

> **CD 3, track 32** — página 5, actividad 2
>
> geografía, Los Ángeles, José

Answers: as in audioscript

AT 2.1	**3 Find the soft ci/ce/z sound and underline it in these Spanish football clubs. Say the words, then listen and check.**

> **CD 3, track 33** — página 5, actividad 3
>
> Barcelona, Albacete, Celta de Vigo, Zaragoza

Answers: as in audioscript

AT 2.1	**4 Find the soft ge/gi/j sound and underline it in these Spanish football clubs. Say the words, then listen and check.**

> **CD 3, track 34** — página 5, actividad 4
>
> Gijón, Getafe, Ejido

Answers: as in audioscript

AT 2.1	**5 Use everything you've learned so far. Underline the tricky bits in these names, then try saying them.** More practice of recognising tricky sounds within words. Listen to students saying these words to ensure that they have fully understood how Spanish pronunciation differs from English pronunciation.

Página 6 Pronunciation, Spanish consonants

- Use with Students' Book, pages 10–11

AT 1.1	**1 Listen, then practise saying these sounds. First on their own, then in words.**

> **CD 3, track 35** — página 6, actividad 1
>
> qu, qu, ¿qué?
> ll, ll, me llamo
> rr, rr, burro
> ch, ch, ocho
> ñ, ñ, España

AT 2.1	**2 In *er*, *ir* and *ar*, do not change the sound of the vowel from 'e', 'i' or 'a'. Try saying these words.** Students practise saying the words. If possible get a few volunteers to say these in class.

AT 2.1	**3 Underline the tricky consonants, then try saying the names of these Spanish football clubs.** Further practice of pronouncing consonants in words.

AT 2.1	**4 Pretend to read the Spanish football results. You will need the following numbers.** Students could also practise this in front of the class – who sounds the most convincing?

¡Vamos!

Página 7 Pronunciation, words and sentences
- Use with Students' Book, pages 114–115

 1 Listen to these words ending in a vowel, 's' or 'n'. Circle the syllable that has the stress.

> 🎧 **CD 3, track 36**   página 7, actividad 1
>
> <u>ca</u>sa, <u>ca</u>sas, <u>ca</u>san, <u>ha</u>bla, <u>ha</u>blas, <u>ha</u>blan

Answers: as in audioscript

 2 Listen to these words ending in a consonant (not 's' or 'n'). Circle the syllable that has the stress.

> 🎧 **CD 3, track 37**   página 7, actividad 2
>
> ho<u>tel</u>, ha<u>blar</u>, profe<u>sor</u>, Ma<u>drid</u>, di<u>ez</u>

Answers: as in audioscript

 3 Listen to these words which have an accent. Circle the syllable that has the stress.

> 🎧 **CD 3, track 38**   página 7, actividad 3
>
> jar<u>dín</u>, mate<u>má</u>ticas, Al<u>me</u>ría, Los <u>Án</u>geles

Answers: as in audioscript

 4 Listen and repeat. Notice how one word can run into the next.

> 🎧 **CD 3, track 39**   página 7, actividad 4
>
> ¿Dónde está? Está en España. Se llama Alberto.

AT 2.1   **5 Be careful with words that look similar to English words. Say these words. Then listen and check.**

> 🎧 **CD 3, track 40**   página 7, actividad 5
>
> hotel, restaurante, tomate, David Beckham

AT 2.2   **6 Read these sentences aloud.**
This activity consolidates what students have learnt so far and provides the opportunity to practise pronouncing tricky vowels and consonants correctly in words and sentences.

Higher Workbook

Página 4 Pronunciation, vowels
- Use with Students' Book, pages 4–5

 1 Listen and practise the vowels with the actions.
The actions will help students who are visual learners.

> 🎧 **CD 4, track 2**   página 4, actividad 1
>
> We are going to practise saying the Spanish vowel sounds. I want you to do actions to go with each vowel, to really fix it in your mind. Let's start with 'a'. Open your mouth wide and make a big wide sound. As you say it, draw a big wide letter a in the air: a, a, a
> 'e' is another nice big sound. Draw a big letter e as you say it: e, e, e
> And the same for 'o'. Open your mouth wide and draw a big letter o: o, o, o
> Now all three: a, e, o

Next the sound 'i'. I want you to do the dot of the i as you say it. It's quite a short sharp sound: i, i, i
And the sound 'u'. You'll have to have your mouth quite closed for this, and even stick your lips out, 'u'. So I want you to draw a little u shaped mouth and concentrate on the 'u' sound: u, u, u
Let's put them all together, with the actions:
big letters: a, e, o; dot: i; mouth: u; a, e, o, i, u; a, e, o, i, u

 2 Practise saying the names of these Spanish football clubs. Listen and check.

> 🎧 **CD 4, track 3**   página 4, actividad 2
>
> Gran Canaria, Salamanca, La Palma, Osasuna, Granada

15

¡Vamos!

AT 2.1 **3** Try these combinations of vowels. Say them separately, then together, then in a word. Listen and check.
Further practice of sounding Spanish vowels correctly.

 CD 4, track 4 página 4, actividad 3

u; a; ua; cuatro
e; i; ei; seis
e; i; ei; veinte
i; e; ie; siete
u; e; ue; nueve

AT 2.1 **4** Now try saying these Spanish football clubs.
Practice of using the combinations of vowels.

AT 2.1 **5** Remember to pronounce all the vowels. Say these words.
Volunteers could say these words in front of the class. Do they sound Spanish?

AT 2.1 **6** Say these Spanish football clubs.
Further practice of pronouncing vowels within words.

Página 5 Pronunciation, soft and hard consonants
- Use with Students' Book, pages 34–35

AT 1.1 **1** Listen and repeat these words. Underline the soft c (pronounced like a 'th').
Students now practise pronouncing consonants. Remind students of the rule for pronouncing the 'c' sound in Spanish.

 CD 4, track 5 página 5, actividad 1

casa, cinco, cocina

Answers: as in audioscript

AT 1.1 **2** Listen and repeat these words. Underline the soft g/j (pronounced like 'ch' in 'loch').
Allow students to listen and repeat as many times as necessary.

CD 4, track 6 página 5, actividad 2

geografía, Los Ángeles, José

Answers: as in audioscript

AT 2.1 **3** Find the soft ci/ce/z sound and underline it in these Spanish football clubs. Say the words, then listen and check.

CD 4, track 7 página 5, actividad 3

Barcelona, Albacete, Celta de Vigo, Zaragoza

Answers: as in audioscript

AT 2.1 **4** Find the soft ge/gi/j sound and underline it in these Spanish football clubs. Say the words, then listen and check.

CD 4, track 8 página 5, actividad 4

Gijón, Getafe, Ejido

Answers: as in audioscript

AT 2.1 **5** Use everything you've learned so far. Underline the tricky bits in these words, and then try saying them.
More practice of recognising tricky sounds within words. If possible, listen to students saying these words to ensure that they have fully understood how Spanish pronunciation differs from English pronunciation.

Página 6 Pronunciation, Spanish consonants
- Use with Students' Book, pages 10–11

AT 1.1 **1** Listen, then practise saying these sounds. First on their own, then in words.

 CD 4, track 9 página 6, actividad 1

qu, qu, ¿qué?
ll, ll, me llamo
rr, rr, burro
ch, ch, ocho
ñ, ñ, España

AT 1.1 **2** Listen carefully to the words. Circle the correct answer.

 CD 4, track 10 página 6, actividad 2

voy, verde, identidad, ciudad

Answers: a bit like a 'b'; a bit like a 'th'

¡Vamos!

 3 In *er*, *ir* and *ar*, do not change the sound of the vowel from 'e', 'i' or 'a'. Try saying these words.
Students practise saying the words. If possible get a few volunteers to say these in class.

 4 Underline the tricky consonants, then try saying the names of these Spanish football clubs.
Further practice of pronouncing consonants in words.

 5 Pretend to read the Spanish football results. You will need the following numbers.
Students could also practise this in front of the class – who sounds the most convincing?

Página 7 Pronunciation, words and sentences
- Use with Students' Book, pages 114–115

AT 1.1 **1** Listen to these words ending in a vowel, 's' or 'n'. Circle the syllable that has the stress.

> 🎧 **CD 4, track 11**   página 7, actividad 1
>
> <u>ca</u>sa, <u>ca</u>sas, <u>ca</u>san, <u>ha</u>bla, <u>ha</u>blas, <u>ha</u>blan

Answers: as in audioscript

AT 1.1 **2** Listen to these words ending in a consonant (not 's' or 'n'). Circle the syllable that has the stress.

> 🎧 **CD 4, track 12**   página 7, actividad 2
>
> ho<u>tel</u>, ha<u>blar</u>, profe<u>sor</u>, Ma<u>drid</u>, di<u>ez</u>

Answers: as in audioscript

 3 Listen to these words which have an accent. Circle the syllable that has the stress.

> 🎧 **CD 4, track 13**   página 7, actividad 3
>
> jar<u>dín</u>, mate<u>má</u>ticas, Al<u>me</u>ría, Los <u>Án</u>geles

Answers: as in audioscript

AT 1.1 **4** Listen and repeat. Notice how one word can run into the next.

> 🎧 **CD 4, track 14**   página 7, actividad 4
>
> ¿Dónde está? Está en España. Se llama Alberto.

 5 Be careful with words that look similar to English words. Say these words. Then listen and check.

> 🎧 **CD 4, track 15**   página 7, actividad 5
>
> hotel, restaurante, tomate, David Beckham

AT 2.2 **6** Read these sentences aloud.
This activity consolidates what students have learnt so far and provides the opportunity to practise pronouncing tricky vowels and consonants correctly in words and sentences.

0 Me presento

Unit Objectives

Contexts and cultural focus: Spanish people and culture
Grammar: Definite and indefinite articles; the verbs *tener* and *ser*
Language learning: Greetings; the alphabet; recording vocabulary accurately; memory games – learning how to learn

- *Aim:* To learn how to introduce and speak about yourself and your family in Spanish
- Each unit has an associated video which will feature throughout the unit. Below is the transcript of the video for this unit.
- As a starter activity to introduce the unit and familiarise students with the language they will meet, you may find it useful for the class to view the video as a whole.

Video script (CD 1, track 12)

Khalid: Buenas tardes, Sra Pérez. ¿Está Montse en casa? ¿No? Ah, vale. Gracias, adiós, adiós.
Marisa: ¿Diga? Sí, papá. Sí, papá. Sí, sí. No, papá, no. Vale, sí, papá. Vale. Adiós, papá.
Khalid: Hola, me llamo Khalid.
Marisa: ¿Ka-?
Khalid: Khalid. K-h-a-l-i-d. Pero me puedes llamar sólo Khal.
Marisa: ¡Khal! Es un nombre muy bonito. ¿No es español, verdad?
Khalid: No. Es marroquí. Mis padres son marroquís. Yo también soy marroquí.
Marisa: Hablas muy bien español.
Khalid: Gracias y tú también. Tú tampoco eres española, ¿verdad?
Marisa: No, soy argentina, de Buenos Aires.
Khalid: ¡Ah! Es verdad, en Argentina también se habla español. Así que eres de Buenos Aires, ¡eso está muy bien! Y tú, ¿cómo te llamas?
Marisa: ¡Oh! Perdona, soy Marisa. Marisa García.
Khalid: ¿Nada más? ¿No María Magdalena López García?
Marisa: No, sólo Marisa García.
Khalid: Encantado de conocerte.
Marisa: Sí, encantada de conocerte a ti también.
[pause]
Khalid: No, no ... se llama Jalal. J-a-l-a-l.
Marisa: Vale. Entonces, tu hermano se llama Elías.
Khalid: Sí.
Marisa: Y tu hermana es Sara y tiene 16 años.
Khalid: Sí.
Marisa: Y tu padre se llama Sidan.
Khalid: No, es Zitane: Z-i-t-a-n-e…
Marisa: ¡Ah, vale! Zitane. Pero, ¿Jalal tiene 17 años?
Khalid: No. Jalal tiene 7 años.
Marisa: Vale, 7 años.
Khalid: Bueno, en realidad tiene siete años y medio.
Marisa: (laughing) Ya, perdona, siete años y medio.
Khalid: Y tú, ¿cuántos años tienes?
Marisa: 15.
Khalid: Pues yo tengo 15 años y medio.
[pause]

Khalid: ¿Tienes hermanos o hermanas?
Marisa: Sí tengo un hermano, se llama Diego.
Khalid: ¿Como Diego Maradona?
Marisa: Sí... tiene 19 años y estudia en Buenos Aires.
Khalid: ¿No tienes ninguna hermana?
Marisa: No, no tengo hermanas. Sólo somos mi hermano y yo.
Khalid: Y ¿qué haces en Barcelona?
Marisa: Mi padre es diplomático. Está aquí por su trabajo, pero sólo estaremos un año.
Khalid: Ah, vale. ¿Y tu madre?
Marisa: Mis padres están divorciados. Mi madre trabaja en Buenos Aires. Es dentista.
Khalid: ¡Ah!
Marisa: Sí.
Khalid: Mi padre es médico. Es cardiólogo.
Marisa: Ah, ya.
Khalid: Y tu madre, ¿en qué trabaja?
Marisa: Mi madre es profesora de francés.
Khalid: ¡Qué bien!
Marisa: No, no está tan bien. Es profesora de francés en mi colegio.
Khalid: Vale, de acuerdo, ya entiendo. La verdad es que no está tan bien.
Marisa: ¿Hablas francés también?
Khalid: Sí, hablo francés y catalán, inglés y entiendo italiano, y también árabe.
Marisa: Impresionante.
[phone rings]
Marisa: Es mi padre. Tengo que irme.
Khalid: ¿Me das tu número de teléfono?
Marisa: Vale.
Khalid: Vale.
Marisa: El 6 66 44 63 24.
Khalid: Vale. 6 66 44 63 24.
Marisa: Perfecto.
Khalid: Mi número es 6 95 05 15 48.
[phone rings]
Marisa: Hola, papá. Sí, papá, no papá. Ya voy … . Bueno, me tengo que ir … Adiós.

Me presento 0

Unit 0 Me presento Overview grid						
Page reference	Contexts and objectives	Language learning	Grammar	Key language	Framework	AT level
Pages 8–9 **Quiz**	• learn facts about Spanish-speaking people and culture • recognise and use greetings correctly			*Buenos días; Buenas tardes; Buenas noches*	1.1, 1.4, 3.1, 4.1	1.2, 2.2, 3.1
Pages 10–11 **Me flipa; me molan**	• talk about things you like, using the alphabet • learn numbers 1–20	• record vocabulary accurately	• use definite and indefinite articles correctly		1.1, 1.4, 2.1, 4.1, 4.3, 5.1, 5.3	1.1–2, 2.1–2, 3.1
Pages 12–13 **La familia**	• talk about family members	• learn how to be an independent learner	• learn and use the verbs *tener* and *ser*	*la familia; los abuelos; el abuelo; la abuela; los padres; el padre; la madre; el padrastro; la madrastra; el marido (el esposo); la mujer (la esposa); los parientes; el tío; la tía; el primo; la prima; los niños; el hermano; la hermana; el hermanastro; la hermanastra; el hijo único; la hija única; casado/a; divorciado/a*	1.1, 1.4, 1.5, 2.1, 2.4, 3.1, 5.1, 5.4	1.3, 2.2–3, 3.1–2, 4.2–3
Pages 14–15 **¿Cuántos años tienes?**	• name family members, say ages and numbers 1–100 • recycle language and verbs from the unit	• practise memory games – learn how to learn!		*veintiuno; veintidós; veintitrés; veinticuatro; veinticinco; veintiséis; veintisiete; veintiocho; veintinueve; treinta; cuarenta; cincuenta; sesenta; setenta; ochenta; noventa; cien*	1.1, 1.4, 2.1, 2.4, 4.1, 5.1, 5.2, 5.8	1.1–3, 2.1–3, 3.3, 4.1–2
Pages 16–17 **Gente y números**	• use the vocabulary of this unit in a wider context	• reinforce the skills you have learnt	• revise and extend the grammar you have learnt		1.1, 1.4, 1.5, 2.1, 2.4, 2.5, 4.1, 5.8	1.1–4, 2.1–3, 3.2–3, 4.2
Pages 18–19 **Labolengua**	• review language and grammar from the unit		• nouns, gender and verbs		1.1, 1.4, 4.1, 4.3, 4.5, 5.1, 5.8	

0 Me presento

Pages 20–21 **Extra Star** **Extra Plus**	• differentiated extension/ homework material				1.1, 1.4, 1.5, 2.1, 2.4, 2.5, 4.1, 4.2, 4.4, 5.6, 5.8	1.2–3, 2.1–2, 3.1–2, 4.2–3
Page 22 **Prueba**	• end-of-spread test				1.1, 1.4, 2.1, 2.4, 3.1, 4.1, 5.4	1.2, 2.1–2, 3.1–2, 4.2–3
Page 23 **Vocabulario**	• a summary of the key language covered in each spread of this unit					
Page 152 **Leer 0**	• practice of longer reading texts based on the theme of the unit				2.1, 3.1, 5.4	3.3

Me presento 0

Week-by-week overview
(Three-year KS3 Route: assuming six weeks' work or approximately 10–12.5 hours)
(Two-year KS3 Route: assuming four weeks' worth or approxmately 6.5-8.5 hours)
*Please note that essential activities are highlighted.
About Unit 0, *Me presento*: Students work in the context of meeting people, talking about themselves and their family and learning about Spanish-speaking people and culture. They find out about Spanish family life and begin to build a personal stock of family-related vocabulary. They learn numbers 1–100 and the Spanish alphabet. They learn to use definite and indefinite articles correctly and learn and use the verbs *tener* and *ser*. The unit also provides tips on language learning techniques.

Three-Year KS3 Route			Two-Year KS3 Route		
Week	**Resources**	**Objectives**	**Week**	**Resources**	**Objectives**
1	0.1 Quiz	learn facts about Spanish-speaking people and culture recognise and use greetings correctly	1	0.1 Quiz omit activity 3	learn facts about Spanish-speaking people and culture recognise and use greetings correctly
2	0.2 Me flipa; me molan 0.6 Lablolengua A (p.18) 0.6 Lablolengua C & D (p.19)	talk about things you like use the alphabet learn numbers 1–20 record vocabulary accurately use definite and indefinite articles correctly	2	0.2 Me flipa; me molan omit activities 4, 5, 9, 11 & Challenge 0.6 Lablolengua A (p.18) 0.6 Lablolengua D (p.19)	talk about things you like use the alphabet learn numbers 1–20 record vocabulary accurately use definite and indefinite articles correctly
3	0.3 La familia 0.6 Lablolengua B (p.18)	talk about family members learn how to be an independent learner learn and use the verbs *tener* and *ser*	3	0.3 La familia omit activities 3, 4, 7, 10 & Challenge 0.6 Lablolengua B (p.18)	talk about family members learn how to be an independent learner learn and use the verbs *tener* and *ser*
4	0.4 ¿Cuántos años tienes? 0.6 Lablolengua E (p.19)	name family members say ages and numbers 1–100 recycle language and verbs from the unit practise memory games – learn how to learn!	4	0.4 ¿Cuántos años tienes? omit activities 3, Think!, 10 & Challenge 1B.8 Prueba (p.22) Vocabulario (p.23)	name family members say ages and numbers 1–100 recycle language and verbs from the unit practise memory games – learn how to learn! recapping on the vocabulary of the unit prepare and carry out assessment in all four skills
5	0.5 Gente y números	use the vocabulary of this unit in a wider context reinforce the skills you have learnt revise and extend the grammar you have learnt			
6	0.7 Extra (Star) (p.20) 0.7 Extra (Plus) (p.21) 0.8 Prueba (p.22) Vocabulario (p.23) Leer (p.152)	further reinforcement and extension of the language of the unit recapping on the vocabulary of the unit prepare and carry out assessment in all four skills further reading to explore the language of the unit and cultural themes			

0.1 Me presento

0.1 Quiz
páginas 8–9

Planner

Objectives
- learn some basic facts about Spanish-speaking people and culture
- recognise and use greetings correctly

Resources
Students' Book, pages 8–9
CD 1, track 7
Foundation Workbook, page 8
Higher Workbook, page 8
Foundation Workbook audio, CD 3, track 41
Higher Workbook audio, CD 4, track 16
Interactive OxBox, Unit 0
Copymasters 1–8
Assessment, Unit 0

Key language
Buenos días; Buenas tardes; Buenas noches

Renewed Framework references
1.1, 1.4, 3.1, 4.1

PLTS
Activity 1: Independent enquirers; Creative thinkers

Starters
- Display the following phrases in a jumbled order and ask students to match each Spanish phrase to its English equivalent.
  My name is… – *Me llamo…*
  What's your name? – *¿Cómo te llamas?*
  How are you? – *¿Qué tal?*
  Goodbye. See you soon. – *Adiós. Hasta pronto.*

Plenaries
- Students work in pairs to practise the dialogues from Activity 2, e.g.
  A: ¡Hola! ¿Cómo te llamas?
  B: Me llamo… . ¿Y tú?
  A: Me llamo Maribel.
  Students could then repeat this exercise, but this time pretending to be famous people, e.g. *Me llamo Rafael Nadal. ¿Y tú?*

Homework/Self-study
Activity 1: Students note down everything they have learnt about Spanish-speaking people and culture so far. They should add to this as the course progresses. Students practise the dialogues from Activity 2 and try to learn them by heart.

AT 3.1 | **PLTS**
1 Completa el quiz: ¿A, B o C?
Students complete the quiz about Spanish-speaking people and culture, choosing A, B or C each time. After completing the third section of the quiz, students make up their own quiz which they share with a partner or the class. Encourage them to use some of their brainstorming ideas from pages 4 and 5.

Answers:
***¿Quién es?:** C, B; **Se llama…:** B, A; **¿Qué es?:** B, C, B, B*

AT 1.2
2 Escucha, lee y repite
Students listen to, read and then repeat the dialogues. Encourage them to learn these dialogues by heart.

 CD 1, track 7 — página 8, actividad 2

A
– ¡Hola! ¿Cómo te llamas?
– Me llamo Abdul. ¿Y tú?
– Me llamo Maribel.

B
– Buenos días. ¿Qué tal?
– Bien, ¿y tú?
– Muy bien, gracias.
– Adiós. Hasta pronto.

Buenos días.
Buenas tardes.
Buenas noches.

AT 1.2
3 Escucha otra vez.
Students listen again and find the items listed.

Answers:
Greetings words/phrases: *¡Hola!; Buenos días.*
'My name is …': *Me llamo…*
'What's your name?': *¿Cómo te llamas?*
'How are you?': *¿Qué tal?*
'Goodbye. See you soon.': *Adiós. Hasta pronto.*

AT 2.2
4 Practica el diálogo.
Students practise the dialogues with a partner. Ask volunteers to perform the dialogues in front of the class.

0.2 Me presento

Think
This encourages students to think about differences in Spanish and English punctuation.

Challenge
Find out more about three of the monuments or personalities you didn't choose as answers.
Students can feed back their findings to the class.

0.2 Me flipa; me molan   páginas 10–11

Planner

Objectives
- talk about things you like, using the alphabet
- use definite and indefinite articles correctly
- learn numbers 1–20
- record vocabulary accurately

Resources
Students' Book, pages 10–11
CD 1, tracks 8–11
Foundation Workbook, pages 6, 9
Higher Workbook, pages 6, 9
Foundation Workbook audio, CD 3, tracks 42–43
Higher Workbook audio, CD 4, tracks 17–18
Interactive OxBox, Unit 0
Copymasters 1–8
Assessment, Unit 0

Key language
uno; dos; tres; cuatro; cinco; seis; siete; ocho; nueve; diez; once; doce; trece; catorce; quince; dieciséis; diecisiete; dieciocho; diecinueve; veinte

Grammar
- gender: definite and indefinite articles

Renewed Framework references
1.1, 1.4, 2.1, 4.1, 4.3, 5.1, 5.3

PLTS
Think!: Independent enquirers
Activities 6 & 7: Reflective learners
Gramática: Reflective learners; Independent enquirers
Activity 12: Reflective learners
Challenge: Independent enquirers; Effective participators

Starters
- Practise counting to twenty in Spanish. Go round the class with each student in turn saying the next number until you reach twenty. Expand on this with a version of 'buzz' where you go round counting to twenty in Spanish, but students must replace any multiples of two with the word ¡Hola!.
- Display a list of words and ask students to decide if they are masculine or feminine from looking at their endings. Check answers as a class.

Plenaries
- Students work in groups to come up with their own alphabet song/rap in Spanish. Each group performs their song and the class votes for the best one.

Homework/Self-study
- Gramática: Students note down any new words they meet, ensuring that they include the definite/indefinite article. Challenge: Students find Spanish words for the letters they didn't include in their list of ten. They add these to their vocabulary list.

 1 El abecedario español. Escucha y canta.
Students listen to the alphabet rap in Spanish and then join in themselves.

 CD 1, track 8   página 10, actividad 1
A, B, C, D, E, F, G, H, I, J, K, L, M, N, Ñ, O, P, Q, R, S, T, U, V, W, X, Y, Z

 2 Escucha y lee el poema.
Students listen to and read the poem. Ask them how many letters sound like English letters and which ones are different. Play a game. Say a group of letters then ask each student in turn round the class to say the next letter.

CD 1, track 9   página 10, actividad 2
A es de amigos – es el número uno
B es de blog – es el número dos
C es de CDs – es el número tres
D es de discotecas o deporte – es el número cuatro
E es de emails o emoticones – es el número cinco
F es de fiestas – seis
G es de mis grupos favoritos – siete
H es de helados y hamburguesas – ocho
I es de iPod e inventos guay – nueve
J es de juegos – diez

0.2 Me presento

AT 3.1 | **3 Lee las palabras.**
Students read the words beginning with A–J and see how many they either know already or can guess because they are similar to English words.

Answers:
amigos – friends; **blog** – blog; **CDs** – CDs; **discotecas** – discos; **deporte** – sport; **emails** – e-mails; **emoticones** – smileys; **fiestas** – parties; **grupos** – groups; **helados** – ice-creams; **hamburguesas** – hamburgers; **iPod** – iPod; **inventos** – inventions; **juegos** – games

AT 2.1 | **4 Deletrea las palabras.**
Students practise spelling the words from the list using the Spanish alphabet. Can their partner guess which word it is?

5 Escribe las palabras que no sabes.
Students write down any of the words from the list that they simply don't know.

Gramática
Explain to students that in Spanish all nouns have a gender: they are either masculine or feminine. Look at the examples given in the Students' Book and explain that the indefinite article in front of the noun shows whether it is masculine or feminine. Point to an example of each indefinite article in turn and ask the class to say if it is masculine or feminine to check understanding.

PLTS | **Think!**
Students look at the words in the grammar box and make a rule to decide if a word is masculine or feminine, singular or plural. They find words on the page which don't follow their rule.

Answers:
masculine singular words tend to end in 'o'; masculine plural words tend to end in 'os'; feminine singular words tend to end in 'a'; feminine plural words tend to end in 'as'
Words that don't follow this rule tend to be cognates and taken from English or other languages, e.g. blog

PLTS | **6 Escribe las palabras.**
Students go back to their list from Activity 3 and, using what they have learned about gender, write down if the words are masculine or feminine.

PLTS | **7 Escribe las palabras.**
Students go back to their list from Activity 5 and, using what they have learned about gender, write down the masculine or feminine form for the words listed. They check their answers with a partner.

AT 1.1 | **8 Escucha y repite.**
Students listen and repeat the numbers.

🎧 **CD 1, track 10**   página 11, actividad 8
1, 2, 3, 4, 5, 6, 7, 8, 9, 10

AT 2.1 | **9 Juega con tu compañero.**
Students refer back to the poem in Activity 3. A says a number. B names the object. They then swap roles.

AT 1.2 | **10 Escucha y lee el poema.**
Students listen to and read the second part of the poem. Encourage them to find cognates.

🎧 **CD 1, track 11**   página 11, actividad 10
Once es la letra K – es de kitesurf
Doce es la letra L – es de Los Simpson
Trece es la letra M – es de móvil y, música
Catorce es la letra N – es de naranjas y ¡no!
Ñ es otra letra en el diccionario español
Quince es la letra O – es de osito
Dieciséis es la letra P – es de pósters y películas
Q es la letra que sigue y es difícil de ilustrar
Diecisiete es la letra R – es de revistas y regalos y la RR doble es difícil de pronunciar
Dieciocho es la letra S – es de siesta y SMS
Diecinueve es la letra T – es de tatuajes y Twitter
Veinte es la letra U – es de universidad
Para finalizar hay
la V de vaqueros y videojuegos
la W es de windsurf y Wally y la Web
la X es por los muchos besos que te quiero dar pero
la Y va sola porque no quiere bailar
Y la letra Z es de zapatos y zumo y zzzzzzzzz ...

PLTS | **Gramática**
Remind students that in Spanish, all nouns are either masculine or feminine and can be singular or plural. Ask them to think back to the work they did on indefinite articles and explain that you are now going to look at definite articles. Work through the examples given in the Students' Book explaining that the definite article in front of the noun shows whether it is masculine or feminine; singular or plural. Add a few more examples if necessary. Finally, explain how to make a noun plural in Spanish.

0.3 Me presento

| AT 2.2 | **11** Habla con tu compañero.
Students refer back to the poem in Activity 10. A makes a statement about it and says a number. B names the object. They then swap roles.

| PLTS | **12 Escribe las palabras.**
Further practice of gender. Students write out the words listed choosing the correct article.

Answers:
1 un videojuego; *2* los zapatos; *3* una siesta; *4* unos regalos; *5* un tatuaje

| PLTS | **Challenge**
Choose ten letters of the alphabet and find ten new words for your Spanish vocabulary list. Swap your list with a partner and see how many meanings you can guess.
Students can record their words in different colours depending on whether they are masculine or feminine, singular or plural.

0.3 La familia   páginas 12–13

Planner

Objectives
- talk about family members
- learn and use the verbs *tener* and *ser*
- learn how to be an independent learner

Video
Video script, Unit 0

Resources
Students' Book, pages 12–13
CD 1, tracks 12–13
Foundation Workbook, page 10
Higher Workbook, page 10
Interactive OxBox, Unit 0
Copymasters 1–8
Assessment, Unit 0

Key language
la familia; los abuelos; el abuelo; la abuela; los padres; el padre; la madre; el padrastro; la madrastra; el marido (el esposo); la mujer (la esposa); los parientes; el tío; la tía; el primo; la prima; los niños; el hermano; la hermana; el hermanastro; la hermanastra; el hijo único; la hija única; casado/a; divorciado/a

Grammar
- the verbs *tener* and *ser*

Renewed Framework references
1.1, 1.4, 1.5, 2.1, 2.4, 3.1, 5.1, 5.4

PLTS
Activity 1: Creative thinkers; Self-managers; Independent enquirers
Challenge: Creative thinkers; Effective participators

Starters
- Display the Spanish vocabulary from Activity 1 and challenge students to write the English translation for each word. You could turn this into a game. You start by saying an item of vocabulary from Activity 1 and then the name of one of the students in the class, e.g. – *el primo* – James. The person you have chosen says what this means in English and then chooses another piece of vocabulary and student, and so on, e.g. – *la familia* – Isabella

Plenaries
- Students take on the role of a famous person, fictional or real, and write a speech bubble in the style of Activity 5 about 'themselves' and their family. Explain that they can make it up.
- Students work in pairs to play a guessing game similar to that in Activity 7. They pretend to be a famous person/fictional character, e.g. *Soy la mujer de David Beckham.* etc. Their partner must guess who they are pretending to be. You could play this as a class with one student playing the famous person and the rest of the class guessing who he/she is.

Homework/Self-study
- In preparation for Activity 5, students write words and phrases that they think would be useful to describe their family. They can refer to reading texts for support. Provide less able students with a list of phrases/adjectives/ages that they can choose from. Gramática: Students use the verbs from the grammar Box in sentences of their own, e.g. *Se llama Madeleine y tiene quince años.*

0.3 Me presento

AT 3.1
PLTS

1 ¿Cuántas palabras conoces?
Students look through the vocabulary list and see how many words they can guess. Encourage them to look at the word endings. Do they follow the masculine/ feminine rule? Explain that in a mixed group of masculine and feminine, masculine will always take priority. Then ask students to write down the English for these words and to add them to their vocabulary book, remembering to colour code them according to gender and number.

Answers:
la familia – *the family;* **los abuelos** – *grandparents;* **el abuelo** – *grandfather;* **la abuela** – *grandmother;* **los padres** – *parents;* **el padre** – *father;* **la madre** – *mother;* **el padrastro** – *stepfather;* **la madrastra** – *stepmother;* **el marido (el esposo)** – *husband;* **la mujer (la esposa)** – *wife;* **los parientes** – *relatives;* **el tío** – *uncle;* **la tía** – *aunt;* **el primo** – *(male) cousin;* **la prima** – *(female) cousin;* **los niños** – *children;* **el hermano** – *brother;* **la hermana** – *sister;* **el hermanastro** – *stepbrother;* **la hermanastra** – *stepsister;* **el hijo único** – *only son;* **la hija única** – *only daughter;* **casado/a** – *married (man/woman);* **divorciado/a** – *divorced (man/woman)*

AT 1.3

2 Mira el video.
Students watch the video and point out the family members in the vocabulary box each time they are mentioned.

 Video script: Unit 0 (CD 1, track 12)

Khalid: Buenas tardes, Sra Pérez. ¿Está Montse en casa? ¿No? Ah, vale. Gracias, adiós, adiós.
Marisa: ¿Diga? Sí, papá. Sí, papá. Sí, sí. No, papá, no. Vale, sí, papá. Vale. Adiós, papá.
Khalid: Hola, me llamo Khalid.
Marisa: ¿Ka-?
Khalid: Khalid. K-h-a-l-i-d. Pero me puedes llamar sólo Khal.
Marisa: ¡Khal! Es un nombre muy bonito. ¿No es español, verdad?
Khalid: No. Es marroquí. Mis padres son marroquís. Yo también soy marroquí.
Marisa: Hablas muy bien español.
Khalid: Gracias y tú también. Tú tampoco eres española, ¿verdad?
Marisa: No, soy argentina, de Buenos Aires.
Khalid: ¡Ah! Es verdad, en Argentina también se habla español. Así que eres de Buenos Aires, ¡eso está muy bien! Y tú, ¿cómo te llamas?
Marisa: ¡Oh! Perdona, soy Marisa. Marisa García.
Khalid: ¿Nada más? ¿No María Magdalena López García?
Marisa: No, sólo Marisa García.
Khalid: Pues, encantado de conocerte.
Marisa: Encantada de conocerte a ti también.
[pause]
Khalid: No, no... se llama Jalal. J-a-l-a-l.
Marisa: Vale. Entonces, tu hermano se llama Elías.
Khalid: Sí.
Marisa: Y tu hermana es Sara y tiene 16 años.
Khalid: Sí.
Marisa: Y tu padre se llama Sidan.
Khalid: No, es Zitane: Z-i-t-a-n-e…
Marisa: ¡Ah, vale! Zitane. Pero, ¿Jalal tiene 17 años?
Khalid: No. Jalal tiene 7 años.
Marisa: Vale, 7 años.
Khalid: Bueno, en realidad tiene siete años y medio.
Marisa: (laughing) Ya, perdona, siete años y medio.
Khalid: Y tú, ¿cuántos años tienes?
Marisa: 15.
Khalid: Pues yo tengo 15 años y medio.
[pause]
Khalid: ¿Tienes hermanos o hermanas?
Marisa: Si, tengo un hermano, se llama Diego.
Khalid: ¿Como Diego Maradona?
Marisa: Sí... tiene 19 años y estudia en Buenos Aires.
Khalid: ¿No tienes ninguna hermana?
Marisa: No, no tengo hermanas. Sólo somos mi hermano y yo.
Khalid: Y ¿qué haces en Barcelona?
Marisa: Mi padre es diplomático. Está aquí por su trabajo, pero sólo estaremos un año.
Khalid: Ah, vale. ¿Y tu madre?
Marisa: Mis padres están divorciados. Mi madre trabaja en Buenos Aires. Es dentista.
Khalid: ¡Ah!
Marisa: Sí.
Khalid: Mi padre es médico. Es cardiólogo.
Marisa: Ah, ya.
Marisa: Y tu madre, ¿en qué trabaja?
Khalid: Mi madre es profesora de francés.
Marisa: ¡Qué bien!
Khalid: No, no está tan bien. Es profesora de francés en mi colegio.
Marisa: Vale, de acuerdo, ya entiendo. La verdad es que no está tan bien.
Marisa: ¿Hablas francés también?
Khalid: Sí, hablo francés y catalán, inglés y entiendo italiano, y también árabe.
Marisa: Impresionante.
[phone rings]
Marisa: Es mi padre. Tengo que irme.
Khalid: ¿Me das tu número de teléfono?
Marisa: Vale.
Khalid: Vale.
Marisa: El 6 66 44 63 24.
Khalid: Vale. 6 66 44 63 24.
Marisa: Perfecto.
Khalid: Mi número es 6 95 05 15 48.
[phone rings]
Marisa: Hola, papá. Sí, papá, no papá. Ya voy… . Bueno, me tengo que ir… Adiós.

0.3 Me presento

Answers:
Family members mentioned: *papá; mis padres; hermano; hermana; padre; madre*

 3 Mira el video otra vez.
Students watch the video again and check the note about Khalid's family to find the two mistakes.

Video script: Unit 0 (CD 1, track 12)

Khalid: No, no... se llama Jalal. J-a-l-a-l.
Marisa: Vale. Entonces, tu hermano se llama Elías.
Khalid: Sí.
Marisa: Y tu hermana es Sara y tiene 16 años.
Khalid: Sí.
Marisa: Y tu padre se llama Sidan.
Khalid: No, es Zitane: Z-i-t-a-n-e…
Marisa: ¡Ah, vale! Zitane. Pero, ¿Jalal tiene 17 años?
Khalid: No. Jalal tiene 7 años.
Marisa: Vale, 7 años.
Khalid: Bueno, en realidad tiene siete años y medio.
Marisa: (laughing) Ya, perdona, siete años y medio.
Khalid: Y tú, ¿cuántos años tienes?
Marisa: 15.
Khalid: Pues yo tengo 15 años y medio.
[pause]
Khalid: ¿Tienes hermanos o hermanas?
Marisa: Si, tengo un hermano, se llama Diego.
Khalid: ¿Como Diego Maradona?
Marisa: Sí... tiene 19 años y estudia en Buenos Aires.
Khalid: ¿No tienes ninguna hermana?
Marisa: No, no tengo hermanas. Sólo somos mi hermano y yo.
Khalid: Y ¿qué haces en Barcelona?
Marisa: Mi padre es diplomático. Está aquí por su trabajo, pero sólo estaremos un año.
Khalid: Ah, vale. ¿Y tu madre?
Marisa: Mis padres están divorciados. Mi madre trabaja en Buenos Aires. Es dentista.
Khalid: ¡Ah!
Marisa: Sí.
Khalid: Mi padre es médico. Es cardiólogo.
Marisa: Ah, ya.
Khalid: Y tu madre, ¿en qué trabaja?
Marisa: Mi madre es profesora de francés.
Marisa: ¡Qué bien!
Khalid: No, no está tan bien. Es profesora de francés en mi colegio.
Marisa: Vale, de acuerdo, ya entiendo. La verdad es que no está tan bien.
Marisa: ¿Hablas francés también?
Khalid: Sí, hablo francés y catalán, inglés y entiendo italiano, y también árabe.
Marisa: Impresionante.

Answers:
His father is called Zitane; his brother is Jalal.

 4 Lee. ¿Quién es?
Students read the speech bubble and say who is speaking.

Answer: Marisa

Gramática
Look at the examples of the verbs *tener* and *ser*. Point out the use of the indefinite article with the verb *tener*: when it is used in a positive statement, the indefinite article is used; when it is used in a negative sentence, the indefinite article isn't needed.

 5 Escribe de ti.
Students use what they have learnt so far to write a speech bubble about themselves and their family. Depending on the class, you may want to do this orally instead. Refer them back to the speech bubble in Activity 4 for support.

 6 ¿Verdad o mentira?
Students study the family tree and then note down whether the statements are true or false.

Answers:
1 true; **2** true; **3** false; **4** false; **5** false

 7 ¿Quién eres?
Students work in pairs to play a guessing game based on the family tree.

 8 Escribe la respuesta correcta.
Students use the family vocabulary they have learned to complete each sentence with the appropriate word.

Answers:
1 tío; **2** abuelos; **3** primo; **4** nieto/nieta

 9 Escucha y lee.
Students listen to and read the dialogue.

CD 1, track 13   página 13, actividad 9

– ¡Hola, soy Tito! ¿Qué tal? Primero, ¿cómo te llamas – tu nombre completo?
– Pues me llamo María Magdalena López García.
– ¿Tienes hermanos?
– Sí, tengo un hermano pero no tengo hermanas.
– Y ¿cómo se llama tu hermano?
– Se llama Diego.
– ¿Tienes abuelos?
– Sí, se llaman Alberto y Beatriz.

0.4 Me presento

Gramática
Point out that the personal pronouns, *yo, tu, el, ella, ellos* and *ellas* are not necessarily used in Spanish if it is obvious from the verb ending which one is meant.

Answers: se llaman; eres; tiene

 10 👥 **Practica el diálogo.**
Students work in pairs to practise reading the dialogue aloud. Ask volunteers to perform the dialogue in front of the class.

 11 👥 **Habla con tu compañero.**
Students interview their partner using the questions in bold in the dialogue.

 👥 **Challenge**
Design an imaginary family tree and then play a guessing game using it.
Encourage students to be creative. They could use their favourite cartoon/TV family, or make up a family.

0.4 ¿Cuántos años tienes?   páginas 14–15

Planner

Objectives
- name family members, say ages and numbers 1–100
- recycle language and verbs from the unit
- practise memory games – learn how to learn!

Resources
Students' Book, pages 14–15
CD 1, tracks 14–18
Foundation Workbook, page 11
Higher Workbook, page 11
Foundation Workbook audio, CD 3, track 44
Higher Workbook audio, CD 4, track 19
Interactive OxBox, Unit 0
Copymasters 1–8
Assessment, Unit 0

Key language
veintiuno; veintidós; veintitrés; veinticuatro; veinticinco; veintiséis; veintisiete; veintiocho; veintinueve; treinta; cuarenta; cincuenta; sesenta; setenta; ochenta; noventa; cien

Renewed Framework references
1.1, 1.4, 2.1, 2.4, 4.1, 5.1, 5.2, 5.8

PLTS
Activity 3: Effective participators
Think!: Independent enquirers; Reflective learners
Activity 9: Reflective learners
Challenge: Reflective learners

Starters
- Revise numbers 1–20. Ask the class to count from 1 to 20 in Spanish. Then call out a sequence of numbers between 1 and 20 and ask students in turn to tell you what the next number is.
- Go round the class asking students how old they are. Each student replies: *Tengo XX años*.

Plenaries
- Challenge students to pretend to be an imaginary Spanish person and to make up a sentence on the theme of the spread, e.g. *¡Hola!, me llamo **Javier/Maria/Roberto**. Soy **el padre/la madre** de Lucas, Pepe y Anita. Tengo **cincuenta y dos/treinta** años.*

Homework/Self-study
Challenge: Students write similar details for a famous/cartoon/imaginary family.

 1 Escucha e indica el número.
Students listen and point to the number mentioned. Repeat this activity as many times as necessary for students to familiarise themselves with the numbers.

🎧 **CD 1, track 14**   página 14, actividad 1

veintiuno, veintidós, veintitrés, veinticuatro, veinticinco, veintiséis, veintisiete, veintiocho, veintinueve, treinta

veintiséis, veintinueve, veintitrés, veintiuno, treinta, veinticuatro, veintisiete, veintidós, veinticinco, veintiocho

 2 Escucha y anota los números.
Students listen and note down the next number in the sequence.

0.4 Me presento

 CD 1, track 15 — página 14, actividad 2

a dos tres cuatro...
b nueve diez once...
c quince dieciséis diecisiete...
d nueve ocho siete...
e quince catorce trece...

Answers:
a cinco; **b** doce; **c** dieciocho; **d** seis; **e** doce

AT 2.1 | **PLTS** — **3 Practica. ¡Contrarreloj!**
Further practice of numbers in Spanish. Students work in pairs. A says a number in Spanish. B says it back in English. Challenge students to go as fast as they can.

AT 2.1 — **4 ¿Cuántos años tienes?**
Students use the prompts to say how old they are. Practise saying a few ages before they start.

Answers:
Tengo trece años. Tengo catorce años. Tengo quince años. Tengo diez años. Tengo doce años.

AT 4.1–2 — **5 ¿Cuántos años tienen?**
Students look at the illustrations to say how old each person is. Practise saying how old other people are before they start.

Answers:
Manolo tiene trece años. Susana tiene quince años. Cristóbal tiene diez años. Dolores tiene doce años. Jorge tiene catorce años. Anita tiene once años.

PLTS — **Think!**
Ask students to study the list of numbers from 30 to 100. Can they relate these to the numbers 3–9? Remind students that from number 31 onwards, *y* is used to join two numbers together. What do they think *y* means?

AT 1.1 — **6 Escucha y repite los números.**
Students listen and repeat the numbers.

 CD 1, track 16 — página 15, actividad 6

treinta, cuarenta, cincuenta, sesenta, setenta, ochenta, noventa, ciento

AT 1.2 — **7 Escucha y anota los nombres y las edades.**
Students look at the family tree on page 13 again. They then listen and note down their names and ages.

 CD 1, track 17 — página 15, actividad 7

1 Buenas tardes. Soy María. Soy la abuela de José. Tengo ochenta y ocho años.
2 Hola, me llamo Javier. Soy el padre de Lucas, Pepe y Anita. Tengo cincuenta y dos años.
3 Saludos; me llamo Irene. Soy la esposa de Armando. Tengo treinta y ocho años.
4 Hola; soy Lucas. Soy el hermano de Pepe y Anita y tengo doce años.
5 Bienos días. Me llamo Roberto y soy el padre de Javier e Irene. Tengo casi noventa años.

Answers:
Maria: 88 years old; **Javier**: 52 years old; **Irene**: 38 years old; **Lucas**: 12 years old; **Roberto**: nearly 90 years old

AT 3.3 — **8 Lee y completa la conversación.**
Students read the conversation and complete it with the correct words from the box.

Answers:
1 tal; **2** única; **3** hermana; **4** hermanos; **5** un; **6** abuelos; **7** abuelos; **8** primos

AT 1.3 | **PLTS** — **9 Escucha y verifica.**
Students listen to check their answers to Activity 8.

 CD 1, track 18 — página 15, actividad 9

– Hola, Patricia! ¿Qué tal?
– ¡Saludos! ¿Eres hija única o tienes hermanos?
– Tengo una hermana y tres hermanos. ¿Y tú?
– Solamente tengo un hermano.
– ¿Tienes abuelos?
– Sí, tengo una abuela y dos abuelos.
– Pues, yo no tengo abuelos pero tengo tíos y una prima y tres primos.

AT 2.3 — **10 Practica el diálogo.**
Students practise the dialogue with a partner.

AT 4.2 | **PLTS** — **Challenge**
Write down the names and ages of your own family members, or those of the family on page 13.
More able students write in full sentences using the verbs they have met earlier in the Students' Book.

0.5 Me presento

0.5 Gente y números
páginas 16–17

Planner

Objectives
- use the vocabulary of this unit in a wider context
- revise and extend the grammar you have learnt
- reinforce the skills you have learnt

Resources
Students' Book, pages 16–17
CD 1, tracks 19–21
Foundation Workbook, page 12
Higher Workbook, page 12
Interactive OxBox, Unit 0
Assessment, Unit 0

Key language
hay; no hay

Grammar
- revise and extend the grammar you have learnt

Renewed Framework references
1.1, 1.4, 1.5, 2.1, 2.4, 2.5, 4.1, 5.8

PLTS
Activity 7: Creative thinkers; Team workers

Starters
- As a class brainstorm as many Spanish words from this unit as possible. Make a list of these.
- Display the list from Starter Activity 1. Go round the class asking each student in turn to spell one of the words from the list. Can the rest of the class guess what it is before he/she has finished? Remind students to use the phrase, *con acento escrito*, if there is an accent on a letter.

Plenaries
- Challenge students to write five sentences on the theme of the spread (remind them that these sentences don't have to be true), e.g. *Tengo tres abuelos – dos abuelos y una abuela. Soy hijo único pero tengo dos hermanastras.*
- Students work in pairs to invent a dialogue similar to that in Activity 6, but this time they should try to invent the most unusual family possible. Students could perform their dialogues in front of the class who votes for the most unusual family.

Homework/Self-study
Students write out the dialogue they invented with their partner in Activity 6.

---

1 Escucha y anota. ¿Cómo se escribe?
Students listen and note down the words that are being spelt out.

> 🎧 **CD 1, track 19**   página 16, actividad 1
>
> a-b-u-e-l-o
> p-a-d-r-e-s
> h-e-r-m-a-n-a-s-t-r-a
> v-e-i-n-t-i-u-n-o
> q-u-i-n-c-e
> o-c-h-e-n-t-a

Answers:
abuelo; padres; hermanastra; veintiuno; quince; ochenta

 2 **Deletrea los nombres.**
Students work in pairs and take it in turns to spell out one of the names listed. Their partner guesses which of the names they are spelling. Before they start, get students to practise saying the phrase, *con acento escrito*, which is what they should say if there is an accent on a letter.

 3 Mira las páginas 10 y 11 otra vez. Lee las frases. ¿Correcto o incorrecto?
Students look back at pages 10 and 11. They then read the statements and decide if they are right or wrong.

Answers:
1 Correcto; **2** Incorrecto (El número cinco es la letra *E*.);
3 Correcto; **4** Incorrecto (El número dieciséis es la letra *P*.);
5 Incorrecto (El número veintidós es la letra *W*.)

 4 Corrige las frases incorrectas.
Students then correct the incorrect sentences.

Answers:
See Activity 3 answers.

 5 Escribe: ¿Cuántos hay?
Students look at the illustrations and note down, using full sentences, how many of each item there are. They should use *hay*, meaning 'there is' or 'there are.

Answers:
a Hay tres ositos. **b** Hay catorce chorizos. **c** Hay veintiún CDs.
d Hay treinta y seis naranjas. **e** Hay cincuenta y cinco aceitunas. **f** Hay cien piñas.

0.6 Me presento

AT 3.3   **6 Escucha y lee.**
Students listen to and read the conversation about Roberto's family.

> **CD 1, track 20**   página 17, actividad 6
>
> – Tengo tres abuelos – dos abuelos y una abuela.
> – ¿Cómo se llaman?
> – Se llaman Alfredo, Mario y Fernanda.
> – ¿Cuántos años tienen?
> – Alfredo tiene ochenta y dos años; Mario tiene setenta y nueve y Fernanda tiene sesenta y siete nada más.
> – ¿Tienes primos?
> – Sí, tengo un primo y tres primas.
> – ¿Tienes hermanos?
> – Pues, no tengo hermanos, soy hijo único pero tengo dos hermanastras.

AT 2.3   **7** **Inventa un diálogo similar.**
PLTS   Students invent a similar dialogue to that in Activity 6 with a partner. Encourage them to reuse phrases and vocabulary from the spread.

AT 3.3   **8 Dibuja el árbol genealógico de Roberto.**
Students read through the dialogue again and then complete as much of Roberto's family tree as possible, adding names and ages.

AT 1.3–4   **9 Escucha y completa el árbol.**
Students listen and complete the family tree.

> **CD 1, track 21**   página 17, actividad 9
>
> – ¿Quién es quién en tu familia?
> – Pues, el padre de mi padre es Alfredo y los padres de mi madre son Mario y Fernanda.
> – ¿Y cómo se llama la esposa de tu abuelo Alfredo?
> – Se llama Mariana.
> – ¿Y tus padres están divorciados?
> – Sí, mi padre Alberto tiene otra esposa que se llama Alicia. Mi madre se llama Cecilia y su hermano Paco es mi tío.
> – Bueno y tus primos son sus hijos ¿verdad?
> – Mi primo Enrique es su hijo pero mis tres primas son las hijas de mi tía Julia que es la hermana de mi padre.
> – Uf qué complicada es tu familia…

AT 1.4   **10 Contesta a las preguntas.**
Students listen to the recording from Activity 9 again and then answer the questions.

Answers:
1 Sí, se llama Mariana. 2 Sí, Fernanda es la esposa de Mario. 3 Paco es el tío de Roberto. 4 Julia es la hermana de Alberto. 5 Roberto tiene cuatro primos.

0.6 Labolengua   páginas 18–19

Planner

Objectives
- review language and grammar from the unit

Resources
Students' Book, pages 18–19
CD 1, tracks 22–23
Foundation Workbook, pages 13–14
Higher Workbook, pages 13–14
Interactive OxBox, Unit 0
Copymasters 9–10
Assessment, Unit 0

Grammar
- nouns, gender and verbs

Renewed Framework references
1.1, 1.4, 4.1, 4.3, 4.5, 5.1, 5.8

PLTS
All activities: Reflective learners/Self-managers

Homework/Self-study
Students try to use some of the conjugated verbs from Activity 5 in sentences.
Activity 10: Students continue to practise pronouncing Spanish vowel sounds.

Comprender – nouns, gender and verbs

> **PLTS**   **1 Do you remember these words? Are they masculine or feminine? Write them using *un*, *una*, *unos*, *unas*.**
> Practice of gender. Remind students of typical masculine and feminine word endings.

Answers:
1 una naranja; 2 un videojuego; 3 una guitarra; 4 un(a) burro; 5 un tatuaje; 6 un email; 7 un póster; 8 un chorizo

0.7 Me presento

PLTS 2 **Explain how you make the plural of words which end in a consonant.**
Revision of plurals. Refer students back to page 11 for support if necessary.

Answer:
Add 'es' if the word ends in a consonant.

PLTS 3 **Write out the verbs on learning cards and add the person doing the action in brackets.**
This activity serves to reinforce students' knowledge of the verbs covered so far.

Aprender – ways to record vocabulary

PLTS 4 **Check your partner has recorded his/her vocabulary correctly.**
Students read the notes on how to record vocabulary and then check that their partner has followed this advice.

PLTS 5 **Write the persons, stem and endings for a verb onto small bits of paper. Place them in a box or envelope. Take out bits and match them up until you have the complete verb again.**
Further practice of conjugating verbs.

PLTS 6 **Complete the word web for *la familia*.**
Students practise the strategy of using a word web to learn new words.

Hablar – pronunciation

PLTS 7 **Listen to the pure sounds and repeat them.**
Students practise pronouncing the vowels.

 CD 1, track 22 página 19, actividad 7
a – e – i – o – u

PLTS 8 **Stand in front of a mirror and look at the shape of your mouth as you pronounce each vowel.**
Students listen again to the vowels and this time practise pronouncing them in front of a mirror.

PLTS 9 **Now listen and repeat these names.**
Futher practice of pronouncing vowels in Spanish.

 CD 1, track 23 página 19, actividad 9
Ana, Armando
Enrique, Elena
Isidoro, Irene
Oswaldo, Olguita
Umberto, Ursula

PLTS 10 **Practise with words from pages 10 and 11.**
Students continue to practise pronouncing vowels in Spanish.

0.7 Extra Star   página 20

Planner

Objectives
- practise spelling names
- practise saying numbers
- give personal information

Resources
Students' Book, page 20
Copymaster 11

Renewed Framework references
1.4, 1.5, 2.1, 4.1, 4.2, 5.6, 5.8

PLTS
Activity 4: Reflective learners

AT 2.1 1 **Deletrea los nombres.**
Students spell out the names and check their answers against the alphabet on page 10.

AT 3.1 2 **Busca las palabras.**
Students study the snake to see how many words they can find. They can look at page 9 for support.

Answers: helado; chorizo; vino; piña; vaqueros; osito; madre; primas; abuelos

0.7 Me presento

AT 2.1 **3 Di los números.**
Students time themselves to see how fast they can say the numbers. You could turn this into a quiz.

AT 2.2 / PLTS **4 Practica el diálogo.**
Students practise the dialogue. When they have practised a few times and are confident, they could record themselves.

0.7 Extra Plus   página 21

Planner

Objectives
- understand information about people's families
- give details about your own family

Video
Video-blog, Unit 0

Resources
Students' Book, page 21
CD 1, tracks 24–25
Copymaster 12

Renewed Framework references
1.1, 2.1, 2.4, 2.5, 4.4

PLTS
Activity 5: Reflective learners; Self-managers

AT 3.2 **1 Empareja las preguntas con las respuestas.**
Students match the questions with the answers to practise greetings.

Answers: **1** c; **2** e; **3** a; **4** d; **5** b

AT 1.2–3 **2 Escucha y anota los nombres de cada familia.**
Students listen and note down the names of each family. They should think of the type of vocabulary they might hear before they start.

> **CD 1, track 24**   **página 21, actividad 2**
>
> 1 Pues yo me llamo Enrique. Tengo una hermana de 14 años y dos hermanos gemelos de 11 años. Mis padres son Álvaro e Isabel y mis abuelos se llaman Federico y Josefa.
> 2 Hola; me llamo Cecilia. Tengo dos hermanas y un hermano. Mis padres se llaman Luís y Ana. Tengo dos abuelos también.
> 3 Bueno, yo me llamo Susana y tengo dos hermanos: Paco que tiene 15 años y José que tiene 10. Mi padre se llama Pepe y mi madre se llama Catalina. Mis abuelos se llaman Fernando y Juana.
> 4 ¿Qué tal? Soy Diego. Solamente tengo un abuelo que se llama Eduardo. Tiene ochenta y cinco años. En mi familia somos tres nada más; yo, mi padre Francisco y mi madre Luisa.

Answers:
Enrique: 14-year-old sister and 11-year-old twin brothers; parents, Álvaro and Isabel; grandparents, Federico and Josefa
Cecilia: two sisters and a brother; parents, Luís and Ana; two grandparents
Susana: two brothers, Paco (15) and José (10); father, Pepe; mother, Catalina; grandparents, Fernando and Juana
Diego: grandfather, Eduardo (85), father, Francisco; mother, Luisa

AT 1.3 **3 Escucha otra vez e identifica a la familia.**
Students listen to the recording from Activity 2 again and this time identify which family the illustration represents.

Answer: Susana's family

AT 1.2–3 **4 Mira el video-blog. ¿Cómo contestan a las preguntas?**
Students watch the video-blog and note in English how each character answers the questions.

> **Video-blog: Unit 0 (CD1, track 25)**
>
> **¿Tienes hermanos o hermanas?**
> Eva: Sí. Tengo un hermano mayor que se llama Jaume y una hermana pequeña que se llama Laura.
> José: No. No tengo ninguna hermana ningún hermano. Soy hijo único.
> Marisa: No tengo hermanas, pero tengo un hermano. Y tú, ¿tienes hermanas o hermanos?
>
> **¿Cuántas personas hay en tu familia?**
> Eva: En mi familia hay cinco personas: mi madre, mi padre y mi dos hermanos y yo también.
> José: Mi madre, mi padre y yo.
> Marisa: En mi familia somos mi madre, mi padre, mi hermano y yo.

0.8 Me presento

¿Cómo se llaman?
Eva: Mi madre se llama Eulalia, mi padre se llama Carlos, mi hermana se llama Laura y mi hermano se llama Jaume.
José: Se llama mi madre Josefa y mi padre Javier.
Marisa: Mi madre se llama Carolina, mi padre se llama Luis y mi hermano se llama Diego.

¿Cuántos años tienen?
Eva: Mi hermana tiene 6 años, mi hermano tiene 19 años y mis padres tienen… mi padre 40 y mi madre tiene 43.
José: Mi madre tiene 47 años y mi padre 50.
Marisa: Mi madre tiene 39 años, mi padre tiene 43 y mi hermano tiene 19.

Answers:
Eva: 1 older brother called Jaume (19) and a younger sister, Laura (6); 5 people in family – mother, father, brother and sister and her; mother (43) called Eulalia; father (40) called Carlos; brother called Jaume and sister called Laura
José: no brothers or sisters; mother, father and him in family; mother (47) called Josefa; father (50) called Javier
Marisa: 1 brother, Diego (19); 4 in family, her, her brother, mother and father; mother (39) called Carolina; father (43) called Luis

 5 Contesta a las preguntas sobre ti.
Students answer the questions for themselves, using full sentences. They can refer back to previous spreads for support. Remind them to embellish to make their answer more interesting and to use a greater variety of language.

0.8 Prueba   página 22

Planner

Resources
Students' Book, page 22
CD 1, track 26

Renewed Framework references
1.1, 1.4, 2.1, 2.4, 3.1, 4.1, 5.4

PLTS
All activities: Reflective learners

Escuchar

 Listen to these six people. What are they talking about?
This activity tests listening skills using the language covered in this unit.

 CD 1, track 26   página 22, Escuchar
1 Hola me llamo Cecilia; tengo dos abuelos y una abuela.
2 No soy hija única porque tengo un hermano que se llama Roberto.
3 Saludos desde Buenos Aires, la capital de Argentina. Soy Rodrigo.
4 Tengo muchos amigos en Barcelona y todos tenemos quince años.
5 Mi padre se llama Rafael y mi madre se llama Susana.
6 Tengo muchos CDs porque me encanta la música.

Answers: 1 e; 2 c; 3 b; 4 a; 5 f; 6 d

Hablar

 A spells out a name and B says the name. A says a country and B names the capital.
This activity tests speaking skills using the language covered in this unit.

Leer

 Read and choose the correct word.
This activity tests reading skills using the language covered in this unit.

Answers: 1 tienes; 2 cómo; 3 se; 4 hermanos; 5 una; 6 los

Escribir

 Write the answers to these questions in full sentences.
This activity tests writing skills using the language covered in this unit.

Answers: Students' own answers

Me presento 0

Leer 0   página 152

Planner

Resources
Students' Book, page 152

Renewed Framework references
2.1, 3.1, 5.4

PLTS
Activity 1: Creative thinkers

Homework/Self-study
All questions

AT 3.3 | **PLTS**   **1** Explain in your own words what the Libro de Familia is. Do you think this is a good idea?

Possible answer:
The Libro de Familia *is an official document held by every family in Spain. It contains the names of any children. All children hold a national identity card. The book is also used by the Spanish Social Security when people get married, divorced or when they die.*

AT 3.3   **2** Answer the questions.

Answers:
1 *Amira;* **2** *22 years old;* **3** *Santiago;* **4** *Jorge Buitrago;* **5** *Peru*

Foundation Workbook

Página 8   0.1 Quiz
- Use with Students' Book, pages 8–9

AT 4.1   **1** Practise writing the Spanish characters. First trace the letter, then write it for yourself.
These will seem very different to most students. You could practise writing them on the board as a class first.

AT 4.1   **2** Now practise writing out these sentences.
Further practice of writing Spanish characters.

AT 1.1   **3** Listen and identify the celebrities in the correct order.

 CD 3, track 41   página 8, actividad 3

1
– ¿Cómo te llamas?
– Me llamo Fernando, Fernando Torres.

2
– Hola. ¿Cómo te llamas?
– Me llamo Penélope.

3
– Buenos días.
– Buenos días.
– ¿Cómo te llamas?
– Me llamo Cesc.

4
– Hola ¿Qué tal?
– Bien ¿Y tú?
– Bien. ¿Como te llamas?
– Me llamo Shakira.

Answers:
1 *Fernando Torres;* **2** *Penélope Cruz;* **3** *Cesc Fàbregas;* **4** *Shakira*

AT 2.1–2   **4** Practise this dialogue for each of the celebrities.
Students practise the dialogue in pairs. Volunteers could perform their dialogue in front of the class.

Página 9   0.2 Me flipa; me molan
- Use with Students' Book, pages 10–11

AT 1.1   **1** Javier is planning a surprise party for his little brother. To keep it secret he spells out the important words. Listen and tick the ones he mentions.
Practice of the alphabet in Spanish.

 CD 3, track 42   página 9, actividad 1

h-a-m-b-u-r-g-u-e-s-a
m-ú-s-i-c-a
a-m-i-g-o-s
f-i-e-s-t-a

0 Me presento

Answers:
hamburguesa, música, amigos, fiesta

 2 Now spell out the other surprises. Listen and check.

> 🎧 **CD 3, track 43**   página 9, actividad 2
>
> h-e-l-a-d-o
> i-P-o-d
> o-s-i-t-o

 3 Read and decode the words.
Work through the example first, if necessary. More able students can decode the words first and you can then go through the answers, explaining anything they do not understand.

Answers:
a móvil; **b** revista; **c** regalo; **d** moda; **e** mascota; **f** naranja; **g** seis; **h** siete

AT 3.1   **4 Colour all the masculine nouns in red and all the feminine ones in blue.**
Remind students that it is important to know the gender of nouns in Spanish and that they should try to learn the gender when they learn the word. Elicit from students what the definite/indefinite article is for a masculine noun and then for a feminine noun.

Answers:
masculine: un amigo; un regalo; un helado; un deporte; un grupo
feminine: una hamburguesa; una fiesta; una naranja; la música

Página 10   0.3 La familia
- Use with Students' Book, pages 12–13

AT 4.1   **1 Complete the grid.**
This provides practice of masculine and feminine forms of nouns.

Answers:
(missing words in order) hermana; tío; madre; padrastro; abuela; primo

AT 3.2-3   **2 Read and name the people in the picture.**
This provides practice of family vocabulary as well as masculine and feminine forms.

Answers:
girl: Ana María; **her brother:** Javier; **Mum:** Violeta; **Dad:** Juan Carlos; **Grandmother:** Ernestina

AT 2.2   **3 Point to each person in this picture and give as much information as you can about them.**
Students should base this on the text in Activity 2, but use the family illustrated, i.e. they should use one *soy* one *tengo* and and one *me llamo* for each person. They can use *se llama* too.

Página 11   0.4 ¿Cuántos años tienes?
- Use with Students' Book, pages 14–15

AT 3.1   **1 Put these animals in order according to their lifespan.**
Have a quick brainstorming session to revise numbers before they do this activity.

Answers: Elefante: 70 años; Cocodrilo: 45 años; Rinoceronte: 40 años; Hipopótamo: 39 años; Serpiente: 23 años; Tigre: 22 años; Canguro: 9 años; Koala: 8 años

AT 3.1-2   **2 Draw lines to match up the answers to the questions.**

Answers:
a ¿Qué tal? Muy bien, gracias. **b** ¿Cómo te llamas? Me llamo Stacey. **c** ¿Cuántos años tienes? Tengo doce años. **d** ¿Tienes hermanos? Tengo una hermana. **e** ¿Tienes abuelos? Tengo una abuela y dos abuelos.

 3 Listen and answer the questions for Stacey. Try not to get caught out.
Students can do this activity using their own information instead of using Stacey's if they prefer. It is also good practise for students to play this with a friend, asking the questions as quickly as they can to try and catch out their partner.

> 🎧 **CD 3, track 44**   página 11, actividad 3
>
> ¿Qué tal?
> ¿Cómo te llamas?
> ¿Qué tal?
> ¿Cuántos años tienes?
> ¿Cuántos años tienes?
> ¿Tienes hermanos?
> ¿Cómo te llamas?
> ¿Cuántos años tienes?
> ¿Tienes hermanos?
> ¿Qué tal?
> ¿Tienes abuelos?
> ¿Qué tal?
> ¿Cómo te llamas?
> ¿Qué tal?
> ¿Cuántos años tienes?
> ¿Cuántos años tienes?
> ¿Tienes hermanos?
> ¿Cómo te llamas?
> ¿Cuántos años tienes?
> ¿Tienes hermanos?

Me presento 0

AT 4.2   **4**   **Now write your own answers to the questions.**
Students write their own answers to the questions from Activity 3. Some students will have already answered for themselves orally, but it will still be of value to write down this information.

Página 12   0.5 Gente y números
- Use with Students' Book, pages 16–17

AT 3.2   **1**   **Follow the word snake round the grid to read the conversation. The snake can go up, down or across, but not diagonally.**
This challenges students' ability to structure texts logically and to predict what might come next in a dialogue.

Answer:
¿Qué tal?
Muy bien.
¿Cómo te llamas?
Me llamo Ben.

AT 3.2   **2**   **Now try this one.**

Answer:
Tengo una hermana, se llama Ana y tengo tres tíos.

AT 4.2   **3**   **Now create your own word snake grid using Spanish you know.**
Encourage students to look back at previous texts for support and ideas. They should try to make their grid as big as they can. They could swap with a partner who tries to work out what the grid says.

Página 13   0.6A Labolengua
- Use with Students' Book, pages 18–19

AT 3.1   **1**   **Circle all the nouns.**

Answers:
una fiesta; un hermano; la música; las naranjas; los helados

2   **How did you decide what was a noun? Put these reasons in order of importance, 1–3.**
Discuss this in class. Remind students that nouns in Spanish can be masculine, feminine or plural and are usually preceded by a definite or an indefinite article.

AT 3.1   **3**   **Sort these nouns into masculine and feminine by writing *un* or *una* in front of them.**
Before students do this activity, discuss typical noun endings.

Answers:
un hermano; una hermana; un osito; un regalo; una hamburguesa; un helado; un abuelo; una familia; una guitarra

AT 3.1   **4**   **'A' or 'the'? Complete the English translations.**

Answers:
a *a;* **b** *the;* **c** *the;* **d** *a;* **e** *a*

Página 14   0.6B Técnica
- Use with Students' Book, pages 18–19

AT 3.1   **1**   **Look at the two different vocabulary pages. Decide who (Alex or Jordan) has …**
This activity encourages students to think about the way in which they record vocabulary. It will also give them ideas about the best way to record vocabulary.

Answers:
Alex; Jordan; Jordan; Jordan; Jordan; Alex; Jordan

2   **What two things do you like about the way Alex has set out the vocabulary? And two things for Jordan?**
Students will be able to take these elements and use them when they record their own vocabulary.

3   **Record Alex and Jordan's vocabulary in the best possible way.**
Encourage students to refer back to this when they next write down a piece of vocabulary.

Higher Workbook

Página 8   0.1 Quiz
- Use with Students' Book, pages 8–9

AT 4.1   **1**   **Practise writing out these sentences, paying attention to the Spanish characters.**
These characters will seem very different for most students so they may want to practise writing out the sentences a few times.

AT 3.1   **2**   **Draw lines to match up.**
This practises students' knowledge of some Spanish phrases.

Answers:
buenos días; buenas tardes; buenas noches

0 Me presento

AT 1.2   **3** **Listen and identify the celebrities.**

> 🎧 **CD 4, track 16**   página 8, actividad 3
>
> – Hola. ¿Cómo te llamas?
> – Me llamo Penélope, Penélope Cruz.
> – Ah, Penélope Cruz. Mucho gusto.
> [Pause]
> – ¿Y tú? ¿Cómo te llamas?
> – Me llamo Shakira.
> – Hola, Shakira, ¿Qué tal?
> – Muy bien.
> [Pause]
> – Buenas tardes. ¿Cómo te llamas?
> – Me llamo Fernando Torres.
> – Buenas tardes, Fernando.
> [Pause]
> – Y ¿cómo te llamas?
> – Me llamo Cesc, Cesc Fàbregas.
> – Hola, Cesc.

Answers:
Penelope Cruz, Shakira, Fernando Torres, Cesc Fàbregas

AT 2.2   **4** **Practise greeting and interviewing celebrities.**
Students can refer back to Activity 3 as well as to the phrases given for support if necessary.

Página 9   0.2 Me flipa; me molan
- Use with Students' Book, pages 10–11

AT 1.1–2   **1** **Javier is planning a surprise party for his little brother. To keep it secret he spells out the important words. Listen and tick the ones he mentions?**
Practice of the Spanish alphabet, including accents.

> 🎧 **CD 4, track 17**   página 9, actividad 1
>
> Vamos a hacer una F-I-E-S-T-A para mi hermano. Vamos a invitar a sus A-M-I-G-O-S. Le gusta comer H-E-L-A-D-O y escuchar M-Ú-S-I-C-A

Answers:
fiesta; amigos; helado; música

AT 2.1   **2** **Now spell out these other surprises. Listen and check.**
Remind students of the phrase, *con acento escrito* before they start.

> 🎧 **CD 4, track 18**   página 9, actividad 2
>
> h-a-m-b-u-r-g-u-e-s-a
> i-P-o-d
> m-ó-v-i-l
> j-u-e-g-o-s
> o-s-i-t-o

AT 3.1   **3** **Read and crack the code.**
Practice of spelling and numbers. This could also work well as a class quiz. Students work individually to try and crack the code. The first one to find all of the words is the winner.

Answers:

tres	cuatro	cinco	seis	siete	ocho	nueve
t	o	r	m	a	e	i

a hamburguesa; **b** revista; **c** regalo; **d** moda; **e** mascota; **f** naranja; **g** seis; **h** siete

4 **Colour all the masculine nouns in red and all the feminine ones in blue.**
Remind students that it is important to know the gender of nouns in Spanish and that they should try to learn the gender when they learn the word. Elicit from students what the definite/indefinite article is for masculine and feminine nouns. Students should also be able to recognise that some of these nouns are plural.

Answers:
masculine: unos amigos; un regalo; un helado; el deporte; un grupo; un pastel
feminine: unas hamburguesas; la fiesta; unas naranjas; la música

Página 10   0.3 La familia
- Use with Students' Book, pages 12–13

AT 3.1   **1** **Complete the grid. What do the words in the Plural column mean?**
Practice of gender and number.

Answers:

Masculine	Feminine	Plural
mi padre	mi madre	mis padres – my parents
mi tío	mi tía	mis tíos – my aunts and uncles
mi hermano	mi hermana	mis hermanos – my brothers and sisters
mi abuelo	mi abuela	mis abuelos – my grandparents
mi primo	mi prima	mis primos – my cousins

Me presento 0

AT 3.3   **2 Read, then draw and label the family.**
Practice of family vocabulary.

Answer:
girl called Ana María, boy (stepbrother) called Javier, Mum called Violeta, Dad called Juan Carlos, Aunt Teresa, male cousin Beto, paternal grandmother Ernestina

AT 3.3   **3 Read and work out the meaning of the words in bold.**
Students use the description and the family tree from Activity 2 to work out the words in bold.

Answers: nieta – granddaughter; sobrina – niece

AT 2.2   **4 Point to someone in your picture for Activity 2. Say five things about them.**
Further practice of talking about families.

Página 11   0.4 ¿Cuántos años tienes?
- Use with Students' Book, pages 14–15

AT 3.1   **1 Put these animals in order according to their lifespan. Use a dictionary to see what the animals are.**
This activity provides practice of higher numbers and dictionary skills.

Answers:
burro (donkey) – 45 años; oso (bear) – 43 años; loro (parrot) – 30 años; pato (duck) – 29 años; venado (deer) – 26 años; gato (cat) – 25 años; murciélago (bat) – 24 años; vaca (cow) – 22 años; lobo (wolf) – 18 años; zorro (fox) – 14 años

AT 4.2–3   **2 Write your own answers to these questions.**
Students use the vocabulary they have learnt to answer the questions for themselves.

AT 1.1–2   **3 Listen and answer the questions. Try not to get caught out. If you can, play the same game with a friend.**
It is good practice for students to play this with a friend, asking the questions as quickly as they can to try and catch out their partner.

CD 4, track 19   página 11, actividad 3

¿Qué tal?
¿Cómo te llamas?
¿Qué tal?
¿Cuántos años tienes?
¿Cuántos años tienes?
¿Tienes hermanos?
¿Cómo te llamas?
¿Cuántos años tienes?
¿Tienes hermanos?
¿Qué tal?
¿Tienes abuelos?
¿Qué tal?
¿Cómo te llamas?
¿Qué tal?
¿Cuántos años tienes?
¿Cuántos años tienes?
¿Tienes hermanos?
¿Cómo te llamas?
¿Cuántos años tienes?
¿Tienes hermanos?

Página 12   0.5 Gente y números
- Use with Students' Book, pages 16–17

AT 3.2   **1 Follow the word snake round the grid to read the conversation. The snake can go up, down or across, but not diagonally.**
This challenges students' ability to structure texts logically and to predict what might come next in a dialogue.

Answer:
¿Qué tal, cómo te llamas?
Me llamo Pedro.
¿Cuántos años tienes?
Tengo trece años.
¿Tienes hermanos?
No, soy hijo único.

AT 4.2   **2 Use this grid to make a Spanish conversation snake for a friend.**
Encourage students to look back at previous texts for support and ideas.

0 Me presento

Página 13 — 0.6A Labolengua
- Use with Students' Book, pages 18–19

AT 3.1 **1 Circle all the nouns.**
Students should read the grammar box before they begin.

Answers:
una fiesta; un hermano; la música; las naranjas; los helados

2 How did you decide what was a noun? Give three ideas.
You may find it useful to discuss students' answers in class after they have finished. Remind students that nouns in Spanish can be masculine, feminine or plural and are usually preceded by a definite or an indefinite article.

3 Sort these nouns into masculine and feminine by writing *un* or *una* in front of them. Use a dictionary to find out what they mean.

Answers:
una casa – a house; un colegio – a school;
una camisa – a shirt; una piscina – a swimming pool;
un chico – a boy; un pulpo – an octopus; un piso – a flat;
una rana – a frog; un bocadillo – a sandwich;

4 'A', 'the' or 'some'? Use the nouns in Activity 3 to translate these phrases into Spanish.
Practice of using the masculine, feminine and plural forms of the definite and indefinite article.

Answers:
la camisa; unas ranas; una piscina; el bocadillo; unos chicos; el piso; las casas; el pulpo

Página 14 — 0.6B Técnica
- Use with Students' Book, pages 18–19

1 Look at the two different vocabulary pages. Decide who (Alex or Jordan) has…
This activity encourages students to think about the way in which they record vocabulary. It will also give them ideas about the best way to record vocabulary.

Answers:
Alex; Jordan; Jordan; Jordan; Jordan; Alex; Jordan

2 What three things do you like about the way Alex has set out the vocabulary? And three things for Jordan?
Students will be able to take these elements and use them when they record their own vocabulary.

3 Record Alex and Jordan's vocabulary in the best possible way.
Encourage students to refer back to this when they next write down a piece of vocabulary.

1A Me describo

Unit Objectives

Contexts and cultural focus: talking about yourself
Grammar: possessive adjectives; adjectival agreement; the present tense of regular verbs; quantifiers
Language learning: recognising when not to use capital letters; working out grammar rules from patterns; pronouncing the Spanish 'c' correctly

- *Aim:* To learn how to speak about yourself in Spanish.
- Each unit has an associated video which will feature throughout the unit. Below is the transcript of the video for this unit.
- As a starter activity to introduce the Unit and familiarise students with the language they will meet, you may find it useful for the class to view the video as a whole.

Video script (CD 1, track 32)

José: ¿Quién es?
Khalid: ¿Quién es quién?
José: Pues, ¡la chica! Khal. ¿Quién es la chica? Siempre hay una chica.
Khalid: Vale, sí, hay una chica. Se llama Marisa.
José: Marisa ¡eh!, bonito nombre.
Khalid: Sí a ti también te caería bien. Es muy maja.
José: ¿Le gusta el fútbol? Ya sabes lo que pienso de las chicas y el fútbol.
Khalid: Lo siento, tío, pero no hablamos de fútbol.
José: Bueno, vale. Cuéntame alguna cosa más.
Eva: Hola, ¿qué hay?
José: Khal ha conocido a una chica.
Eva: ¿A otra?
José: Se llama Marisa.
Khalid: Sí, es muy lista y algo tímida… lo cual tiene su encanto.
Eva: Yo también soy muy inteligente y tímida… a veces.
Khalid: También es alta. Bueno, bastante alta aunque no demasiado.
Eva: Vale, entonces ¿cómo es? ¿Alta o baja?
Khalid: ¡Es perfecta! Y además, es guapa.
Eva: ¡Por el amor de Dios! ¡Basta ya! Es lista y tímida y encantadora y alta y baja y guapa y fantástica y maravillosa y… Vale, ¡vale ya! ¡Es estupenda! Ya lo hemos entendido.

[Pause]

Khalid: El color favorito de Marisa es el blanco…
Eva: Ya. ¿Sabíais que el color favorito de Gaudí era el azul? ¡Ese sí que es un color interesante! ¿No te parece que el blanco es un color un poco aburrido?
José: ¡Totalmente!
Khalid: Y también, Marisa habla portugués.
Eva: Sí, eso es muy útil.
Khalid: Y obviamente, también habla inglés.
Eva: ¿Es americano su padre?
Khalid: No, es argentino. Su madre es americana.
Eva: Pero en casa hablaran español, ¿no?
Khalid: Español e inglés.
Eva: Y… ¿habla catalán? Porque saber hablar catalán en Barcelona es muy importante. Alguien se lo debería decir a la Srta. Trilingüe.
Khalid: ¿Qué te pasa, Eva? ¿Qué problema tienes? Estás de mal humor, desagradable y lo criticas todo.
Eva: Sí, porque sólo hablas de Marisa, Marisa, Marisa, Marisa. Sabes más de ella que sabes de mí y, ¿cuánto tiempo hace que nos conocemos?
Khalid: Eh… 10 años.
Eva: En realidad son 11 años.
Eva: ¿Tengo algún animal en casa?
Khalid: Tienes un perro o… no, tienes un gato, no… no ¿un pez de colores? No, tienes un conejo de indias, eso es, tienes un conejo de indias, ¿no es verdad?
Eva: No. No tengo animales.
Khalid: ¡Ah!
Eva: Y ¿de dónde son mis padres?
Khalid: Ehh… de España.
Eva: Vale, eso es verdad, pero ¿qué idioma hablan?
Khalid: ¡Español!
Eva: En casa hablan catalán y sólo hablan español con gente que no entiende catalán.
Khalid: Ah, ahí está Marisa. ¡Estupendo!
Eva: Si, ¡estupendo!, ¡verdaderamente estupendo!

1A Me describo

Unit 1A Me describo Overview grid						
Page reference	Contexts and objectives	Language learning	Grammar	Key language	Framework	AT level
Pages 24–25 **Cumpleaños y fiestas**	• say dates and birthdays	• recognise when not to use capital letters	• use possessive adjectives correctly	enero; febrero; marzo; abril; mayo; junio; julio; agosto; septiembre; octubre; noviembre; diciembre; lunes; martes; miércoles; jueves; viernes; sábado; domingo	1.1, 1.4, 2.4, 3.1, 4.1, 5.1, 5.4, 5.8	1.1–2, 2.1–2, 3.1–2, 4.2–3
Pages 26–27 **Mis mascotas**	• say what pets you have and what colour they are	• work out grammar rules from patterns	• make adjectives agree correctly	un ratón; un pájaro; un gato; una rata; una tortuga; un perro; una araña; un pez; un conejo; un caballo; blanco/a; negro/a; rojo/a; azul; verde; amarillo/a; naranja; gris; marrón; rosa; morado/a	1.1, 1.4, 4.1, 4.3, 5.1, 5.3, 5.4	1.1–3, 2.2, 3.1, 4.1–3
Pages 28–29 **Lenguas y nacionalidades**	• give your nationality and say what languages you speak	• pronounce Spanish 'c' correctly	• use the present tense of regular verbs	inglés/inglesa; escocés/escocesa; irlandés/irlandesa; galés/galesa; francés/francesa; español(a); portugués/portuguesa; italiano/a	1.1, 1.4, 4.1, 2.1, 2.4, 3.1, 3.2, 4.5, 5.1, 5.4, 5.6	1.3–4, 2.2–3, 3.2–3, 4.2–3
Pages 30–31 **¿Cómo eres?**	• describe yourself and others	• extend sentences using simple connectives	• use quantifiers to enhance description	el pelo; largo; corto; liso; rizado; ondulado; de punta; los ojos; bigote; barba; pecas; llevo gafas; alto/a; bajo/a; delgado/a; gordo/a; de talla mediana; ordenado/a; desordenado/a; simpático/a; antipático/a; paciente; impaciente; estudioso/a; perezoso/a; testarudo/a; extrovertido/a; tímido/a; inteligente; bobo/a; maduro/a; inmaduro/a	1.1, 1.5, 2.1, 2.4, 4.3, 4.4, 5.1, 5.4, 5.8	1.2–4, 2.2–3, 3.1–2, 4.2–3
Pages 32–33 **En otros lugares**	• recognise words for additional animals, countries and nationalities			Paquistán; Marruecos; Polonia; Rumanía; Senegal; Somalia; Turquía; Estados Unidos; India; Grecia serpientes; ovejas; patos; cabras; cobayas; cerdos; vacas	1.1, 1.4, 2.1, 2.4, 2.5, 3.1, 4.2	1.2, 2.1–2, 3.1, 4.2–3
Pages 34–35 **Labolengua**	• review language and grammar from the unit				1.1, 1.4, 2.4, 4.1, 4.2, 4.4, 4.5, 5.1, 5.8	

Me describo 1A

Pages 36–37 **Extra Star** **Extra Plus**	• differentiated extension/ homework material	• revise and consolidate all vocabulary and grammar covered in the unit	• revise and consolidate all vocabulary and grammar covered in the unit		2.1, 2.4, 2.5, 4.2, 4.4, 4.5	3.2–3, 4.2–3
Page 38 **Prueba**	• end-of-spread test				1.1, 1.4, 1.5, 2.1, 2.4, 2.5, 4.4, 4.5	1.4, 2.2–4, 3.3, 4.3
Page 39 **Vocabulario**	• a summary of the key language covered in each spread of this unit					
Page 153 **Leer 1A**	• practice of longer reading texts based on the theme of the unit				2.1, 2.4, 2.5, 5.4	3.4, 4.4

1A Me describo

Week-by-week overview
(Three-year KS3 Route: assuming six weeks' work or approximately 10–12.5 hours)
(Two-year KS3 Route: assuming four weeks' worth or approximately 6.5-8.5 hours)
*Please note that essential activities are highlighted.

About Unit 1A, *Me describo*: Students work in the context of describing themselves and others. They talk about when their and other people's birthdays are, any pets they have (type, age, colour), say what nationality they are and which languages they speak. Students learn how to use possessive adjectives correctly, make adjectives agree correctly, use the present tense of regular verbs and use quantifiers to enhance description, etc. The unit also provides tips on language learning techniques.

	Three-Year KS3 Route			Two-Year KS3 Route	
Week	Resources	Objectives	Week	Resources	Objectives
1	1A.1 Cumpleaños y fiestas 1A.6 Lablolengua A (p.34) 1A.6 Lablolengua C (p.35)	say dates and birthdays recognise when not to use capital letters use possessive adjectives correctly	1	1A.1 Cumpleaños y fiestas omit activities 5, 8 & Challenge 1A.6 Lablolengua A (p.34) 1A.6 Lablolengua C (p.35)	say dates and birthdays recognise when not to use capital letters use possessive adjectives correctly
2	1A.2 Mis mascotas 1A.6 Lablolengua B (p.34)	say what pets you have and what colour they are work out grammar rules from patterns make adjectives agree correctly	2	1A.2 Mis mascotas omit activities 4, Think!, 7 & Challenge 1A.6 Lablolengua B (p.34) Omit activity 3	say what pets you have and what colour they are work out grammar rules from patterns make adjectives agree correctly
3	1A.3 Lenguas y nacionalidades 1A.6 Lablolengua E (p.35)	give your nationality and say what languages you speak pronounce Spanish 'c' correctly use the present tense of regular verbs	3	1A.3 Lenguas y nacionalidades omit activities 5, 6 & Challenge 1A.6 Lablolengua E (p.35)	give your nationality and say what languages you speak pronounce Spanish 'c' correctly use the present tense of regular verbs
4	1A.4 ¿Cómo eres? 1A.6 Lablolengua D (p.35)	describe yourself and others extend sentences using simple connectives use quantifiers to enhance description	4	1A.4 ¿Cómo eres? omit activities 3, 8 & Challenge 1A.6 Lablolengua D (p.35) 1B.8 Prueba (p.38) Vocabulario (p.39)	describe yourself and others extend sentences using simple connectives use quantifiers to enhance description recapping on the vocabulary of the unit prepare and carry out assessment in all four skills
5	1A.5 En otros lugares	recognise words for additional animals, countries and nationalities			
6	1A.7 Extra (Star) (p.36) 1A.7 Extra (Plus) (p.37) 1A.8 Prueba (p.38) Vocabulario (p.39) Leer (p.153)	further reinforcement and extension of the language of the unit recapping on the vocabulary of the unit prepare and carry out assessment in all four skills further reading to explore the language of the unit and cultural themes			

1A.1 Me describo

1A.1 Cumpleaños y fiestas
paginas 24–25

Planner

Objectives
- say dates and birthdays
- use possessive adjectives correctly
- recognise when not to use capital letters

Resources
Students' Book, pages 24–25
CD 1, tracks 27–29
Foundation Workbook, page 16
Higher Workbook, page 16
Foundation Workbook audio, CD 3, tracks 45–46
Higher Workbook audio, CD 4, tracks 20–21
Interactive OxBox, Unit 1A
Copymasters 14–21
Assessment, Unit 1A

Key language
enero; febrero; marzo; abril; mayo; junio; julio; agosto; septiembre; octubre; noviembre; diciembre
lunes; martes; miércoles; jueves; viernes; sábado; domingo

Grammar
- use possessive adjectives correctly

Renewed Framework references
1.1, 1.4, 2.4, 3.1, 4.1, 5.1, 5.4, 5.8

PLTS
Think!: Creative thinkers
Activity 5: Reflective learners
Challenge: Reflective learners

Starters
- Practise the months of the year in Spanish. Go round the class with each student in turn saying the next month in the sequence, i.e. *enero, febrero, marzo*, etc. Then say a sequence of months, i.e. *septiembre, octubre, noviembre…* and ask a volunteer to finish the sequence with the appropriate month – in this case, *diciembre*.
- Go round the class with each student telling you when their birthday is. Depending on the ability of the class, you may want to display the months in Spanish along with the phrase, *Mi cumpleaños es el XXX de XXX*. Does anyone share the same birthday?

Plenaries
- Students write five sentences using the possessive adjectives they have met in the spread. If necessary, display the possessive adjectives for support.
- Play a guessing game. Write down a birth date on a piece of paper. Don't show the class. The class tries to guess which date you have written down, e.g. *¿Tu cumpleaños es el 10 de marzo?* Whoever guesses correctly writes down a new date and the class guesses again.

Homework/Self-study
Think!: Students write out the months and illustrate each one to help them remember them. They can highlight the endings to illustrate the pattern they follow.
Students rewrite the sentences they have translated in the Challenge Activity, changing the date and month in each.

AT 1.1 **1 Escucha y repite.**
Students listen and repeat the months of the year.

CD 1, track 27 — página 24, actividad 1
enero, febrero, marzo, abril, mayo, junio, julio, agosto, septiembre, octubre, noviembre, diciembre

AT 1.2 **2 Anota el día y el mes.**
Students listen and note down the day(s) and the months of the festivals mentioned.

CD 1, track 28 — página 24, actividad 2
1. El día de Reyes es el 6 de enero.
2. Las Fallas culminan el 19 de marzo.
3. La Diada de Cataluña es el 11 de septiembre.
4. El día de la Hispanidad se celebra el 12 de octubre.
5. Los Sanfermines se celebran el 7 de julio.
6. El 1 de noviembre se celebra el día de Todos los Santos.

Answers:
1 6 de enero; **2** 19 de marzo; **3** 11 de septiembre; **4** 12 de octubre; **5** 7 de julio; **6** 1 de noviembre

1A.1 Me describo

AT 3.1   **3 Pon los días de la semana en el orden correcto.**
Students use the calendar to put the days of the week in the correct order.

Answers:
lunes, martes, miércoles, jueves, viernes, sábado, domingo

AT 1.1   **4 Escucha y verifica.**
Students then listen to check their answers.

🎧 **CD 1, track 29**   página 24, actividad 4

lunes, martes, miércoles, jueves, viernes, sábado, domingo

PLTS   **Think!**
Students look carefully at the how the months and days are spelled in Spanish. Can they see any patterns?

Answers:
The months in Spanish are not usually written with a capital letter, except at the beginning of a sentence.
The months up until August all end in the letter 'o'; from September on, they end in 'bre'.
The week days all end in 'es'; Saturday and Sunday end in 'o' in Spanish.

AT 2.1   **5 Repaso: Decid los números 1–31 en voz alta.**
PLTS   Students work with a partner to say the numbers from 1–31 out loud as fast as possible.

AT 3.2   **6 Lee.**
Students read the speech bubbles and note what they mean?

Answers:
¿Cuándo es tu cumpleaños? When is your birthday?
Mi cumpleaños es el catorce de febrero. My birthday is on 14th February.

AT 4.2   **7 Escribe las frases.**
Students use the prompts to write their own sentences on the subject of birthdays.

Answers:
18/7: Mi cumpleaños es el dieciocho de julio.
30/1: Mi cumpleaños es el treinta de enero.
9/11: Mi cumpleaños es el nueve de noviembre.
31/3: Mi cumpleaños es el treinta y uno de marzo.
25/2: Mi cumpleaños es el veinticinco de febrero.
13/4: Mi cumpleaños es el trece de abril.

AT 2.2   **8 Citas rápidas.**
Students ask six of their classmates when their birthday is and note their answers.

AT 3.2   **9 Mira los dibujos. ¿Cómo se dice…?**
Students look at the cartoons and work out how to say each of the possessive adjectives in Spanish.

Answers:
my – mi (sing.); mis (pl)
your – tu (sing.); tus (pl)
his/her – su (sing.); sus (pl)
our – nuestro (masc. sing.), nuestra (fem. sing.); nuestros (masc. pl.), nuestras (fem. pl.)
your – vuestro (masc. sing.), vuestra (fem. sing.); vuestros (masc. pl.), vuestras (fem. pl.)
their – su (sing.); sus (pl.)

AT 4.2–3   **Challenge**
PLTS   **Translate these sentences into Spanish.**
Students use the language and grammar covered in the spread to translate the sentences listed into Spanish.

Answers:
1 Su cumpleaños es el tres de marzo. **2** Nuestro cumpleaños es el diecisiete de julio. **3** Tu cumpleaños es el veintiocho de enero. **4** Su cumpleaños es el veinte de septiembre. **5** Su cumpleaños es el nueve de junio.

1A.2 Me describo

1A.2 Mis mascotas
páginas 26–27

Planner

Objectives
- say what pets you have and what colour they are
- make adjectives agree correctly
- work out grammar rules from patterns

Resources
Students' Book, pages 26–27
CD 1, tracks 30–31
Foundation Workbook, page 17
Higher Workbook, page 17
Foundation Workbook audio, CD 3, track 47
Higher Workbook audio, CD 4, track 22
Interactive OxBox, Unit 1A
Copymasters 14–21
Assessment, Unit 1A

Key language
un ratón; un pájaro; un gato; una rata; una tortuga; un perro; una araña; un pez; un conejo; un caballo blanco/a; negro/a; rojo/a; azul; verde; amarillo/a; naranja; gris; marrón; rosa; morado/a

Grammar
- make adjectives agree correctly

Renewed Framework references
1.1, 1.4, 4.1, 4.3, 5.1, 5.3, 5.4

PLTS
Think! (1): Independent enquirers
Think! (2): Independent enquirers
Activity 6: Reflective learners
Challenge: Team workers

Starters
- Go round the class asking each student in turn if they have a pet. They can make up a pet if they don't have one, e.g. *Tengo dos leones!*
- Display some adjectives from the spread and challenge students to write out all of their forms. Check answers as a class.

Plenaries
- Play a memory game using animal vocabulary and adjectives. You start with a sentence, e.g. *Tengo un perro negro y blanco.* Students continue in turn with each one repeating what has already been said and adding a new sentence of their own, e.g. *Tengo un perro negro y blanco y tengo un pez naranja*. etc. Remind students that they don't have to tell the truth – they could say they have a blue spider, for example!
- Display the adjectives from Starter Activity 2 and challenge students to use them in sentences on the theme of the spread, paying particular attention to adjectival agreement. Volunteers could read their sentences out to the class.

Homework/Self-study
Students find examples of plurals in the spread to illustrate the rules they formulated in the first Think! box. Provide less able students with a list of plurals to categorise.
Activity 6: Students use the key language from the spread to practise writing sentences including adjectives. They must make sure that the adjectives agree. Provide less able students with gapped sentences and adjectives to choose from.

AT 1.1 1 Escucha y escribe.
Students listen and write down the animal mentioned each time.

🎧 **CD 1, track 30** página 26, actividad 1
1 Tengo un gato.
2 Tengo un perro.
3 Tengo un pez.
4 Tengo un conejo.
5 Tengo un caballo.
6 Tengo un pájaro.
7 Tengo una rata.
8 Tengo una tortuga.
9 Tengo un ratón.
10 Tengo una araña.

Answers:
1 un gato; *2* un perro; *3* un pez; *4* un conejo; *5* un caballo; *6* un pájaro; *7* una rata; *8* una tortuga; *9* un ratón; *10* una araña

AT 4.1 2 Escribe el singular.
Students write down the singular of the plural forms listed. Encourage them to think back to Activity 1 for support.

Answers:
1 un perro; *2* un gato; *3* un ratón; *4* un pez; *5* una araña; *6* un león

1A.2 Me describo

PLTS **Think!**
Students try to work out the rules to make a word plural in Spanish. Point out that it makes a difference if a word ends in a vowel or in a consonant. Depending on the ability of the class, you may also want to add that some words add or lose an accent in the plural (*ratón = ratones*).

Answers:
If a word ends in a vowel just add –s to make it plural.
If a word ends in a consonant add –es to make it plural
Note: *If a word ends in z, change this to c and add –es (un pez = cinco peces)*

AT 4.1 **3 Haz el plural.**
Students draw upon what they have learnt to write out the plural of the animals in the house. They should write M (masculine) or F (feminine) accordingly.

Answers:
1 un gato – dos gatos (M); 2 un perro – dos perros (M); 3 un pez – dos peces (M); 4 un conejo – dos conejos (M); 5 un caballo – dos caballos (M); 6 un pájaro – dos pájaros (M); 7 una rata – dos ratas (F); 8 una tortuga – dos tortugas (F); 9 un ratón – dos ratones (M); 10 una araña – dos arañas (F)

AT 2.2 **4 Conversación.**
Students act out the conversation with a partner, taking it in turns to be A or B. You could display the animals in Spanish, if necessary.

AT 3.1 **5 ¿Conoces los colores?**
Students use the text and picture to work out 11 colours in Spanish. They then write down what they are in English.

Answers:
naranja – *orange;* **rojo** – *red;* **rosa** – *pink;* **gris** – *grey;* **negro** – *black;* **verde** – *green;* **amarillo** – *yellow;* **azul** – *blue;* **marrón** – *brown;* **morado** – *purple;* **blanco** – *white*

PLTS **Think!**
Students focus on adjectival agreement in Spanish. They look carefully at the colours they have noted down from the Noah's Ark passage. What did they notice about Spanish adjectives? Explain that you will look at this in detail in the grammar box.

Gramática
Work through the grammar box as a class. Ensure that students understand that in Spanish all adjectives all have a masculine and feminine form, and that they change to agree with the noun they are describing, according to whether it is masculine or feminine. Look at the table showing adjective endings and work through some examples to illustrate this. Remind students that they must also make adjectives plural when describing a plural noun.

AT 4.1 **6 Haz una tabla con los colores.**
PLTS Students complete the table with the colours from Activity 5. Refer them back to the grammar box for support if necessary.

Answers:
white: *blanco, blanca, blancos, blancas*
orange: *naranja, naranja, naranja, naranja*
red: *rojo, roja, rojos, rojas*
pink: *rosa, rosa, rosa, rosa*
grey: *gris, gris, grises, grises*
black: *negro, negra, negros, negras*
green: *verde, verde, verdes, verdes*
yellow: *amarillo, amarilla, amarillos, amarillas*
blue: *azul, azul, azules, azules*
brown: *marrón, marrón, marrónes, marrónes*
purple: *morado, morada, morados, moradas*

AT 1.2–3 **7 Escucha y rellena la tabla (1–6).**
This practises the language and grammar covered in the spread. Students listen and fill in the table.

🎧 **CD 1, track 31** página 27, actividad 7

1 ¿Tienes animales en casa, Jorge?
  Sí, tengo tres perros negros.
2 ¿Y tú, Elisa? ¿Tienes también perros?
  No, no tengo perros. Tengo un gato blanco.
3 María, ¿tienes animales en casa?
  Sí, tengo un hámster marrón y blanco y ocho peces de colores: tres azules y cinco naranjas.
4 Josema, ¿y tú? ¿Tienes animales?
  Sí, tengo dos tortugas verdes.
5 Maricati, ¿tú tienes animales en casa?
  Tengo dos caballos negros en el establo y en casa tengo un conejo blanco.
6 Susana, ¿tienes animales en casa?
  Sí, tengo una rata blanca, dos gatos grises y un perro marrón.

Answers:
Jorge: perros, 3, negros
Elisa: gato, 1, blanco
María: hámster/peces, 1/8, marrón y blanco/3 azules, 5 naranja
Josema: tortugas, 2, verdes
Maricati: caballos/conejo, 2/1, negros/blanco
Susana: rata/gatos/perro, blanca/grises/marrón

1A.3 Me describo

4.2-3 PLTS Challenge
Ask five of your classmates about their pets by using the questions in Activity 4. Write out your findings.
Students ask five of their classmates about their pets, using the questions in Activity 4. They then write out their findings as fully as possible, paying particular attention to plurals and adjectival agreement.

1A.3 Lenguas y nacionalidades   páginas 28–29

Planner

Objectives
- give your nationality and say what languages you speak
- use the present tense of regular verbs
- pronounce Spanish 'c' correctly

Video
Video script, Unit 1A
Video-blog, Unit 1A

Resources
Students' Book, pages 28–29
CD 1, tracks 32–35
Foundation Workbook, page 18
Higher Workbook, page 18
Foundation Workbook audio, CD 3, track 48
Higher Workbook audio, CD 4, track 23
Interactive OxBox, Unit 1A
Copymasters 14–21
Assessment, Unit 1A

Key language
inglés/inglesa; escocés/escocesa; irlandés/irlandesa; galés/galesa; francés/francesa; español(a); portugués/portuguesa; italiano/a

Grammar
- use the present tense of regular verbs

Renewed Framework references
1.1, 1.4, 4.1, 2.1, 2.4, 3.1, 3.2, 4.5, 5.1, 5.4, 5.6

PLTS
Activity 3: Independent enquirers
Challenge: Team work

Starters
- Students work in pairs or small groups to tell each other what country they are from, what nationality they are and which language(s) they speak.
- Display a list of Spanish words all containing either of the 'c' sounds. Go round the class pointing to one of the words and asking students to read it out, taking care to pronounce the 'c' correctly. Alternatively, or in addition to this, go round each student in turn calling out either 'k' or 'th'. Each student should give you a Spanish word containing that sound.

Plenaries
- Display some infinitives from the spread and challenge students to write them out in the present tense. Check answers as a class.
- Students write a few sentences about a famous person of their choice saying what country they are from, what nationality they are, where they live now and which languages they speak. They could also incorporate language from previous spreads and say how old they are and when their birthday is. Volunteers read their sentences out to the class who tries to guess who they are describing.

Homework/Self-study
Gramática: Students write sentences in the present tense about somebody else they know.

AT 1.3–4 PLTS 1 Mira el video. ¿Cuál es la nacionalidad de Eva y Marisa? ¿Qué idiomas hablan?
Students note down Eva and Marisa's nationalities and the languages they speak. Allow them to watch the video again if necessary.

Video script: Unit 1A (CD1, track 32)
Khalid: El color favorito de Marisa es el blanco…
Eva: Ya. ¿Sabíais que el color favorito de Gaudí era el azul? ¡Ese sí que es un color interesante! ¿No te parece que el blanco es un color un poco aburrido?
José: ¡Totalmente!
Khalid: Y también, Marisa habla portugués.

1A.3 Me describo

Eva: Sí, eso es muy útil.
Khalid: Y obviamente, también habla inglés.
Eva: ¿Es americano su padre?
Khalid: No, es argentino. Su madre es americana.
Eva: Pero en casa hablaran español, ¿no?
Khalid: Español e inglés.
Eva: Y… ¿habla catalán? Porque saber hablar catalán en Barcelona es muy importante. Alguien se lo debería decir a la Srta. Trilingüe.
Khalid: ¿Qué te pasa, Eva? ¿Qué problema tienes? Estás de mal humor, desagradable y lo criticas todo.
Eva: Sí, porque sólo hablas de Marisa, Marisa, Marisa, Marisa, Marisa. Sabes más de ella que sabes de mí y, ¿cuánto tiempo hace que nos conocemos?
Khalid: Eh… 10 años.
Eva: En realidad son 11 años.
Eva: ¿Tengo algún animal en casa?
Khalid: Tienes un perro o… no, tienes un gato, no no… ¿un pez de colores? No, tienes un conejo de indias, eso es, tienes un conejo de indias, ¿no es verdad?
Eva: No. No tengo animales.
Khalid: ¡Ah!
Eva: Y ¿de dónde son mis padres?
Khalid: Ehh… de España.
Eva: Vale, eso es verdad, pero ¿qué idioma hablan?
Khalid: ¡Español!
Eva: En casa hablan catalán y sólo hablan español con gente que no entiende catalán.

Answers:
Eva: *Spanish; speaks Catalan and Spanish*
Marisa: *Argentine; speaks Spanish, Portuguese and English*

AT 3.3   **2 Lee e identifica.**
Students read what the young people say and identify three countries, three nationalities and five languages.

Answers:
countries: *Spain, Guatemala, Paraguay;* **nationalities:** *Columbian, Guatemalan, Paraguayan;* **languages:** *Spanish, Catalan, English, French, Guarani*

PLTS   **3 Rellena la tabla.**
Students fill in the table with the appropriate country, nationality or language. Refer them back to Activity 2 for support if necessary.

Answers:
Inglaterra; inglés; inglés; inglesa
Escocia; escocés/inglés; escocés; escocesa
Irlanda; irlandés/inglés; irlandés; irlandesa
Francia; francés; francés; francesa
España; español; español; española
Alemania; alemán; alemán; alemana
Italia; italiano; italiano; italiana

Think!
Students practise pronouncing the letter 'c' in Spanish. Work through the examples in the box checking that all students understand when to pronounce 'c' like 'k' and when to pronounce it like 'th'. Students then work in pairs and read one of the reading passages from the spread to each other, taking care to pronounce 'c' correctly whenever it occurs.

🎧 **CD 1, track 33**   página 28, Think!

capitán, concierto, curioso
centro, cine
cereal, cerámica, catástrofe, círculo, escocés, cámara, color, francés, ceremonia

AT 4.2   **4 ¿Qué significan…?**
Students note down the meaning of the verbs listed. They then use these verbs to write a few sentences about themselves.

Answers:
soy – *I am;* **vivo** – *I live;* **hablo** – *I speak;* **aprendo** – *I learn*

AT 3.3   **5 Lee. ¿Qué pasó con *soy, vivo, hablo* y *aprendo*?**
Students read the speech bubble. They then note down what has happened to the verbs listed. They consider reasons why these verbs have changed their form.

Answers:
They have changed to the 3rd person singular forms: **es, vive, habla** *and* **aprende***.*

1A.3 Me describo

Gramática

Work through the grammar explanation as a class. First concentrate on infinitives. List some of the infinitives students have already met and ask them to look them up in the dictionary. Next look at the grid showing the present tense of some familiar verbs. Pay attention to the regular verb endings. Point out the pattern for each infinitive ending and ask students to compare these regular endings with the irregular verb *ser* – can they see why this is considered an irregular verb? To check understanding, ask students to write sentences either about you, or about a friend.

AT 1.4 **6 Escucha y completa la información.**
Students listen and fill in the information.

CD 1, track 34 — página 29, actividad 6

1 Me llamo Aurora y tengo 16 años. Aunque soy americana vivo en Madrid con mi padre y mi hermano. Hablo inglés y español y ahora en el colegio aprendo francés también.

2 Hola, soy Magaluz. Se escribe M-A-G-A-L-U-Z. Acabo de cumplir trece años y vivo aquí en Sevilla en España pero soy chilena. Sólo hablo el español pero en el instituto aprendo inglés, aunque se me da bastante mal.

3 Hola, ¿qué tal? Somos Ken y Will. Tenemos dieciocho años, nuestro cumpleaños fue el dieciséis de septiembre. Somos chinos pero vivimos en Dublín en Irlanda. Hablamos inglés, español y chino y en la universidad aprendemos japonés.

4 ¡Buenas! Soy Pablo aunque toda mi familia me llama Pablito. Soy mejicano y vivo en Cancún en Méjico. Mi madre es mejicana pero mi padre es inglés así que hablo español y por supuesto inglés también. Tengo trece años y en el instituto no estudio idiomas.

Answers:
1 Aurora; 16 años; americana; Madrid, España; inglés y español; francés
2 Magaluz; 13 años; chilena; Sevilla, España; español; inglés
3 Ken y Will; 18 años; chinos; Dublín, Irlanda; inglés, español y chino; japonés
4 Pablo; 13 años; mejicano; Cancún, Méjico; español y inglés; no estudio idiomas

AT 1.3 **7 Mira el video-blog. ¿Cómo contestan a las preguntas?**
Students watch and note down the answers for each person.

Video–blog: Unit 1A (CD 1, track 35)

¿Dónde vives?
Eva: Vivo en Barcelona, en el centro, cerca de la catedral de la Sagrada Familia.
José: Vivo en las afueras de Barcelona, en Badalona.
Khalid: Vivo aquí en Barcelona, en el barrio de Gràcia.
Marisa: Vivo en el norte de Barcelona, cerca del Parque Güell.

¿Cuál es tu nacionalidad?
Eva: Soy española y catalana también.
José: Mi nacionalidad es española.
Khalid: Soy marroquí.
Marisa: Soy de Argentina.

¿Qué idiomas hablas?
Eva: En casa hablo catalán pero también hablo español e inglés y un poco de latín.
José: Hablo español, un poco de francés e un poco de inglés.
Khalid: Hablo español, catalán, francés, inglés, árabe y entiendo italiano.
Marisa: Hablo español, portugués e inglés.

Answers:
Eva: lives in the centre of Barcelona; is Spanish and Catalan; speaks Catalan, Spanish, English and a little Latin
José: lives on the outskirts of Barcelona; is Spanish; speaks Spanish, a little French and English
Khalid: lives in Barcelona; is Moroccan, speaks Spanish, Catalan, French, English, Arabic and understands Italian
Marisa: lives in the North of Barcelona; is Argentine; speaks Spanish, Portuguese and English

AT 4.2–3 PLTS **Challenge**
Ask a friend the questions in Activity 7 and note their answers. Then write a paragraph about them.
Students should take care to use the correct verbs. Encourage able students to use connectives.

1A.4 Me describo

1A.4 ¿Cómo eres?
páginas 30–31

Planner

Objectives
- describe yourself and others
- use quantifiers to enhance description
- extend sentences using simple connectives

Resources
Students' Book, pages 30–37
CD 1, tracks 36–37
Foundation Workbook, page 19
Higher Workbook, page 19
Foundation Workbook audio, CD 3, tracks 49–50
Higher Workbook audio, CD 4, tracks 24–25
Interactive OxBox, Unit 1A
Copymasters 14–21
Assessment, Unit 1A

Key language
el pelo; largo; corto; liso; rizado; ondulado; de punta; los ojos; bigote; barba; pecas; llevo gafas; alto/a; bajo/a; delgado/a; gordo/a; de talla mediana ordenado/a; desordenado/a; simpático/a; antipático/a; paciente; impaciente; estudioso/a; perezoso/a; testarudo/a; extrovertido/a; tímido/a; inteligente; bobo/a; maduro/a; inmaduro/a

Grammar
- use quantifiers to enhance description

Renewed Framework references
1.1, 1.5, 2.1, 2.4, 4.3, 4.4, 5.1, 5.4, 5.8

PLTS
Activity 4: Reflective learners
Grammar: Reflective learners
Challenge: Creative thinkers; Reflective learners

Starters
- Display some adjectives from the spread in the masculine form. Give students a time limit (of your choosing) to write down the feminine and plural forms of the adjectives listed. Check answers as a class.
- Play a 'description' game as a class. Ask students to think of a famous person. Explain that they are going to pretend to be this person and will describe themselves (as the famous person). They write the description out on paper first. A volunteer reads out his/her description. The class tries to guess who he/she is pretending to be.
- Call out a personality trait, e.g. *inteligente* and ask students to give you the opposite trait, e.g. *bobo/a*. The first student to answer correctly gets to call out the next trait, and so on.

Plenaries
- Challenge students to write five sentences using quantifiers to make them more sophisticated. Compare the sentences which include quantifiers with sentences without these to illustrate the difference they can make.
- Challenge students to come up with the most unusual description (physical and personality).

Homework/Self-study
Activity 2: Students write a sentence describing their own hair. More able students can also describe other people's hair. Provide less able students with a model sentence to adapt.
Challenge: Students go on to describe a nightmare teacher. They should be as creative as possible.

AT 1.2 **1 Escucha y elige.**
Students listen to the customers and note down which of the wigs they have bought.

Answers:
a 4; **b** 5; **c** 8; **d** 2; **e** 6; **f** 1; **g** 3; **h** 7

AT 3.1 **2 ¿Qué significa…?**
Students draw upon what they have heard in Activity 1 to work out the English meaning of the words in the vocabulary box.

Answers:
rubio – blond; **pelirrojo** – red-headed; **castaño** – brunette; **largo** – long; **corto** – short; **liso** – straight; **rizado** – curly; **ondulado** – wavy; **de punta** – spiky

🎧 **CD 1, track 36** página 30, actividad 1

a Tengo el pelo pelirrojo, largo y rizado.
b Tengo el pelo castaño, largo y liso.
c Tengo el pelo negro de punta.
d Tengo el pelo rubio, corto y liso.
e Tengo el pelo castaño, corto y ondulado.
f La peluca me ha costado 55€.
g Tengo el pelo pelirrojo, largo y ondulado.
h Tengo el pelo negro, corto y rizado.

1A.4 Me describo

AT 3.2 **3 ¿Verdad o mentira?**
Students look at the illustration and answer 'true' or 'false' to each of the statements.

Answers:
1 Mentira: Tengo los ojos verdes. **2** Verdad; **3** Mentira: Tengo los ojos azules. **4** Mentira: Tengo los ojos grises. **5** Verdad; **6** Mentira: Tengo los ojos rojos.

AT 4.2 / PLTS **4 ¿Cómo eres? ¡Descríbete!**
Students use the vocabulary they have learnt on the page to write a description of themselves.

AT 3.2 **5 ¿Qué dicen las chicas?**
Students look at what the boys say. They then note down what the girls would say.

Answers:
1 Soy alta. **2** Soy baja. **3** Soy gorda. **4** Soy delgada. **5** No soy ni alta ni baja, ni gorda ni delgada: soy de talla mediana.

PLTS **Gramática**
Explain to students that quantifiers are words such as 'very', 'too', 'quite', 'a little', 'extremely', etc. Encourage them to think about the difference these could make in an English sentence. Explain that it is by using words such as these that they will get higher marks in Spanish.

AT 3.1 **6 Empareja los contrarios. ¿Qué significan?**
Students find the eight pairs of opposite personality adjectives and then note down what they mean. They can use a dictionary to help them.

Answers:

ordenado/a – tidy
simpático/a – friendly
paciente – patient
estudioso/a – studious
extrovertido/a – outgoing
inteligente – intelligent
flexible – easy-going
maduro/a – mature

desordenado/a – untidy
antipático/a – unfriendly
impaciente – impatient
perezoso/a – lazy
tímido/a – shy
bobo/a – silly
testarudo/a – stubborn
inmaduro/a – immature

AT 1.4 **7 Escucha. ¿Es el chico a o el chico b?**
Students listen and note down who is being described. They also make a list of all of the adjectives they hear.

🎧 **CD 1, track 37**   página 31, actividad 7

¿Pepe? ¿Cómo es Pepe? Bueno, ummm… la verdad es que es bastante inteligente pero no es ni estudioso ni responsable y eso puede ser un problema. En mi opinión, pienso que Pepe es un poco inmaduro para su edad: siempre discute con sus padres y es demasiado testarudo. Deberías ver su dormitorio… ¡buff! Es super desordenado. ¡Ah! Y es muy, ¡pero que muy perezoso!

Answer:
Person being described: Pepe; He is quite intelligent (inteligente), but isn't studious (estudioso) or responsible (responsable); a little bit immature (inmaduro); too stubborn (testarudo); untidy (desordenado); lazy (perezoso)

AT 2.2–3 **8 Describe al otro chico.**
Students describe the boy from the other photo.

AT 4.2–3 / PLTS **Challenge**
Students use what they have learnt in the spread to prepare a written description of one of their teachers. In small groups, they take it in turns to read their description out loud and work out who others have described. Remind students to try to use one or more of the connectives listed.

1A.5 Me describo

1A.5 En otros lugares
páginas 32–33

Planner

Objectives
- recognise words for additional animals, countries and nationalities

Resources
Students' Book, pages 32–33
CD 1, track 38
Foundation Workbook, page 20
Higher Workbook, page 20
Foundation Workbook audio, CD 3, tracks 51–52
Higher Workbook audio, CD 4, tracks 26–27
Interactive OxBox, Unit 1A
Assessment, Unit 1A

Key language
Paquistán; Marruecos; Polonia; Rumanía; Senegal; Somalia; Turquía; Estados Unidos; India; Grecia
serpientes; ovejas; patos; cabras; cobayas; cerdos; vacas

Renewed Framework references
1.1, 1.4, 2.1, 2.4, 2.5, 3.1, 4.2

PLTS
Challenge: Creative thinkers; Reflective learners

Starters
- Display the key language from the spread in one column and the English translations in jumbled order in a second column. Split the class into two teams. The first team to match each piece of key language to its correct translation wins.

Plenaries
- Following on from the Challenge Activity, students work in pairs to carry out a role play. Each partner pretends to be the character they have invented for the Challenge Activity. In character, they speak about themselves and ask each other questions. Volunteers could perform their role play in front of the class.

Homework/Self-study
Activity 2: Students write the same sentences again, but this time with just one of each animal. Check answers in class.
Challenge: Students improve what they have written about their invented character. Encourage them to use extended sentences and to make their work flow better.

AT 1.2 **1 Escucha y verifica. ¿Qué falta?**
Students listen to Les and note down the animals he has forgotten.

> **CD 1, track 38** — página 32, actividad 1
> El granjero Simón tiene dos serpientes y diez ovejas. También tiene seis patos, ocho cabras y tres cobayas. Además tiene cuatro cerdos y doce vacas.

Answers:
He has forgotten the bulls.

AT 4.1–2 **2 ¡Traduce!**
Students translate the phrases into Spanish.

Answers:
1 dos serpientes verdes; **2** tres ovejas negras; **3** cuatro cobayas blancos; **4** cinco cabras marrónes; **5** seis vacas negras y blancas; **6** siete patos amarillas

AT 3.1 **3 Empareja.**
Students match the descriptions to the flags.

Answers:
1 a; **2** d; **3** b; **4** h; **5** i; **6** j; **7** g; **8** f; **9** c; **10** e

AT 3.1 **4 Descifra y completa.**
Students work out the nationalities within the snake and then use them to complete the table.

Answers:
in snake: paquistaní; polaco; rumano; marroquí; somalí; senegalés; griego; estadounidense; turco; indio
table: Pakistan; Paquistán; paquistaní; paquistaní; paquistanís; paquistanís
Poland; Polonia; polaco; polaca; polacos; polacas
Romania; Rumanía; rumano; rumana; rumanos; rumanas
Morocco; Marruecos; marroquí; marroquí; marroquís; marroquís
Somalia; Solmalia; somalí; somalí; somalís; somalís
Senegal; Senegal; senegalés; senegalesa; senegalés; senegalesas
Greece; Grecia; griego; griega; griegos; griegas
United States; Estado Unidos; estadounidense; estadounidense; estadounidenses; estadounidenses
Turkey; Turquía; turco; turca; turcos; turcas
India; India; indio; india; indios; indias

AT 2.1–2 **5 ¡Bingo!**
Students play Bingo with a twist! They write down nine of the nationalities they have learnt on these pages and pages 28 and 29. There is no nominated caller for this bingo game. Instead, students take

turns to call out a full sentence using one of their unmarked nationalities. Any other students who also have this nationality can cross it off. Students raise their hand when they have a line/house. Explain to students that only full sentences with correct gender are valid.

> [AT 4.2–3] [PLTS]
> **Challenge**
> **Write what the young people would say and invent one other character.**
> Students write what the young people would say and then invent one other character of their own. Remind students to pay particular attention to word order and agreement and to be inventive.

Possible answers:
1 *Me llamo Layla, tengo trece años y mi cumpleaños es el tres de enero. Vivo en España pero soy marroquí. Hablo inglés y español y tengo tres gatos negros.*
2 *Me llamo Kenneth, tengo catorce años y mi cumpleaños es el dieciséis de agosto. Vivo en Francia pero soy chino. Hablo francés, inglés y chino y tengo tres caballos blancos y un hámster gris.*
3 *Me llamo Agnieszka, tengo doce años y mi cumpleaños es el dos de noviembre. Vivo en Italia pero soy polaca. Hablo polaco, italiano y inglés y tengo dos perros blancos y negros.*

1A.6 Labolengua   páginas 34–35

> ### *Planner*
>
> **Objectives**
> - review language and grammar from the unit
>
> **Resources**
> Students' Book, pages 34–35
> CD 1, track 39
> Foundation Workbook, pages 21–22
> Higher Workbook, pages 21–22
> Foundation Workbook audio, CD 3, track 53
> Higher Workbook audio, CD 4, track 28
> Interactive OxBox, Unit 1A
> Copymasters 22–23
> Assessment, Unit 1A
>
> **Grammar**
> - Possessive adjectives
> - Verbs
> - Quantifiers and connectives
>
> **Renewed Framework references**
> 1.1, 1.4, 2.4, 4.1, 4.2, 4.4, 4.5, 5.1, 5.8
>
> **PLTS**
> All activities: Reflective learners/Self-managers
>
> **Homework/Self-study**
> Activity 2: Students find an example of each type of verb from the Students' Book and conjugate them in the present tense.
> Activity 5: Students write some more sentences of their own including months of the year, days of the week, nationalities and languages remembering not to use capital letters for these.

Comprender – possessive adjectives and verbs

A Possessive adjectives

> [PLTS] **1 Add the correct possessive adjective.**
> Practice of using possessive adjectives correctly.

Answers: **1** *mi*; **2** *su*; **3** *vuestra*; **4** *mis*

B Verbs

> [PLTS] **2 Look at this table and the table on page 29. Can you identify the pattern? Based on what you see, write rules to explain how regular verbs work.**
> Practice of conjugating regular verbs. Point out to students that the *-ar* ending is the most common. There are more verbs ending in *-ar* than any other ending.

Answers:
For regular *–ar*, *–er*, and *–ir* verbs: take the infinitive, remove the ending and add the following endings:
– *ar* verbs: (yo) o, (tú) as, (él/ella/usted) a, (nosotros) amos, (vosotros) áis, (ellos/ellas/ustedes) an
– *er* verbs: (yo) o, (tú) es, (él/ella/usted) e, (nosotros) emos, (vosotros) éis, (ellos/ellas/ustedes) en
– *ir* verbs: (yo) o, (tú) es, (él/ella/usted) e, (nosotros) imos, (vosotros) ís, (ellos/ellas/ustedes) en

> [PLTS] **3 Write in Spanish.**
> Further practice of conjugating verbs in the present tense. Students translate the sentences into Spanish.

1A.7 Me describo

Answers:
1 Beben Coca-Cola. **2** Escuchamos rap. **3** Tú enseñas el francés. **4** Llamo por teléfono a su hermana.

Aprender – spellings, quantifiers and connectives

C Spelling

> **PLTS** **4** Rewrite these sentences, correcting the errors.
> Practice of using capital letters correctly in Spanish.

Answers:
1 Vivo en Inglaterra pero soy **e**spañol. **2** Hoy es **m**artes tres de octubre. **3** Abril es mi mes favorito. **4** En **a**gosto visito a mis abuelos en Italia pero no hablo **i**taliano.

D Quantifiers and connectives

> **PLTS** **5** Improve Phoebe's work by rewriting what she says using quantifiers and connectives. You should use at least five different ones.
> Practice of using quantifiers and connectives.

Possible answer:
Me llamo Phoebe. Soy americana **pero** vivo en Canadá. Soy **muy** alta **y bastante** delgada. Soy **muy** simpática **y además** soy **bastante** estudiosa **aunque** soy **también** divertida. Tengo un perro. Es viejo **sin embargo** es **demasiado** bobo. Además es **bastante** grande.

Hablar – pronunciation

D The letter 'c'

> **PLTS** **6** Listen to these phrases. Who is speaking?
> Practice of recognising regional pronunciation of the letter 'c' in Spanish.

> 🎧 **CD 1, track 39**   página 35, actividad 6
> 1 La cocinera olvidó el cochecito del niño en la cocina.
> 2 La cocinera olvidó el cochecito del niño en la cocina.
> 3 Cintia quería ir al cine pero no tenía ni un centavo.
> 4 Cintia quería ir al cine pero no tenía ni un centavo.
> 5 Cecilia quería cerezas pero la cocina estaba cerrada.
> 6 Cecilia quería cerezas pero la cocina estaba cerrada.
> 7 Francisco comía cereales en un bol de cerámica cerca del circo.
> 8 Francisco comía cereales en un bol de cerámica cerca del circo.

Answers:
1 Pablo; **2** Jordi; **3** Jordi; **4** Pablo; **5** Jordi; **6** Pablo; **7** Pablo; **8** Jordi

1A.7 Extra Star   página 36

Planner

Objectives
- practise saying birthdays
- understand/give basic information about others

Resources
Students' Book, page 36

Copymaster 24

Renewed Framework references
2.1, 2.4, 4.2, 4.4

PLTS
Activity 3: Creative thinkers; Reflective learners

AT 3.2   **1 ¿De quién se trata?**
Students read the list of birthdays and then note down which celebrity each sentence is referring to.

Answers:
1 Britney Spears; **2** Daniel Radcliffe; **3** Cesc Fàbregas; **4** Rafael Nadal; **5** Fernando Torres; **6** Leona Lewis

AT 3.2   **2 ¿De qué famoso del calendario se trata?**
Students read the descriptions and decide which person from the calendar each one refers to.

Answers:
1 Fernando Torres; **2** Dannii Minogue; **3** Shakira;

AT 4.3   **3 ¡Tu turno!**
PLTS Students choose four famous people from the calendar and write similar passages to the ones in Activity 2. Encourage them to include connectives and quantifiers where possible to make their writing more interesting.

1A.8 Me describo

1A.7 Extra Plus
página 37

Planner

Objectives
- revise the unit's vocabulary by reading information about others

Resources
Students' Book, page 37
Copymaster 25

Renewed Framework references
2.1, 2.4, 2.5, 4.4, 4.5

PLTS
Activity 2: Reflective learners; Creative thinkers

AT 3.2–3 **1 ¿Qué se le preguntó?**
Students match the answers to the questions.

Answers:
A 7; B 8; C 6; D 1; E 5; F 2; G 9; H 3; I 4

AT 4.2–3 PLTS **2 Escribe sobre Cecilia.**
Students write a paragraph about Cecilia using the information from Activity 1. Remind them to use the third person of the verb. Also encourage students to use connectives and quantifiers.

AT 3.2–3 **3 Problema de lógica.**
Students copy the table and then use their logic to fill it in by reading the sentences.

Answers:

Nombre	Ana	Marta	Rory	Federico
Cumpleaños	2 marzo	8 julio	3 diciembre	15 agosto
Descripción física	rubia	ojos verdes	alto	pelo largo
Personalidad	traviesa	simpática	impaciente	extrovertido
Nacionalidad	chilena	colombiana	irlandés	escocés
Mascotas	-	conejo	tigre	-

1A.8 Prueba
página 38

Planner

Resources
Students' Book, page 38
CD 1, track 40

Renewed Framework references
1.1, 1.4, 1.5, 2.1, 2.4, 2.5, 4.4, 4.5

PLTS
All activities: Reflective learners

Escuchar

AT 1.4 **Listen and fill in the table.**
This activity tests listening skills using the language covered in this unit.

CD 1, track 40 — página 38, Escuchar

1 Hola, me llamo Abdul-Wahid y soy amigo de Khalid. Tengo quince años y mi cumpleaños es el seis de agosto. Soy marroquí como Khalid aunque vivo en Barcelona en España. Físicamente soy alto y bastante delgado y creo que soy muy simpático pero no soy estudioso. En casa tengo un perro negro.

2 Hola, me llamo Martha y tengo dieciséis años. Mi cumpleaños es el tres de febrero. Soy americana pero vivo en Canadá con mi hermana. No soy muy alta y tengo los ojos verdes. Soy un poco testaruda e impaciente como mi gato Sisi. Sisi es blanco y precioso.

1A Me describo

3 Hola, me llamo Salvatore y soy italiano. Vivo en Roma en Italia. Mi cumpleaños es el trece de abril y tengo doce años. Tengo el pelo largo y castaño y los ojos negros. No soy el típico italiano extrovertido, yo soy bastante tímido pero responsable. No tengo animales en casa porque mi hermano les tiene alergia.

Answers:
Martha: 16; 3/2; American; Canada; not very tall/green eyes; a little bit stubborn and impatient; beautiful white cat (Sisi)
Salvatore: 12; 3/4; Italian; Italy; long brown hair/black eyes; quite shy/responsible; no animals as brother is allergic

Hablar

AT 2.2–4 **Choose a picture and give your teacher as much information as you can about the person shown.**
This activity tests speaking skills using the language covered in this unit.

Leer

AT 3.3 **Read the letters and write the name of the person each sentence refers to.**
This activity tests reading skills using the language covered in this unit.

Answers:
1 Shayne; 2 Shayne; 3 Shayne; 4 Sofía; 5 Sofía; 6 Sofía

Escribir

AT 4.3 **Write three short sentences describing your best friend.**
This activity tests writing skills using the language covered in this unit.

Answers:
Students' own answers

Leer 1A   página 153

Planner

Resources
Students' Book, page 153

Renewed Framework references
2.1, 2.4, 2.5, 5.4

PLTS
Activity 3: Creative thinkers; Reflective learners; Self-managers

Homework/Self-study
Students make up their own soap opera character. The description can be very detailed or quite simple depending on ability. Volunteers describe their character to the class.

AT 3.4 **1 Read and choose the correct answer.**

Answers:
1 b; 2 a; 3 b; 4 b; 5 a

AT 3.4 **2 Read again and find the following:**

Answers:
10 countries that watch Ugly Betty: (10 of) Germany, Belgium, China, Spain, France, Greece, India, Israel, Russia, Turkey, Vietnam; 5 physical attributes of Bea: (5 of) thin, average height, black eyes, long black hair, glasses, not very attractive; 4 personality attributes: studious, responsible, very intelligent, brilliant

AT 4.4 / PLTS **3 Your turn!**
Students draw upon what they have read and what they have learnt from the unit as a whole to describe their favourite character from a soap opera, cartoon or sitcom.

Foundation Workbook

Página 16   1A.1 Cumpleaños y fiestas
- Use with Students' Book, pages 24–25

AT 1.1 **1 Play *Bópelo*. Listen and bop the words on the page as you hear them.**
This is a fun way to practise days of the week. Students can play on their own, or in pairs (who can bop the word first).

Me describo 1A

> 🎧 **CD 3, track 45**　　　　　　　página 16, actividad 1
>
> lunes; miércoles; martes; martes; miércoles; jueves; domingo; sábado; sábado; lunes; lunes; jueves; martes; jueves; viernes; viernes; viernes; sábado; viernes; domingo; jueves; lunes; jueves

AT 1.1–2　**2 Read the dates of these people's birthdays. Then listen, and when you hear one of the dates, shout 'Feliz Cumpleaños' and the person's name.**
A fun class game, ideal for practising dates.

> 🎧 **CD 3, track 46**　　　　　　　página 16, actividad 2
>
> Here's an example of how to play the game:
> El dos de febrero
> Feliz Cumpleaños, Shakira!
>
> Now your turn:
> el cuatro de mayo
> el nueve de marzo
> el dieciocho de diciembre
> el veintiuno de noviembre
> el dos de febrero
> el tres de enero
> el cinco de agosto
> el siete de noviembre
> el ocho de octubre
> el veinte de marzo

AT 4.2　**3 Write a sentence in Spanish saying when each celebrity's birthday is.**

Página 17　　　　　　1A.2 Mis mascotas
- Use with Students' Book, pages 26–27

AT 1.1–2　**1 Listen to the English and Spanish ways of describing things, and try to tick which animal is being talked about.**
Hearing the description in English and then Spanish will help students understand how the position of Spanish adjectives differs from the position of English adjectives.

> 🎧 **CD 3, track 47**　　　　　　　página 17, actividad 1
>
> It is a small, grey, friendly, smelly, young…
> Es una tortuga pequeña, gris, amistosa y joven, que huele mal…

Answer: tortoise/tortuga

AT 3.2　**2 Read and underline all the pets, colours and numbers.**
This practises vocabulary from the unit as well as focusing students' attention on adjectival agreement.

Answers:
pets: tortuga; perros; gato; perros; pez; gato; perro; gato; conejo; pájaro; ratón; pez; pájaro; ratón; pez
colours: marrones; negros; blanco; marrón; negro; blanco; verde; gris; rojo
numbers: una; dos; un; dos; un; un; un; dos; un; un; un; un; un

AT 3.2　**3 Read again. Who has …**
Students look at the text in more detail. The work they have done in Activity 2 should help them.

Answers:
a Nacho; **b** Paz; **c** Álvaro; **d** Álvaro; **e** Beto

AT 4.2　**4 Choose two of the people from Activity 2. Draw and label their pets.**
This checks that students have understood the text.

Página 18　　　　1A.3 Lenguas y nacionalidades
- Use with Students' Book, pages 28–29

AT 1.1　**1 Listen and tick the words in the clouds as you hear them.**
Listening out for specific words gives students something to focus on and will help them to make sense of the listening passage.

> 🎧 **CD 3, track 48**　　　　　　　página 18, actividad 1
>
> – Me llamo Marta. Soy española. Hablo español y aprendo inglés. Vivo en España.
> – Me llamo Ed. Soy escocés. Hablo inglés y aprendo español. Vivo en Escocia.
> – Me llamo Tiago. Soy portugués. Hablo portugués y español. Aprendo inglés porque vivo en Inglaterra.

AT 4.2　**2 Use the clouds to introduce each of these people.**
Remind students that they will need to use the third person singular here.

AT 4.2–3　**3 Write your own answers to these questions.**
Students use their work from Activities 1 and 2 to produce sentences of their own.

1A Me describo

Página 19   1A.4 ¿Cómo eres?
- Use with Students' Book, pages 30–31

AT 1.1   **1 Listen to the descriptions of agents X, Y, Z and 0. Write the correct letter under each picture.**
Practice of recognising descriptions.

> 🎧 **CD 3, track 49**   página 19, actividad 1
>
> Agente X: el pelo largo y rubio
> Agente Y: el pelo corto y rubio
> Agente Z: el pelo largo y castaño
> Agente cero: el pelo corto, rizado y castaño

Answers: Agent X = d; Agent Y = b; Agent Z = c; Agent 0 = a

AT 3.1–2   **2 Read, and draw the disguise on each agent.**
Students should draw a long white beard on Agent X; a black moustache on Agent Y; glasses on Agent Z and a black beard, a moustache, glasses, a long blonde wig and freckles on Agent 0.

AT 1.2   **3 Listen. Which agent has been caught?**

> 🎧 **CD 3, track 50**   página 19, actividad 3
>
> Hemos detenido a un espía. Tiene el pelo largo y rubio. Tiene pecas, una barba negra, bigote y gafas.

Answer: Agent 0

AT 4.1–2   **4 Draw and label in Spanish a picture of yourself before and after a disguise.**
Encourage students to be creative and to draw upon the vocabulary they have met so far. Remind them to add colour and to remember to make adjectives agree correctly when labelling their drawings. More able students could write short sentences to describe their disguise.

Página 20   1A.5 En otros lugares
- Use with Students' Book, pages 32–33

AT 3.1   **1 Draw lines to match up the name of the country with the nationality.**
Point out to students that in Spain they spell *México* with a 'j'. In Mexico it is spelled with an 'x'.

Answer:
Méjico = mejicano; Argentina = argentino; Colombia = colombiano; Perú = peruano; Venezuela = venezolano; Guatemala = guatemalteco; Honduras = hondureño; Chile = chileno

AT 1.2   **2 Listen and fill in the grid.**
Further practice of nationality, countries and languages.

> 🎧 **CD 3, track 51**   página 20, actividad 2
>
> – Hola. Me llamo Igor. Soy mejicano y vivo en Méjico. Hablo español.
> – Hola. Me llamo Marta. Soy chilena, pero vivo en Argentina. Hablo español.
> – Me llamo Carlos. Soy venezolano pero vivo en Inglaterra. Hablo español e inglés.
> – Me llamo Claudia. Soy peruana y vivo en Perú. Hablo español.

Answers:
Igor: Mexican, Mexico, Spanish; **Marta:** Chilean, Argentina, Spanish; **Carlos:** Venezuelan, England, Spanish and English; **Claudia:** Peruvian, Peru, Spanish

AT 1.2, 2.1   **3 In Latin America, a 'z' or soft 'c' are pronounced like an 's'. In Spain, they are pronounced like an English 'th'. Read and listen to these sentences. Which is spoken in European Spanish, and which is American Spanish? Try saying them both ways.**
It is useful for students to recognise the difference between Latin American and Spanish pronunciation. Point out that in general they should use the Spanish pronunciation.

> 🎧 **CD 3, track 52**   página 20, actividad 3
>
> 1 Me llamo Azucena y soy venezolana. Vivo en Venezuela.
> 2 Me llamo Cecilia y vivo en Cádiz, una ciudad española.

Answer:
1 is American Spanish; 2 is European Spanish

Página 21   1A.6A Labolengua
- Use with Students' Book, pages 34–35

1 Put the verbs into the correct columns.
This practises recognising types of verbs.

Answers:
–ar *verbs:* visitar, hablar; –er *verbs:* leer, beber; –ir *verbs:* escribir, vivir

2 Put the persons of the verb in the correct order on the grid.
Doing this in English will help students understand how to conjugate verbs in Spanish.

Me describo 1A

Answers:

Singular		Plural	
1st person	I	1st person	we
2nd person	you (sing.)	2nd person	you (plur.)
3rd person	he/she/it	3rd person	they

3 Listen and follow the instructions.
This is a good way to help students remember verb endings. You could extend this to play a class version of 'Simon Says'.

🎧 **CD 3, track 53**　　　página 21, actividad 3

We are going to practise the verb endings for ar verbs. As you do it, make sure you do the right actions. Here we go.
First point at yourself and say "o". Now point forwards and say "as". Now point away to the side and say "a". "o" point to yourself, "as" point forwards, "a", point away. "o", that's I; "as", that's you; "a", that's he or she over there. Keep doing it: "o", "as", "a". "o", "as", "a". "o", "as", "a".
Now we are going to do the plural, so point with two hands this time:
"amos" point at yourself with two hands; "áis" point forward with two hands; "an" point to the side with two hands.
That's "amos" – we; "áis" – you plural; "an" – they "amos", "áis", "an". "amos", "áis", "an".
Now all together. Start with one hand: o, as, a; two hands now amos, áis, an
o, as, a; amos, áis, an; o, as, a; amos, áis, an; o, as, a; amos, áis, an

[AT 3.2] **4 Draw lines to match up.**
Students to check that they know the verb endings. If they are unsure of any of them, they should refer back to previous activities, or to the grammar section.

Answers:
a Hablamos español – We speak Spanish. **b** Visitan a la familia – They are visiting the family. **c** Hablo inglés – I speak English. **d** Visitamos a mi abuela – We are visiting my grandmother.

Página 22　　　**1A.6 Técnica**
- Use with Students' Book, pages 34–35

[AT 3.1–2] **1 Be the teacher. Elena has had some problems with getting capital letters right. Get out your red pen and correct her work.**
Remind students that they should always read through their work to correct any mistakes.

Answers:
Me llamo Elena. Vivo en **e**spaña y soy **e**spañola. Hablo español y **f**rancés. En el instituto tengo francés los **j**ueves y martes.

[AT 4.2–3] **2 Read Ryan's Spanish work. He has written a long list of pets. Can you rewrite it with connectives to make it a better piece of work?**
Students can read their revised version of Ryan's work to the class. Who has made the best use of connnectives in order to make the work flow better?

[AT 3.2] **3 Look at the pictures. Choose the best quantifier to complete each sentence.**
Explain to students that any of the quantifiers from the box could be used in each sentence, but that for each sentence there is one that fits best.

Suggested answers:
1 El perro es un poco grande. **2** El pájaro es muy inteligente. **3** El gato es demasiado pequeño

Higher Workbook

Página 16　　　**1A.1 Cumpleaños y fiestas**
- Use with Students' Book, pages 24–25

[AT 1.2] **1 Listen and play finger twister. When you hear a month, put a finger on it. Keep your fingers on the page. You will need all 10 fingers.**
Practice of the months in Spanish.

🎧 **CD 4, track 20**　　　página 16, actividad 1

Mi cumpleaños es el tres de febrero.
Hoy es el cuatro de julio.
El cumpleaños de Emma es el tres de mayo.
La Navidad cae en diciembre.
Es el veinte de octubre.
Mi cumpleaños es el cuatro de abril.
Estamos en junio.
Es el cinco de marzo.
En agosto estamos de vacaciones.
En septiembre vamos al instituto.

[AT 1.3] **2 Eva and José María are having a competition to see who knows the celebrities' birthdays. Listen and keep score.**
Students listen and check against the birthdays illustrated to see if Eva and José Maria have answered correctly each time.

1A Me describo

CD 4, track 21 — página 16, actividad 2

- Bueno, Eva. ¿Cuándo es el cumpleaños de Shakira?
- Es fácil, el cumpleaños de Shakira es el dos de febrero.
- José María. ¿Cuándo es el cumpleaños de Fernando Torres?
- Es el veinte de marzo.
- Eva. ¿Sabes cuándo es el cumpleaños de Cesc Fàbregas?
- ¿Es el cinco de abril?
- Una pregunta para José María. ¿Cuándo es el cumpleaños de… Madonna?
- ¿Maradona?
- Maradona, no. Madonna.
- ¿Es el cinco de febrero?
- Y una última pregunta para Eva: ¿Cuál es el cumpleaños de Cristina Aguilera?
- Diciembre… el dieciocho de diciembre.
- Y José María. ¿Cuándo es el cumpleaños de Rio Ferdinand?
- ¿Rio Ferdinand? ¿Quién es? ¿Es un cantante?

Answers:
Eva: 2; José María: 1

AT 4.2 **3 Write a sentence in Spanish saying when each celebrity's birthday is.**
Students practise the language they have learnt.

Página 17 — 1A.2 Mis mascotas
- Use with Students' Book, pages 26–27

AT 1.1–2 **1 Listen to the English and Spanish ways of describing things, and try to tick which animal is being talked about.**
Hearing the description in English and then Spanish will help students understand how the position of Spanish adjectives differs from the position of English adjectives.

CD 4, track 22 — página 17, actividad 1

It is a small, grey, friendly, smelly, young…
Es una tortuga pequeña, gris, amistosa y joven, que huele mal…

Answer: a tortoise

2 Explain the difference between Spanish and English word order. Which order was more helpful in Activity 1 and why?

Answer:
In Spanish the noun comes before the adjective.
The Spanish version is more helpful because it tells you straightaway that it is a tortoise, whereas in the English version you never found out which animal it was.

AT 3.2 **3 Read and underline all the pets, colours and numbers. These people are neighbours. How many pets do you think there are altogether?**

Answers:
pets and numbers: una tortuga; cinco perros; cinco gatos; un conejo; un pájaro; un ratón, dos peces
colours: blanco; verdes; negros; blanco; marrón; blancos; blanco
There could well be 12 pets altogether, as we suspect it's the same cat visiting different owners! If you put 15 you could be right too.

AT 3.1 **4 Draw lines to match up the colours to the animals and then draw them.**
Practice of adjectival agreement.

Answers:
a un gato negro; **b** dos perros blancos; **c** una tortuga verde; **d** tres arañas rojas

Página 18 — 1A.3 Lenguas y nacionalidades
- Use with Students' Book, pages 28–29

AT 1.1–2 **1 Listen and tick the words in the clouds as you hear them.**
Listening out for specific words gives students something to focus on and will help them to make sense of the listening passage.

CD 4, track 23 — página 18, actividades 1 y 2

- Me llamo Tiago. Soy portugués. Vivo en Inglaterra. Hablo portugués y francés porque mi madre es francesa. También estudio inglés y español en el instituto. Mi padre es portugués. Mi madre vive en Inglaterra y mi padre vive en Portugal.
- Me llamo Violeta. Soy española y vivo en España. Hablo español y catalán. Mi padre es español pero vive en Francia. Aprende francés. Mi madre es española y vive en España.

AT 1.3 **2 Listen again and fill in the information.**
Students listen the the recording from Activity 1 again, this time for more details.

Answers:
Nombre: Tiago; **Nacionalidad:** portugués; **Residencia:** Inglaterra; **Idiomas:** portugués, francés, inglés, español; **Madre:** francesa – Inglaterra; **Padre:** portugués – Portugal

Nombre: Violeta; **Nacionalidad:** española; **Residencia:** España; **Idiomas:** español, catalán; **Madre:** española – España; **Padre:** español – Francia, aprende francés

Me describo 1A

AT 2.2–3   **3 Be Tiago or Violeta. Talk about yourself and your family in Spanish using the information you heard.**

AT 4.3   **4 Write up the information for the other person in full sentences.**
This is following on from the previous speaking exercise, so students answer in the first person. However, if they want to transfer it into the third person, they can.

Página 19   1A.4 ¿Cómo eres?
- Use with Students' Book, pages 30–31

AT 1.3   **1 Listen to the descriptions of agents X, Y, Z and 0. Write the correct letter under each picture.**
Practice of recognising descriptions.

> 🎧 **CD 4, track 24**   página 19, actividad 1
>
> Escucha atentamente la descripción de estos agentes. Son espías muy peligrosos.
>
> Primero, el agente X. El agente X tiene el pelo largo y rubio. Es ruso y habla el inglés perfectamente.
>
> Agente Y. El agente Y tiene el pelo corto y rubio. No habla inglés.
>
> Agente Z. Es muy peligrosa. Tiene el pelo largo y castaño.
>
> Agente cero. El agente cero es el más peligroso de todos. Tiene el pelo corto, rizado y castaño, pero cuidado, porque muchas veces va disfrazado.

Answers:
a 0; b Y; c Z; d X

AT 3.2   **2 Read the descriptions. Then draw the disguise on each agent.**
Students should draw a long white beard on Agent X; a black moustache on Agent Y; glasses on Agent Z and a black beard, a moustache, glasses, a long blonde wig and freckles on Agent 0.

AT 1.2   **3 Listen. Which agent has been caught?**

> 🎧 **CD 4, track 25**   página 19, actividad 3
>
> Hemos detenido a un espía. Tiene el pelo largo y rubio. Tiene pecas, una barba negra, bigote y gafas.

Answer: Agent 0

AT 4.2–3   **4 Draw a picture of yourself before and after a disguise. Write a description in Spanish.**
Students could present these disguises in class to see who has come up with the funniest/scariest, etc.

Página 20   1A.5 En otros lugares
- Use with Students' Book, pages 32–33

AT 3.1   **1 Draw lines to match up the name of the country with the nationality.**
Point out to students that in Spain they spell México with a 'j'. In Mexico it is spelled with an 'x'.

Answers:
Méjico – mejicano; Argentina – argentino; Colombia – colombiano; Perú – peruano; Venezuela – venezolano; Guatemala – guatemalteco; Honduras – hondureño; Chile – chileno

AT 1.2   **2 Listen and fill in the grid.**
Further practice of nationality, countries and languages

> 🎧 **CD 4, track 26**   página 20, actividad 2
>
> – Hola. Me llamo Igor. Soy mejicano y vivo en Méjico. Hablo español.
> – Hola. Me llamo Marta. Soy chilena, pero vivo en Argentina. Hablo español.
> – Me llamo Carlos. Soy venezolano pero vivo en Inglaterra. Hablo español e inglés.
> – Me llamo Claudia. Soy peruana y vivo en Perú. Hablo español.

Answers:
Igor: *Mexican, Mexico, Spanish;* **Marta:** *Chilean, Argentina, Spanish;* **Carlos:** *Venezuelan, England, Spanish and English;* **Claudia:** *Peruvian, Peru, Spanish*

AT 1.2, 2.1   **3 In Latin America, a 'z' or a soft 'c' are pronounced like an 's'. In Spain, they are pronounced like an English 'th'. Try saying these sentences both ways, then listen to how Azucena and Cecilia say them.**
It is useful for students to recognise the difference between Latin American and Spanish pronunciation. Point out that in general they should use the Spanish pronunciation.

> 🎧 **CD 4, track 27**   página 20, actividad 3
>
> 1 Me llamo Azucena y soy venezolana. Vivo en Venezuela.
> 2 Me llamo Cecilia y vivo en Cádiz, una ciudad española.

Answers:
1 Latin American; 2 European Spanish

1A Me describo

Página 21   1A.6A Labolengua
- Use with Students' Book, pages 34–35

1 Find the infinitives and put them into three groups.
This practises recognising infinitives and the different types of verb.

Answers:
–ar – visitar; hablar; –er – beber; leer; –ir – vivir; escribir

PLTS 2 Listen and follow the instructions.
This is a good way to help students remember verb endings. You could extend this to play a class version of 'Simon Says'.

> 🎧 **CD 4, track 28**   página 21, actividad 2
>
> We are going to practise the verb endings for ar verbs. As you do it, make sure you do the right actions. Here we go. First point at yourself and say "o". Now point forwards and say "as". Now point away to the side and say "a". "o" point to yourself, "as" point forwards, "a", point away.
>
> "o", that's I; "as", that's you; "a", that's he or she over there.
>
> Keep doing it: "o", "as", "a". "o", "as", "a". "o", "as", "a".
>
> Now we are going to do the plural, so point with two hands this time: "amos" point at yourself with two hands; "áis" point forward with two hands; "an" point to the side with two hands.
>
> That's "amos" – we; "áis" – you plural; "an" – they
>
> "amos", "áis", "an". "amos", "áis", "an".
>
> Now all together. Start with one hand: o, as, a; two hands now: amos, áis, an.
>
> o, as, a; amos, áis, an; o, as, a; amos, áis, an; o, as, a; amos, áis, an

3 Look at the *er* column. Highlight what is different from the *ar* endings. Now look at the *ir* column. Highlight what is different from the *er* endings.

Answers (differences in bold):

ar	er	ir
o	o	o
as	e**s**	e**s**
a	**e**	**e**
amos	**e**mos	**i**mos
áis	**é**is	**í**s
an	e**n**	en

4 Write out the verbs with the correct ending to complete the sentences.

Answers:
a Visito a mis padres. **b** Hablamos español. **c** Bebe agua. **d** Aprenden francés.

Página 22   1A.6B Técnica
- Use with Students' Book, pages 34–35

AT 3.2 1 Be the teacher. Elena has had some problems with getting capital letters right. Get out your red pen and correct her work.
Remind students that they should always read through their work to correct any mistakes.

Answers:
Me llamo Elena. Vivo en **E**spaña y soy **e**spañola. Hablo español y **f**rancés. En el instituto tengo francés los **j**ueves y martes.

AT 4.2–3 2 Read Ryan's Spanish work. He has written a long list of pets. Can you rewrite it with connectives to make it a better piece of work?
Students can read their revised version of Ryan's work to the class. Who has made the best use of connnectives in order to make the work flow better?

AT 4.2 3 Look at the pictures. Write a sentence for each one, using a quantifier.
Explain to students that any of the quantifiers from the box could be used in each sentence, but that for each sentence there is one that fits best.

Suggested answers:
1 El perro es un poco grande. **2** El pájaro es muy inteligente.
3 El gato es demasiado pequeño.

1B El insti

Unit Objectives

Contexts and cultural focus: school in Spanish-speaking countries: subjects, uniform and facilities
Grammar: verbs and adjectival agreement, the verb *tener*, the verb *ser* with telling the time, the present tense, adjectives
Language learning: learning how to work out meanings from cognates, transferring previous knowledge, understanding the subject pronouns are not used much in Spanish, developing ways of learning vocabulary, predicting and checking

- *Aim:* to talk about school subjects and give an opinion of them, say what time it is and when lessons are, talk about what there is to do in your school, talk about school uniform and give an opinion of it, learn how Spanish-speaking schools differ from your school.
- Each unit has an associated video which will feature throughout the unit. Below is the transcript of the video for this unit.
- As a starter activity to introduce the Unit and familiarise students with the language they will meet, you may find it useful for the class to view the video as a whole.

Video script (CD 1, track 41)

Eva: ¿Dónde está Khal?
José: Está en el comedor del colegio.
Eva: ¿Está con Marisa?
José: No. Marisa está en la biblioteca.
Eva: ¿Está estudiando?
José: Sí, para el examen de mañana.
Eva: ¡Vaya! ¿Te gusta el horario de este año?
José: Bueno, no está mal.
Eva: Tenemos inglés todos los días. ¿No te parece estupendo?
José: ¡Sí, estupendo! Tener deberes de inglés los lunes, los martes, los miércoles, los jueves, y también los viernes. ¡Realmente estupendo!
Eva: Este año nos da clases de geografía el Sr. Hernández.
José: Sí, ¡es un tío guay!
Eva: Ya, pero a mí, la geografía no me gusta. Me parece aburridísima.
José: ¿Aburrida? ¡Para nada!
Eva: Y ¿no te parece fantástica la nueva profesora de matemáticas?
José: ¿Estás de broma, no?
Eva: ¿No te cae bien la Señorita Rodríguez?
José: ¡Eh, Eva, que soy yo, José! Me gustan los deportes. Me gusta la geografía. Me gusta el inglés. Pero odio las matemáticas.
Eva: Así como no te gustan las matemáticas, ¿no te gusta la Señorita Rodriguez?
José: Pues... sí, así es.
Eva: Vaya, me tengo que ir.
José: ¿Adónde? ¿Vas a clases de teatro?
Eva: No, voy a una exposición con mi padre.
José: ¿Adónde si no?
Eva: Bueno... me tengo que ir. ¡Nos vemos mañana!
[Pause]

Marisa: Eva a veces es una pesada, ¿no te parece?
Khalid: No, sólo es... sólo es Eva.
Marisa: Pero le gusta tocar el piano, le gusta la ópera, le gusta ir a museos.
Khalid: Creo que también le gusta hacer deberes.
Marisa: ¿No ves?, ¿eso no te parece eso una pesadez?
Khalid: Ah mira, ahí está José.

Khalid: ¿Qué? ¿Haciendo los deberes de matemáticas?
José: ¡Hola!
Khalid: La Señorita Rodríguez está muy buena, ¿no te parece? Bueno quiero decir que es muy inteligente, muy buena con las matemáticas porque a nosotros nos gustan las matemáticas *(imitating the Sesame Street characters when they start counting)* "¡Saludos!, y ahora, vamos a contar, uno, dos, tres."
Marisa: Vale, Khal, de acuerdo. No pasa nada. Es verdad, la Señorita Rodríguez es muy guapa.
Khalid: Sí, y se pone ropa preciosa.
Marisa y José: ¿Qué?
Khalid: Bueno, preciosa no, pero bonita, ¿no?
Marisa: ¡Anda, ya venga, hombre! Una falda azul marino, una blusa blanca y una chaqueta azul marino. ¡Esto es horrible!
Khalid: Aun así, es muy maja.
Marisa y José: Sí, aparte de las matemáticas.
Khalid: ¿Hay algún momento en el que no estés comiendo?
José: *[shakes his head]*

1B El insti

Unit 1B El insti Overview grid

Page reference	Contexts and objectives	Language learning	Grammar	Key language	Framework	AT level
Pages 40–41 **Mis asignaturas**	• talk about school subjects and your opinions of them	• learn how to work out meanings from cognates	• use verbs and adjectival agreements correctly	la educación física; el español; el inglés; la geografía; la historia; la informática; la technología; las ciencias; las matemáticas; fácil; difícil; útil; aburrido/a; divertido/a; interesante; un poco; bastante; tan; muy; demasiado; para mí; pero; me gusta; te gusta; correcto; mentira	1.1, 1.4, 2.1, 2.4, 2.5, 3.1, 3.2, 4.3, 4.5, 5.3, 5.4	1.2–4, 2.2–3, 3.1–2, 4.2–3
Pages 42–43 **La hora y el horario**	• say what time it is and when your lessons are	• tell the time, transfer previous knowledge	• practise using the verb *tener*, use the verb *ser* with telling the time	Es la una …y cinco,…y cuarto, …y veinte, …y media; Son las dos … menos veinticinco, … menos cuarto, …menos diez; Es el mediodía; Es la medianoche	1.1, 1.4, 2.1, 2.4, 4.2, 4.3, 4.5, 5.5, 5.8	1.1–2, 2.2, 4.2–3
Pages 44–45 **Las instalaciones**	• talk about what there is in your school	• understand that subject pronouns are not used much in Spanish	• use verbs correctly in the present tense	el aula; el gimnasio; el laboratorio; el patio; la biblioteca; la oficina; la oficina del director; grande; pequeño/a; moderno/a; antiguo/a; bonito/a; feo/a; cómodo/a; hay; leer un libro; comer un bocadillo; estudiar ciencias; charlar con amigos; practicar deporte; escribir cartas	1.1, 1.4, 2.1, 2.4, 2.5, 3.1, 4.4, 4.5, 5.1, 5.2	1.2, 2.2, 3.2–3, 4.2–3
Pages 46–47 **La ropa**	• talk about your school uniform and your opinion of it	• develop ways of learning vocabulary	• use adjectives correctly	llevar; un jersey; una camisa; una camiseta; una corbata; una falda; una sudadera; unas zapatillas; unos calcetines; unos pantalones; unos vaqueros; unos zapatos; incómodo/a; elegante; práctico/a; formal; cómodo/a; feo/a; ridículo/; informal	1.1, 1.4, 1.5, 2.1, 2.4, 2.5, 3.1, 3.2, 4.3, 4.5	1.2–4, 2.2, 3.2–3, 4.1–4
Pages 48–49 **Me gusta**	• learn the names for more school subjects, talk about patterns on clothes		• use more adjectival agreements correctly		1.1, 1.4, 2.1, 2.4, 2.5, 4.3, 4.5, 5.8	1.2–3, 2.2, 3.2–3, 4.2–3

El insti 1B

Pages 50–51 **Labolengua**	• review language and grammar from the unit				2.1, 2.4, 4.1, 4.2, 4.3, 4.4, 4.5, 5.3, 5.4	
Pages 52–53 **Extra Star** **Extra Plus**	• differentiated extension/ homework material	• revise and consolidate all vocabulary and grammar covered in the unit	• revise and consolidate all vocabulary and grammar covered in the unit		1.1, 2.1, 2.4, 2.5, 3.1, 3.2, 4.2, 4.3, 4.4, 4.5, 5.4	3.1–4, 4.2–4
Page 54 **Prueba**	• end-of-spread test				1.1, 1.4, 1.5, 2.1, 2.4, 2.5, 3.1, 3.2	1.3, 2.2–3, 3.4, 4.3–4
Page 55 **Vocabulario**	• a summary of the key language covered in each spread of this unit					
Page 154 **Leer 1B**	• practice of longer reading texts based on the theme of the unit				2.1, 3.1, 3.2, 5.4	3.4

1B El insti

Week-by-week overview
(Three-year KS3 Route: assuming six weeks' work or approximately 10–12.5 hours)
(Two-year KS3 Route: assuming four weeks' worth or approximately 6.5-8.5 hours)
*Please note that essential activities are highlighted.

About Unit 1B, *El insti*: Students work in the context of schools. They talk about school subjects and give their opinion of them. They say what time it is and when lessons are. They also talk about what there is to do in their school, and describe and discuss school uniform. They learn about Spanish-speaking schools. Students practise using verbs and practise adjectival agreement. They also practise using the verb tener and the verb ser with telling the time as well as the present tense. The unit also provides tips on language learning techniques.

	Three-Year KS3 Route			Two-Year KS3 Route	
Week	**Resources**	**Objectives**	**Week**	**Resources**	**Objectives**
1	1B.1 Mis asignaturas (p.40)	talk about school subjects and your opinion of them use verbs and adjectival agreement correctly learn how to work out the meaning from cognates	1	1B.1 Mis asignaturas omit activities 3, 5 & Challenge 1B.6 Lablolengua A (p.50)	talk about school subjects and your opinion of them use verbs and adjectival agreement correctly learn how to work out the meaning from cognates
2	1B.2 La hora y el horario	say what time it is and when your lessons are practise using *tener* and *ser* tell the time	2	1B.2 La hora y el horario omit activities Think!, 3, 5 & Challenge	say what time it is and when your lessons are practise using *tener* and *ser* tell the time
3	1B.3 Las instalaciones 1B. 6 Lablolengua B (p.50)	talk about what there is in your school use verbs correctly in the present tense understand subject pronouns	3	1B.3 Las instalaciones omit activities 2, Gramática & Challenge 1B. 6 Lablolengua B (p.51)	talk about what there is in your school use verbs correctly in the present tense understand subject pronouns
4	1B.4 La ropa 1B. 6 Lablolengua C (p.51)	talk about school uniform and give your opnion use adjectives correctly develop ways of learning vocabulary	4	1B.4 La ropa omit activities Gramática, Think!, Challenge 1B. 6 Lablolengua C (p.50) 1B.8 Prueba (p.54) Vocabulario (p.55)	talk about school uniform and give your opnion use adjectives correctly develop ways of learning vocabulary recapping on the vocabulary of the unit prepare and carry out assessment in all four skills
5	1B.5 Me gusta…	learn more about school and clothes further work on adjectival agreements predicting and checking your work			
6	1B.7 Extra (Star) (p.52) 1B.7 Extra (Plus) (p.53) 1B.8 Prueba (p.54) Vocabulario (p.55) Leer (p.154)	further reinforcement and extension of the language of the unit recapping on the vocabulary of the unit prepare and carry out assessment in all four skills further reading to explore the language of the unit and cultural themes			

1B.1 El insti

1B.1 Mis asignaturas

páginas 40–41

Planner

Objectives
- talk about school subjects and your opinions of them
- use verbs and adjectival agreements correctly
- learn how to work out meaning from cognates

Video
Video script, Unit 1B

Resources
Students' Book, pages 40–41
CD 1, tracks 41–42
Foundation Workbook, page 24
Higher Workbook, page 24
Foundation Workbook audio, CD 3, track 54
Higher Workbook audio, CD 4, track 29
Interactive OxBox, Unit 1B
Copymasters 27–34
Assessment, Unit 1B

Key language
la educación física; el español; el inglés; la geografía; la historia; la informática; la technología; las ciencias; las matemáticas; fácil; difícil; útil; aburrido/a; divertido/a; interesante; un poco; bastante; tan; muy; demasiado; para mí; pero; me gusta; te gusta; correcto; mentira

Grammar
- use verbs and adjectival agreement correctly

Renewed Framework references
1.1, 1.4, 2.1, 2.4, 2.5, 3.1, 3.2, 4.3, 4.5, 5.3, 5.4

PLTS
Activity 1: Team workers; Indpendent enquirers; Creative thinkers
Gramática: Reflective learners; Independent enquirers
Think!: Reflective learners
Activity 7: Creative thinkers
Challenge: Effective participators

Starters
- Go round the class giving each student in turn a school subject. He/She must give you an adjective which describes this subject for them, e.g. *interesante*, etc. More able students use quantifiers, or can reply using a full sentence, e.g. *No me gusta la historia, es demasiado difícil*. Remind students that the adjective must agree with the school subject.
- Students take it in turns to describe a 'mystery' subject to the rest of the class, e.g. *Son muy útiles pero tan difíciles*. You can provide them with a subject or they can think of one themselves. The class tries to guess which subject they are talking about.

Plenaries
- Display the key language from the spread and challenge students to write five sentences describing school subjects. Less able students could just use nouns and adjectives; more able students could include *un poco, bastante, tan, muy, demasiado, para mí, pero, me gusta* in their sentences.
- Students interview one another about school subjects, e.g. *¿Te gusta inglés?* etc. Encourage more able students to give as full an answer as possible.

Homework/Self-study
Gramática: Students write sentences saying which subjects they like/dislike using the phrases from the grammar box. Provide less able students with a model sentence to adapt, e.g. *Me gusta _____.* etc.
Think!: Students use at least three of the adjectives from the vocabulary box in their masculine, feminine and plural forms. With less able students, provide nouns and adjectives for them to change accordingly.
Activity 5: Students rewrite the sentences so that they reflect their own opinion. Even if they agree with the original sentences, encourage students to lie in order to practise their Spanish!

AT 3.1
PLTS

1 Adivina las asignaturas.
Students work individually, with a partner or in a group to see how many of the subjects listed in the vocabulary box they can work out. They can compare notes to see how many subjects they guessed, or compete with another group to see who got the most correct. You could make this a *Contrareloj* activity – how many subjects can they guess in 2 minutes, etc. With less able students, provide the words in Spanish and English for them to match them up.

Answers:
el español – Spanish; **el inglés** – English; **la educación física** – PE; **la geografía** – geography; **la historia** – history; **la informática** – ICT; **la technolgía** – design and technology; **las ciencias** – science; **las matemáticas** – maths

1B.1 El insti

AT 1.4 **2 Mira el video.**
Students watch the video to check if Eva and José like or dislike the subjects shown in the pictures. They can make notes, draw symbols, tick a list, or put their hand up mid-video as they spot the differences.

Video script: Unit 1B (CD1, track 41)

Eva: ¿Dónde está Khal?
José: Está en el comedor del colegio.
Eva: ¿Está con Marisa?
José: No. Marisa está en la biblioteca.
Eva: ¿Está estudiando?
José: Sí, para el examen de mañana.
Eva: ¡Vaya! ¿Te gusta el horario de este año?
José: Bueno, no está mal.
Eva: Tenemos inglés todos los días. ¿No te parece estupendo?
José: ¡Sí, estupendo! Tener deberes de inglés los lunes, los martes, los miércoles, los jueves, y también los viernes. ¡Realmente estupendo!
Eva: Este año nos da clases de geografía el Sr. Hernández.
José: Sí, ¡es un tío guay!
Eva: Ya, pero a mí, la geografía no me gusta. Me parece aburridísima.
José: ¿Aburrida? ¡Para nada!
Eva: Y ¿no te parece fantástica la nueva profesora de matemáticas?
José: ¿Estás de broma, no?
Eva: ¿No te cae bien la Señorita Rodríguez?
José: ¡Eh, Eva, que soy yo, José! Me gustan los deportes. Me gusta la geografía. Me gusta el inglés. Pero odio las matemáticas.
Eva: Así, como no te gustan las matemáticas, ¿no te gusta la Señorita Rodríguez?
José: Pues… sí, así es.
Eva: Vaya, me tengo que ir.
José: ¿Adónde? ¿Vas a clases de teatro?
Eva: No, voy a una exposición con mi padre.
José: ¿Adónde si no?
Eva: Bueno… me tengo que ir. ¡Nos vemos mañana!

Answers:
Eva likes English; she doesn't like geography, but likes maths; José likes sport, he likes geography, he likes English but he hates maths.

AT 2.2 **3 Habla con tu compañero.**
Students work with a partner and tell him/her which subjects they like/dislike. Their partner makes notes. More advanced students could vary the activity by speaking very slowly/ quickly/quietly to make it harder for their partner.

PLTS **Gramática**
Draw students' attention to *me gusta* and *me gustan* and check they understand. Ask them which other subject they would use *me gustan* or *no me gustan* with (*las matemáticas*). Get them to make up some examples using vocabulary from previous units, e.g. *me gusta el perro, no me gustan los gatos*.

AT 1.3 **4 Rellena la tabla.**
Students listen to the students talking and fill in the table.

🎧 **CD 1, track 42**   página 41, actividad 4

Cristina: Me llamo Cristina. Me gustan las matemáticas porque son interesantes.
Antonio: Hola, soy Antonio. No me gusta nada la historia, es demasiado difícil.
Pedro: Me llamo Pedro, y me gusta mucho el deporte. Es bastante fácil.
Susana: Soy Susana, y no me gusta la informática. Es tan aburrida.
Pedro: Cristina, ¿te gustan las ciencias?
Cristina: Sí, Pedro, me gustan mucho, son muy útiles.
Susana: Antonio, ¿te gusta el inglés?
Antonio: Sí, Susana, me gusta. Es bastante fácil.

Answers:

	♥♥	♥	✗	✗✗
Cristina	ciencias	matemáticas		
Antonio		inglés		historia
Pedro	deporte			
Susana			informática	

PLTS **Think!**
Read through the *Think!* box as a class. Elicit from pupils that adjective endings change depending on gender and number.

AT 3.2 **5 ¿Positivo o negativo?**
Students decide if the opinions are positive (✓) or negative (✗).

Answers:
1 ✓; 2 ✓; 3 ✗; 4 ✓; 5 ✗; 6 ✓

1B.1 El insti

AT 1.2–3

6 Escucha otra vez.
Students listen to Activity 4 again and note down why students like or dislike the subjects. Students can respond in English or Spanish as appropriate to their ability, using a single word or a whole phrase. They can give the answer orally or write it down if you wish to practise spelling the words.

Answers:
Cristina: *interesantes – interesting; muy útiles – very useful;*
Antonio: *demasiado difícil – too difficult; bastante fácil – quite easy;* **Pedro:** *bastante fácil – quite easy;* **Susana:** *tan aburrida – so boring*

AT 4.2–3 / PLTS

7 Escribe unas frases.
Students write their opinion of their school subjects. They can write as much or little as they feel able. The finished pieces of work could be displayed anonymously for the rest of the class to identify who wrote what. This is a good opportunity to introduce more able students to little phrases like *para mí* to make their work sound more natural, but less able students can keep things simple.

AT 2.2–3 / PLTS

Challenge
Tell your friends what you think of a subject. Can they decide if you are telling the truth or not?
This is a version of 'Call My Bluff'. Individual students could take it in turns to give a statement, or you could set up a panel of three or four students of whom only one is telling the truth. The rest of the class have to decide which one it is. If the class guesses incorrectly, that player stays on the panel for an extra turn. Once students are familiar with the game and comfortable with the language, it could be played in smaller groups.

1B.2 El insti

1B.2 La hora y el horario
páginas 42–43

Planner

Objectives
- say what time it is and when your lessons are
- practise using the verb *tener*, use the verb *ser* with telling the time
- tell the time, transfer previous knowledge

Resources
Students' Book, pages 42–43
CD 1, tracks 43–44
Foundation Workbook, page 25
Higher Workbook, page 25
Interactive OxBox, Unit 1B
Copymasters 27–34
Assessment, Unit 1B

Key language
Es la una …y cinco,…y cuarto, …y veinte, …y media; Son las dos …menos veinticinco, …menos cuarto, …menos diez; Es el mediodía; Es la medianoche

Grammar
- practise using the verb *tener*, use the verb *ser* with telling the time

Renewed Framework references
1.1, 1.4, 2.1, 2.4, 4.2, 4.3, 4.5, 5.5, 5.8

PLTS
Think!: Reflective learners
Activity 3: Team workers
Gramática: Independent enquirers
Challenge: Creative learners; Self-managers

Starters
- Display some school subjects either in words or using symbols. Go round the class and for each student point to one of the subjects. The student says at what time and on what day they have this subject. If they don't do a particular subject, they can either make up a time and day, or pick a different subject.
- Display some blank clock faces at the front of the class which students will be able to write on. Split the class into two teams. Explain that you will call out a time and that each team must allocate a member to go to the front and draw the correct time on one of the clock faces; their team members can help them decide on what time has been called out. The first team to draw on the correct time gets a point. Continue, using the other clock faces, as many times as you feel useful. At the end, the team with the most points wins.

Plenaries
- Challenge students to write a sentence for each part of the verb *tener* in the present tense. The sentences should be on the theme of the spread. Volunteers then read their sentences to the class.
- Students write a description of their ideal school day saying which subjects they have and at what time. They could either do this in the form of a timetable, as in the Challenge Activity but only with subjects they like, or as a written description. In both cases, students should try to add opinions and, if they can, quantifiers and adjectives.

Homework/Self-study
Students make up their own examples of sentences using 'it's X o'clock' and 'at X o'clock' to practise these phrases from Activity 6.
Students add to their list from the last Think! box any other phrases using the verb *tener* that they come across later in the book.

🎧 **1 Identifica el reloj.**

AT 1.1–2

Students listen and note down which clock is mentioned each time. Present the clocks and the times to the class before doing the listening activity so they know what the different times sound like. Various practice games can be played to familiarise the students with the times – call out a time and ask students to give the letter; say a time and a letter and ask students to say if it is true or false, etc.

🎧 **CD 1, track 43** página 42, actividad 1

1 Es la una y media.
2 Son las dos.
3 Es la una y veinte.
4 Son las dos menos cuarto.
5 Son las dos menos veinticinco.
6 Es la una y cinco.

Answers:
1 e; **2** i; **3** d; **4** g; **5** f; **6** b

1B.2 El insti

PLTS **Think!**
Students could discuss this in small groups and feed back their conclusions. Alternatively, you could discuss this as a class.

AT 3.2 **2 Identifica el reloj.**
Students look at the clocks and match them to the sentences.

Answers:
1 d; **2** e; **3** a; **4** b; **5** c; **6** f

PLTS **Think!**
Elicit from students that these phrases mean midday and midnight. Have students noticed that *medio/a* is spelt differently in each of these terms? Elicit from them that as *día* is masculine, *medio* is written in its masculine form to make *mediodía* and as *noche* is feminine, *media* is written in its feminine form to make *medianoche*.

AT 2.2 **3 Habla con tu companero.**
PLTS This can also be played the other way round, with one student pointing to a clock and the other saying the time. This second option works better as a group competition, with different groups trying to be the first to give the correct answer.

AT 1.2 **4 ¿Verdad o mentira?**
Students listen and decide if what Pablo is saying is correct or not. They should listen for times, days and school subjects.

🎧 **CD 1, track 44** página 43, actividad 4
1 El lunes tengo inglés a las diez y cuarto.
2 Tengo matemáticas el martes a las doce.
3 El miércoles tengo español a las nueve.
4 Tengo deporte el martes a las tres menos cuarto.
5 Tengo informática el lunes a las tres menos cuarto.
6 El martes tengo tecnología a las nueve.

Answers:
1 ✓; **2** ✗; **3** ✗; **4** ✗; **5** ✓; **6** ✓

2.2 **5 Identifica la asignatura.**
Students use Pablo's timetable to play a game with a partner. Partner A says a day and time; B looks at the timetable says which lesson takes place on that day at that time. They then swap roles. This could also be a team game, where different groups compete to be the first to give the correct answer.

PLTS **Gramática**
Look at the grammar box as a class. Work through a few examples using as many parts of *tener* as possible to ensure that all students fully understand how to form this verb. To check understanding, ask students to give you some examples of their own.

PLTS **6 Copia y completa las frases.**
Students complete the sentences with the correct part of the verb *tener*. Highlight how to say 'at one o'clock', etc.

Answers:
1 tenemos; **2** tiene; **3** tenéis; **4** Tengo; **5** tiene; **6** tienen

PLTS **Think!**
This is an ideal opportunity for students to revise what they learnt earlier in the book.

AT 4.2–3 **Challenge**
PLTS Draw out your own timetable. Personalise it by adding opinions as Pablo has done. Write a few sentences about it.
This can be as simple or complicated as you like. Students could add pictures to show the different subjects and look up additional opinion words.

73

1B.3 El insti

1B.3 Las instalaciones
páginas 44–45

Planner

Objectives
- talk about what there is in your school
- use verbs correctly in the present tense
- understand that subject pronouns are not much used in Spanish

Resources
Students' Book, pages 44–45
CD 1, track 45
Foundation Workbook, page 26
Higher Workbook, page 26
Foundation Workbook audio, CD 3, track 55
Higher Workbook audio, CD 4, track 30
Interactive OxBox, Unit 1B
Copymasters 27–34
Assessment, Unit 1B

Key language
el aula; el gimnasio; el laboratorio; el patio; la biblioteca; la oficina; la oficina del director; grande; pequeño/a; moderno/a; antiguo/a; bonito/a; feo/a; cómodo/a; hay; leer un libro; comer un bocadillo; estudiar ciencias; charlar con amigos; practicar deporte; escribir cartas

Grammar
- use verbs correctly in the present tense

Renewed Framework references
1.1, 1.4, 2.1, 2.4, 2.5, 3.1, 4.4, 4.5, 5.1, 5.2

PLTS
Activity 3: Effective participators
Gramática: Independent enquirers
Think!: Reflective learners
Challenge: Self-managers

Starters
- Call out an activity, e.g. *leer un libro, estudiar ciencias*, etc. and ask students to reply with the appropriate place in school. You could turn this into a game by splitting the class into two teams. The team who says the most correct places wins. Keep a list of the activities and places mentioned.
- Play a class game. As a class, you are going to describe a school. Ask a student to begin by saying one thing about the school, e.g. *En mi colegio hay un gimnasio*. The next student must say what activity you can do in the gym, i.e. *Practicamos deporte en el gimnasio*. The next student gives an opinion of this, e.g. *No me gusta mucho*. And so on with another place in school. Support less able students by displaying some places in school, some activities and some opinion phrases.

Plenaries
- Display the list of activities and places from Starter Activity 1. Explain to students that you will call out a 'person', e.g. 'I', and point to an activity, e.g. *comer un bocadillo*. They use this information to write down a sentence with the verb conjugated correctly and with an appropriate place at the end, e.g. *Como un bocadillo en el comedor*. Check answers as a class.
- Students describe their ideal school. They should mention how big it is, whether it is old or new, what it has, e.g. *Hay un bonito patio*., and what it doesn't have *No hay laboratorio*. Students should also include what activities they can do in the different places and add an opinion, e.g. *Practicamos deporte en el gimnasio. Me gusta mucho*.

Homework/Self-study
Activity 2/Gramática: Students adapt the description from Activity 2 for their school. Less able students could just do the first sentence.
Gramática: Students find an example of a regular *–ar*, *–er*, and *–ir* verb and write each one out in the present tense. More able students could do this be writing short sentences; less able students may need you to give them verbs to conjugate, rather than finding their own.

AT 1.2 **1 Escucha a Fernando.**
Students listen and note down which part of the school Fernando is talking about each time. The audioscript can be also used as a reading activity – cut the sentences in half and ask students to match up the places and the activities in preparation for the work on page 45.

CD 1, track 45 — página 44, actividad 1
1. En el patio charlo con mis amigos.
2. En la oficina trabaja la secretaria.
3. En el comedor como la comida a mediodía.
4. En la biblioteca hay libros y ordenadores.
5. En el laboratorio estudio ciencias.
6. ¡No me gusta ir a la oficina del director!
7. En las aulas estudio español, inglés, matemáticas, historia ... todo.

1B.3 El insti

Answers:
1 el patio (the playground); 2 la oficina (the office); 3 el comedor (the dining room); 4 la biblioteca (the library); 5 el laboratorio (the laboratory); 6 la oficina del director (the headteacher's office); 7 las aulas (classrooms)

AT 3.3 — **2 Lee la carta.**
Students read the description and note down whether it refers to school A or school B.

Answer: School A

AT 2.2 / PLTS — **3 Juega con tu compañero o en grupo.**
This can be played in pairs or small groups. More advanced students can find out the names of other places in the school (the hall, the toilets, technology workshop) and use them in the game too.

Gramática
Read through the grammar box as a class. To check that students have understood, ask them to use *hay* with some examples of their own, e.g. *hay un bonito patio*, etc. Have they noticed anything different about *no hay*? Elicit from students that you don't use the article with *no hay*.

AT 3.2 — **4 Lee las frases.**
Students use the grid to identify the component parts of the sentence. This provides practice of recognising the different parts of the verb, and which 'person' is identified with each one.

Answers:
1 d, iii, B; 2 f, iv, C; 3 b, i, A; 4 c, vi, E; 5 e, v, F

PLTS — **Gramática**
Explain to students that is is important that they learn the present tense endings of these three types of regular verb.

PLTS — **Think!**
This is a concept that will probably need a lot of reinforcing. To help with this, students could write out the pronouns and the verbs in full on separate pieces of card, and then cut off the verb endings and play "jigsaws" matching the correct person to the ending.

AT 4.2 — **5 Escribe la frase. ¿Es ridículo?**
Students use the grid to work out if the sentences are absurd or not. This can be extended by students writing their own absurd sentences about themselves and their classmates. Personalising the verbs in this way will also help students to remember their different parts.

Answers:
1 Paloma y Francisco charlan con amigos en la oficina. – ¡Es ridículo!
2 Sofía, ¿estudias ciencias en el laboratorio? – No es ridículo.
3 Trinidad y yo practicamos deporte en la biblioteca – ¡Es ridículo!
4 Practico deporte en el gimnasio. – No es ridículo.
5 ¿Coméis un bocadillo en el gimnasio? – ¡Es ridículo!

AT 4.2–3 / PLTS — **Challenge**
With a partner, describe your school. Take pictures of your school, label them in Spanish, and write about what you do in the different places.
Students could use pictures from a prospectus rather than taking their own. More able students can add opinions of the activities they do as well. The finished pieces of work could be displayed on the school website, sent to a partner school or given to another class who have to match up the pictures and the descriptions.

1B.4 El insti

1B.4 La ropa
páginas 46–47

Planner

Objectives
- talk about school uniform and your opinion of it
- use adjectives correctly
- develop ways of learning vocabulary

Resources
Students' Book, pages 46–47
CD 1, tracks 46–48
Foundation Workbook, page 27
Higher Workbook, page 27
Foundation Workbook audio, CD 3, track 56
Higher Workbook audio, CD 4, track 31
Interactive OxBox, Unit 1B
Copymasters 27–34
Assessment, Unit 1B

Video
Video-blog, Unit 1B

Key language
llevar; un jersey; una camisa; una camiseta; una corbata; una falda; una sudadera; unas zapatillas; unos calcetines; unos pantalones; unos vaqueros; unos zapatos; incómodo/a; elegante; práctico/a; formal; cómodo/a; feo/a; ridículo/a; informal

Grammar
- use adjectives correctly

Renewed Framework references
1.1, 1.4, 1.5, 2.1, 2.4, 2.5, 3.1, 3.2, 4.3, 4.5

PLTS
Think!: Reflective learners
Activity 4: Reflective learners; Creative thinkers; Self-managers
Activity 5: Effective participators
Challenge: Creative thinkers/Team workers

Starters
- Display some items of clothing in Spanish and some adjectives. Students match the adjectives to the clothing, making sure that the adjectives agree. Compare answers as a class.
- Ask a volunteer to come to the front of the class. Explain that you are going to describe an outfit and that they must draw it on the board as you describe it, using the correct colours. When they have finished, ask the rest of the class if they think the drawing is correct or not. Alternatively, you could ask a different student to draw each item of clothing.

Plenaries
- Display the following: *the class, Loreto, Rafael, you, I, we* along with some items of clothing, colours and adjectives (you can display all of these in English or in Spanish depending on the level of the class). Students write as many sentences as they can to describe what the different people are wearing using the verb *llevar*. Remind them to ensure that they use the correct part of *llevar* and to make any adjectives agree with the noun(s) they are describing. Volunteers read their sentences out to the class.
- Students describe their ideal uniform using the vocabulary from the spread. More able students should include colours and adjectives. They read their descriptions to the class who votes for the best one.

Homework/Self-study
Think!: Students write out in full the verb *llevar* and then make sentences saying who is wearing what, and illustrating these.
Gramática: Students write an adjective to describe each item of clothing in the vocabulary box, ensuring that they make the adjective agree each time. Provide less able students with a list of adjectives to help them.

AT 3.3 **1 ¿Sam o Carlos?**
Students listen and decide who is speaking each time, Sam or Carlos. The pictures and texts at the top of the Students' Book page will help them.

CD 1, track 46 — página 46, actividad 1
1 Llevo una camisa blanca.
2 Llevo una corbata azul, amarilla y roja.
3 Llevo unos vaqueros.
4 Llevo un jersey azul.
5 Llevo una camiseta.
6 Llevo zapatillas de deporte.

Answers:
1 Sam; **2** Sam; **3** José; **4** Sam; **5** José; **6** José

1B.4 El insti

PLTS **Think!**
Elicit from pupils the answers *Llevamos zapatos.* and *Llevan pantalones.* Conduct a quick-fire quiz along the same lines to practice *llevar* further, e.g. How would you say, 'He/They/I/You... wear/wears a shirt/a sweater/trainers/jeans...?

AT 1.4 **2 Mira el video-blog.**
Students watch Marisa, José and Khalid and fill in the table saying what they like/dislike about what they wear to school.

🎥 Video-blog: Unit 1B (CD 1, track 47)

¿Llevas uniforme al colegio?
José: No. No llevo uniforme en el colegio. Llevo mis vaqueros y mi camiseta.
Khalid: No. No llevo uniforme. Llevo tejanos, camiseta.
Marisa: No. No llevo uniforme. Normalmente llevo una camiseta y una falda de color rojo, negro, azul.

¿Te gusta? ¿Por qué?
José: Sí, me gusta llevar mi ropa porque me siento cómodo.
Khalid: Me gusta porque puedo ir a mi estilo.
Marisa: Me gusta no llevar uniforme porque así no somos todos iguales.

¿Qué prefieres llevar el fin de semana?
José: Mi camiseta El Barça y ropa normal, como los vaqueros.
Khalid: El fin de semana prefiero ir más arreglado, con camisas, tejanos...
Marisa: El fin de semana me gusta llevar ropa cómoda, un vestido para salir con los amigos.

Answers:
Marisa: likes not wearing a uniform as it means they don't all look the same.
José: likes wearing his own clothes as he feels more comfortable.
Khalid: likes not wearing a uniform as he can wear his own style of clothing.

AT 3.2 **3 ¿Verdad o mentira?**
Students read the texts at the top of the page 46 and then note down if the sentences about Sam and Carlos are true or not.

Answers:
1 verdad; *2* verdad; *3* mentira; *4* verdad; *5* mentira; *6* mentira

Gramática
Ask students to find examples of other adjectives on this page and to write them down. Look at how they agree.

PLTS **Think!**
Refer students back to Unit 0 – learning vocabulary, or on to the *Labolengua* spread for some ideas.

AT 4.1–2 **4 Dibuja tu propio mapa mental.**
PLTS Students draw up a clothes mind map using clothes and opinions of their own. Alternatively students can work in groups to draw up mind maps which they then compare with the whole class – who has the same/different words? Who has been the most inventive?

AT 2.2 **5 👥 Habla con tu compañero.**
PLTS Students play 20 questions with a partner using the clothing they included in their mind map. More able students can include colours as well, e.g. *una camisa blanca.*

AT 1.2 **6 👥 Escucha. Escoge el dibujo correcto.**
Students listen and choose the correct item of clothing each time.

🎧 CD 1, track 48 — página 47, actividad 6

1 Llevo zapatillas de deporte y un chándal rojo y cómodo.
2 Llevamos uniforme – unos pantalones grises y una camisa azul. ¡Qué incómodo y feo!
3 Julio lleva vaqueros y una camiseta blanca. Es muy informal.
4 Pilar lleva una falda verde y un jersey negro bastante elegante.

Answers:
1 b; *2* d; *3* a; *4* c

AT 4.2–4 **Challenge**
PLTS **Design a new school uniform; show your design to the class and describe it.**
This could be a solo homework activity with students producing a picture and description on a sheet of A4 for display. Alternatively, pairs or groups could produce a large poster design and written description to present to the class. Or you could do a fashion parade. The designs don't have to be serious – they could have an eco theme, a space age theme, the unifom for a school of super-heros...

1B.5 El insti

1B.5 Me gusta
páginas 48–49

Planner

Objectives
- learn the names for more school subjects, talk about patterns on clothes
- use more adjectival agreements correctly

Resources
Students' Book, pages 48–49
CD 1, tracks 49–51
Foundation Workbook, page 28
Higher Workbook, page 28
Foundation Workbook audio, CD 3, track 57
Higher Workbook audio, CD 4, track 32
Interactive OxBox, Unit 1B
Assessment, Unit 1B

Renewed Framework references
1.1, 1.4, 2.1, 2.4, 2.5, 4.3, 4.5, 5.8

PLTS
Activity 3: Creative thinkers; Effective participators
Activity 6: Self-managers
Activity 7: Effective participators

Starters
- Display some expressions to show how well you are doing and then some opinions. Students match the opinions to the expressions, e.g. *saco buenas notas – es fácil; me esfuerzo en – es muy interesante*, etc.
- Students play a memory game on the theme of clothes. You start with *Llevo una camiseta con mangas cortas*. A student continues, *Llevo una camiseta con mangas cortas y una corbata negra a puntos blancos*, and so on. Play until someone forgets one of the ítems mentioned.

Plenaries
- Challenge students to write five sentences on the theme of the spread using the vocabulary and ideas covered. These sentences can be as simple or extended as appropriate. Encourage more able students to write extended sentences giving opinions and reasons.
- Students design a whole outfit including details of patterns. This could be for a famous person of their choice or something quite unusual, i.e. a very colourful, patterned wedding dress. They write out their description, do a drawing to go with it and then present this to the class.

Homework/Self-study
After listening to the recording in Activity 2, students write a sentence about a school subject of their choice saying if they like it or not and why. Provide less able students with a model sentence to adapt. You can display school subjects, opinions and reasons to choose from.
After completing Activity 7, students write some descriptions of items of clothing. These descriptions can be very simple or quite detailed according to ability, but students should try to use the words from the vocabulary box. Students then read their descriptions to a partner in class. The partner draws the item of clothing.

AT 3.2–3 **1 Lee lo que opinan los estudiantes.**
Students read the sentences and note down which subject is mentioned each time and if the person likes it or not.

Answers:
1 b ✓; **2** d ✓; **3** e ✗; **4** g ✗; **5** c ✗

AT 1.2–3 **2 Escucha. Copia y completa la tabla.**
Students listen to the people speaking about school subjects and fill in the table. Encourage students to predict the vocabulary they are likely to hear.

🎧 **CD 1, track 49** página 48, actividad 2

Mari-Carmen: Mi asignatura preferida es la música. Es interesante y el profe es simpático.
Isabel: No me interesa mucho el arte. La profesora es muy estricta.
Rosita: ¿El alemán? Pues, me interesa un poco, pero es difícil.
Alfonso: ¿La religión? ¡Qué va! Es aburrida.
Miguel Ángel: Me fascina la literatura española. Es muy interesante y la profe es muy simpática.

Answers:
Isabel: arte; no se interesa mucho; profesora estricta
Rosita: alemán; se interesa un poco; difícil
Alfonso: religión; ¡Qué va!; aburrida
Miguel Ángel: literatura española; se fascina; interesante, profe simpática

1B.6 El insti

AT 4.2-3
PLTS

3 Escribe lo que piensa tu compañero.
Students write down what they think their friends would say about the subjects from Activity 2. The number and complexity of sentences can vary according to ability. Less able students can make notes, e.g. *John – música – profe simpatico*. Students check their guesses by asking their friends *¿Te gusta la música?* or *¿Qué opinas de la música?*.

AT 1.2

4 Escucha a los estudiantes.
Students listen and choose the appropriate illustration. More advanced students can note down the subject they speak about as well. Before they begin, ask students to read through the first vocabulary box and to try to guess what each phrase means.

CD 1, track 50 — página 49, actividad 4
1 Soy fuerte en matemáticas.
2 Trabajo bien en ciencias.
3 Saco malas notas en francés.
4 Voy muy mal en historia.
5 Hago un esfuerzo en geografía.
6 Saco buenas notas en literatura.

Answers:
1 c; 2 e; 3 b; 4 d; 5 f; 6 a

AT 4.2-3
PLTS

5 Escribe tu opinión.
Students use the phrases from Activity 4 and the vocabulary box to write down how well they think they are doing in different subjects. More able students can add an opinion about the subjects, e.g. *Saco buenas notas en inglés – es fácil, pero saco malas notas en geografía – es abburrida.* Less able students could just write notes, e.g. *Las matemáticas – interesantes*.

AT 1.2
PLTS

6 Escucha y anota la ropa.
Work through the second vocabulary box with the class. Students then listen and note down the item of clothing they hear each time. Less able students just note down the style – stripy, checked, etc. This could be made into a game – students listen and draw a quick sketch of the item.

CD 1, track 51 — página 49, actividad 6
1 Llevo una camisa azul con mangas largas.
2 Llevo unos pantalones rojos a rayas.
3 Llevo una falda verde a flores.
4 Llevo una camiseta con un logo.
5 Llevo un vestido amarillo sencillo.
6 Llevo una corbata negra a puntos blancos.
7 Llevo una camisa naranja sin mangas.

Answers:
1 blue shirt, long sleeves; *2* trousers, red, stripy; *3* skirt, green, flowers; *4* T-shirt, logo; *5* dress, plain, yellow; *6* tie, black, white spots; *7* shirt, orange, sleeveless

AT 2.2
PLTS

7 Juega al tres en raya.
Students play noughts and crosses using the grid in the Students' Book. In order to place their nought or cross, they must say what they are wearing. With less able students, go through possible descriptions again before they start playing. This can be played as a class team game on OHP/interactive whiteboard, and then in pairs. You will either need multiple copies of the grid, or small Os and Xs cut out of card to place on the book.

1B.6 Labolengua — páginas 50–51

Planner

Objectives
- review language and grammar from the unit

Resources
Students' Book, pages 50–51
CD 1, track 46
Foundation Workbook, pages 29–30
Higher Workbook, pages 29–30
Interactive OxBox, Unit 1B
Copymasters 35–36
Assessment, Unit 1B

Grammar
- adjectives
- verbs

Renewed Framework references
2.1, 2.4, 4.1, 4.2, 4.3, 4.4, 4.5, 5.3, 5.4

PLTS
All activities: Reflective learners/Self-managers

Homework/Self-study
Activity 1: Students make up an imaginative brain-jogger cartoon.
Activity 4: Students make up some more absurd sentences of their own.

1B.6 El insti

Comprender – adjectives and verbs

A Adjectival agreements

PLTS 1 Write the sentences using the following nouns and adjectives. Remember to make them agree.

To encourage students to recognise masculine and feminine nouns, set up a class competition. Give groups 5 minutes to see how many different masculine nouns ending in 'o'/not ending in 'o'/feminine nouns ending in 'a'/not ending in 'a' they can find in the Students' Book. Sort the nouns into categories. Drawing quick cartoons can help students remember which non-'o' ending nouns are masculine, e.g. a picture of a pencil wearing trousers and a crew cut to illustrate *un lápiz*. Writing a sentence practises using and making adjectives agree, e.g. *El lápiz es rojo*. The sillier the sentence, the more likely it is to be remembered.

Answers:
La falda es corta. Las aulas son viejas. Los patios son bonitos. El inglés es interesante.
Students can also mix and match the words to make other sentences.

B Regular verbs

PLTS 2 How would you say...?
Practice of conjugating regular verb.

Answers:
1 María habla español. 2 Marcos come en el comedor. 3 Rafael vive en Madrid.

PLTS 3 Transfer your skills. How would you say...?
Further practice of conjugating regular verbs.

Answers:
1 Practicamos deporte. 2 Lees un libro. 3 Abren sus cuadernos.

PLTS 4 Why are these sentences absurd?
Practice of translating verbs.

Answers:
These are absurd as they mean: **a** I live in the canteen. **b** We eat black trousers. **c** They speak IT.

Aprender – learning vocabulary

C Language learning tricks

PLTS 5 Look back through the book. How many cognates can you find? Make a list.
Using cognates to learn new vocabulary.

PLTS 6 What does this mean?
Using word association to learn new words.

Answer: b

PLTS 7 Look back through the book again. Make a list of words that look similar to something in English but have a slightly different meaning.
Practice of recognising 'false friends' and translating them correctly.

Hablar – pronunciation

D Pronunciation – emphasis

PLTS 8 Where do you emphasise these words? Copy them and underline where you think the emphasis should go. Then listen and check.
Practice of pronouncing words in Spanish. Items 7–12 of the recording can be used to provide context for the words, or used on their own for more able pupils.

🎧 **CD 1, track 52** página 51, actividad 8

practicar
falda
pantalones
inglés
comemos
interesante
Me gusta practicar deporte.
Llevo una falda verde.
Tengo unos pantalones negros.
El profesor de inglés es muy simpático.
Normalmente, comemos a las dos.
La historia es muy interesante.

Answers:
practic**ar**; **fa**lda; panta**lo**nes; ingl**és**; com**e**mos; interes**a**nte

1B.7 El insti

1B.7 Extra Star   página 52

Planner

Objectives
- practise telling the time
- practise using –ar verbs
- work independently

Resources
Students' Book, page 52
Copymaster 37

Renewed Framework references
2.1, 2.4, 2.5, 4.3, 4.5, 5.4

PLTS
Activity 2: Reflective learners

AT 3.1
AT 4.2

1 Escoge el dibujo y copia y completa la frase.
This practises telling the time in Spanish. Students match the sentences to the pictures and then complete each sentence with the correct time.

Answers:
1 f – las cuatro; 2 a – las nueve y media; 3 d – las tres menos veinticinco; 4 b – las once y cuarto; 5 c – las doce y veinte

AT 4.2–3
PLTS

2 Mira tu horario.
Do a few examples in class first to check students understand what they have to do. Give less able students sentences to complete, e.g. *Tengo inglés a …, tengo deporte a …*

AT 4.2
PLTS

3 Copia y completa las frases.
Students complete the sentences with the correct part of *estudiar*.

Answers:
1 estudio; 2 estudiamos; 3 estudias; 4 estudia

1B.7 Extra Plus   página 53

Planner

Objectives
- understand how schools in Spain work
- understand *desde … hasta*
- compare schools in different countries

Resources
Students' Book, page 53
Copymaster 38

Renewed Framework references
1.1, 2.1, 2.4, 2.5, 3.1, 3.2, 4.2, 4.4

PLTS
Activity 2: Independent enquirers
Activity 4: Self-managers

AT 3.3–4

1 Lee el correo electrónico.
Students read the email and answer the questions. Questions are in English because although this page is designed for independent access, it could be the starting point for a cultural discussion on the differences in Spanish and English schools. It is worth pointing out that not all schools operate this system – some work till 2pm without a lunch break – but many do. The long lunch hour is a very Spanish feature.

Answers:
1 9am; 2 5pm; 3 15 minutes; 4 1pm; 5 at home with his family; 6 3pm; 7 play sport; 8 big and modern; 9 many are nice, some are very strict

AT 3.3–4
PLTS

2 ¿Como se dice…?
Students find the Spanish for the phrases listed.

1B.8 El insti

Answers:
1 desde las nueve de la mañana; *2* hasta las cinco de la tarde;
3 de quince minutos; *4* normalmente; *5* en casa; *6* el miércoles;
7 con; *8* pero; *9* unos; *10* muchos

AT 4.3 **3 Escribe en español.**
Students use what they have learnt in Activity 2 to translate the sentences listed into Spanish. The most able students could be given more complex sentences to translate. Once they have understood that all the vocabulary they need is in Felipe's letter, you could have a competition to see how long a sentence they can translate.

Answers:
1 Tengo clases desde las nueve y media de la mañana.
2 Tenemos un recreo de veinte minutos.
3 Normalmente como en el comedor.
4 Unos profesores son divertidos.

AT 4.3–4 **PLTS** **4 Describe tu instituto.**
Students draw upon the vocabulary and structures in Felipe's email to describe their school and their school day. More able students can add opinions, quantifiers and connectives.

1B.8 Prueba   página 54

Planner

Resources
Students' Book, page 54
CD 1, track 47

Renewed Framework references
1.1, 1.4, 1.5, 2.1, 2.4, 2.5, 3.1, 3.2

PLTS
All activities: Reflective learners
Hablar: Reflective learners; Creative thinkers
Escribir: Reflective learners; Creative thinkers

Escuchar

AT 1.3 **PLTS** **1 Listen, copy and complete the timetable. Add a smiley or frowning face to show if Luisa likes each subject or not.**
This activity tests listening skills using the language covered in this unit. Students can answer in Spanish or English as you prefer.

🎧 **CD 1, track 53**   página 54, Escuchar

Example: Tengo matemáticas el lunes a las ocho y media. Me gusta mucho – ¡el profe es muy divertido!
1 A las nueve y media tengo informática. Es muy aburrida.
2 A las diez y media hay un recreo, y despúes tenemos deporte. ¡Me encanta el deporte!
3 A las doce menos diez tengo inglés. No me gusta porque es difícil.
4 A la una menos diez hay la hora de comer. Despúes, a las dos y cuarto tengo historia. La profesora es muy simpática.
5 Finalmente a las tres y cuarto tengo español. El profesor de español es demasiado estricto.

Answers:
1 informática/IT – ☹; *2* deporte/PE – ☺; *3* inglés/English – ☹;
4 historia/history – ☺; *5* español/Spanish – ☹

El insti 1B

Hablar

AT 2.3 **PLTS** **Choose one of these people. Imagine what their favourite subject is and explain what they like and dislike and why.**
Students use the stimulus pictures or, if you prefer, they can talk about their own personal experiences. Remind students to try to give opinions, and to use connectives as this will lead to higher marks.

Leer

AT 3.4 **PLTS** **3 Read Eva's email and decide if the statements are true or false.**
This activity tests reading skills using the language covered in this unit.

Answers:
1 false – she has English 5 days a week; *2* true; *3* false – she finds it boring; *4* false – she has it on Tuesday at 2pm; *5* true; *6* false – she finds it interesting

Escribir

AT 4.3–4 **PLTS** **4 Describe this uniform. What do you think of it?**
This activity tests writing skills using the language covered in this unit. It might be interesting to discuss the fact that some Spanish pupils do have to wear uniform. What do students think of this?

Leer 1B   página 154

Planner

Resources
Students' Book, page 154

Renewed Framework references
2.1, 3.1, 3.2, 5.4

PLTS
Activity 4: Independent enquirers

Homework/Self-study
Students carry out further research on the schools featured using the Internet. They make notes about each of them in Spanish/English/note form/full sentences depending on their ability. They then feed back their findings to the class.

AT 3.3–4 **1 Match the school descriptions to the photos.**
There will be words here that students have not met, but many can be worked out by context and cognates. All the schools mentioned are real places and can be researched further. This could be the starting point for a discussion of the differences between the schools, the areas they are in, and what students think of all this.

Answers:
a 1; *b* 2; *c* 3; *d* 4

AT 3.4 **2 Who…?**
Answering these questions will help students to understand the texts better.

Answers:
1 Rodrigo; *2* Beatriz; *3* Delia; *4* Iván; *5* Iván/Delia; *6* Beatriz

AT 3.4 **3 What is amazing about the Peruvian islands mentioned?**
Encourage students to comment on/discuss this further. How do the schools described compare to their school?

Answer: they are floating islands.

AT 3.4 **PLTS** **4 Why do you think the students in Madrid and Tenerife mention friends, but those from Colombia and Peru talk about education?**
This is a very open question about values which is designed to get students thinking about cultural differences. This ties in with the suggested homework/self-study task of researching the schools further as students will be better able to answer this question if they know more about the schools and countries featured.

83

1B El insti

Foundation Workbook

Página 24   **1B.1 Mis asignaturas**
- Use with Students' Book, pages 40–41

AT 1.1, 2.1   **1 Listen to the pronunciation on the CD, then read these words aloud.**

> 🎧 **CD 3, track 54**   página 24, actividad 1
>
> **a** el inglés, la geografía, las matemáticas, la informática, la tecnología
> **b** las ciencias, el español, la tecnología, la geografía, la historia

2 Masculine, feminine, singular, plural. Put the words below into the chart.
This practises typical masculine, feminine and plural endings as well as adjectival agreement.

Answers:

	Asignaturas
EL	inglés, español, dibujo, deporte
LA	historia, música, geografía, informática, tecnología
LAS	ciencias; matemáticas

AT 2.2   **3 Use the chart in Activity 2 to read aloud different opinions on school subjects. How many can you do in one minute?**
More able students can use more than one adjective for each subject and can also use connectives to extend sentences, e.g. *La historia es divertida pero el deporte es ....*

AT 4.2   **4 Use the chart again to help you complete these sentences.**
This will help students to give reasons when writing in order to make their sentences more interesting.

Página 25   **1B.2 La hora y el horario**
- Use with Students' Book, pages 42–43

AT 4.2   **1 Complete with the correct times.**
Practice of telling the time in Spanish.

Answers:
Row 1: seis; las dos; son las ocho
Row 2: y cuarto; seis y cuarto; las siete y cuarto
Row 3: media; cuatro y media; son las diez y media
Row 4: menos; menos cuarto; seis menos cuarto

AT 3.3   **2 Read and underline the times and the lessons. Then fill in the timetable.**
Practice of telling the time in the context of a school timetable.

Answers:
<u>A las nueve</u>, tengo <u>inglés</u>. Tengo <u>matemáticas a las diez menos cuarto</u>. <u>A las once</u> tengo <u>geografía</u> y <u>a las doce menos cuarto</u> tengo <u>historia</u>. <u>A la una y cuarto</u> tengo <u>ciencias</u>. Tengo <u>música a las tres menos cuarto</u>.

9.00	inglés
9.45	matemáticas
11.00	geografía
11.45	historia
1.15	ciencias
2.45	música

Página 26   **1B.3 Las instalaciones**
- Use with Students' Book, pages 44–45

AT 1.2   **1 Listen. True (T) or false (F)?**

> 🎧 **CD 3, track 55**   página 26, actividad 1
>
> **a** Mi instituto es antiguo.
> **b** El patio es grande.
> **c** Tenemos una aula especial para informática.
> **d** Hay cuatro oficinas.
> **e** La oficina del director es grande.
> **f** No me gusta el instituto.
> **g** Hay un gimnasio.
> **h** Trabajo en la biblioteca.
> **i** Como en el patio.

Answers:
a T; *b* F; *c* F; *d* F; *e* T; *f* F; *g* F; *h* T; *i* F

AT 3.2   **2 Circle the option that best describes your own school.**
Students can choose options that describe their ideal school if they prefer.

AT 4.1–2   **3 Draw a plan of your school and label it in Spanish.**
This brings together what students have learnt in this spread. Encourage more able students to write sentences when labelling their plan and to add opinions as well. Less able students can label the plan with the appropriate words. If you prefer, students could draw a plan of and label their ideal school.

El insti 1B

Página 27 — 1B.4 La ropa
- Use with Students' Book, pages 46–47

1 Carry out an experiment to evaluate different ways of learning clothes vocabulary.
There are many ways of learning vocabulary and different strategies will suit different students. Explain to students that they should try to find the best way for them.

2 When you have had time to learn all the words, do the test on the CD. Listen to the words and write them in English. Record your score for each set of words.
This will give students an idea of the best way for them to learn new vocabulary.

> **CD 3, track 56** — página 27, actividades 2 y 3
> a un jersey, una corbata, una falda
> b un vestido, una camisa, unos vaqueros
> c unos zapatos, unos pantalones, una gorra
> d unos calcetines, una sudadera, una chaqueta

3 Use the technique that worked best for you to learn all the words on this page. Test yourself again with the CD.

Página 28 — 1B.5 Me gusta…
- Use with Students' Book, pages 48–49

[AT 3.1–2] 1 Put these expressions into the correct column.
Students can record these useful expressions in their vocabulary books. Using these will make their writing more interesting and increase their marks.

Answers:
Positive: me fascina; me interesa; es interesante; me gusta; soy fuerte en…; saco buenas notas; es fácil; me encanta; el profesor es; simpático
Negative: es difícil; es aburrido/a; voy mal en…; saco malas notas

[AT 1.3] 2 Listen to Pilar. Complete the grid with ☺ or ☹.
This provides the opportunity to hear the expressions from Activity 1 in context.

> **CD 3, track 57** — página 28, actividad 2
> Soy fuerte en historia. Saco buenas notas y me gusta. También me interesa la geografía, y el profesor es muy simpático. Soy fuerte en inglés. Me gusta y es importante. La música es más difícil. Voy mal en música. No es interesante. Me fascina el deporte y me encanta la educación física.

Answers:
la historia ☺; la geografía ☺; el inglés ☺; la música ☹; la educación física ☺

[AT 4.2] 3 Give your own opinions of these subjects.
Encourage students to try and use connectives.

Página 29 — 1B.6A Labolengua
- Use with Students' Book, pages 50–51

[AT 3.2] 1 Complete each sentence with the correct adjective.
Students who finish this quickly could finish the sentences with a different adjective as well, ensuring that they use the correct ending each time.

Answers:
a divertida; **b** divertidas; **c** divertido; **d** divertidos

[AT 3.2] 2 Translate into English.
Refer students back to previous grammar boxes or the Grammar Section for support if necessary.

Answers:
a We eat in the canteen. **b** The headteacher eats in his office. **c** I don't wear uniform. **d** I talk with my friends. **e** Do you study Spanish? **f** My grandparents live in Spain.

[AT 4.2–3] 3 Use the words from Activity 2 to write about your own school.
Students could also write about their ideal school or the worst school they can think of.

Página 30 — 1B.6B Técnica
- Use with Students' Book, pages 50–51

[AT 3.1] 1 Which are English and which are Spanish? Highlight the Spanish words.
When students have done this, ask them to say all of the Spanish words out loud being careful to pronounce them in a Spanish way.

Answers:
English words: technology; geography; mathematics; history; music; science
Spanish words: tecnología; geografía; matemáticas; historia; música; ciencias

[AT 4.1] 2 Copy out the Spanish words from Activity 1. Write two important things to remember about how to spell each one.

Possible answers:
geografía has an 'f' not a 'ph' and an accent on the 'ía'; matemáticas has no 'h' and has an accent on the 'áticas'; historia has an 'ia' at the end but there is no accent; música has an accent on the 'u' and ends in 'a'; ciencias doesn't start with an 's', but it does end in one

1B El insti

3 A cognate is a word you can re<u>cog</u>nise from a language you already know. How many of these words are cognates? Tick the ones that are.

Answers:
gimnasio; laboratorio; patio; oficina; director

4 Cognates help when you see the written word, but can be tricky when you need to use them yourself. Think about the words you ticked in Activity 3 and put them into the table in the correct column.

Answers:

Watch the spelling	Watch the pronunciation	Mean something slightly different
gimnasio; laboratorio; oficina	gimnasio; oficina	patio; director

Higher Workbook

Página 24   1B.1 Mis asignaturas
- Use with Students' Book, pages 40–41

AT 1.1, 2.1   **1** Read aloud these words and then compare your pronunciation with the CD.
Practice of pronouncing tricky words in Spanish.

> **CD 4, track 29**   página 24, actividad 1
> a el inglés, la geografía, las matemáticas, la informática, la tecnología
> b las ciencias, el español, la tecnología, la geografía, la historia

2 Masculine, feminine, singular, plural. Put the words below into the chart.
This practises typical masculine, feminine and plural endings as well as adjectival agreement.

Answers:

	Asignaturas		Adjetivos
EL	inglés; español; deporte; dibujo	ES	divertido; interesante; aburrido; difícil; fácil; útil
LA	música; historia; geografía; tecnología; informática		divertida; interesante; aburrida; difícil; fácil; útil
LOS		SON	divertidos; interesantes; difíciles
LAS	ciencias; matemáticas		divertidas; interesantes; aburridas; difíciles; fáciles; útiles

AT 4.2   **3** Use the chart in activity 2 to help you complete these sentences.
Discuss the sentences in class to ensure that students have fully understood gender and adjectival agreement.

AT 2.2   **4** Now read out your sentences from Activity 3, using these expressions to sound more personal.

Página 25   1B.2 La hora y el horario
- Use with Students' Book, pages 42–43

AT 3.2   **1** Complete with the correct times.

Answer:
Row 1: cuatro, 6 o'clock, 2 o'clock, 8 o'clock
Row 2: cinco, quarter past 2, quarter past 6, quarter past 7
Row 3: dos, half past 3, half past 4, half past 10
Row 4: cinco, quarter to 3, quarter to 8, quarter to 6

AT 3.3   **2** Read and work out how many lessons Paula has each day. How long are the lessons? What time does she go home for lunch?
Understanding the time in Spanish in context.

Answers:
8 lessons of 45 minutes, goes home at 12.00

Página 26   1B.3 Las instalaciones
- Use with Students' Book, pages 44–45

AT 1.2, 3.2   **1** Guess the answers, then listen and see if you were right!
Listening out for specific answers will help students to focus on what is being said.

> **CD 4, track 30**   página 26, actividad 1
> a Mi instituto es antiguo.
> b El patio es grande.
> c Tenemos una aula especial para informática.
> d Hay cuatro oficinas.
> e La oficina del director es grande.
> f No me gusta el instituto.
> g Hay un gimnasio.
> h Trabajo en la biblioteca.
> i Como en el patio.

Answers: see audioscript

El insti 1B

AT 3.3-4

2 Read this description and then draw and label a plan of the school.
The layout of students' plans will vary, but they must include all of the elements mentioned (five classrooms; small library; computer suite; big playground; two offices: one for the headteacher and one for the receptionist. Students can either label in English to show comprehension of the text, or in Spanish instead.

AT 4.3-4

3 Adapt the ideas on this page to write a description of what there is in your own school.

Página 27   1B.4 La ropa
- Use with Students' Book, pages 46–47

1 Carry out an experiment to evaluate different ways of learning clothes vocabulary.
There are many ways of learning vocbaulary and different strategies will suit different students. Explain to students that they should try to find the best way for them.

2 When you have had time to learn all the words, do the test on the CD. Listen to the words and write them in English. Record your score for each set of words.
This will give students an idea of the best way for them to learn new vocabulary.

> 🎧 **CD 4, track 31**   página 27, actividades 2 y 3
>
> a un jersey; una corbata; una falda
> b un vestido; una camisa; un chándal
> c unos zapatos; unos pantalones; una gorra
> d unos calcetines; una sudadera; una chaqueta
> e unos vaqueros; una camiseta; un cinturón

3 Use the technique that worked best for you to learn all the words on this page. Test yourself again with the CD.

Página 28   1B.5 Me gusta...
- Use with Students' Book, pages 48–49

AT 3.1-2

1 Put these expressions into the correct column.
Students can record these useful expressions in their vocabulary books. Using these will make their writing more interesting and increase their marks.

Answers:
Positive: me fascina(n); me interesa(n); es/son interesante(s); me gusta(n); soy fuerte en...; saco buenas notas; es/son fácil(es); me encanta(n); el profesor es; simpático; la profesora es simpática
Negative: es/son difícil(es); es/son aburrido/a/os/as; voy mal en...; saco malas notas

2 Explain why some of the words in the table have different options.
For verbs singular/plural: is/are, interests me/interest me and for adjectives sing/plur/m/f.

AT 1.4

3 Listen to Pilar. Complete the grid with ☺ or ☹.
This provides the opportunity to hear the expressions from Activity 1 in context.

> 🎧 **CD 4, track 32**   página 28, actividad 3
>
> Mis asignaturas preferidas son la historia y la geografía. Me encantan, porque son muy interesantes. Las matemáticas son más difíciles, y el profesor no es simpático. Soy fuerte en inglés. Es muy importante y me gusta. Las ciencias me fascinan. Es una asignatura que me encanta. Me gusta mucho el deporte, así que saco muy buenas notas en las clases de educación física.

Answers:
la historia ☺; la geografía ☺; las matemáticas ☹; el inglés ☺; las ciencias ☺; la educación física ☺

AT 4.2-3

4 Give your own opinions of these subjects.
Students put into practice what they have learnt from this spread. Encourage students to try and use connectives to make their writing flow better.

Página 29   1B.6A Labolengua
- Use with Students' Book, pages 50–51

1 Complete each sentence with an adjective. Make sure the ending agrees.

AT 4.2

2 Translate into English.
Practice of recognising different verb endings.

Answers:
a We eat in the canteen. **b** The headteacher eats in his office. **c** I don't wear uniform. **d** I talk with my friends. **e** Do you study Spanish? **f** My grandparents live in Spain.

AT 4.2

3 Now change the sentences in Activity 2 to say the following.
Practice of conjugating verbs correctly.

Answers:
a Comen...; **b** Los profesores comen...; **c** No llevamos...; **d** Habla...; **e** ¿Estudiáis...; **f** Vive...

1B El insti

Página 30 1B.6B Técnica
• Use with Students' Book, pages 50–51

1 Copy out these words. Write three important things to remember about how to spell or pronounce each one.

Possible answers:
geografía: *has an 'f' not a 'ph'; has an accent on the 'ía'; has a soft 'g' and then a hard 'g' sound.*
matemáticas: *has no 'h'; has an accent on the 'áticas'; make sure you don't say the 'e' as an 'i'*
historia: *has an 'ia' at the end but there is no accent; silent 'h'*
música: *has an accent on the 'u'; and ends in 'a'; Don't put a 'i' sound before the 'u'.* **ciencias** *doesn't start with an 's', but it does end in one; plural in Spanish but singular in English.*

2 A cognate is a word you can re<u>cogn</u>ise from a language you already know. How many of these words are cognates? Tick the ones that are.

Answers:
gimnasio; laboratorio; patio; oficina; director; jersey; chaqueta

3 Cognates help when you see the written word, but can be tricky when you need to use them yourself. Think about the words you ticked in Activity 2 and put them into the table in the correct column.

Watch the spelling	Watch the pronunciation	Mean something slightly different
gimnasio; laboratorio; oficina; chaqueta	gimnasio; oficina; jersey; chaqueta	patio; director

2A Mi semana

Unit Objectives

Contexts and cultural focus: sport and leisure activities
Grammar: radical-changing verbs; *gustar* + verb; reflexive verbs; the verb *ir* – to go
Language learning: using sequencing to add interest and cohesion to what you write and say

- *Aim:* talk about what you do in your freetime and daily routine whilst incorporating the grammar and vocabulary covered in the spread.
- Each unit has an associated video which will feature throughout the unit. Below is the transcript of the video for this unit.
- As a starter activity to introduce the Unit and familiarise students with the language they will meet, you may find it useful for the class to view the video as a whole.

Video script (CD 2, track 2)

José: Bueno, éste es el Camp Nou, el campo del mejor equipo del mundo, el FC Barcelona.
Marisa: ¿Tienes fiebre, o qué te pasa? Parece que delires.
José: Vengo aquí con mi padre cada dos sábados, granice, llueva o nieve ¡no importa!, siempre venimos.
Marisa: Pero, ¿normalmente hace bastante buen tiempo aquí, no? Estamos en Barcelona, aquí no llueve muy a menudo.
José: Bueno, normalmente no llueve pero ¡se hace mucho viento!
Marisa: ¿Te da miedo del viento?
José: Bueno, vale, tienes razón, normalmente hace buen tiempo. ¿Sabes que juego al fútbol?
Marisa: ¿Sí? Eso está muy bien. ¿Juegas a menudo?
José: Dos veces por semana. Los martes y los jueves.
Marisa: No está mal.
José: No, no está mal. Oye, ¿has visto ya el puerto?

[Pause]

José: Oye, como eres la hija de un diplomático, ¿te gustará hacer esas cosas que hacen los ricos: ir en yate, jugar al golf en verano e ir a esquiar en invierno…? Bueno, ¿te gusta eso o no?
Marisa: ¿Qué, ir en yate? ¡No, por Dios! Sí me mareo si voy en barco.
José: ¿Y golf?
Marisa: ¿Tengo pinta de vieja o qué?
José: Entonces, ¿esquiar?
Marisa: No, demasiado frío…
José: ¿Montañismo?
Marisa: Mucho esfuerzo.
José: ¿Escalada?
Marisa: Demasiado peligroso.
José: ¡Ya sé… ballet! Bueno, por lo menos tendrás una profesora de música que te enseña a tocar el piano los sábados por la mañana y te echa la bronca por no aprenderte la lección.
Marisa: ¡No! No hay lecciones de música.
José: Entonces ¿qué haces en tu tiempo libre?
Marisa: Lo normal… ver fútbol, ir al cine, salir con los amigos.

[Pause]

Marisa: ¿Qué? ¿Te estoy aburriendo?
José: ¡Desde luego que no! Es sólo que… bueno… eres muy diferente a Eva. Ella se levanta por la mañana hacer yoga y meditar.
Marisa: ¿De verdad?
José: Y luego practica con el oboe.
Marisa: Sí, la verdad es que somos bastante distintas.
Marisa: Bueno y ahora… ¿Adónde vamos?
José: ¿Te refieres al tour por Barcelona, especialidad de José? Bueno, había pensado en ir hacer algunas compras por el centro en una tienda de deportes.
Marisa: ¡Me parece estupendo! Vamos.
José: Pero, ¿no te vas a probar ropa como hacen todas esas chicas, no?
Marisa: Mmm… depende, depende… depende de la ropa, de los zapatos, del precio.

2A Mi semana

Unit 2A Mi semana Overview grid						
Page reference	Contexts and objectives	Language learning	Grammar	Key language	Framework	AT level
Pages 56–57 **El tiempo**	• talk about the weather • recognise and use idioms with the verb *hacer*		• use the radical-changing verb *jugar (ue)*	*buen tiempo; mal tiempo; frío; calor; sol; viento* *Hay… tormenta/niebla/nubes/llueve/nieva* *la primavera; el verano; el otoño; el invierno* *el fútbol; el golf; el baloncesto; el tenis; el ciclismo; el atletismo; el boxeo; la pelota vasca; el windsurf; el voleibol*	1.1, 1.4, 2.1, 2.4, 2.5, 3.1, 3.2, 4.1, 4.3, 4.5, 5.4, 5.5	1.2–4, 2.2–3, 3.3, 4.2–3
Pages 58–59 **Tiempo libre**	• talk about what you do in your free time		• use *gustar* + verb • recognise and learn patterns in radical-changing verbs	*jugar al ajedrez; tocar la guitarra; ir al cine; montar a caballo; bailar salsa; jugar con videojuegos; me gusta; me encanta; me apasiona; me interesa; me flipa; me mola; no me gusta; me aburre; me molesta; me fastidia*	1.1, 1.4, 2.4, 2.5, 3.1, 3.2, 4.1, 4.2, 4.3, 4.5, 5.1, 5.3	1.2–4, 2.2–3, 3.3, 4.2–3
Pages 60–61 **Por la mañana**	• say what you do in the morning		• use reflexive verbs • explain patterns in verbs	*desayuno; me ducho; me lavo los dientes; me levanto; me peino; me pongo (el uniforme)*	1.1, 1.4, 2.1, 2.4, 3.1, 3.2, 4.3, 4.4, 4.5, 5.1	1.2–4, 2.3–4, 3.2
Pages 62–63 **Por la tarde**	• talk about what you do after school	• use sequencing to add interest and cohesion to what you write and say	• use the full verb *ir* – to go	*descansar; merendar (ie); ver la tele; pasear el perro; hacer los deberes; cenar; acostarse (ue); dormirse; en punto; a eso de*	1.1, 1.4, 2.1, 2.4, 2.5, 4.2, 4.3, 4.4, 4.5, 5.1	1.3–4, 2.2, 3.4, 4.3–4
Pages 64–65 **El fin de semana**	• talk about weekend activities • recognise and use additional vocabulary on sports and hobbies			*¿Qué te gusta hacer los sábados? ¿Qué te fastidia de los sábados? ¿Qué te flipa? ¿Qué odias?*	1.1, 1.4, 2.1, 2.4, 2.5, 4.2, 4.3, 4.4, 4.5, 5.4	1.4, 2.2–3, 3.3–4, 4.4
Pages 66–67 **Labolengua**	• review language and grammar from the unit				1.1, 1.4, 2.4, 4.1, 4.2, 4.3, 4.4, 4.5, 5.1	

Mi semana 2A

Pages 68–69 **Extra Star** **Extra Plus**	• differentiated extension/ homework material	• revise and consolidate all vocabulary and grammar covered in the unit	• revise and consolidate all vocabulary and grammar covered in the unit		1.1, 1.4, 2.1, 2.4, 2.5, 4.3, 4.4, 4.5, 5.8	1.2–3, 2.2–3, 3.2–3, 4.2–4
Page 70 **Prueba**	• end-of-spread test				1.1, 1.4, 2.1, 2.4, 2.5, 5.4	1.3–4, 2.2–3, 3.4, 4.4
Page 71 **Vocabulario**	• a summary of the key language covered in each spread of this unit					
Page 155 **Leer 2A**	• practice of longer reading texts based on the theme of the unit				2.1, 3.1, 5.4, 5.5	3.4

2A Mi semana

Week-by-week overview
(Three-year KS3 Route: assuming six weeks' work or approximately 10–12.5 hours)
(Two-year KS3 Route: assuming four weeks' worth or approxmately 6.5-8.5 hours)
*Please note that essential activities are highlighted.

About Unit 2A, *Mi semana*: Students work in the context of sport and leisure activities. They talk about the weather and learn to recognise and use idioms with the verb *hacer*. They say what they do in the morning, after school and at the weekend. Students learn how to use radical-changing verbs as well as reflexive verbs and the verb *ir*. The unit also provides tips on language learning techniques.

Three-Year KS3 Route

Week	Resources	Objectives
1	2A.1 El tiempo 2A.6 Lablolengua A (p.66)	talk about the weather recognise and use idioms with the verb *hacer* use the radical-changing verb *jugar (ue)*
2	2A.2 Tiempo libre 2A.6 Lablolengua C (p.67)	talk about what you do in your free time use *gustar* + verb recognise and learn patterns in radical-changing verbs
3	2A.3 Por la mañana 2A.6 Lablolengua B (p.66)	say what you do in the morning use reflexive verbs explain patterns in verbs
4	2A.4 Por la tarde	talk about what you do after school use sequencing to add interest and cohesion to what you write and say use the full verb *ir* – to go
5	2A.5 El fin de semana	talk about weekend activities recognise and use additional vocabulary on sports and hobbies
6	2A.7 Extra (Star) (p.68) 2A.7 Extra (Plus) (p.69) 2A.8 Prueba (p.70) Vocabulario (p.71) Leer (p.155)	further reinforcement and extension of the language of the unit recapping on the vocabulary of the unit prepare and carry out assessment in all four skills further reading to explore the language of the unit and cultural themes

Two-Year KS3 Route

Week	Resources	Objectives
1	2A.1 El tiempo omit activities 3, 5 & Challenge 2A.6 Lablolengua A (p.66)	talk about the weather recognise and use idioms with the verb *hacer* use the radical-changing verb *jugar (ue)*
2	2A.2 Tiempo libre omit activities 4 & 5 2A. 6 Lablolengua C (p.67)	talk about what you do in your free time use *gustar* + verb recognise and learn patterns in radical-changing verbs
3	2A.3 Por la mañana omit activities 4 & Challenge 2A.6 Lablolengua B (p.66)	say what you do in the morning use reflexive verbs explain patterns in verbs
4	2A.4 Por la tarde omit activities 1, 4, Gramática 2A.8 Prueba (p.70) Vocabulario (p.71)	talk about what you do after school use sequencing to add interest and cohesion to what you write and say use the full verb *ir* – to go recapping on the vocabulary of the unit prepare and carry out assessment in all four skills

2A.1 Mi semana

2A.1 El tiempo
páginas 56–57

Planner

Objectives
- talk about the weather
- use the radical-changing verb *jugar (ue)*
- recognise and use idioms with the verb *hacer*

Video
Video script, Unit 2A

Resources
Students' Book, pages 56–57
CD 2, tracks 2–4
Foundation Workbook, page 32
Higher Workbook, page 32
Foundation Workbook audio, CD 3, track 58
Higher Workbook audio, CD 4, track 33
Interactive OxBox, Unit 2A
Copymasters 40–47
Assessment, Unit 2A

Key language
*buen tiempo; mal tiempo; frío; calor; sol; viento
Hay… tormenta/niebla/nubes/llueve/nieva
la primavera; el verano; el otoño; el invierno
el fútbol; el golf; el baloncesto; el tenis; el ciclismo; el atletismo; el boxeo; la pelota; vasca; el windsurf; el voleibol*

Grammar
- the radical-changing verb *jugar (ue)*

Renewed Framework references
1.1, 1.4, 2.1, 2.4, 2.5, 3.1, 3.2, 4.1, 4.3, 4.5, 5.4, 5.5

PLTS
Activity 4: Creative thinkers
Challenge: Reflective learners; Creative thinkers

Starters
- Display some of the key vocabulary from the spread. Next to this display the English translations but in jumbled order. Give students a time limit to match the Spanish to the English. Check answers as a class.
- Practice talking about sport in Spanish. Start by asking a student if they play a certain sport, e.g. *¿Juegas al golf/al fútbol/al tenis?* He/She replies as appropriate, e.g. *No, no juego al golf pero sí juego al baloncesto.* and then asks another student if he/she plays a certain sport, and so on around the class. Encourage students to use conjunctions to make their sentences more interesting, e.g. *pero, también, sin embargo, en cambio.*

Plenaries
- Display some simple idiomatic phrases in Spanish from this and previous units and ask students to translate these. Volunteers then say what the phrases mean. Remind students that it is not possible to translate idiomatic phrases literally.
- Choose a confident volunteer to think of a season. He/She mustn't tell the rest of the class. He/She then describes this season without mentioning the season itself, e.g. *En […] normalmente hace buen tiempo; hace calor y sol.* Students put up their hand to guess which season it is. The student who guesses first then has a go at describing a season.

Homework/Self-study
- Students write about a season they haven't yet written about in Activity 6. They could also illustrate it accordingly and students' work could be displayed around the classroom. Provide less able students with a model sentence with gaps for them to fill in a season/month/type of weather. You could also provide a list of seasons, etc. in Spanish for them to choose from. Gramática: More able students write a couple of sentences using the structure, *jugar a….* Less able students copy out the verb *jugar* in the present tense again paying attention to the spellings.

AT 1.4 **1 Mira el video.**
Students watch the video and note down when they hear phrases mentioned.

Video script: Unit 2A (CD2, track 2)

José: Bueno, éste es el Camp Nou, el campo del mejor equipo del mundo, el FC Barcelona.
Marisa: ¿Tienes fiebre, o qué te pasa? Parece que delires.
José: Vengo aquí con mi padre cada dos sábados, granice, llueva o nieve ¡no importa!, siempre venimos. Marisa: Pero, ¿normalmente hace bastante buen tiempo aquí, no? Estamos en Barcelona, aquí no llueve muy a menudo.
José: Bueno, normalmente no llueve pero ¡se hace mucho viento!
Marisa: ¿Te da miedo del viento?
José: Bueno, vale, tienes razón, normalmente hace buen tiempo. ¿Sabes que juego al fútbol?

2A.1 Mi semana

Marisa: ¿Sí? Eso está muy bien. ¿Juegas a menudo?
José: Dos veces por semana. Los martes y los jueves.
Marisa: No está mal.
José: No, no está mal. Oye, ¿has visto ya el puerto?

AT 1.2

2 Escucha, repite e identifica el dibujo.
Students listen to and repeat the phrases. They then match each phrase to the appropriate weather picture.

🎧 **CD 2, track 3** — página 56, actividad 3
- Hoy hace buen tiempo.
- Hace sol.
- Hace calor.
- No hace frío.
- No llueve.

Answers:
a; e; d; c; b

AT 2.2

3 Habla con tu compañero.
Students work with a partner to practise the weather expressions they have just heard.

Think!
This is a good opportunity to discuss looking up verbs in a dictionary and the possible pitfalls of this. It is also a chance to look at set phrases and to explain to students that they can't translate idiomatic language literally.

Answers:
Hace...
1 buen tiempo – the weather is fine; **2** mal tiempo – the weather is bad; **3** frío – it is cold; **4** calor – it is hot; **5** sol – it is sunny; **6** viento – it is windy
Hay...
7 tormenta – it is stormy; **8** niebla – it is foggy; **9** nubes – it is cloudy
10 llueve – it is rainy; **11** nieva – it is snowy

AT 4.2–3 / PLTS

4 Lee y escribe un texto similar.
Students read the extract. They guess what *primavera* means. Then look at the illustration of the other seasons and elicit from students what *verano*, *otoño* and *invierno* mean. Ask them to choose one of these three seasons and to produce a similar text.

AT 1.3

5 Escucha. ¿Qué tiempo hace? ¿En qué día?
Students listen and identify the weather on each day.

🎧 **CD 2, track 4** — página 57, actividad 5
- Lunes: mal tiempo; hay tormenta y nubes.
- Martes: sigue el mal tiempo; llueve mucho.
- Miércoles hay viento.
- Jueves por fin hace sol y buen tiempo.
- Viernes hace calor pero hay viento otra vez.
- Sábado y domingo continuamos con tormentas.

Answers:
Monday: bad weather, stormy, cloudy
Tuesday: still bad weather with lots of rain
Wednesday: windy
Thursday: finally sunny and good weather
Friday: hot but windy again
Saturday and Sunday: stormy

AT 2.2–3

6 Habla con tu compañero.
Read through the vocabulary box as a class. Check understanding by calling out each sport in a random order and ask students to say what it is in English or to describe the sport if there is no English equivalent. Students then work in pairs and ask their partner which sports he/she plays.

AT 3.3

7 Lee el diálogo y contesta a las preguntas.
Students read the dialogue and answer the questions.

Answers:
1 Marisa; **2** when it rains; **3** José plays football; **4** Los Vampiros; **5** it's good

Gramática
Explain to students that in Spanish, some verbs change their spelling in all the persons except *nosotros* (we) and *vosotros* (you plural). These are called radical-changing verbs. Work through the examples given in the Students' Book and ask students to copy out the verb *jugar* with the personal pronouns for each part of the verb. Ask more able students to write a couple of sentences using the structure, *jugar a...*

AT 4.2–3 / PLTS

Challenge
Write about what sports are played in each season. List all the sports you can think of in Spanish under the following headings.
Students practise what they have learnt in this spread. They list all of the sports they can think of in Spanish under the headings given. They then choose four of the sports listed and write a sentence about when you would play each one (weather and season), and why.

2A.2 Mi semana

2A.2 Tiempo libre
paginas 58–59

Planner

Objectives
- talk about what you do in your free time
- use *gustar* + verb
- recognise and learn patterns in radical-changing verbs

Video
Video script, Unit 2A

Resources
Students' Book, pages 58–59
CD 2, tracks 2, 5–6
Foundation Workbook, page 33
Higher Workbook, page 33
Interactive OxBox, Unit 2A
Copymasters 40–47
Assessment, Unit 2A

Key language
jugar al ajedrez; tocar la guitarra; ir al cine; montar a caballo; bailar salsa; jugar con videojuegos; me gusta; me encanta; me apasiona; me interesa; me flipa; me mola; no me gusta; me aburre; me molesta; me fastidia

Grammar
- *gustar* + verb
- patterns in radical-changing verbs

Renewed Framework references
1.1, 1.4, 2.4, 2.5, 3.1, 3.2, 4.1, 4.2, 4.3, 4.5, 5.1, 5.3

PLTS
Gramática (2): Reflective learners
Think!: Independent enquirers
Challenge: Creative thinkers

Starters
- Display a list of hobbies in Spanish and the English translations for these jumbled up next to them. Give students a time limit to match the Spanish to the English. Can they add any more hobbies to the list?
- Display the list from Starter Activity 1 along with the following verbs: *me gusta; me encanta; me apasiona; me interesa; me flipa; me mola; no me gusta; me aburre; me molesta; me fastidia*. Call out a hobby and make either a 'thumbs up' sign (like) or a 'thumbs down' (dislike). Pick a student to make up a sentence using the hobby you have chosen and an appropriate verb.

Plenaries
- Display the list of hobbies from Starter Activity 1. Challenge students to write three sentences, using a different hobby each time, and to say if they like or dislike each one. Remind them of the different verbs they could use and encourage them to use conjunctions, e.g. *Me gusta tocar la guitarra pero me aburre la tele.*
- Students play a memory game on the theme of hobbies/weather. You start, e.g. *Si hace sol prefiero jugar al tenis*. The next person must repeat your sentence and add a similar one of their own, e.g. *Si hace sol prefiero jugar al tenis. Si hay viento puedo hacer windsurf.* And so on.

Homework/Self-study
Gramática: Students write a couple of sentences using *gustar* with a verb. They should try to use a different 'person' each time. Provide less able students with some sentences to complete, e.g. *Me gusta … música pop. Les gusta … salsa. Te gusta … de música pop.* etc. It is up to you whether you want to provide the missing words, i.e. *escuchar; bailar; los conciertos*, etc.
Students adapt the tweets from Activity 6 to make them relevant to them. With less able students, brainstorm possible activities they could use and list them.
Think!: Students add these words to their vocabulary list, highlighting differences between the Spanish and the English. They practise pronouncing the Spanish words.

AT 1.4   **1 Mira el video. ¿Qué deportes y pasatiempos se mencionan?**
Students watch the second part of the video and note down any sports or hobbies that are mentioned.

Video script: Unit 2A (CD2, track 2)

José: Oye, como eres la hija de un diplomático, ¿te gustará hacer esas cosas que hacen los ricos: ir en yate, jugar al golf en verano e ir a esquiar en invierno…? Bueno, ¿te gusta eso o no?

Marisa: ¿Qué, ir en yate? ¡No, por Dios! Sí me mareo si voy en barco.

José: ¿Y golf?

2A.2 Mi semana

Marisa: ¿Tengo pinta de vieja o qué?
José: Entonces, ¿esquiar?
Marisa: No, demasiado frío…
José: ¿Montañismo?
Marisa: Mucho esfuerzo.
José: ¿Escalada?
Marisa: Demasiado peligroso.
José: ¡Ya sé… ballet! Bueno, por lo menos tendrás una profesora de música que te enseña a tocar el piano los sábados por la mañana y te echa la bronca porque no aprenderte la lección.
Marisa: ¡No! No hay lecciones de música.
José: Entonces ¿qué haces en tu tiempo libre?
Marisa: Bueno, lo normal… ver fútbol, ir al cine, salir con los amigos.

Answers:
yachting; golf; skiing; mountaineering; rock climbing; music (piano); ballet; cinema; going out with friends; football

Gramática
Remind students how to use *gustar* with a noun and ask volunteers to say a sentence using *gustar* with a noun. Explain that *gustar* can also be used with a verb and look at the examples given in the Students' Book. Ask students to write a couple of sentences using *gustar* with a verb.

AT 1.2 2 Escucha e indica el pasatiempo.
Students listen and point to the hobby mentioned.

CD 2, track 5 página 58, actividad 2
1. Me gusta tocar la guitarra.
2. Me encanta montar a caballo.
3. Me apasiona jugar al ajedrez.
4. Me fascina ir al cine.
5. Me mola jugar con videojuegos.
6. Me flipa bailar salsa en la disco.

Answers:
1 b; 2 d; 3 a; 4 c; 5 f; 6 e

AT 2.2–3 3 Habla con tu compañero.
Students work with a partner to practise speaking about sports and hobbies.

AT 4.2–3 4 Escribe.
Students use what they learnt about their partner in Activity 3 to write a sentence saying which of the activities their partner likes doing.

AT 1.4 5 Escucha el diálogo.
Students listen to the conversation between Elena and Carlos and decide which statements apply to each of them.

CD 2, track 6 página 59, actividad 5
Carlos: Te digo que me mola mi nuevo iPod – es fenomenal.
Elena: Pues a mí me molestan todos esos aparatos, sobre todo los videojuegos nuevos.
Carlos: Ay, ¡qué aburrida eres! A mí me fascina el cine pero a ti no te interesa.
Elena: También me aburre la tele.
Carlos: Bueno, no te interesa nada. A mí, en cambio, me apasiona todo: me fascina la natación y me encanta navegar por Internet.
Elena: Uf, ¡tú me fastidias mucho!

Answers:
1 Carlos; 2 Elena; 3 Carlos; 4 Elena; 5 Carlos; 6 Carlos

PLTS Gramática
Remind students of the radical-changing verb they have already looked at (*jugar*) and explain that you are going to look at some more, *poder (ue)* (to be able), *preferir (ie)* (to prefer) and *querer (ie)* (to like/want). Look at how these are conjugated and how they compare with the verb *jugar*. Ask students to list all the radical-changing verbs used in Activity 6.

Answers:
prefiero; prefiero; puedo; podemos; puedo; jugar

AT 3.3 6 Lee y contesta a las preguntas.
Students read the 'tweets' about hobbies and answer the questions.

Answers:
1 go to the cinema; 2 all year round; 3 when it is sunny; 4 they can't go surfing; 5 cold or hot

PLTS Think!
Students look at the spelling of all the sports and hobbies that look like the English equivalent. They then make a note of the difference and how the pronunciation changes.

AT 4.2–3 PLTS Challenge
List five of your favourite hobbies and sports and give a reason why you like each one.
Remind students that they can embellish to make their writing more interesting and to use a variety of verbs and structures.

2A.3 Mi semana

2A.3 Por la mañana
páginas 60–61

Planner

Objectives
- say what you do in the morning
- use reflexive verbs
- explain patterns in verbs

Video
Video script, Unit 2A

Resources
Students' Book, pages 60–61
CD 2, tracks 2, 7–8
Foundation Workbook, page 34
Higher Workbook, page 34
Foundation Workbook audio, CD 3, track 59
Higher Workbook audio, CD 4, track 34
Interactive OxBox, Unit 2A
Copymasters 40–47
Assessment, Unit 2A

Key language
desayuno; me ducho; me lavo los dientes; me levanto; me peino; me pongo (el uniforme)

Grammar
- use reflexive verbs
- explain patterns in verbs

Renewed Framework references
1.1, 1.4, 2.1, 2.4, 3.1, 3.2, 4.3, 4.4, 4.5, 5.1

PLTS
Activity 1: Creative thinkers
Gramática (2): Reflective learners
Think!: Independent enquirers; Reflective learners
Challenge: Creative thinkers

Starters
- Display a list of reflexive pronouns and one of personal pronouns and ask students to match them up. Check answers as a class. Next, display a list of the reflexive verbs from this spread and ask students to write out at least two of these verbs in full. Compare answers as a class.
- Display the verbs from Activity 5 and challenge students to write five sentences using each of them.

Plenaries
- Students write a few sentences describing their morning routine. They should include the time they do each activity. They then compare their morning routine with that of their partner.
- Students pretend to be a famous person and write a paragraph describing their morning routine. Encourage them to make it as interesting as possible. Volunteers then read their paragraph to the class.

Homework/Self-study
Think!: Students use this verb in a sentence to say when they, and others, have lunch. Depending on the level of the class, you may find it useful to brainstorm possible times. More able students could also add places, e.g. *en la cantina*.
Challenge: Students write out the dialogue they made up with a partner.

Gramática
Read through the grammar box on reflexive verbs as a class. Ensure that students know what the reflexive pronouns are and that they are positioned before the verb. Students then match the personal pronouns to the correct part of the verb.

Answers:
me levanto = yo; te levantas = tú; se levanta = él, ella; nos levantamos = nosotros; os levantáis = vosotros; se levantan = ellos, ellas

AT 3.2 | PLTS **1 Empareja.**
Students match each of the phrases in the vocabulary box with one of the illustrations a–f. They then translate each of the phrases into English.

Answers:
desayuno – I have breakfast – f
me ducho – I have a shower – d
me lavo los dientes – I clean my teeth – a
me levanto – I get up – e
me peino – I comb my hair – c
me pongo (el uniforme) – I put on my uniform – b

AT 1.2 **2 Escucha y anota la hora.**
Students listen and make a note of the time for each activity. They then note down what Lucho has forgotten to do.

2A.3 Mi semana

CD 2, track 7 — página 60, actividad 2

Me levanto a las 06:45.
A las 07:00 desayuno.
A las 07:05 me ducho.
A las 07:15 me lavo los dientes.
A las 07:25 me peino.

Answers:
gets up at 6.45am; has breakfast at 7am; showers at 7.05am; brushes teeth at 7.15am; combs hair at 7.25am
Lucho has forgotten to put on his uniform.

AT 1.3 — 3 Mira el video.
Students watch the video and note down what Eva does in the morning. Remind students to listen for the verbs they have practised in Activities 1 and 2.

Video script: Unit 2A (CD2, track 2)

Marisa: ¿Qué? ¿Te estoy aburriendo?
José: ¡Desde luego que no! Es sólo que… bueno… eres muy diferente a Eva. Ella se levanta por la mañana hacer yoga y meditar.
Marisa: ¿De verdad?
José: Luego practica con el oboe.

Answers:
She gets up, does yoga, meditates and then practises the oboe.

AT 1.4 — 4 Escucha a Lucía. ¿Verdad o mentira?
Students listen to Lucía and decide if the statements listed are true (verdad) or false (mentira)?

CD 2, track 8 — página 61, actividad 4

Me despierto a las seis en punto y me ducho. Luego hago yoga. Después desayuno algo ligero y luego me visto para ir al instituto. Tengo clase de guitarra a las cinco de la tarde y a las seis voy al club de teatro. Los sábados me encanta tener clase de alemán con mi abuelo.

Answers:
1 verdad; 2 mentira; 3 mentira; 4 mentira; 5 verdad; 6 mentira

PLTS Gramática
Read through the grammar box as a class. Remind students what the reflexive pronouns are and about radical-changing verbs. Can they remember the other radical-changing verbs they have met in this unit? Students then note down what the verbs listed mean.

Answers:
nos despertamos = we wake up; **te despiertas** = you wake up; **se visten** = they get dressed; **os vestís** = you get dressed

PLTS Think!
Students use what they have learnt about conjugating radical-changing verbs to write out the verb 'to have lunch' in Spanish.

Answers:
almorzar – to have lunch
yo almuerzo; tú almuerzas; él almuerza; nosotros almorzamos; vosotros almorzáis; ellos almuerzan

PLTS 5 Copia el texto. Escribe los verbos correctos.
Further practice of conjugating verbs and writing on the theme of the spread. Students copy the text and write out the verbs in the first person singular.

Answers:
1 me despierto; 2 me baño; 3 me pongo; 4 desayuno; 5 juego; 6 almuerzo

PLTS 6 Escribe los verbos en la 3. persona.
Students write the verbs from Activity 5 in the third person singular.

Answers:
1 se despierta; 2 se baña; 3 se pone; 4 desayune; 5 juega; 6 almuerza

AT 2.3–4 PLTS Challenge
Create a dialogue with a partner about your morning routine. Ask about times and try to use all the verbs on these two pages.
Remind students that they can embellish to make their dialogue more interesting. They should use a variety of verbs and structures.

2A.4 Mi semana

2A.4 Por la tarde
páginas 62–63

Planner

Objectives
- talk about what you do after school
- use the full verb *ir* – to go
- use sequencing to add interest and cohesion to what you write and say

Video
Video-blog, Unit 2A

Resources
Students' Book, pages 62–63
CD 2, tracks 9–11
Foundation Workbook, page 35
Higher Workbook, page 35
Foundation Workbook audio, CD 3, track 60
Higher Workbook audio, CD 4, track 35
Interactive OxBox, Unit 2A
Copymasters 40–47
Assessment, Unit 2A

Key language
descansar; merendar (ie); ver la tele; pasear al perro; hacer los deberes; cenar; acostarse (ue); dormirse en punto; a eso de

Grammar
- use the full verb *ir* – to go

Renewed Framework references
1.1, 1.4, 2.1, 2.4, 2.5, 4.2, 4.3, 4.4, 4.5, 5.1

PLTS
Gramática: Reflective learners; Self-managers
Think!: Creative thinkers; Reflective learners
Challenge: Creative thinkers; Self-managers

Starters
- Display a list of irregular verbs students have met. Each student says a sentence using one of the irregular verbs listed.
- Go round the class asking students to say one sport they like and one they don't. Depending on the ability of the class, they could give reasons why.

Plenaries
- Students write a paragraph describing what they do after school. They should use as much vocabulary from the spread as possible.
- Display a list of sequencing words and challenge students to use them in at least five sentences on the theme of the spread.

Homework/Self-study
Gramática: Students find as many examples of sentences containing *ir* as they can. More able students can also write a sentence of their own using *ir* in the present tense.
Students write sentences containing the sequencing words from the Think! box. They can use Manuela and Rebeca's texts as models. Provide less able students with possible activities they could include in their sentences.

AT 2.2   **1**   **Juega.**
Students play a game with a partner. Partner A says a time. Partner B says what happens in school at that time.

AT 1.4   **2**   **Escucha y contesta a las preguntas.**
Students listen to Bartolomé talking about his daily routine and answer the questions.

CD 2, track 9   página 62, actividad 2

¡Guay! Son las cuatro – las dieciséis horas en punto. No más clases hoy – fenomenal.
Normalmente meriendo pan con un vaso de leche ¡pero hoy quiero merendar chocolate!
Primero veo la tele – mi programa favorito – luego descanso media hora.
Hmmm… puedo hacer los deberes en diez minutos a eso de las dieciocho horas y a las dieciocho y quince paseo al perro.
Siempre cenamos en familia a las diecinueve horas en punto.
Me acuesto a las veinte horas y me duermo en cinco minutos a eso de las …

2A.4 Mi semana

Answers:
1 4pm; **2** eats bread and a glass of milk; **3** watches TV and then rests; **4** 6.15pm; **5** after; **6** an hour and a half; **7** 8pm; **8** 8.05pm

> **AT 3.4** **3 Lee los textos. ¿Adónde van Manuela y Rebeca?**
> Students read Manuela and Rebeca's texts and note down in the third person where they go.

Answers:
Primero Manuela va al centro comercial; luego va a la piscina; después va a casa a cenar; más tarde quiero ir al cine con José y Felix; ¡y finalmente va a casa a dormir!
Primero Rebeca va a la biblioteca; luego va al Museo de Arte Contemporáneo; por último va a cenar.

> **AT 1.3** **4 Escucha. ¿Quién habla, Manuela o Rebeca?**
> Students listen and note down who is speaking, Manuela or Rebeca.

> 🎧 **CD 2, track 10** página 63, actividad 4
> Bueno, hoy no tengo tiempo para leer – voy a practicar deporte. Luego voy a tener mucha hambre. ¡A ver qué va a cocinar mi padre cuando llego a casa!

Answer: Manuela

> **PLTS** **Gramática**
> Ask students if anyone can remember what irregular verbs are and which irregular verbs they have already met. Remind them that they have already learnt the irregular verbs *tener* and *ser* and ask them to write out these verbs to check that they remember them. Explain that they are going to meet another irregular verb, *ir* (to go) that they also need to learn by heart.

> **PLTS** **Think!**
> Students try to guess what each of the sequencing words means. They check these in a dictionary or with you. Students then work with a partner and think of a way to try to remember these words. They could make up a rap or a game.

> **AT 1.4** **5 Mira el video-blog. ¿Qué contestan Eva, José y Marisa?**
> Students watch Eva, José and Marisa chatting about sports and note down their answers to the questions listed. Students can answer in Spanish, but remind them to change the verbs into the third person singular.

> 🎥 **Video blog: Unit 2A (CD 2, track 11)**
> **¿Qué deporte practicas?**
> Eva: Practico yoga y tenis.
> Marisa: Juego al voleibol dos veces a la semana.
> José: Practico el fútbol. ¿Y tú, qué deporte practicas? ¿Qué deporte prefieres?
> Eva: Prefiero el yoga porque es más relajante.
> José: El fútbol.
> Marisa: Prefiero el fútbol.
> **¿Quién es tu deportista preferido?**
> Eva: Aunque no me gustan los deportes, mi deportista favorito es Rafael Nadal.
> José: Mi deportista preferido es Bojan que es jugador del Barça.
> Marisa: Mi deportista preferido es el tenisstar, Roger Federer.
> **¿Cuál es tu equipo de fútbol preferido?**
> Eva: No me gusta el fútbol y no sé tener ningún equipo.
> Marisa: Mi equipo preferido es El Barça que es el fútbol club Barcelona.
> José: El Barça.

Answers:
Eva: *Practica yoga y tenis. Prefiere el yoga porque es más relajante. Su deportista favorito es Rafael Nadal. No se gusta el fútbol.*
José: *Practica el fútbol. Prefiere el fútbol. Su deportista preferido es Bojan que es jugador del Barça. Su equipo preferido es El Barça.*
Marisa: *Juega al voleibol dos veces a la semana. Prefiere el fútbol. Su deportista preferido es el tenisstar, Roger Federer. Su equipo preferido es El Barça.*

> **AT 4.3–4** **PLTS** 👥 **Challenge**
> Write a blog about what you do after school. Use the sequencing words and the times of day. Make sure you include some radical-changing verbs as well. Swap papers with a partner and ask questions about what is written. See how much you can answer from memory.
> Students draw upon the grammar and vocabulary they have met in the spread to write a blog about what they do after school.

2A.5 Mi semana

2A.5 El fin de semana
páginas 64–65

Planner

Objectives
- talk about weekend activities
- recognise and use additional vocabulary on sports and hobbies

Resources
Students' Book, pages 64–65
CD 2, track 12
Foundation Workbook, page 36
Higher Workbook, page 36
Foundation Workbook audio, CD 3, track 61
Higher Workbook audio, CD 4, track 36
Interactive OxBox, Unit 2A
Assessment, Unit 2A

Key language
¿Qué te gusta hacer los sábados? ¿Qué te fastidia de los sábados? ¿Qué te flipa? ¿Qué odias?

Renewed Framework references
1.1, 1.4, 2.1, 2.4, 2.5, 4.2, 4.3, 4.4, 4.5, 5.4

PLTS
Think!: Creative thinkers; Indepedent enquirers
Challenge: Self-managers; Creative thinkers

Starters
- Go round the class asking each student to give an activity that you could do at the weekend. List these.
- Display the list from Starter Activity 1 and explain that you are going to play a memory game as a class. You start by saying one of the activities, e.g. *Practico ciclismo*. The student nearest to you continues by repeating your activity and adding one of his/her own, e.g. *Practico ciclismo y me acuesto tarde* and so on until somebody forgets one of the activities.

Plenaries
- Students write a paragraph similar to that in Activity 3 saying what they like/dislike doing at the weekend. They should use as much vocabulary from the spread as possible and draw upon the grammar from the unit. Volunteers could read their paragraph to the class. Who do the class think does the most interesting things over the weekend?

Homework/Self-study
Activity 2: Students write out their answers to the questions. More able students should use full sentences and include sequencing words. Less able students could use note form.

AT 1.4 **1 Escucha y anota. ¿Qué les gusta hacer los sábados y qué no les gusta hacer?**
Students listen and note down what each speaker likes and dislikes doing on Saturdays.

CD 2, track 12 — página 64, actividad 1

1
Prof: Sergio, ¿qué te gusta hacer los sábados?
Sergio: Bueno, primero me encanta dormir hasta tarde – las diez por ejemplo. Odio levantarme temprano los sábados.

2
Prof: De acuerdo. ¿Y a ti, Javier?
Javier: Bueno, practico ciclismo casi todos los sábados por la mañana, por eso no me gusta cuando llueve, porque si llueve, no puedo montar en bicicleta.

3
Profe: Luz Elena, ¿a ti qué te gusta de los domingos?
Luz Elena: Bueno, lo que más me gusta es ir a casa de mis abuelos y almorzar con toda la familia, como es costumbre aquí en España.
Profe: Vale, eso a mí también me encanta. ¿Y qué te molesta de los domingos?
Luz Elena: Pues a ver, me fastidia ponerme ropa elegante. Prefiero unos vaqueros y una camiseta sencilla.

4
Profe: Tienes razón. Olguita, ¿te gusta ir al cine los domingos?
Olguita: No, profe. Odio ir al cine – no me interesa nada.
Profe: Bueno, pues, ¿qué te interesa entonces?
Olguita: Me flipa tocar la batería con mi grupo de amigas, Las Sirenas. Me mola cantar y tocar. Hacemos un ruido fenomenal.

Answers:
1 likes getting up late (10am for example), dislikes getting up early; 2 likes cycling in the morning, doesn't like it when it rains as he can't go on his bike; 3 likes going to grandparents' house to have lunch with all the family, dislikes having to wear smart clothes; 4 likes playing the drums and singing with her group, Las Sirenas, dislikes going to the cinema

2A.6 Mi semana

2 👥 **Habla con tu compañero. Da tres respuestas para cada pregunta.**
Students work with a partner. They take turns to ask and answer the questions listed. They should give three answers for each question.

3 Copia y completa el texto con los verbos correctos de la casilla.
Students copy and complete the text with the correct verbs from the box.

Answers:
es; encanta; puedo; desayuno; me baño; soy; jugar; vamos; tenemos; me acuesto

4 Lee el diario de Eva y contesta a las preguntas.
Students read Eva's diary and answer the questions.

Answers:
1 Grandmother's birthday, going to eat in a restaurant, La Santa María; **2** it is easier and can drink and eat without worrying; **3** good; **4** there is a dining room inside where you can eat; **5** she is called Clarissa, is 82 years old, is very active and loves all her grandchildren; **6** she is going to wear a smart floral dress; **7** Yes – she says she loves going out with her family and always has a great time.

Think!
Students follow the advice given in the Think! box to help them get used to analysing texts. They try to find the items listed.

Challenge
Write a blog about what you like to do best on a Sunday or on family occasions. Give reasons and try to describe in detail what you do.
Students draw upon what they have learnt in the spread to write their blog. They can embellish to make their writing more interesting and should use as much vocabulary from the spread as possible.

2A.6 Labolengua   páginas 66–67

Planner

Objectives
- review language and grammar from the unit

Resources
Students' Book, pages 66–67
CD 2, track 13
Foundation Workbook, pages 5, 37–38
Higher Workbook, pages 5, 37–38
Interactive OxBox, Unit 2A
Copymasters 48–49
Assessment, Unit 2A

Grammar
- Radical-changing verbs
- Reflexive verbs
- Pronouns and verb patterns

Renewed Framework references
1.1, 1.4, 2.4, 4.1, 4.2, 4.3, 4.4, 4.5, 5.1

PLTS
All activities: Reflective learners/Self-managers

Homework/Self-study
Activities 3 & 4: Students think of a regular –ar, –ir, and –er verb and write them out in the present tense, trying to remember the endings. They can refer to a verb table, however, if necessary.

Comprender – verbs

1 Copy the sentence and choose the correct form of the verb.
Practice of conjugating radical-changing verbs.

Answers:
1 quiere; **2** prefieren; **3** puede; **4** jugamos; **5** jugáis

B Reflexive verbs

2 Use reflexive verbs to say the following in Spanish.
Practice of using and forming reflexive verbs.

Answer:
1 Nos despertamos a las seis y media. **2** Se levantan a las siete menos cuarto. **3** Primero me ducho. **4** Después me visto. **5** Se acuestan a las diez y media. **6** Se duermen a eso de las once.

2A.7 Mi semana

Aprender – learning verbs

C Pronouns and verb patterns

> **PLTS 3** Can you write down the personal pronouns in sequence? Start with *yo* (I).
> Remind students that in Spanish they don't need these pronouns in order to know who is doing the action.

Answer:
yo, tú, él, ella, usted, nosotros, vosotros, ellos, ellas, ustedes

> **PLTS 4** Now write out the pattern sequence for regular verbs ending in *-er* and *-ir*.
> Students look at the pattern for regular verbs ending in *–ar* and then write out the pattern for regular *-er* and *-ir* verbs.

Answers:
-er: –o, –es, –e, –emos, –éis, –en
-ir: –o, –es, –e, –imos, –ís, –en

> **PLTS 5** Now do the same for ser and *tener*. What else do you have to remember about the verb *tener*? Can you think of more ways to help you learn verbs?
> More practice of conjugating verbs.

Answers:
ser: yo soy, tú eres, él es, nosotros somos, vosotros sois, ellos son
tener: yo tengo, tú tienes, él tiene, nosotros tenemos, vosotros tenéis, ellos tienen
tener is a radical-changing verb

> **PLTS 6** Find the Spanish sequencing words that go with these English ones. Why do you think it is helpful to use words like this when you speak or write?
> Using strategies to make writing more interesting.

Answers:
last – por último; **later** – más tarde; **next** – después; **first** – primero; **then** – pues; **afterwards** – después/más tarde

Hablar – pronunciation

D The sounds of the letters j and g

> **PLTS 7** Listen and repeat these sounds.
> Students practise the *ja, je, ji, jo* and *ju* sounds in Spanish.

🎧 **CD 2, track 13**   página 67, actividad 7

ja – je – ji – jo – ju

Javier
Jerónimo
Jiménez
Jorge
Julio

gato
gorila
gusano
gerbo
gigante

La tortuga gigante juega con la guapa jirafa al ajedrez.

2A.7 Extra Star   página 68

Planner

Objectives
- revise sports and hobbies
- practise using radical-changing verbs
- follow an example to begin to write independently

Resources
Students' Book, page 68
CD 2, tracks 14–15
Copymaster 50

Renewed Framework references
1.1, 1.4, 2.1, 2.4, 2.5, 4.3, 4.5

PLTS
Activity 4: Reflective learners
Activity 7: Creative thinkers

> **AT 1.2 1** Escucha e identifica el deporte.
> Students listen and identify each sport.

2A.7 Mi semana

CD 2, track 14 — página 68, actividad 1 y 2

1. Me encanta jugar al fútbol.
2. A mí me fastidia practicar la natación.
3. Me mola el ciclismo.
4. ¿Qué día juegas al baloncesto?
5. Juego al tenis todos los martes por la tarde.

Answers:
1 football = c; **2** swimming = d; **3** cycling = a; **4** basketball = f; **5** tennis = e

AT 1.2 **2 ¿Qué deporte no se menciona?**
Students listen again and note down which of the sports illustrated isn't mentioned.

Answer: boxing

AT 3.3 **3 Completa el diálogo con el verbo adecuado.**
Students complete the conversation with the appropriate verbs.

Answers:
a bailar; **b** ver; **c** tocar; **d** escuchar; **e** leer; **f** jugar; **g** hacer

AT 1.3 / PLTS **4 Escucha y verifica.**
Students listen and check their answers.

CD 2, track 15 — página 68, actividad 4

– Me encanta bailar salsa pero no me gusta ver la tele.
– Pues a mí me fascina tocar la trompeta y también me apasiona escuchar música.
– Bueno, a mí me aburre leer libros y me molesta mucho jugar al fútbol.
– Vale, pero entonces ¿qué te interesa hacer en tu tiempo libre?

AT 3.2–3 **5 Lee el anuncio. ¿Quién es? Identifica a la persona.**
Students read the advert and identify who the writer is.

Answer:
A twelve-year-old looking for penpals from all over the world.

AT 2.2–3 **6 Juega: Adivina quién soy.**
Students work in pairs and to play 'Guess who I am'. Partner A chooses one of the people from the illustrations. Partner B asks questions to guess who Partner A has chosen. You may find it useful to work through the example given in the Students' Book first.

AT 4.2–3 / PLTS **7 Escribe un anuncio similar para ti.**
Students write a text similar to that in Activity 5.

2A.7 Extra Plus   página 69

Planner

Objectives
- revise sports and hobbies in a wider context
- prepare a dialogue
- write independently

Resources
Students' Book, page 69
CD 2, tracks 16–17
Copymaster 51

Renewed Framework references
1.1, 1.4, 2.1, 2.4, 2.5, 4.4, 5.8

PLTS
Activity 4: Reflective learners
Challenge: Creative thinkers

AT 1.2–3 **1 Escucha. ¿Verdad (✓) o mentira (X)?**
Students listen and note down of each statement is true or false.

CD 2, track 16 — página 69, actividades 1 y 2

a Me gusta jugar al fútbol – los lunes
b Me aburre jugar al golf – los martes
c Me apasiona jugar al baloncesto – los miércoles
d Me molesta jugar al tenis – los jueves
e Me interesa jugar al voleibol – los viernes
f No me gusta jugar a la pelota vasca – los sábados
g Me flipa hacer windsurf – los domingos
h Me fastidia hacer boxeo – todos los lunes
i Me encanta hacer ciclismo – los martes
j Me mola hacer atletismo – los miércoles

Answers:
1 X – Wednesdays; **2** ✓; **3** X – Mondays; **4** ✓; **5** X – Wednesdays

2A.8 Mi semana

| AT 1.2 | **2 Escucha otra vez.**
Students listen again to the recording from Activity 1 and this time answer the questions. |

Answers:
1 Saturdays: pelota; Sundays: windsurfing; 2 pelota: doesn't like playing; windsurfing: loves it

| AT 3.2 | **3 Lee la entrevista. Empareja las respuestas con las preguntas.**
Students read the interview and match up the questions and answers. |

Answers:
1 d; 2 a; 3 f; 4 b; 5 e; 6 c

| AT 1.2
PLTS | **4 Escucha y verifica.**
Students listen to check their answers to Activity 3. |

> 🎧 **CD 2, track 17** página 69, actividad 4
>
> – ¿Quién es tu deportista preferido/a?
> – Se llama Lionel Messi.
>
> – ¿Qué deporte practica?
> – Juega al fútbol.
>
> – ¿Cómo es (físicamente)?
> – Tiene el pelo largo y liso – es guapo.
>
> – ¿Cuál es tu equipo preferido?
> – Prefiero el Barça.
>
> – ¿Qué colores tiene?
> – Rojo y azul grana.
>
> – ¿Qué deporte prefieres tú?
> – Me encanta el surf.

| AT 2.3 | **5 👥 Haz un diálogo usando las preguntas 1–6 de la Actividad 3.**
Students work with a partner. They have a conversation using the questions from Activities 3 and 4 above. |

| AT 3.3 | **6 Lee la ficha. Contesta a las preguntas.**
Students read the form and answer the questions. Encourage them to write full sentences. |

Answers:
1 Se llama Rafael Nadal. 2 Tiene 24 años. 3 Tiene una hermana. 4 Pratica tenis. 5 Peso 85 kg; mide 185 cm; zurdo (usa la mano izquierda); pelo negro y liso; su apodo es el torito español.

| AT 4.4
PLTS | **7 Rellena una ficha para tu deportista preferido/a.**
Students fill in a form about their favourite sports person. They should draw upon the vocabulary and structures from the spread for support. |

2A.8 Prueba   página 70

Planner

Resources
Students' Book, page 70
CD 2, track 18

Renewed Framework references
1.1, 1.4, 2.1, 2.4, 2.5, 5.4

PLTS
All activities: Reflective learners

Escuchar

| AT 1.3–4 | **Listen and say whether it's Sergio or Lorena.**
This activity tests listening skills using the language covered in this unit. |

> 🎧 **CD 2, track 18** página 70, Escuchar
>
> Sergio: Oye, Lorena. ¿Te gusta la revista Bravo?
> Lorena: Sí, me encanta leer revistas pero me molesta hacer la natación los domingos por la mañana. Y a ti, ¿qué es lo que no te gusta hacer?
> Sergio: Pues me fastidia jugar al fútbol cuando llueve, en cambio me gusta ir al museo.
> Lorena: Vale, a mí también me gusta hacer deporte en el verano, y me apasiona tocar la batería con mi grupo.

2A Mi semana

Answers:
1 Lorena; 2 Sergio; 3 Lorena; 4 Sergio; 5 Lorena; 6 Lorena

Hablar

> **AT 2.2–3** **Complete these sentences to speak about yourself.**
> This activity tests speaking skills using the language covered in this unit.

Leer

> **AT 3.4** **Read the text and spot six differences in the picture.**
> This activity tests reading skills using the language covered in this unit.

Answers:
1 text: Tuesday 13th/picture: Friday 13th; 2 text: 13 years old/picture: 15 years old; 3 text: favourite sports person is Cesc Fàbregas/picture: favourite sports person is Rafael Nadal; 4 text: favourite team is Real Madrid/picture: favourite team is Arsenal; 5 text: plays trumpet/picture: plays guitar; 6 text: likes horse riding/picture: likes windsurfing

Escribir

> **AT 4.4** **Write the weather report.**
> This activity tests writing skills using the language covered in this unit.

Answers:
Students' own answers

Leer 2A   página 155

Planner

Resources
Students' Book, page 155

Renewed Framework references
2.1, 3.1, 5.4, 5.5

PLTS
Activity 2: Creative thinkers, Reflective learners
Self-study: Independent enquirers, Self-managers

Homework/Self-study
All activities – students could find out about the *Vuelta a España*, Pau Gassol or a Spanish pop group.

PLTS Note to teachers: the *Vuelta a España* is a cycle race similar to the *Tour de France*. Pau Gassol is the internationally famous basket ball player currently in the NBA.

AT 3.4 **1 Read and find the Spanish for the words listed.**

Answers:
1 equipo; 2 ciclismo; 3 tenista; 4 circuito; 5 campeones; 6 trofeo

AT 3.4 **2 Read and work out...**
PLTS

Answers:
1 Barcelona and Real Madrid; 2 in May; 3 on the Costa del Sol; 4 the International Pop Music Festival at the end of June; 5 last two weeks of September and end of November; 6 very old, very fast (can reach speeds of up to 220 km/h)

Mi semana 2A

Foundation Workbook

Página 32 — 2A.1 El tiempo
- Use with Students' Book, pages 56–57

AT 3.1 **1 Put the weather words into the correct column.**

Answers:
hace…: *sol; calor; frío; viento*
hay…: *tormenta; niebla*
llueve; nieva

AT 1.1 **2 Listen and tick the correct answer.**
This provides students with the opportunity to hear the weather expressions.

> 🎧 **CD 3, track 58** página 32, actividad 2
> 1 Hace calor.
> 2 Nieva.
> 3 Hace frío.
> 4 Llueve.
> 5 Hay niebla.

Answers: 1 hot; 2 snow; 3 cold; 4 rain; 5 fog

AT 2.1 **3 Roll a dice and see how quickly you can say the correct weather.**
Students should try to sound as Spanish as possible when pronoucing these words making sure they pronounce the 'c' correctly.

Página 33 — 2A.2 Tiempo libre
- Use with Students' Book, pages 58–59

AT 4.1 **1 Copy these activities in Spanish, in order of personal preference.**
Encourage students to say these to themselves as they write them in order to think about the pronunciation of each.

AT 4.2 **2 Go down your list of activities, giving an opinion about each one in Spanish.**
Students can write sentences and then discuss with a partner. How many activities do they agree on?

AT 4.2–3 **3 Finish these sentences, saying what you do and don't like to do.**
Students could start by writing sensible answers and then do it again with ridiculous answers.

Página 34 — 2A.3 Por la mañana
- Use with Students' Book, pages 60–61

AT 3.2 **1 Match up the captions to the pictures.**

Answers:
a *me despierto;* **b** *me levanto;* **c** *me lavo;* **d** *me ducho;* **e** *me visto;* **f** *me lavo los dientes;* **g** *me peino;* **h** *desayuno*

AT 1.2 **2 Listen to Javier playing a dice game. What has he 'forgotten' to do when he says he goes to school?**

> 🎧 **CD 3, track 59** página 34, actividad 2
> Tres. Desayuno. Muy bien.
> Dos. Me ducho. Sí…
> Uno. Me lavo los dientes…
> Tres. Desayuno ¿Otra vez?
> Cinco. Me peino. Hmm…
> Dos. ¡Me ducho otra vez!
> Seis. Voy al colegio. ¡O no!

Answer: He has forgotten to get dressed!

AT 2.2 **3 Now play the dice game yourself.**
Students could play this in pairs – who gets all of the numbers and leaves for school first?

Página 35 — 2A.4 Por la tarde
- Use with Students' Book, pages 62–63

AT 3.1 **1 Read the list of activities. Are they things you do after school? Put a tick or a cross.**
This is good revision of daily activities.

AT 1.3 **2 Listen to Miriam. Does she do the same things as you? Tick the boxes for her.**
Students could go on to compare what they do after school with what a partner does. What are the most popular activities?

> 🎧 **CD 3, track 60** página 35, actividad 2
> Después del instituto… pues, descanso y… luego… meriendo. Veo la televisión… luego salgo un rato con los amigos… Más tarde ceno con mis padres. No paseo al perro y no hago mis deberes.

2A Mi semana

AT 2.2 **3 Use your list to say what you do in the evening.**
Encourage students to try and use extended sentences where possible.

AT 4.2–3 **4 Read these times and write what you are usually doing then.**
Volunteers can read their sentences out to the class to see if students do similar things at similar times.

Página 36   2A.5 El fin de semana
• Use with Students' Book, pages 64–65

AT 3.2 **1 What do you do at the weekend? Put these activities into the grid.**
When students have finished this activity, they can compare grids. Do most students agree on which activities go where? As an extension to this activity, students could add any other activities they can think of into each box.

AT 1.3 **2 Listen to Miriam. How would you describe her weekends? Explain why.**
Remind students to listen out for connectives that can change the meaning of a sentence, i.e. *pero*.

> 🎧 **CD 3, track 61**   página 36, actividad 2
>
> Los fines de semana, prefiero dormir hasta las diez, pero no puedo. Nos levantamos temprano.
> Me fastidia porque tengo que salir con mi familia. No me gusta comer en un restaurante con mis padres.
> Prefiero el fútbol, pero no puedo ver a mis amigos. No puedo hacer deporte.

Answer:
Frustrating: She can't stay in bed, see her friends or practise sport. She has to get up and go out with her family and eat in a restaurant.

AT 4.2–3 **3 Use the grid in Activity 1 to write sentences about your own weekends.**
Students should think about how Miriam described her weekend and the structures and verbs she used.

Página 37   2A.6A Labolengua
• Use with Students' Book, pages 66–67

1 Spot the odd one out. Explain why it is different.

Answer:
desayuno, as it is not a reflexive verb – you don't eat yourself for breakfast!

2 Think like a Spanish person. Complete the grids.
As an extension activity, students could write a similar grid for other reflexive verbs.

Answers:
I get washed, I wash myself, *me lavo*; I wake up, I wake myself up, *me despierto*; I have a shower, I shower myself, *me ducho*; I am called, I call myself, *me llamo*

AT 3.1 **3 Draw lines to match up the Spanish and English.**

Answers:
a *Me despierto* – I wake up; **b** *Se levanta* – He gets up; **c** *Se visten* – They get dressed; **d** *¿Te duchas?* – Do you have a shower?

Página 38   2A.6B Técnica
• Use with Students' Book, pages 66–67

1 How would you write these verbs in your vocabulary list?
Students have already started to look at how best to format their vocabulary list and this will help them further.

Answers: *preferir (ie), querer (ie), poder (ue)*

2 Give three reasons why it might be better to write *jugar (ue)* instead of writing out the whole verb.

Suggested answers:
takes up less space, quicker, makes you think and notice, you know what to do when you meet another verb

3 Translate into Spanish.
Practice of using radical-changing verbs.

Answers:
a *prefiero*; **b** *preferimos*; **c** *quieres*; **d** *quiere*; **e** *puedo*; **f** *podemos*

Mi semana 2A

Higher Workbook

Página 32 — 2A.1 El tiempo
- Use with Students' Book, pages 56–57

AT 3.1 **1** Put the weather words into the correct column.

Answers:
hace…: *sol; calor; frío; viento; buen tiempo; mal tiempo*
hay…: *tormenta; niebla*
llueve; nieva

AT 1.2 **2** Listen and tick the correct weather for each day.
This provides students with the opportunity to hear the weather expressions as some are tricky to pronounce.

> 🎧 **CD 4, track 33** — página 32, actividad 2
>
> El Lunes hace calor, pero el martes nieva. El miércoles hace frío, y el jueves llueve. ¿Y el viernes? El viernes hay niebla.

Answers:
lunes: hot; martes: snow; miércoles: cold; jueves: rain; viernes: fog

AT 2.1 **3** Roll a dice and see how quickly you can say the correct weather.
Students should try to sound as Spanish as possible when pronouncing these words.

Página 33 — 2A.2 Tiempo libre
- Use with Students' Book, pages 58–59

AT 4.1 **1** Copy these activities, in order of personal preference.
Encourage students to say these to themselves as they write them in order to think about the pronunciation of each.

AT 4.2 **2** Go down your list of activities, giving an opinion about each one in Spanish.
Students can write sentences and then discuss with a partner. How many of the activities do they agree on? Students should try to use as many of the words listed as possible in their sentences.

AT 4.2–3 **3** Finish these sentences, saying what you do and don't like to do.
Students could start by writing sensible answers and then do it again with ridiculous answers.

Página 34 — 2A.3 Por la mañana
- Use with Students' Book, pages 60–61

AT 4.2 **1** Write a Spanish caption under each picture.

Answers:
a *me despierto;* **b** *me levanto;* **c** *me lavo;* **d** *me ducho;* **e** *me visto;* **f** *me lavo los dientes;* **g** *me peino;* **h** *desayuno*

AT 1.2 **2** Listen to Javier playing a dice game. What has he 'forgotten' to do when he says he goes to school?

> 🎧 **CD 4, track 34** — página 34, actividad 2
>
> Tres. Desayuno. Muy bien.
> Dos. Me ducho. Sí…
> Uno. Me lavo los dientes…
> Tres. Desayuno ¿Otra vez?
> Cinco. Me peino. Hmm…
> Dos. ¡Me ducho otra vez!
> Seis. Voy al colegio. ¡O no!

Answer: He has forgotten to get dressed!

AT 2.2 **3** Now play the dice game yourself.
Students could play this in pairs – who gets all of the numbers and leaves for school first?

AT 4.2 **4** Write up your random day from Activity 3.
Students could compare their day with that of a partner. Who has created the most unusual day?

Página 35 — 2A.4 Por la tarde
- Use with Students' Book, pages 62–63

AT 3.1 **1** Read the list of activities. Are they things you do after school? Put a tick or a cross.
This is good revision of daily activities.

AT 1.3 **2** Listen to Miriam. Does she do the same things as you? Tick the boxes for her.
Students could go on to compare what they do after school with what a partner does. What are the most popular activities?

> 🎧 **CD 4, track 35** — página 35, actividad 2
>
> Pues después del instituto, primero voy a casa y descanso un poco. Luego meriendo algo y veo la tele un rato, aunque nunca hay nada interesante. Después salgo por ahí con mis amigos y vuelvo a casa un poco más tarde. Ceno con mis padres a eso de las nueve. Nunca paseo al perro, y no hago mis deberes.

2A   Mi semana

AT 2.2–3 **3 Use your list to say what you do and don't do in the evening.**
Encourage students to try and use extended sentences where possible.

AT 4.3–4 **4 Write about what you do in the evening.**
Remind students that they can embellish in order to use a wide range of vocabulary. They could also add opinions.

Página 36   2A.5 El fin de semana
- Use with Students' Book, pages 64–65

AT 3.2 **1 What do you do at the weekend? Put these activities into the grid.**
Practice of daily activities. When students have finished this activity, they can compare grids. Do most students agree on which activities go where? As an extension to this activity, students could add any other activities they can think of into each box.

AT 1.3 **2 Listen to Miriam. How would you describe her weekends? Explain why.**
Remind students to listen out for connectives that can change the meaning of a sentence, i.e. *pero*.

> 🎧 **CD 4, track 36**   página 36, actividad 2
>
> Los fines de semana, prefiero dormir hasta las diez, pero no puedo. Siempre nos levantamos temprano. Me fastidia porque tengo que salir con mi familia. Comemos en un restaurante con mis padres y no me gusta. Lo que yo prefiero es el fútbol, pero no puedo hacer deporte o ver a mis amigos, porque tengo que estar con mi familia.

Answer:
Frustrating: She can't stay in bed, see her friends or practise sport. She has to get up and go out with her family and eat in a restaurant.

AT 4.3 **3 Use the grid in Activity 1 to write a paragraph about your own weekends.**
Students should think about how Miriam described her weekend and the structures and verbs she used.

Página 37   2A.6A Labolengua
- Use with Students' Book, pages 66–67

1 Explain why these words all have the same ending. Explain why they don't all start with *me*.
Practise of recognising verb endings and types of verb.

Answer:
Because they are all "I" (first person singular present tense). Because you don't eat yourself for breakfast – this isn't a reflexive verb.

2 Think like a Spanish person. Complete the grids.
As an extension activity, students could write a similar grid for other reflexive verbs.

Answers:
I get washed, I wash myself, me lavo; I wake up, I wake myself up, me despierto; he has a shower, he showers himself, se ducha; I am called, I call myself, me llamo

3 Translate into Spanish.
Practice of using reflexive verbs.

Answers:
a Se levanta. b Me despierto. c ¿Te duchas? d Se visten.

Página 38   2A.6B Técnica
- Use with Students' Book, pages 66–67

1 Write out this verb in full: *preferir (ie)*
Practice of conjugating a radical-changing verb.

Answer:
prefiero, prefieres, prefiere, preferimos, preferís, prefieren

2 Note the change in these verbs and write them out in the simplified way recommended in the box at the top of the page.

Answers: querer (ie), poder (ue)

3 Give three reasons why it might be better to write *jugar (ue)* instead of writing out the whole verb.

Suggested answers:
takes up less space, quicker, makes you think and notice, you know what to do when you meet another verb

4 Translate into Spanish.
Students put into practice what have learnt about radical-changing verbs.

Answers:
a prefiero; b preferimos; c quieres; d quiere; e puedo; f podemos

2B Donde vivo yo

Unit Objectives

Contexts and cultural focus: where you live: house and region
Grammar: *ser* and *estar*, imperatives; prepositions
Language learning: pronouncing cognates correctly; extending sentences using frequency adverbs; improving speaking and writing using adjectives; working out the gender of new words

- *Aim:* to describe and give your opinion of your house and the area where you live whilst incorporating the grammar and vocabulary covered in the spread.
- Each unit has an associated video which will feature throughout the unit. Below is the transcript of the video for this unit.
- As a starter activity to introduce the Unit and familiarise students with the language they will meet, you may find it useful for the class to view the video as a whole.

Video clip (CD 2, track 23)

Khalid: ¡Mira al otro lado de la calle! Esa es la Casa Milà.
Marisa: ¡Impresionante!
Khalid: La mayoría de la gente la llama La Pedrera que en catalán quiere decir 'La cantera'. Cuando la estaban construyendo la gente creía que era una cantera.
Marisa: ¡Qué interesante!
Khalid: Sí. Según Eva, Gaudí la construyó para un matrimonio llamado Milà. Se acabó de construir en 1912.
Marisa: Me gusta.
Khalid: Sí, a mí también. Ha sido declarada Patrimonio de la Humanidad por la Unesco.
Marisa: ¡Es realmente impresionante…!
Khalid: Sí… Eh, creo que aquí estamos en el medio… ¿quieres ir a una cafetería? Conozco una que está muy bien.
Marisa: Vale. La verdad es que tengo algo de sed.
Khalid: Está por allí, todo recto…

[in the café]

Marisa: ¿Cómo es tu piso?
Khalid: Pues… igualita a La Pedrera. Más o menos del mismo tamaño también.
Marisa: Venga, en serio…
Khalid: Bueno, mi piso también está bien. Y tengo mi propia habitación.
Marisa: ¿Cómo es?
Khalid: Pues lo normal: tengo una cama, un escritorio, una estantería, un armario.
Marisa: Y ¿en las paredes? ¿Qué tienes en las paredes?
Khalid: No tengo ninguna foto del FC Barcelona, pero tengo un par de posters de Marruecos. Y, justo encima de la puerta, la bandera de Marruecos.
Marisa: Y ¿tienes un balcón?
Khalid: Sí, tengo un balcón pequeño, muy pequeño. Y ¿la tuya? ¿Cómo es tu habitación?
Marisa: Pues, igual que la tuya, sólo que yo tengo dos armarios.
Khalid: ¿Y tienes mucha ropa?
Marisa: ¡No están llenos de libros!
Khalid: Te creo. Y ¿tienes balcón?
Marisa: No. No hay balcón.
Khalid: Entonces, ¡gano yo!
Marisa: No, porque yo tengo jardín.
Khalid: Vale, tú ganas. Así que vives en una casa. ¡Qué bien!
Marisa: Si, está muy bien. A mi padre y a mí nos gusta mucho.
Khalid: ¿Es grande?
Marisa: Es bastante grande. Tenemos dos habitaciones de sobra.
Khalid: ¿Sólo dos? ¿y cuántas salas de estar tenéis?
Marisa: Sólo una, pero tenemos un comedor y por supuesto, una cocina muy grande donde podemos comer.
Khalid: ¡Debe ser difícil vivir en un espacio tan reducido!
Marisa: Sí, la verdad es que mi padre y yo estamos buscando un sitio más grande.
Khalid: Vale, lo entiendo. La familia de José tiene una finca a las afueras de Figueres. Es… ¡Oh!... Creo que tu teléfono está sonando.
Marisa: Pero ¿dónde está?
Khalid: ¿En el bolsillo de tus vaqueros?
Marisa: No.
Khalid: ¿En la mochila?
Marisa: No está allí.
Khalid: Busca en el fondo, debajo de los libros.
Marisa: No lo veo.
Khalid: Creo que está allí, entre tu cámara de fotos y el libro de inglés.
Marisa: Ah sí. Aquí está. ¡Típico!

2B Donde vivo yo

Unit 2B ¡Aquí vivo! Overview grid							
Page reference	Contexts and objectives	Language learning	Grammar	Key language	Framework	AT level
Pages 72–73 **Vivo en…**	• say where you live	• pronounce cognates correctly	• differentiate between *ser* and *estar*	*está en …; la montaña; la costa; el campo; la ciudad; un pueblo; una aldea; un barrio; las afueras; un supermercado; un restaurante; un parque; una estación; un hospital; un banco; un museo; una catedral; un zoo; un colegio; una discoteca; un cine; un parque de atracciones; la bolera; el polideportivo; la piscina; la oficina de Correos; el ayuntamiento; la iglesia; los grandes almacenes; la parada de autobús; las tiendas; delante de; enfrente de; detrás de; encima de; debajo de; entre; al lado de; cerca de; lejos de*	1.1, 1.4, 2.1, 2.4, 2.5, 4.1, 4.3, 4.5, 5.3, 5.4	1.1–2, 2.1–2, 3.3–4, 4.3–4
Pages 74–75 **¿Dónde está?**	• give and understand directions	• extend sentences using frequency adverbs	• use simple imperatives	*el parque de atracciones; la bolera; el polideportivo; la piscina; la oficina de Correos; el ayuntamiento; la iglesia; los grandes almacenes; la parada de autobús; las tiendas; siempre; todos los días; a menudo; a veces; nunca; una vez a la semana; dos veces a la semana; de vez en cuando; Sigue/Siga; Todo recto; Tuerza/Tuerce; Cruza/Cruce; Toma/Tome; el puente; la primera/segunda/tercera; la calle; a la derecha; a la izquierda*	1.1, 2.1, 2.4, 2.5, 4.2, 4.3, 4.4, 4.5, 5.1, 5.6, 5.8	1.2–4, 2.2–3, 3.3, 4.2–3
Pages 76–77 **Mi casa**	• name the rooms in a house	• improve your speaking and writing using adjectives	• use prepositions correctly	*una entrada; unas escaleras; una cocina; un salón; un comedor; un dormitorio; un cuarto de baño; una ducha; un aseo; un despacho; un garaje; un jardín; un balcón; una piscina; un sótano; la planta baja; la primera planta; el ático; una granja; un chalet; un bloque de pisos; una casa; un piso; delante de; enfrente de; detrás de; encima de; debajo de; entre; al lado de; cerca de; lejos de*	1.1, 1.4, 2.1, 2.4, 2.5, 3.1, 3.2, 4.2, 4.4, 4.3, 5.1, 5.5	1.2–4, 2.3–4, 3.2–4, 4.3–4

Donde vivo yo 2B

Pages 78–79 **Mi dormitorio**	• say what furniture is in your bedroom	• work out the gender of new words	• use more prepositions	un armario; una cama; un escritorio; unas estanterías; una mesita de noche; una alfombra; una cómoda; una silla; unas cortinas; una puerta; una ventana; una lámpara grande; pequeño; bonito; moderno; cómodo; simple; elegante; demasiado; muy; bastante; un poco; delante de; enfrente de; detrás de; encima de; debajo de; entre; al lado de; cerca de; lejos de	1.1, 1.4, 2.1, 2.4, 2.5, 4.2, 4.3, 4.4, 5.1, 5.4, 5.8	1.4, 2.2, 3.4, 4.2–4
Pages 80–81 **¿Cómo es tu región?**	• give your opinion about the region where you live			animado; pintoresco; histórico; turístico; ruidoso; agrícola; industrial; residencial	1.1, 1.4, 1.5, 2.1, 4.2, 4.3, 4.4, 5.1	1.4, 2.4, 3.1–3
Pages 82–83 **Labolengua**	• review language and grammar from the unit				1.1, 1.4, 4.1, 4.2, 4.3, 4.4, 4.5, 5.1	
Pages 84–85 **Extra Star Extra Plus**	• differentiated extension/ homework material	• revise and consolidate all vocabulary and grammar covered in the unit	• revise and consolidate all vocabulary and grammar covered in the unit		1.4, 1.5, 2.1, 2.4, 2.5, 4.2, 4.3, 4.4, 5.1, 5.4	2.2–3, 3.1–4, 4.2–4
Page 86 **Prueba**	• end-of-spread test				1.1, 1.4, 1.5, 2.1, 2.4, 2.5, 4.2, 4.4	1.3, 2.2–3, 3.3, 4.3–4
Page 87 **Vocabulario**	• a summary of the key language covered in each spread of this unit					
Page 156 **Leer 2B**	• practice of longer reading texts based on the theme of the unit				2.1, 2.4, 2.5, 5.4	3.4, 4.4

2B Donde vivo yo

Week-by-week overview
(Three-year KS3 Route: assuming six weeks' work or approximately 10–12.5 hours)
(Two-year KS3 Route: assuming four weeks' worth or approxmately 6.5-8.5 hours)
*Please note that essential activities are highlighted.

About Unit 2B, *Donde vivo yo*: Students work in the context of where you live. They talk about and give their opinion of their area and also give and listen to directions. They name the rooms in a house, saying where they are located in the house and name the furniture in their bedroom, also giving its position using prepositions. Students learn how to pronounce cognates correctly, differentiate between *ser* and *estar*, use imperatives and prepositions. The unit also provides tips on language learning techniques.

Three-Year KS3 Route

Week	Resources	Objectives
1	2B.1 Vivo en… 2B.6 LaboIengua B (p.82)	say where you live pronounce cognates correctly differentiate between *ser* and *estar*
2	2B.2 ¿Dónde está? 2B.6 LaboIengua A (p.82) 2B.6 LaboIengua C (p.83)	give and understand directions extend sentences using frequency adverbs use simple imperatives
3	2B.3 Mi casa	name the rooms in a house improve your speaking and writing using adjectives use prepositions correctly
4	2B.4 Mi dormitorio	say what furniture is in your bedroom work out the gender of new words use more prepositions
5	2B.5 ¿Cómo es tu región?	give your opinion about the region where you live
6	2B.7 Extra (Star) (p.84) 2B.7 Extra (Plus) (p.85) 2B.8 Prueba (p.86) Vocabulario (p.87) Leer (p.156)	further reinforcement and extension of the language of the unit recapping on the vocabulary of the unit prepare and carry out assessment in all four skills further reading to explore the language of the unit and cultural themes

Two-Year KS3 Route

Week	Resources	Objectives
1	2B.1 Vivo en… omit activities Think!, 3 & Challenge 2B.6 LaboIengua B (p.82) Omit activity 3	say where you live pronounce cognates correctly differentiate between *ser* and *estar*
2	2B.2 ¿Dónde está? omit activities Think!, 4 & Challenge 2B. 6 LaboIengua A (p.82)	give and understand directions extend sentences using frequency adverbs use simple imperatives
3	2B.3 Mi casa omit activities Think!, 4 & Challenge	name the rooms in a house improve your speaking and writing using adjectives use prepositions correctly
4	2B.4 Mi dormitorio omit activities Think! & Challenge 2B.8 Prueba (p.86) Vocabulario (p.87)	say what furniture is in your bedroom work out the gender of new words use more prepositions recapping on the vocabulary of the unit prepare and carry out assessment in all four skills

2B.1 Donde vivo yo

2B.1 Vivo en ...
páginas 72–73

Planner

Objectives
- say where you live
- differentiate between *ser* and *estar*
- pronounce cognates correctly

Resources
Students' Book, pages 72–73
CD 2, tracks 19–20
Foundation Workbook, page 40
Higher Workbook, page 40
Foundation Workbook audio, CD 3, track 62
Foundation Workbook audio, CD 4, track 37
Interactive OxBox, Unit 2B
Copymasters 53–60
Assessment, Unit 2B

Key language
está en …; la montaña; la costa; el campo; la ciudad; un pueblo; una aldea; un barrio; las afueras; un supermercado; un restaurante; un parque; una estación; un hospital; un banco; un museo; una catedral; un zoo; un colegio; una discoteca; un cine; un parque de atracciones; la bolera; el polideportivo; la piscina; la oficina de Correos; el ayuntamiento; la iglesia; los grandes almacenes; la parada de autobús; las tiendas; delante de; enfrente de; detrás de; encima de; debajo de; entre; al lado de; cerca de; lejos de

Grammar
- differentiate between *ser* and *estar*

Renewed Framework references
1.1, 1.4, 2.1, 2.4, 2.5, 4.1, 4.3, 4.5, 5.3, 5.4

PLTS
Activity 2: Creative thinkers
Challenge: Creative thinkers; Reflective learners

Starters
- Display a list of cognates and as a class practise pronouncing these correctly in Spanish. Then ask students to work in pairs to add more cognates to the list. In their pair, they practise pronouncing these words.
- Students work with a partner to say what there is in their town/village/suburb. Display the key vocabulary for support, if necessary.

Plenaries
- Display some of the key language from the spread and challenge students to write at least five sentences incorporating these words. Compare sentences as a class.
- Students write a passage describing their ideal town/village. Where would it be? Countryside, coast, city? What would there be there? Volunteers read their description to the class who votes for the best sounding one.

Homework/Self-study
Students use at least two of the phrases from Activity 2 in simple sentences of their own.
Gramática: Ask students to write a couple of sentences using both of these verbs (*ser* and *estar*)

AT 1.2

1 Escucha y empareja.
Students listen and match the speakers to the pictures. They then draw an arrow for the compass points mentioned.

Answers:
1 e ←; 2 a ↑; 3 f ↓; 4 c ↖; 5 d ↗; 6 b →

🎧 **CD 2, track 19** página 72, actividad 1

1 Vivo en un pueblo pequeño al oeste de la capital.
2 Vivo en las montañas al norte de la ciudad.
3 Vivo en una aldea al sur de Madrid.
4 Vivo en el campo al noroeste de la costa.
5 Vivo al noreste del país, en la ciudad.
6 Vivo en la costa al este de las montañas.

AT 3.3 / PLTS

2 ¿Qué significan las palabras subrayadas?
Students use the map to help them work out what the underlined words mean.

Answers:
el barrio – area/suburb/neighbourhood; **las afueras** – outskirts; **lejos de** – far from

2B.1 Donde vivo yo

Gramática
Read through the grammar box on *ser* and *estar* as a class. Look at the examples in Activity 2 and ask students if they can think of any more of their own. Then move on to the activity ¿*Es* or *está*?. With more able classes you could also ask students to write a couple of sentences using both of these verbs.

Answers:
Madrid **está** en España. El Parque del Retiro **es** muy bonito. Barcelona **es** una ciudad bastante grande. Andalucía **está** al sur del país.

Think!
This is a good opportunity to practise pronouncing Spanish words correctly. Go round the class getting students to pronounce the vowel sounds.

AT 1.1 **3 Escucha y repite.**
Students listen to and repeat the places in town.

🎧 **CD 2, track 20** página 73, actividad 3

un supermercado
un restaurante
un parque
una estación
un banco
un museo
una catedral
un instituto
una discoteca
un cine

AT 3.4 **4 Lee. ¿Verdad, mentira o no se menciona?**
Students read what Javier says and then note down whether each statement is true, false or not mentioned.

Answers:
1 false; **2** false; **3** not mentioned; **4** true; **5** false

AT 2.2 **5 Habla. ¿Qué hay en tu barrio? ¡Practica!**
Students work with a partner and use the prompts to discuss what there is where they live. Encourage them to think back to Activities 3 and 4 for support if necessary.

AT 4.3–4 **Challenge**
PLTS **Copy the letter and replace the pictures with words. Then write a similar passage about where you live.**
Remind students to refer back to previous activities and point out that they can embellish to make their writing more interesting.

Answers:
Vivo en Bolivia en una ciudad que se llama La Paz. Vivo cerca del centro de la ciudad al **norte** del país. Mi barrio está cerca de la **catedral** de Nuestra Sra. de la Paz. En mi ciudad hay dos **cines**, un **supermercado** y muchos **restaurantes**. También hay un **museo** y una **estación** pero no hay **hospital**. Me **gusta** mi barrio porque es muy turístico.

2B.2 Donde vivo yo

2B.2 ¿Dónde está?

páginas 74–75

Planner

Objectives
- give and understand directions
- use simple imperatives
- extend sentences using frequency adverbs

Resources
Students' Book, pages 74–75
CD 1, tracks 21–22
Foundation Workbook, page 41
Higher Workbook, page 41
Foundation Workbook audio, track 63
Higher Workbook audio, track 38
Interactive OxBox, Unit 2B
Copymasters 53–60
Assessment, Unit 2B

Key language
el parque de atracciones; la bolera; el polideportivo; la piscina; la oficina de Correos; el ayuntamiento; la iglesia; los grandes almacenes; la parada de autobús; las tiendas; siempre; todos los días; a menudo; a veces; nunca; una vez a la semana; dos veces a la semana; de vez en cuando Sigue/Siga; Todo recto; Tuerza/Tuerce; Cruza/Cruce; Toma/Tome; el puente; la primera/segunda/tercera; la calle; a la derecha; a la izquierda

Grammar
- use simple imperatives

Renewed Framework references
1.1, 2.1, 2.4, 2.5, 4.2, 4.3, 4.4, 4.5, 5.1, 5.6, 5.8

PLTS
Activity 2: Self-managers; Creative thinkers; Reflective learners
Activity 5: Reflective learners
Challenge: Reflective learners; Creative thinkers

Starters
- Have a quick class quiz. Split the class into small groups. Display directions in Spanish and ask the groups to compete against one another to note down the English translations of these directions. The first group to translate all of the directions correctly is the winner.
- Display a basic sentence on the theme of the spread. Go round the class asking each student how it could be improved upon. Depending on the class, you may want to display a list of connectives/opinions for support.

Plenaries
- Display the map from Activity 4 and the list of places. Split students into pairs. Partner A chooses a place in secret and gives directions to get there. Partner B follows these directions and says where they have ended up. Partner A confirms whether this is correct. They then swap roles.
- To practise directions, ask students to tell the class the directions they take to get to school. Explain that students can simplify the route and that it is practising Spanish that is important here, rather than giving completely accurate directions!
- Students pretend to be a celebrity and make up sentences saying where they go and how often. They then present their sentences to the class.

Homework/Self-study
Gramática: Students write two sentences, one including *voy al*, the other, *voy a la*.
Gramática: Students write an instruction in the familiar form and one in the polite form.

AT 1.4 **1 ¿Adónde va Javier? Escucha y rellena la tabla en inglés.**
Students listen and fill in the table in English.

🎧 **CD 2, track 21** página 74, actividad 1

Voy a la piscina tres veces a la semana.
Nunca voy al ayuntamiento.
Voy a los grandes almacenes a menudo.
A veces voy a la bolera.
De vez en cuando voy al parque de atracciones.
Voy al polideportivo todos los días.
Voy a la iglesia una vez a la semana.
Siempre voy a la parada del autobús.

Answers:
1 swimming pool: three times a week; **2** town hall: never; **3** department store: often; **4** bowling alley: sometimes; **5** theme park: from time to time; **6** sports centre: every day; **7** church: once a week; **8** bus stop: always

AT 4.2–3 **PLTS** **2 Escribe. ¿Adónde vas?**
Students use the vocabulary from Activity 1 to write a few sentences of their own saying where they go and how often.

2B.2 Donde vivo yo

Gramática
Read through the Grammar box as a class, pointing out how *a* works with *el* and *la*. Ask students to try and find examples of this in reading passages. When you are happy that all students understand how to use *voy a* ask them to write two sentences, one including *voy al*, the other, *voy a la*.

Think!
Read through the Think! box as a class. You could ask students to look at an old piece of writing they have produced and to see if they can improve on it using connectives and/or opinions. Alternatively, you could display a basic sentence on the theme of the spread and ask students to improve upon it.

AT 1.2 **3** Escucha. ¿En qué orden se mencionan?
Students listen and note down the order in which the phrases are mentioned. They then state where each speaker wants to go.

CD 2, track 22   página 75, actividad 3

1. ¿Para ir a la piscina, por favor?
   Cruza la calle.
2. ¿Para ir al polideportivo?
   Sigue todo recto.
3. ¿Cómo se va al ayuntamiento?
   Toma la tercera calle a la derecha.
4. ¿Para ir a las tiendas, por favor?
   Toma la primera calle a la derecha.
5. ¿Cómo se va a la bolera?
   Tuerce a la derecha.
6. ¿La oficina de Correos, por favor?
   Cruza el puente.
7. ¿Cómo se va a los grandes almacenes?
   Toma la segunda calle a la izquierda.
8. ¿Cómo se va a la iglesia?
   Toma la primera calle a la izquierda.
9. ¿El parque de atracciones, por favor?
   Tuerce a la izquierda.

Answers:
1 e, piscina; **2** a, polideportivo; **3** i, ayuntamiento; **4** g, tiendas; **5** c, bolera; **6** d, oficina de Correos; **7** h, grandes almacenes; **8** f, iglesia; **9** b, parque de atracciones

Think!
Students consider the best way to ask for directions in Spanish. They could discuss this as a class.

Gramática
Students look at the familiar and polite ways of giving instructions in Spanish.

AT 3.3 **4** Lee las frases. ¿Adónde van?
Students read the sentences and look at the map to say where the people are going?

Answers:
1 estación; **2** instituto; **3** parque de atracciones; **4** tiendas

AT 2.2–3 **PLTS** **5** Hablar. ¿Cómo se va a...?
With a partner, take it in turns to ask and answer how to get to the different places in town. Use the map in Activity 4.

AT 4.2–3 **PLTS** **Challenge**
Write directions to get from your school to a nearby place your classmates and teachers will know. Read them out loud and see who can work out where they are going.
Depending on the level of the class, you may decide to display the directions and places in town for support.

2B.3 Donde vivo yo

2B.3 Mi casa
páginas 76–77

Planner

Objectives
- name the rooms in a house
- use prepositions correctly
- improve your speaking and writing using adjectives

Video
Video clip, Unit 2B

Resources
Students' Book, pages 76–77
CD 2, tracks 23–24
Foundation Workbook, page 42
Higher Workbook, page 42
Foundation Workbook audio, CD 3, track 64
Higher Workbook audio, CD 4, track 39
Interactive OxBox, Unit 2B
Copymasters 53–60
Assessment, Unit 2B

Key language
una entrada; unas escaleras; una cocina; un salón; un comedor; un dormitorio; un cuarto de baño; una ducha; un aseo; un despacho; un garaje; un jardín; un balcón; una piscina; un sótano; la planta baja; la primera planta; el ático; una granja; un chalet; un bloque de pisos; una casa; un piso

Grammar
- use prepositions correctly

Renewed Framework references
1.1, 1.4, 2.1, 2.4, 2.5, 3.1, 3.2, 4.2, 4.4, 4.3, 5.1, 5.5

PLTS
Think!: Creative thinkers; Reflective learners
Challenge: Creative thinkers

Starters
- Challenge students to come up with as many words as possible which enhance adjectives, e.g. *muy, bastante*. List these words.
- Display the key vocabulary from the spread and go round the class asking each student to produce a sentence using a piece of the key vocabulary, e.g. *Tenemos una cocina muy grande*.

Plenaries
- Display a list of adjectives from the spread and challenge students to use as many of them as possible in a paragraph on the theme of the spread. Remind students to enhance the adjectives with words from the list from Starter Activity 1.
- Students write a paragraph describing the floor plan of their ideal house. Refer them back to Activity 4 for ideas and vocabulary. Volunteers read their paragraph out. Who has described the best floor plan?

Homework/Self-study
After reading the Think! box, students write sentences including adjectives and think of ways in which they can enhance these. Provide less able students with basic sentences to which they should add adjectives.

AT 1.4 **1 Mira el video. ¿Qué dice Marisa de su casa?**
Students watch the video and note down what Marisa says about her house. Which rooms does she mention?

Video clip: Unit 2B (CD2, track 23)

Khalid: ¡Mira al otro lado de la calle! Esa es la Casa Milà.
Marisa: ¡Impresionante!
Khalid: La mayoría de la gente la llama La Pedrera que en catalán quiere decir 'La cantera'. Cuando la estaban construyendo la gente creía que era una cantera.
Marisa: ¡Qué interesante!
Khalid: Sí. Según Eva, Gaudí la construyó para un matrimonio llamado Milà. Se acabó de construir en 1912.
Marisa: Me gusta.
Khalid: Sí, a mí también. Ha sido declarada Patrimonio de la Humanidad por la Unesco.
Marisa: ¡Es realmente impresionante…!
Khalid: Sí… Eh, creo que aquí estamos en el medio… ¿quieres ir a una cafetería? Conozco una que está muy bien.
Marisa: Vale. La verdad es que tengo algo de sed.
Khalid: Está por allí, todo recto…

[in the café]

Marisa: ¿Cómo es tu piso?
Khalid: Pues… igualita a La Pedrera. Más o menos del mismo tamaño también.
Marisa: Venga, en serio…
Khalid: Bueno, mi piso también está bien. Y tengo mi propia habitación.
Marisa: ¿Cómo es?
Khalid: Pues lo normal: tengo una cama, un escritorio, una estantería, un armario.
Marisa: Y ¿en las paredes? ¿Qué tienes en las paredes?

2B.3 Donde vivo yo

Khalid:	No tengo ninguna foto del FC Barcelona, pero tengo un par de posters de Marruecos. Y, justo encima de la puerta, la bandera de Marruecos.
Marisa:	Y ¿tienes un balcón?
Khalid:	Sí, tengo un balcón pequeño, muy pequeño. Y ¿la tuya? ¿Cómo es tu habitación?
Marisa:	Pues, igual que la tuya, sólo que yo tengo dos armarios.
Khalid:	¿Y tienes mucha ropa?
Marisa:	¡No están llenos de libros!
Khalid:	Te creo. Y ¿tienes balcón?
Marisa:	No. No hay balcón.
Khalid:	Entonces, ¡gano yo!
Marisa:	No, porque yo tengo jardín.
Khalid:	Vale, tú ganas. Así que vives en una casa. ¡Qué bien!
Marisa:	Si, está muy bien. A mi padre y a mí nos gusta mucho.
Khalid:	¿Es grande?
Marisa:	Es bastante grande. Tenemos dos habitaciones de sobra.
Khalid:	¿Sólo dos? ¿Y cuántas salas de estar tenéis?
Marisa:	Sólo una, pero tenemos un comedor y por supuesto, una cocina muy grande donde podemos comer.
Khalid:	¡Debe ser difícil vivir en un espacio tan reducido!
Marisa:	Sí, la verdad es que mi padre y yo estamos buscando un sitio más grande.
Khalid:	Vale, lo entiendo. La familia de José tiene una finca a las afueras de Figueres. Es… ¡Oh!... Creo que tu teléfono está sonando.
Marisa:	Pero ¿dónde está?
Khalid:	¿En el bolsillo de tus vaqueros?
Marisa:	No.
Khalid:	¿En la mochila?
Marisa:	No está allí.
Khalid:	Busca en el fondo, debajo de los libros.
Marisa:	No lo veo.
Khalid:	Creo que está allí, entre tu cámara de fotos y el libro de inglés.
Marisa:	Ah sí. Aquí está. ¡Típico!

Answers:
Her house is similar to Khalid's.
Rooms mentioned: living room, dining room, kitchen

AT 3.2 2 Copia y completa.
Students copy the text, replacing the pictures with the appropriate words.

Answers:
En casa tenemos un **sótano** muy oscuro donde mi padre tiene su vino. En la planta baja hay un **garaje** enorme, una **cocina** bastante moderna y grandísima y un **salón** muy acogedor, pero no tenemos **comedor**. También hay un **aseo** nuevo. En la primera planta hay dos **dormitorios**. El **dormitorio** de mis padres es azul y el mío es de color rosa. Además hay un **cuarto de baño** antiguo pero limpio y un **despacho** pequeño. Mi casa no tiene **ático** pero tiene un **balcón** bastante espacioso. Fuera hay un **jardín** muy bonito.

Think!
Students read the paragraph from Activity 2 again and consider how the adjectives have been enhanced.

AT 1.2 3 Escucha y verifica
Students listen to check their answers.

CD 2, track 24 *página 76, actividad 3*

En casa tenemos un sótano muy oscuro donde mi padre tiene su vino. En la planta baja hay un garaje enorme, una cocina bastante moderna y grandísima y un salón muy acogedor, pero no tenemos comedor. También hay un aseo nuevo. En la primera planta hay dos dormitorios. El dormitorio de mis padres es azul y el mío es de color rosa. Ádemas hay un baño antiguo pero limpio y un despacho pequeño. Mi casa no tiene ático pero tiene un balcón bastante espacioso. Fuera hay un jardín muy bonito.

AT 3.3 4 Identifica los 13 adjetivos de la Actividad 2.
Students find the 13 adjectives in Activity 2. They look up their meaning in the dictionary if they don't already know them.

Answers:
oscuro – dark; **enorme** – enormous; **moderna** – modern; **grandísima** – big; **acogedor** – welcoming; **nuevo** – new; **azul** – blue; **rosa** – pink; **antiguo** – old; **limpio** – clean; **pequeño** – small; **espacioso** – spacious; **bonito** – pretty/nice

Think!
Originating from Miguel de Cervantes 17th Century novel *El ingenioso hidalgo don Quijote de la Mancha*, Don Quijote and Sancho are the most prominent characters of Spanish literature.
Don Quijote is a middle-aged gentleman from the region of La Mancha who is obsessed with chivalrous ideals of the books he has read. With his imagination and little sanity, he takes his lance and sets off to defend the helpless and destroy the wicked aided by his baffled labourer Sancho, his squire in the adventures they face together. Famously, Don Quijote sees giants where there are windmills and he truly believes that *Dulcinea*, the peasant woman whose love he yearns, is a princess.

AT 3.3–4 5 Escribe las habitaciones en el plano.
Students read the description and label the floor plans.

Answers:
1 la entrada; **2** el salón; **3** un aseo; **4** la cocina; **5** el comedor; **6** el cuarto de baño; **7** el dormitorio de mis padres; **8** mi dormitorio; **9** el despacho; **10** el dormitorio de mi hermano

2B.4 Donde vivo yo

PLTS **Think!**
Students look at the description from Activity 4 and make a note of how to say 'my parents' bedroom' (*el dormitorio de mis padres*) and 'my brother's bedroom' (*el dormitorio de mi hermano*). They use these phrases as models to help them translate similar English phrases into Spanish.

Answers:
my dad's office – *la officina de mi padre*; **my sister's friend** – *la amiga de mi hermana*; **my friend's cat** – *el gato de mi amigo*

AT 2.3–4 **Challenge**
PLTS
Prepare a detailed description of where you live and the floor plan. Describe it to a partner who will make notes and draw the plan. Do the same for them.
Students can be as inventive as possible. They should refer back to Activity 4 for ideas and vocabulary.

2B.4 Mi dormitorio
páginas 78–79

Planner

Objectives
- say what furniture is in your bedroom
- use more prepositions
- work out the gender of new words

Video
Video-blog, Unit 2B

Resources
Students' Book, pages 78–79
CD 2, tracks 25–26
Foundation Workbook, page 43
Higher Workbook, page 43
Foundation Workbook audio, CD 3, track 65
Higher Workbook audio, CD 4, track 40
Interactive OxBox, Unit 2B
Copymasters 53–60
Assessment, Unit 2B

Key language
un armario; una cama; un escritorio; unas estanterías; una mesita de noche; una alfombra; una cómoda; una silla; unas cortinas; una puerta; una ventana; una lámpara
grande; pequeño; bonito; moderno; cómodo; simple; elegante
demasiado; muy; bastante; un poco
delante de; enfrente de; detrás de; encima de; debajo de; entre; al lado de; cerca de;
lejos de

Grammar
- use more prepositions

Renewed Framework references
1.1, 1.4, 2.1, 2.4, 2.5, 4.2, 4.3, 4.4, 5.1, 5.4, 5.8

PLTS
Challenge: Creative thinkers

Starters
- Play a game to practise prepositions. All students stand up. Call out a preposition, e.g. *delante*. Students stand in front of their desks. Call out another preposition, e.g. *detrás de* or *al lado de*. Students stand behind or next to their desks. Continue in this way. It is up to you whether or not students who stand in the wrong place are out of the game. You could also turn this into a version of 'Simon Says'.

Plenaries
- Display the key language and challenge students to write five sentences on the theme of the spread incorporating this vocabulary. Remind them to enhance sentences by including adjectives and quantifiers. They could also include prepositions.
- Challenge students to write a paragraph describing the worst bedroom they can think of. They should use adjectives, prepositions and quantifiers to make their writing more sophisitcated. Volunteers read their descriptions to the class. Who has described the worst bedroom?

Homework/Self-study
Think!: students note down a few examples of masculine, feminine, singular and plural nouns. Depending on the level of the class, they could then add adjectives in the appropriate form.

AT 4.2 **1** **¿Qué hay en el dormitorio? Descríbelo.**
Students study the illustration of a bedroom and then write a description detailing what is in the bedroom. They should add *un/una/unos/unas* as appropriate.

Answers:
En el dormitorio hay:
una cama, un armario, un escritorio, unas estanterías, una mesita de noche, una alfombra, una cómoda, una silla, unas cortinas, una puerta, una ventana y una lámpara

2B.4 Donde vivo yo

Think!
Students look at the items listed in Activity 1 and think about whether they are masculine or feminine, singular or plural. Remind them that determiners (*el/la/los/las* or *un/una/unos/unas*) and describing words (*blanco, bonito* etc.) agree with the noun.

AT 4.3

2 Mejora la descripción y da tu opinión.
Students enhance their answer from Activity 1 using adjectives (including colours) and quantifiers. There are some ideas in the box. They then give their opinion of the bedroom.

AT 1.2, 4.2

3 ¿Dónde está Don Quijote? Escucha y corrige los errores.
Students listen and correct the mistakes.

CD 2, track 25 página 79, actividad 3

1 Don Quijote está detrás del armario.
2 Don Quijote está al lado de la cómoda.
3 Don Quijote está encima del escritorio.
4 Don Quijote está enfrente de Sancho Panza.

Answers:
1 Don Quijote está **dentro del** armario. 2 Don Quijote está **encima de la** cómoda. 3 Don Quijote está **debajo del** escritorio. 4 Don Quijote está **delante del** Sancho Panza.

AT 2.4

4 Hablar. Tres en raya.
Students play a game to practise using prepositions. They take it in turns with a partner to describe one of the pictures in the grid, using the vocabulary and prepositions they have learnt. The object of the game is to get three in a row. Students only have twenty seconds per turn and the first one to get three in a row wins.

Answers:
A1: El teléfono móvil está debajo de la cama.
B1: El teléfono móvil está detrás de las cortinas.
C1: El teléfono móvil está al lado de la lámpara.
A2: El teléfono móvil está detrás de la puerta.
B2: El teléfono móvil está dentro del armario.
C2: El teléfono móvil está debajo de la silla.
A3: El teléfono móvil está detrás del escritorio.
B3: El teléfono móvil está entre dos lámparas.
C3: El teléfono móvil está encima de la cama.

AT 3.4

5 Lee la descripción y dibuja el plano.
Students read the description and draw a plan of Soraya's bedroom.

AT 1.3–4

6 Mira el video-blog. Toma notas en inglés.
Students listen to the young people and make notes in English about their house, bedroom and opinions. They note down how each person answers the questions listed.

Video-blog: Unit 2B (CD 2, track 26)

¿Vives en una casa o en un piso?
Eva: Vivo en un piso en el centro de Barcelona, cerca de la Sagrada Familia.
José: Vivo en un piso situado en el barrio de Gràcia.
Marisa: Vivo en una casa.

¿Cómo es tu piso?
Eva: Mi piso es pequeño pero es muy acogedor y tiene dos baños, dos dormitorios, una cocina y un salón.
José: Mi piso es pequeño pero es muy acogedor. Tengo tres dormitorios, una cocina, un comedor y un pequeño balcón donde entra mucha luz.
Marisa: Mi casa es bastante grande. Tiene un jardín con terraza. Hay una cocina, un salón, tres dormitorios.

Describe tu dormitorio.
Eva: Tiene tres camas y al lado de mi cama hay el armario y tenemos también una mesilla de noche y un escritorio enfrente.
Marisa: Mi dormitorio tiene una cama. Al lado de la cama hay un pequeño sofá… y la cama es muy alta para que debajo de la cama quepa el escritorio.

Answers:
Eva: lives in a flat in the centre of Barcelona; flat is small but very welcoming; there are two bathrooms, two bedrooms, a kitchen and a living room; she has three beds next to her bed she has a wardrobe; also has a bedside table and a desk opposite.
José: lives in a flat in the Gràcia neighbourhood; flat is small but welcoming; has three bedrooms, a kitchen, a dining room, a small balcony which lets in a lot of light.
Marisa: lives in a house; quite big; has garden with a terrace; has a kitchen, a living room and three bedrooms; in her bedroom she has a bed; next to her bed is a small sofa; the bed is very high so that the desk can go underneath.

AT 4.4
PLTS

Challenge
Write a detailed description of your bedroom.
Students use the grammar and vocabulary they have met in the spread for support. They can embellish in order to make their writing more interesting.

2B.5 Donde vivo yo

2B.5 ¿Cómo es tu región?
páginas 80–81

Planner

Objectives
- give your opinion about the region where you live

Resources
Students' Book, pages 80–81
CD 1, track 27
Foundation Workbook, page 44
Higher Workbook, page 44
Interactive OxBox, Unit 2B
Assessment, Unit 2B

Key language
animado; pintoresco; histórico; turístico; ruidoso; agrícola; industrial; residencial

Renewed Framework references
1.1, 1.4, 1.5, 2.1, 4.2, 4.3, 4.4, 5.1

PLTS
Challenge: Creative thinkers

Starters
- Practise adjectives. Describe a location, e.g. *Hay muchos sitios famosos para visitar*. Students say which adjective best fits the description. The student who answered then comes up with his/her own description. And so on.
- Further practise of adjectives. Go round the class with you saying the name of a well known city/town/attraction and students giving an appropriate adjective to describe it.

Plenaries
- Display the key vocabulary and challenge students to use all of the adjectives in a paragraph of their own.
- Students write a description of their ideal location and house using ideas and vocabulary from the spread for support. They then read their paragraphs to the class who votes for the best description.

Homework/Self-study
Students use the phrases from Activity 4 in sentences of their own.

AT 3.1 **1 Escoge un adjetivo para cada foto.**
Students choose an adjective from the list for each of the photographs.

Answers:
1 f; **2** d; **3** a; **4** g; **5** c; **6** e; **7** h; **8** b

AT 3.3 **2 Lee y elige un adjetivo para cada frase.**
Students read the sentences and choose an adjective from Activity 1 for each of them.

Answers:
1 c; **2** h; **3** f; **4** b; **5** d; **6** e; **7** g; **8** a

AT 1.4 **3 Escucha. ¿En qué orden se mencionan los adjetivos de la Actividad 1?**
Students listen and note down the order in which the adjectives from Activity 1 are mentioned.

🎧 **CD 2, track 27** página 81, actividad 3

La ciudad de Barcelona lo tiene casi todo. Sagrada Familia es un barrio muy <u>turístico</u> a causa de la famosa catedral de Gaudí. ¡Siempre hay muchos autobuses llenos de turistas sacando fotos! Las zonas del centro y el puerto están siempre muy <u>animadas</u> y hay gente y fiesta hasta muy tarde por la noche. La verdad es que vivir en el centro puede ser muy <u>ruidoso</u>. No me gusta nada la Zona Franca porque es muy <u>industrial</u> pero sí me gusta Gracia, donde vivo, porque es una zona más bien <u>residencial</u>. Pienso que el barrio más <u>pintoresco</u> quizás está alrededor del Parc Güell donde todo es muy bonito. Si buscas edificios antiguos, supongo que el mejor lugar es el Barrio Gótico que es muy <u>histórico</u>. Las zonas <u>agrícolas</u> están a las afueras de la ciudad.

Answers:
as underlined in the audio script

AT 3.4 **4 Lee. ¿Cómo se dice en español?**
Students read the text about Marisa and note down how to say the words and phrases listed in Spanish.

Answers:
1 un televisor de pantalla plana; **2** moqueta; **3** en una esquina; **4** literas; **5** paredes; **6** rosa claro; **7** una impresora; **8** un portátil; **9** un altavoz

AT 2.4 PLTS **Challenge**
Prepare a short presentation about where you live. Ensure you mention all the following points.
Students use what they have learnt in the spread to prepare their presentation, making sure to include all of the points listed in the Students' Book. You could use this as a class listening activity where students deliver their presentation in front of the other students who note down what they hear.

2B.6 Donde vivo yo

2B.6 Labolengua
páginas 82–83

Planner

Objectives
- review language and grammar from the unit

Resources
Students' Book, pages 82–83
CD 1, track 70
Foundation Workbook, pages 45–46
Higher Workbook, pages 45–46
Foundation Workbook audio, CD 3, track 66
Higher Workbook audio, CD 4, track 41
Interactive OxBox, Unit 2B
Copymasters 61–62
Assessment, Unit 2B

Grammar
- Ordinal numbers
- *Ser* and *estar*

Renewed Framework references
1.1, 1.4, 4.1, 4.2, 4.3, 4.4, 4.5, 5.1

PLTS
All activities: Reflective learners/Self-managers

Homework/Self-study
Students practise reading out loud in Spanish, paying particular attention to the vowel sounds. They could read some of the texts from the Students' Book.

Comprender – more numbers and verbs

A Ordinal numbers

> **PLTS** **1 How would you say the following in Spanish?**
> Practice of using ordinal numbers.

Answers:
1 el séptimo libro; 2 el cuarto hermano; 3 la sexta calle;
4 los primeros días; 5 la puerta doce; 6 la segunda piscina

B *Ser* and *estar*

> **PLTS** **2 Choose the correct verb and say why you have made that choice.**
> Practice of using *ser* and *estar* correctly. A useful video (in the form of a fun rap) on the use of *ser* and *estar* can be found at: http://www.youtube.com/watch?v=lY10_T_ROq4

Answers:
1 es – description; 2 está – temporary state; 3 son – origin;
4 es – description; 5 está – position; 6 es – what things are made of

> **PLTS** **3 Translate the following sentences.**
> Further practice of using *ser* and *estar*.

Answers:
1 Es de Málaga. 2 El autobús está en la parada de autobús.
3 La casa está en la montaña. 4 La aldea es muy bonito;
5 El hermano de Maria es estudiante.

Aprender – sending a letter

C Spanish addresses

Students read the advice on writing letters in Spain. They could practise writing a Spanish letter themselves, either to a penpal or to an imaginary or famous Spanish person.

Hablar – pronunciation

D Vowel sounds

> **PLTS** **4 Practise pronouncing these words. Then listen and check your pronunciation.**
> Students practise saying the vowel sounds in Spanish.

> 🎧 **CD 2, track 28**   página 83, actividad 4
> feo; curioso; fuera; viudo; aeropuerto; euros; autobús; autocar; marea; idolo; tierra; guía; violín, Europa

2B.7 Donde vivo yo

2B.7 Extra Star
página 84

Planner

Objectives
- practise using prepositions and giving directions

Resources
Students' Book, page 84
Copymaster 63

Renewed Framework references
1.4, 1.5, 2.1, 2.4, 4.2, 4.3, 4.4, 5.1

PLTS
Question 1: Creative thinkers; Reflective learners

AT 3.1 / PLTS

1 Busca la palabra diferente.
Students find the odd one out each time. They should give reasons for their choice.

Answers:
1 polideportivo – all the others are rooms in a house;
2 dormitorio – this is a noun, the others are adjectives;
3 puerta – this is a noun, the others are prepositions;
4 bolera – the others are all types of landscape;
5 ventana – it's not furniture

AT 3.2, 4.2

2 Completa las frases.
Students complete the sentences with the correct preposition.

Answers:
1 encima; 2 detrás; 3 dentro; 4 entre; 5 debajo; 6 al lado

AT 3.2

3 ¿Adónde van?
Students read the sentences and look at the map to find out which place is being described each time.

Answers:
1 el instituto; 2 el cine; 3 la bolera; 4 la iglesia; 5 el polideportivo; 6 el parque de atracciones

AT 2.3

4 Elige cuatro lugares del mapa. ¿Cómo se va?
Students choose four places on the street map and give directions from the red star.

2B.7 Extra Plus
página 85

Planner

Objectives
- practise giving directions and describing where things are

Resources
Students' Book, page 85
Copymaster 64

Renewed Framework references
2.1, 2.4, 2.5, 4.2, 4.3, 5.1, 5.4

PLTS
Activity 2: Reflective learners; Self-managers
Activity 4: Creative thinkers; Self-managers; Reflective learners

---

AT 3.3–4

1 Mira el mapa. ¿Adónde van?
Students read the directions and use the map to find out where the directions lead.

Answers:
1 Van al ayuntamiento. 2 Van a la catedral. 3 Van al parque. 4 Van al cine. 5 Van a las tiendas. 6 Van al parque de atracciones.

AT 3.2 / PLTS

2 Categoriza estas palabras. Escribe un/una/unos/unas.
Students categorise the words under the headings listed. They then add *un, una, unos* or *unas* as appropriate.

Answers:
Lugares en la ciudad: una bolera; una piscina; un polideportivo; unas tiendas; unos grandes almacenes
Viviendas: un piso; una granja; una casa; un chalet; una castillo
Habitaciones en la casa: un dormitorio; un cuarto de baño; una entrada; unas escaleras; un salón
Muebles del dormitorio: una silla; una cómoda; un armario; una cama; unas estanterías

2B.8 Donde vivo yo

AT 2.2

3 ¿Dónde están?
Students look at the picture and say where each of the items listed is. They should answer using full sentences.

Answers:
1 El niño está delante del cine. **2** El pájaro está dentro de la tienda. **3** La tienda está entre el cine y el Correos. **4** El banco está delante de la tienda. **5** El perro está debajo de la mesa; **6** El colegio de idiomas está encima del Correos. **7** El coche está delante del Correos. **8** Los libros están debajo del banco.

Think!
Explain to students that words, such as *banco* in the last activity, can have more than one meaning. Ask them to note down the two meanings of *el banco* ('bank' and 'bench') and as a class have a brainstorming session to find other Spanish words with more than one meaning.

AT 4.3–4 PLTS

4 Describe tu dormitorio ideal.
Students use the vocabulary and grammar they have learnt to write a description of their ideal bedroom. They should be as inventive as possible.

2B.8 Prueba   página 86

Planner

Resources
Students' Book, page 86
CD 2, track 29

Renewed Framework references
1.1, 1.4, 1.5, 2.1, 2.4, 2.5, 4.2, 4.4

PLTS
All activities: Reflective learners
Hablar: Team workers

Escuchar

AT 1.3
Where do they live? Choose the correct pictures, give their opinion and say why they like/don't like it.
This activity tests listening skills using the language covered in this unit.

🎧 **CD 2, track 29**   página 86, Escuchar

1. Vivo en una aldea en la costa. Vivo en una casa pequeña al lado del mar. Me gusta mucho porque es tranquila.
2. Vivo en las montañas, cerca de la ciudad en un pueblo que se llama La Seu. No me gusta mucho porque siempre hace frío.
3. Vivo en el centro de la ciudad en un bloque antiguo de veintitrés plantas. Odio mi barrio porque hay mucho tráfico.
4. Vivo en el campo con mi familia en una granja enorme. Me encanta vivir en una granja porque me gustan mucho los animales.
5. Mi abuela y yo vivimos en un piso pequeño en un pueblo en la costa. Me gusta pero preferiría vivir en la ciudad.

Answers:
1 c, f, h, likes a lot, quiet; **2** a, d, e, doesn't like it much, always cold; **3** d, g, hates it, a lot of traffic; **4** b, i, loves it, likes animals a lot; **5** j, e, c, likes it but would prefer to live in the city

Hablar

AT 2.2–3 👥 **Answer the questions.**
Students use what they have learnt in this unit in order to use the map to give directions. They should aim to give as much detail as possible, remembering to use prepositions as well.

Leer

AT 3.3–4 **Read Clara's text and answer the questions.**
This activity tests reading skills using the language covered in this unit.

Answers:
1 In the Andes; **2** any three of: visit museums, monuments, the cathedral; eat in one of the many restaurants; go to the sports centre on the outskirts of the city; **3** a big house close to the centre; three floors, a pretty garden behind the house; **4** on the first floor; **5** She loves her bedroom because she has a very big bed and posters of her favourite artists everywhere. **6** wardrobes and windows; **7** next to the door; **8** under the bed

Escribir

AT 4.3–4 **Write a paragraph about where you live.**
This activity tests writing skills using the language covered in this unit.

Answers: Students' own answers

Donde vivo yo 2B

Leer 2B
página 156

> **Planner**
>
> **Resources**
> Students' Book, page 156
>
> **Renewed Framework references**
> 2.1, 2.4, 2.5, 5.4
>
> **PLTS**
> Activity 2: Creative thinkers
> Activity 3: Reflective learners; Creative thinkers
>
> **Homework/Self-study**
> All questions

AT 3.4   **1** Read the adverts. How do you say the following?

Answers:
1 calefacción central; **2** aire acondicionado; **3** vistas de las montañas; **4** muebles incluidos; **5** amenidades locales

AT 3.4 / PLTS   **2** Which house would you recommend to these people?

Answers:
1 chalet; **2** piso; **3** casa de campo; **4** apartamento

AT 4.4 / PLTS   **3** Design a similar advert to sell your house.

Foundation Workbook

Página 40   2B.1 Vivo en…
- Use with Students' Book, pages 72–73

AT 3.1   **1** Match up the captions and the pictures.

Answers:
a la ciudad; **b** la costa; **c** la montaña; **d** el campo

AT 1.2   **2** Listen. Where do they live? Write the correct number in each box.

> 🎧 **CD 3, track 62**   página 40, actividad 2
>
> 1 Me llamo Enrique, vivo en el campo.
> 2 Me llamo Elena. Vivo en Barcelona, una ciudad en España.
> 3 Vivo en Loarre, en la montaña en España.
> 4 Vivo en Puerto Vallarta, en la costa pacífica del Pacífico.

Answers:
a la ciudad – 2; **b** la costa – 4; **c** la montaña – 3; **d** el campo – 1

AT 2.2   **3** Randomsville: Toss a coin to see what is in the town.
Students should try to get through all of the places listed. Remind them to add *una piscina* and *una bolera* to their vocabulary lists in the style they have decided upon.

AT 4.2–3   **4** Use these words to write sentences about Randomsville.
Students pick their own words to describe the town. Remind them to ensure that the adjectives agree with the noun and that the resulting sentence is logical, i.e. *una ciudad grande* or *un pueblo pequeño*.

Página 41   2B.2 ¿Dónde está…?
- Use with Students' Book, pages 74–75

1 Do the maths.
Remind students of the importance of using prepositions correctly.

Answers:
a + el = al; a + la = a la; a + los = a los; a + las = a las

AT 4.2   **2** Use this grid to make up sentences.
Students should make up as many sentences as they can using a variety of places.

AT 1.2   **3** Listen and do the actions.
Students should listen to the recording several times as it is a good way to remember these directions.

2B Donde vivo yo

CD 3, track 63 — página 41, actividad 3

As you hear the words, point or step in the right direction, so 'a la izquierda' is to the left, 'a la derecha' is to the right, and 'todo recto' is forwards. Here we go.

A la izquierda, that's it, left.
A la derecha, to the right.
A la izquierda, a la izquierda, a la izquierda, todo recto.
Did you go forward?
A la derecha, a la derecha, a la derecha, todo recto.
A la izquierda, a la izquierda, a la izquierda, todo recto.
Todo recto, todo recto, a la derecha, a la derecha.
A la derecha, todo recto, todo recto, STOP.

AT 4.2–3

4 Put on your favourite song. Make up 'a la izquierda' actions to go with it. Write down the instructions.
Confident volunteers could perform their actions in front of the class to their favourite song. Alternatively, students could swap instructions with a partner who must try to act them out.

Página 42 — 2B.3 Mi casa
- Use with Students' Book, pages 76–77

AT 3.3

1 Read and underline all the names of rooms.
This is good revision of daily activities.

Answers:
Hola, soy Carmen. Me gusta mi casa. A la izquierda hay <u>una cocina</u>. Enfrente de la cocina está <u>el salón</u>. En el centro está <u>mi dormitorio</u> y <u>el dormitorio de mis padres</u>. Mis padres tienen <u>el dormitorio grande</u>. Finalmente, a la derecha está <u>el cuarto de baño</u>.

AT 3.3

2 Read again, and draw in the rooms on this plan.
Point out to students that the directions given are as if you are looking straight at the plan, and not starting at a certain point in the house.

Answers:

Lounge	Carmen's room	bathroom
kitchen	parents' bedroom	

AT 1.3

3 Listen and add the three extra details to the plan.
Students will hear a passage similar to the reading one in Activity 1, but with some added details. They listen carefully for these and add them to the plan.

CD 3, track 64 — página 42, actividad 3

Hola, soy Carmen. Me gusta mi casa. A la izquierda hay una cocina. Enfrente de la cocina está el salón. En el centro está mi dormitorio y el dormitorio de mis padres. Mis padres tienen el dormitorio grande con el balcón. Finalmente, a la derecha está el cuarto de baño ducha. Afuera hay un jardín con una piscina.

Answers:
add a balcony to parents' bedroom, a shower in the bathroom and a garden with swimming pool

Página 43 — 2B.4 Mi dormitorio
- Use with Students' Book, pages 78–79

AT 3.1, 4.1

1 Use these words to label the pictures.

Answers:
a estantería, libros; **b** escritorio, ordenador; **c** televisor, póster; **d** armario, ropa

AT 1.3

2 Listen to the four friends. Number each picture correctly.

CD 3, track 65 — página 43, actividad 2

1 Mi dormitorio no está muy ordenado. Tengo una cama. Tengo un armario para la ropa. Tengo una silla y un escritorio para mi ordenador. En mi dormitorio estudio, duermo y escucho música.
2 En mi dormitorio tengo un televisor, un armario para mi ropa, y un póster de mi equipo de fútbol favorito.
3 Mi dormitorio es muy pequeño y tengo muchas cosas. Tengo tres armarios porque tengo mucha ropa.
4 En mi dormitorio, tengo muchos libros. Tengo libros en estanterías, y tengo más libros en los armarios con la ropa.

Answer:
Isabelle – 4; Iñaki – 1; Alejandro – 2; Lola – 3

AT 2.3

3 Use this grid to talk about your own bedroom.
Students should try to use connectives where possible. They could also write out their sentences.

Página 44 — 2B.5 ¿Cómo es tu región?
- Use with Students' Book, pages 80–81

AT 3.1

1 Find four words to describe each picture.
This is subjective to a degree so accept different slightly different answers from each student as long as they are sensible.

Suggested answers:
a museos, monumentos, turistas, pintoresco;
b tranquilo, verde, paisaje, granjas; **c** animado, tráfico, gente, industrial

Donde vivo yo 2B

AT 3.2 **2 Find the sentences in these word snake grids.**
Students should try to predict what they might be looking for by thinking back to the words in Activity 1.

Answer: Es tranquilo y verde.

AT 4.2 **3 Now make up your own word snake to describe a place.**
Students can give their word snake to a partner to try to solve. They should try to make their sentence as interesting as possible using the words in the box.

Página 45   2B.6A Labolengua
- Use with Students' Book, pages 82–83

1 Fill in the grids with the words below.
Practice of conjugating the two Spanish forms of 'to be'.

Answers:
ser: I am – soy; you are – eres; he/she/it is – es; we are – somos; you are (plural) – sois; they are – son
estar: I am – estoy; you are – estás; he/she/it is – está; we are – estamos; you are (plural) – estáis; they are – están

2 Listen and check. Then listen and repeat with actions.
Students check that they have conjugated the verbs correctly. They then join in with the appropriate actions.

> 🎧 **CD 3, track 66**   página 45, actividad 2
>
> soy, eres, es, somos, sois, son
> estoy, estás, está, estamos, estáis, están

3 Decide which group of words goes with *soy*... and which goes with *estoy*... Then write out the words in sentences.
Writing the words out in sentences will help students to remember when to use which form of 'to be'. As an extension activity, ask students to adapt each sentence, e.g. *Soy inglés/esa*, etc.

Answers:
Soy español(a). Soy bastante inteligente. Soy de Madrid. Soy estudiante.
Estoy en mi casa. Estoy enfermo/a. Estoy en la cama. Estoy triste.

Página 46   2B.6B Técnica
- Use with Students' Book, pages 82–83

AT 3.2 **1 Find the information in this Spanish address.**

Answers:
Her first name is <u>Ana</u>.
Her surnames are <u>García</u> (her father's surname) and <u>López</u> (her mother's surname).
She lives at number <u>23</u> on <u>Luís Roldán</u> Street, on the <u>3rd</u> floor, <u>2nd</u> door.
Her postcode is <u>50012</u>.
The city is <u>Zaragoza</u>.
The region is <u>Aragón</u>.

2 Now write out the name and address of someone you know, using the Spanish style.
This will make students think about the differences between Spanish and English conventions.

Higher Workbook

Página 40   2B.1 Vivo en...
- Use with Students' Book, pages 72–73

AT 4.2 **1 Write a caption for each picture.**

Answers:
a la ciudad; **b** la costa; **c** la montaña; **d** el campo

AT 1.2–3 **2 Listen. Where do they live? Write the correct number in each box.**

> 🎧 **CD 4, track 37**   página 40, actividad 2
>
> 1 Me llamo Enrique. Soy de Roballedo. Vivo en una aldea pequeña en el campo.
> 2 Me llamo Elena. Vivo a las afueras de Barcelona, una ciudad en Catalunia, España.
> 3 Vivo en Loarre, en el Pirineo, en la montaña en el norte de España.
> 4 Vivo en Puerto Vallarta, en la costa pacífica de México.

Answers:
a la ciudad – 2; **b** la costa – 4; **c** la montaña – 3; **d** el campo – 1

AT 2.2 **3 Randomsville: Toss a coin to see what is in the town.**
Students should try to get through all of the places listed. Remind them to add *una piscina* and *una bolera* to their vocabulary lists in the style they have decided upon.

AT 4.2–3 **4 Use these words to write sentences about Randomsville.**
Students pick their own words to describe the town. Remind them to ensure that the adjectives agree with the noun and that the resulting sentence is logical, i.e. *una ciudad grande* or *un pueblo pequeño*.

2B Donde vivo yo

Página 41　　　　　　**2B.2 ¿Dónde está ...?**
- Use with Students' Book, pages 74–75

1 Do the maths.

Answers:
a + el = al; a + la = a la; a + los = a los; a + las = a las

AT 4.2 2 Put the words into the grid. Then use it to make up sentences.
Students should try to use all of the items in the last column in their sentences.

Answers:
al: supermercado; institutio; parque
a la: piscina; bolera; oficina de Correos
a los: grandes almacenes
a las: tiendas

AT 1.2 3 Listen and do the actions.
Students should listen to the recording several times as it is a good way to remember these directions.

> 🎧 **CD 4, track 38**　　　　　página 41, actividad 3
> A la izquierda.
> A la derecha.
> A la izquierda, a la izquierda, a la izquierda, todo recto.
> A la derecha, a la derecha, a la derecha, todo recto.
> A la izquierda, a la izquierda, a la derecha, todo recto.
> Todo recto, todo recto, a la derecha, a la derecha.
> A la derecha, todo recto, todo recto, STOP.

AT 4.2–3 4 Put on your favourite song. Make up 'a la izquierda' actions to go with it. Write down the instructions.
Confident volunteers could perform their actions in front of the class to their favourite song. Alternatively, students could swap instructions with a partner who must try to act them out.

Página 42　　　　　　**2B.3 Mi casa**
- Use with Students' Book, pages 76–77

AT 3.4 1 Read and underline all the names of rooms.

Answers:
Hola, soy Carmen. Voy a describir mi casa. La entrada está en la planta baja. Al entrar, a la izquierda está la cocina, y enfrente está el comedor. Al lado del comedor, o sea la segunda habitación a la derecha, está el salón. Es un salón muy grande. Enfrente del salón hay el despacho de mi padre y un cuarto de baño.

En la primera planta están los dormitorios. Mis padres tienen el dormitorio grande. Enfrente del dormitorio de mis padres hay otro cuarto de baño y un salón con un televisor grande. Al final, a la izquierda hay el dormitorio de mi hermano, y a la derecha tengo mi dormitorio.

AT 3.4 2 Read again, and draw in the rooms on this plan.
Students must pay attention to where the entrance is in order to ensure they label the rest correctly.

Answers:

kitchen	office	bathroom [shower]
dining room	lounge	

[double garage] [garden with swimming pool]

Carmen's room	tv room [big TV]	bathroom
brother's room	parents' bedroom [with balcony]	

AT 1.4 3 Listen and add the five extra details to the plan.
Before students begin, remind them to listen out for cognates and to try to predict what extra details might be mentioned.

> 🎧 **CD 4, track 39**　　　　　página 42, actividad 3
> Hola, soy Carmen. Voy a describir mi casa. La entrada está en la planta baja. Al entrar, a la izquierda está la cocina, y enfrente está el comedor. Al lado del comedor, o sea la segunda habitación a la derecha, está el salón. Es un salón muy grande. Enfrente del salón hay el despacho de mi padre y hay un cuarto de baño con una ducha. También hay un garaje para dos coches.
>
> En la primera planta están los dormitorios. Mis padres tienen el dormitorio grande con el balcón. Enfrente del dormitorio de mis padres hay otro cuarto de baño y un salón con un televisor grande. Al final, a la izquierda está el dormitorio de mi hermano, y a la derecha tengo mi dormitorio. Afuera, hay un jardín grande con una piscina.

Answers: marked on the plan

Donde vivo yo 2B

Página 43 — 2B.4 Mi dormitorio
- Use with Students' Book, pages 78–79

AT 1.3 **1 Listen to the four friends. Number each picture correctly.**

> 🎧 **CD 4, track 40** — página 43, actividad 1
>
> 1 Mi dormitorio no está muy ordenado. Tengo una cama. Tengo un armario para la ropa. Tengo una silla y un escritorio para mi ordenador. En mi dormitorio estudio, duermo y escucho música.
> 2 En mi dormitorio tengo un televisor, un armario para mi ropa, y un póster de mi equipo de fútbol favorito.
> 3 Mi dormitorio es muy pequeño y tengo muchas cosas. Tengo tres armarios porque tengo mucha ropa.
> 4 En mi dormitorio, tengo muchos libros. Tengo libros en estanterías, y tengo más libros en los armarios con la ropa.

Answers:
Isabelle – 4; Iñaki – 1; Alejandro – 2; Lola – 3

AT 2.3–4 **2 Use this grid to talk about your own bedroom.**
Volunteers could talk about their bedroom to the class. The class listen carefully to make sure that they have made adjectives agree correctly and that they have used a variety of connectives and quantifiers.

AT 4.3–4 **3 Write a short description of your room.**
Students base their description on the work they did in Activity 2.

Página 44 — 2B.5 ¿Cómo es tu región?
- Use with Students' Book, pages 80–81

AT 3.1 **1 Find four words to describe each picture.**
This is subjective to a degree so accept different slightly different answers from each student as long as they are sensible.

Suggested answers:
a museos, monumentos, turistas, pintoresco;
b tranquilo, verde, paisaje, granjas; **c** animado, tráfico, gente, industrial

AT 3.2 **2 Follow the word snake round the grid to find the sentence. Then make up your own word snake sentence to describe a place.**
Students should think about the theme of the spread and try to predict what kind of words the sentence may contain.

Answer:
Es muy pintoresco, con muchos monumentos y museos.

Página 45 — 2B.6A Labolengua
- Use with Students' Book, pages 82–83

1 Write out the two verbs.

Answers:
ser: I am – soy; you are – eres; he/she/it is – es; we are – somos; you are (plural) – sois; they are – son
estar: I am – estoy; you are – estás; he/she/it is – está; we are – estamos; you are (plural) – estáis; they are – están

2 Listen and check. Then listen and repeat with actions.
Students check that they have conjugated the verbs correctly. They then join in with the appropriate actions.

> 🎧 **CD 4, track 41** — página 45, actividad 2
>
> soy, eres, es, somos, sois, son
> estoy, estás, está, estamos, estáis, están

3 Decide which words go with *soy*… and which go with *estoy*… Then write out the words in sentences with *soy* and *estoy*.
Writing the words out in sentences will help students to remember when to use which form of 'to be'. As an extension activity, ask students to adapt each sentence, e.g. *Soy inglés/esa*, etc.

Answers:
Soy española. Soy bastante inteligente. Soy de Madrid. Soy estudiante.
Estoy en mi casa. Estoy enfermo/a. Estoy en mi cama. Estoy triste.

Página 46 — 2B.6B Técnica
- Use with Students' Book, pages 82–83

AT 3.2 **1 Find the information in this Spanish address.**

Answers:
Her first name is <u>Ana</u>.
Her surnames are <u>García</u> (her father's surname) and <u>López</u> (her mother's surname).
She lives at number <u>23</u> on <u>Luís Roldán</u> Street, on the <u>3rd</u> floor on the <u>left</u>.
Her postcode is <u>50012</u>.
The city is <u>Zaragoza</u>.
The region is <u>Aragón</u>.

2 Now write out the name and address of someone you know, using the Spanish style.
This will make students think about the differences between Spanish and English conventions.

3A Me gusta comer ...

Unit Objectives

Contexts and cultural focus: food: likes and dislikes; different types of food
Grammar: nouns and verbs; *más que* and *menos que*; *tú* and *usted*; *ir a*; adjectives and *se come mucho*
Language learning: *tengo hambre* and *tengo sed*; saying who you are on the telephone and complaining politely

- *Aim:* to talk about your food likes and dislikes and learn about different types of food whilst incorporating the grammar and vocabulary covered in the spread.
- Each unit has an associated video which will feature throughout the unit. Below is the transcript of the video for this unit.
- As a starter activity to introduce the Unit and familiarise students with the language they will meet, you may find it useful for the class to view the video as a whole.

Video script (CD 2, track 33)

José:	¡Tengo hambre! Hoy no he comido nada.
Eva:	Yo he desayunado un montón. Pa amb tomàquet.
José:	¿Pa amb qué?
Eva:	Pa amb tomàquet. Es un desayuno típico catalán. Es una tostada de pan, con tomate y ajo untados por encima. Añades un poco de aceite de oliva y sal y ¡ya está!
José:	Tiene que estar muy bueno.
Eva:	Lo está. En Madrid no se come eso, ¿eh?
José:	No. Creo que voy a comprarme una manzana.
Eva:	¿Una manzana? Venga, José, prueba algo más exótico; mira este mango de aquí. Tienen más buena pinta que esas manzanas.
José:	Pero es muy difícil de comer.
Eva:	Entonces, ¡cómprate un melocotón!
José:	Pero, no me gustan demasiado.
Eva:	¿Cómo es posible que no te gusten los melocotones?
José:	¿Me pone esta manzana?
Vendedor:	Cincuenta.
José:	Gracias.
[Pause]	
Eva:	Me encanta el pescado. ¡Mi favorito es el pez espada!
José:	Sí, a mí también me gusta el pescado pero en cambio el marisco, no.
Eva:	¿Cómo? ¿Así que no te gusta la paella, o los mejillones a la marinera?
José:	Sí, la paella, sí, pero no me como los mejillones.
Eva:	¡Mira lo grande que es ese calamar!
José:	Sí, es impresionante. Y ese atún también es muy grande.
Eva:	Creo que es un salmón.
José:	Vaya, tú lo sabes todo, ¿eh?
[Pause]	
José:	¡Son ya las seis!
Eva:	¿De verdad? El tiempo vuela. Oye, que tengo que volver a casa para cenar.
José:	¿Tan pronto?
Eva:	Esta noche echan un documental de Dalí por la tele.
José:	Nunca he oído hablar de ella. Bueno, ¿tienes claro lo que vas a pedir?
Eva:	Sí. Creo que voy a pedir unas tapas. Aquí las hacen muy bien.
José:	¡Perfecto! Yo pediré una de olivas y una de patatas.
Eva:	¿Y no vas a probar los montaditos?
José:	Bueno, vale.
Eva:	Vale. Y, ¿para beber…? ¿Coca Cola?
José:	Sí, me parece bien.
Eva:	Vamos a pedir.
José:	Vamos.

Me gusta comer ... 3A

Unit 3A Me gusta comer ... Overview grid						
Page reference	Contexts and objectives	Language learning	Grammar	Key language	Framework	AT level
Pages 88–89 **Es la hora de comer**	• talk about what you eat at different mealtimes • understand the differences between Spanish and English mealtimes		• use nouns and verbs to talk about mealtimes	la cena; la comida; la merienda; el desayuno; a eso de; el chocolate; el pan de ajo; la carne; las verduras; los cereales; los churros; un bocadillo de queso; un paquete de patatas fritas; un pollo asado; una paella; una pizza	1.1, 1.4, 2.1, 2.4, 2.5, 3.1, 3.2, 4.3, 4.4, 4.5	1.2, 2.1–2, 3.3, 4.2–3
Pages 90–91 **Comida sana**	• talk about food you like and dislike, and say what is healthy • give a short presentation in Spanish		• use *más que* and *menos que*	el atún; los mariscos; el pescado; el salmón; las gambas; los calamares; un melocotón; un plátano; una ensalada verde; una manzana; una naranja; contiene mucha grasa; contiene mucho azúcar; es (muy) ...; ... sano/a; ... malsano/a; ... soso/a; ... delicioso/a; son (muy) ...; ... sanos/as; ... malsanos/as; ... sosos/as; ... deliciosos/as; no soporto; no me importa comer; odio; me encanta	1.1, 1.4, 1.5, 2.4, 2.5, 3.1, 3.2, 4.3, 4.5, 5.1, 5.3, 5.4, 5.5	1.2–4, 2.2–4, 4.3–4
Pages 92–93 **¡Tengo hambre!**	• ask for food in a café • understand language used when ordering food	• use *tengo hambre* and *tengo sed*	• use *tú* and *usted*	una coca-cola; una fanta naranja; un café solo; un café con leche; un vaso de vino tinto; un vaso de vino blanco; una cerveza; un agua mineral con gas; un agua mineral sin gas; tengo hambre; tengo sed; para comer; para beber	1.1, 1.4, 2.1, 2.4, 2.5, 3.1, 3.2, 4.2, 4.3, 4.5, 5.3, 5.4	1.2–4, 2.2, 3.4, 4.2–4
Pages 94–95 **¡Oiga, camarero!**	• invite someone to go out with you, order food and complain	• say who you are on the telephone, and complain politely	• use *ir a*	una cuchara; un tenedor; un cuchillo; ¿Dónde está...? pedí; hay; una mosca; lo siento; lo traigo; en seguida; traigo otro	1.1, 1.4, 1.5, 2.1, 2.4, 2.5, 4.3, 4.5, 5.4	1.3, 2.2–4, 3.3, 4.3
Pages 96–97 **Me encanta la comida**	• discuss different types of food • be aware of foods in different cultures		• practise using adjectives and *se come mucho*	el arroz; la pasta; las especias; es muy/es poco; contiene mucho; contiene poco; utiliza mucho; utiliza poco	1.1, 1.4, 1.5, 2.4, 2.5, 4.3, 4.5, 3.2, 3.2, 5.5	1.2–4, 2.2–4, 4.2–3
Pages 89–99 **Labolengua**	• review language and grammar from the unit				1.1, 1.4, 3.1, 3.2, 4.2, 4.3, 4.4, 5.1, 5.2, 5.4	

3A Me gusta comer ...

Pages 100–1 **Extra Star** **Extra Plus**	• differentiated extension/ homework material	• revise and consolidate all vocabulary and grammar covered in the unit	• revise and consolidate all vocabulary and grammar covered in the unit		2.1, 2.4, 2.5, 3.1, 3.2, 4.3	3.2, 4.2–4
Page 102 **Prueba**	• end-of-spread test				1.1, 1.4, 2.1, 2.4, 2.5, 3.1, 3.2, 4.3, 4.4, 4.5	1.2, 2.3–4, 3.3, 4.3
Page 103 **Vocabulario**	• a summary of the key language covered in each spread of this unit					
Page 157 **Leer 2A**	• practice of longer reading texts based on the theme of the unit				2.1, 3.1, 3.2, 5.4	3.4

Week-by-week overview
(Three-year KS3 Route: assuming six weeks' work or approximately 10–12.5 hours)
(Two-year KS3 Route: assuming four weeks' worth or approxmately 6.5-8.5 hours)
*Please note that essential activities are highlighted.

About Unit 3A, *Me gusta comer ...*: Students work in the context of food likes and dislikes and different types of food. They talk about what they eat when and learn about the differences between English and Spanish mealtimes. They discuss their food likes and dislikes and learn to order and complain in a café or restaurant. Students learn how to use *más que* and *menos que* correctly as well as *tú* and *usted* and *ir a*. They also practise using adjectives and *se come mucho*. The unit also provides tips on language learning techniques.

Three-Year KS3 Route			Two-Year KS3 Route		
Week	Resources	Objectives	Week	Resources	Objectives
1	**3A.1 Es la hora de comer**	talk about what you eat at different mealtimes understand the differences between Spanish and English mealtimes use nouns and verbs to talk about mealtimes	1	**3A.1 Es la hora de comer** omit activities 5, 6, Think! & Challenge	talk about what you eat at different mealtimes understand the differences between Spanish and English mealtimes use nouns and verbs to talk about mealtimes
2	**3A.2 Comida sana** **3A.6 Lablolengua A** (p.98)	talk about food you like and dislike, and say what is healthy give a short presentation in Spanish use *más que* and *menos que*	2	**3A.2 Comida sana** omit activities 3, Think! & Challenge **3A.6 Lablolengua A** (p.82)	talk about food you like and dislike, and say what is healthy give a short presentation in Spanish use *más que* and *menos que*

Me gusta comer ... 3A

3	3A.3 ¡Tengo hambre! 3A.6 Lablolengua B (p.98) 3A.6 Lablolengua C (p.99)	ask for food in a café understand language used when ordering food use *tengo hambre* and *tengo sed* use *tú* and *usted*	3	3A.3 ¡Tengo hambre! omit activities Gramática, Think! & Challenge 3A.6 Lablolengua B (p.98) Omit activity 3	ask for food in a café understand language used when ordering food use *tengo hambre* and *tengo sed* use *tú* and *usted*
4	3A.4 ¡Oiga, camarero! 3A.6 Lablolengua E (p.99)	invite someone to go out with you, order food and complain say who you are on the telephone, and complain politely use *ir a*	4	3A.4 ¡Oiga, camarero! omit activities 2, Think!, Gramática (2) & 6 3A.6 Lablolengua E (p.99) omit activity 6 3A.8 Prueba (p.102) Vocabulario (p.103)	invite someone to go out with you, order food and complain say who you are on the telephone, and complain politely use *ir a* recapping on the vocabulary of the unit prepare and carry out assessment in all four skills
5	3A.5 Me encanta la comida	discuss different types of food be aware of foods in different cultures practise using adjectives and *se come mucho*			
6	3A.7 Extra (Star) (p.100) 3A.7 Extra (Plus) (p.101) 3A.8 Prueba (p.102) Vocabulario (p.103) Leer (p.157)	further reinforcement and extension of the language of the unit recapping on the vocabulary of the unit prepare and carry out assessment in all four skills further reading to explore the language of the unit and cultural themes			

3A.1 Me gusta comer ...

3A.1 Es la hora de comer
páginas 88–89

Planner

Objectives
- talk about what you eat at different mealtimes
- use nouns and verbs to talk about mealtimes
- understand the differences between Spanish and English mealtimes

Resources
Students' Book, pages 88–89
CD 2, tracks 30–32
Foundation Workbook, page 48
Higher Workbook, page 48
Interactive OxBox, Unit 3A
Copymasters 66–73
Assessment, Unit 3A

Key language
la cena; la comida; la merienda; el desayuno; a eso de; el chocolate; el pan de ajo; la carne; las verduras; los cereales; los churros; un bocadillo de queso; un paquete de patatas fritas; un pollo asado; una paella; una pizza

Grammar
- use nouns and verbs to talk about mealtimes

Renewed Framework references
1.1, 1.4, 2.1, 2.4, 2.5, 3.1, 3.2, 4.3, 4.4, 4.5

PLTS
Activity 1: Independent enquirers
Activity 7: Effective participators
Think!: Reflective learners

Challenge: Self-managers; Creative thinkers

Starters
- Display names of mealtimes in English and give students a time limit to write down the Spanish equivalent for each one. With less able classes, display the English equivalents in jumbled order for students to match to the Spanish mealtimes.
- Go round the class asking each student to give you a Spanish food. With more able students, ask them to say for which meal they would eat this food. Then play a game. Split the class into groups. Display the different meals in Spanish and challenge students to write as many items of food as possible for each meal. Compare answers as a class.

Plenaries
- Students write a few sentences describing their ideal meal. They then compare this with others in the class. Which food types are the most popular? Does the class like Spanish food?
- Students practise using the verbs from the grammar box. They write at least five sentences, e.g. *Desayuno a las siete.*

Homework/Self-study
Activity 1: Students carry out further research on mealtimes in Spain.
Students find out about the Spanish foods listed in Activity 7 and some other typical Spanish foods. They also consider if there is any big difference between the foods eaten in Spain and in Britain.

PLTS 1 Mira los dibujos.
Students look at the pictures and discuss what they think the different mealtimes are. This should lead on to a class discussion/explanation about the difference in times and type of meals in Spain as compared to the UK. The idea here is to establish the mealtimes and the style of meal rather than a detailed analysis of the food.

AT 1.2 2 Escucha y elige la palabra adecuada.
Students listen and match the mealtimes to the pictures. First, check that they understand the sound of the meal words. Call out *la merienda*, and students say *número 3*. They could then practise this in pairs. Remind students that in Spain *la tarde* is used to cover the afternoon and most of the evening.

CD 2, track 30 página 88, actividades 2 y 3

– Normalmente tomo el desayuno a las siete de la mañana.
– Tomo la cena con mi familia a las ocho y media de la tarde.
– Después del instituto, tomo la merienda a eso de las cinco.
– Tomo la comida a las dos de la tarde.

Answers: 1, 4, 3, 2

AT 1.2 3 Escucha otra vez.
Students listen again and note down how to say 'at about 5 o'clock'.

Answer: a eso de las cinco

3A.1 Me gusta comer ...

AT 2.2-3 **4 Habla con tu compañero.**
Students work in pairs to tell their partner what time they eat their meals. Their partner notes down the time. They then swap roles. You could start by saying what time you eat your meals and checking that students have understood. More advanced students could feed back after the pairwork activity and change the verb accordingly, e.g. *Sarah toma la cena a las seis de la tarde.*

AT 1.2 **5 Escucha e identifica.**
Students listen and note down which mealtime they are speaking about each time.

🎧 **CD 2, track 31** *página 88, actividad 5*
1 Son las ocho y media de la tarde.
2 Son las siete y cuarto de la mañana.
3 Son las cinco menos cuarto de la tarde.
4 Son las dos de la tarde.

Answers:
1 la cena; 2 el desayuno; 3 la merienda; 4 la comida

Gramática
Read through the grammar explanation as a class. Ask students to translate phrases 1, 2 and 3 to check that they have understood. Go through the answers as a class. Point out that *merendar* is a radical-changing verb and check students remember how to form these types of verb. They covered radical changing verbs in Unit 2A.

Answers:
1 Como; 2 Cena; 3 Meriendan

AT 4.2-3 **6 Escribe**
Students write down what time they have their meals and compare this with someone else. More able students should use full sentences. Next, play a game. Call out a mealtime e.g. *la cena*. Students find other people who eat dinner at the same time as them and stand with them. Alternatively, ask students to organise themselves into a line with the earliest breakfast first, etc.

AT 2.1-2 / PLTS **7 ¿El desayuno, la comida, la merienda o la cena?**
Students look at the pictures and say for which meal they would be most likely to eat each item of food. They could discuss this in small groups and feed back to the class. This is a good opportunity to explain about typical dishes such as *churros* and *paella* and when they would normally be eaten, e.g. *churros* in a *churrería* probably on a weekend morning. Explain to students that certain answers are up for debate.

Answers:
1 la merienda; 2 el desayuno; 3 la cena/la comida; 4 la comida; 5 la merienda; 6 la comida/la cena; 7 la comida/la cena; 8 el desayuno

AT 1.2 **8 ¿Verdadero o falso?**
Students listen and decide if the speakers are telling the truth or not. For further language exploitation ask students to explain what is wrong with the incorrect answers, and suggest alternatives.

🎧 **CD 2, track 32** *página 89, actividad 8*
1 En España, se come carne con verduras en el desayuno.
2 En Gran Bretaña se come pizza y pan de ajo en la comida.
3 En Gran Bretaña se come paella en la merienda.
4 En España se come chocolate con churros en la cena.
5 En España se come un bocadillo de queso en la merienda.
6 En Gran Bretaña se come pollo asado en la cena.

Answers:
1 falso, 2 verdad, 3 falso, 4 falso, 5 verdad, 6 verdad

PLTS **Think!**
Read through the box as a class. The use of *se come* is to highlight that things are said in different ways in different languages, not translated word for word. It also gives the students a useful bit of Spanish shorthand. The passive will be looked at again in Unit 4A.

AT 3.3 **9 Lee. Copia y completa.**
Students read the description and fill in the blanks. More able students could be given a copy of the text with the mealtimes missing also, or the foods only showing a letter in the middle of the word. Highlight words they can re-use in the *Challenge* such as *normalmente, pero, a eso de, preferida*, etc.

Answers:
cereales; chocolate con churros; carne y verduras; bocadillo de queso; paella; pollo asado

AT 4.2-3 / PLTS **Challenge**
Design a poster showing what you eat for different meals and at what time. Add comparisons with what a Spanish person might eat and when. Use pictures from magazines, food packets or Internet research.
The posters could be displayed as part of a Spanish week exhibition or something similar.

3A.2 Me gusta comer ...

3A.2 Comida sana
páginas 90–91

Planner

Objectives
- talk about food you like and dislike, and say what is healthy
- use *más que* and *menos que*
- give a short presentation in Spanish

Video
Video script, Unit 3A
Video-blog, Unit 3A

Resources
Students' Book, pages 90–91
CD 2, tracks 33–35
Foundation Workbook, page 49
Higher Workbook, page 49
Foundation Workbook audio, CD 3, track 67
Higher Workbook audio, CD 4, track 42
Interactive OxBox, Unit 3A
Copymasters 66–73
Assessment, Unit 3A

Key language
el atún; los mariscos; el pescado; el salmón; las gambas; los calamares; un melocotón; un plátano; una ensalada verde; una manzana; una naranja; contiene mucha grasa; contiene mucho azúcar; es (muy) …; … sano/a; … malsano/a; … soso/a; … delicioso/a; son (muy) …; … sanos/as; … malsanos/as; … sosos/as; … deliciosos/as; no soporto; no me importa comer; odio; me encanta

Grammar
- use *más que* and *menos que*

Renewed Framework references
1.1, 1.4, 1.5, 2.4, 2.5, 3.1, 3.2, 4.3, 4.5, 5.1, 5.3, 5.4, 5.5

PLTS
Activity 3: Self-managers; Effective participators
Activity 4: Independent enquirers
Challenge: Team workers

Starters
- Split the class into small groups. Challenge each group to write down an item of food in Spanish beginning with each letter of the alphabet. Time is up either when the first group finishes or when you decide. The groups then feed back. They score a point for each correct item of food and two points if no other group has chosen the same item.
- Display the headings *sanos/as* and *malsanos/as*. Also display a list of food items in Spanish. Give students a time limit to categorise these foods under the headings. Compare answers as a class. You could repeat this with different, more subjective categories, e.g. *sosos/as* and *deliciosos/as* which would encourage a variety of answers.

Plenaries
- Display the names of different items of food in Spanish. Students say as many sentences as they can to compare these foods, using the expressions *más que* and *menos que*. With less able students, ask questions using the items listed instead, e.g. *Una naranja contiene menos o más grasa que una hamburguesa?*
- Students play the part of a celebrity and write a few sentences describing what they think are his/her food preferences – healthy or unhealthy, typically Spanish/English/American, etc. They read their description to the class who tries to guess who the celebrity might be. If necessary, display example sentences as well as the names of food items in Spanish.

Homework/Self-study
Activity 5: For further practice of the expressions *más que* and *menos que*, students write out the sentences the other way round e.g. *Una naranja contiene menos grasa que una hamburguesa*. They can also make up their own examples.

AT 1.4   **1 Mira el video.**
Students watch the first two sections of the video and note down which of the items listed they see. First, check that students understand the vocabulary. In pairs, get them to decide how to say the different words using their knowledge of Spanish pronunciation. Then ask for volunteers to say the words and get the rest of the class to decide how Spanish they sound.

Video script: Unit 3A (CD2, track 33)

José: ¡Tengo hambre! Hoy no he comido nada.
Eva: Yo he desayunado un montón. Pa amb tomàquet.
José: ¿Pa amb qué?
Eva: Pa amb tomàquet. Es un desayuno típico catalán. Es una tostada de pan, con tomate y ajo untados por encima. Añades un poco de aceite de oliva y sal y ¡ya está!

3A.2 Me gusta comer …

José: Tiene que estar muy bueno.
Eva: Lo está. En Madrid no se come eso, ¿eh?
José: No. Creo que voy a comprarme una manzana.
Eva: ¿Una manzana? Venga, José, prueba algo más exótico; mira este mango de aquí. Tienen más buena pinta que esas manzanas.
José: Pero es muy difícil de comer.
Eva: Entonces, ¡cómprate un melocotón!
José: Pero, no me gustan demasiado.
Eva: ¿Cómo es posible que no te gusten los melocotones?
José: ¿Me pone esta manzana?
Vendedor: Cincuenta.
José: Gracias.
[Pause]
Eva: Me encanta el pescado. ¡Mi favorito es el pez espada!
José: Sí, a mí también me gusta el pescado pero en cambio el marisco, no.
Eva: ¿Cómo? ¿Así que no te gusta la paella, o los mejillones a la marinera?
José: Sí, la paella, sí, pero no me como los mejillones.
Eva: ¡Mira lo grande que es ese calamar!
José: Sí, es impresionante. Y ese atún también es muy grande.
Eva: Creo que es un salmón.
José: Vaya, tú lo sabes todo, ¿eh?

Answers:
1 el atún; **2** los mariscos; **4** el pescado; **5** el salmón; **8** los calamares; **9** un melocotón; **12** una manzana

AT 1.4 2 Mira el video-blog.
Students watch the video and answer the questions.

Video-blog: Unit 3A (CD 2, track 34)

¿Qué te gusta comer y por qué?
Eva: Me gusta comer pescado, pollo, pizza, pasta, verduras. Me gusta casi todo.
José: Me gustan mucho las manzanas porque son muy sanas.
Khalid: Me gusta comer pizza, zarzuela y paella.
Marisa: Me gusta comer mucha ensalada pero también me gusta mucho el chocolate.

¿Qué no te gusta comer?
Eva: No me gustan nada las cosas dulces como los pasteles, por ejemplo.
José: Odio el marisco, y el por qué, no lo sé.
Khalid: No me gusta comer verdura.
Marisa: No me gusta comer calamares.

¿Qué comes para el desayuno?
Eva: Para desayunar, normalmente como pa amb tomàquet que es un desayuno tradicional catalán.
José: Para el desayuno tostadas con mermelada y un zumo de naranja.
Khalid: Para desayunar bebo un vaso de leche con galletas.
Marisa: Normalmente, para el desayuno como pan con mantequilla y mermelada y me tomo un té.

Answers:
Eva: *likes to eat fish, chicken, pizza, pasta, vegetables; doesn't like sweet things like cakes; for breakfast she has pa amb tomàquet a traditional catalan breakfast; does eat healthily.*
José: *likes apples; doesn't like shellfish; for breakfast has toast with jam and orange juice; seems to eat healthily.*
Khalid: *likes pizza, zarzuela and paella; doesn't like vegetables; for breakfast had a glass of milk with biscuits; his diet doesn't seem very healthy.*
Marisa: *likes salad and chocolate; dislikes squid; for breakfast has bread with butter and jam and drinks tea.*

AT 2.2–3 PLTS 3 Haz un sondeo.
Students carry out a survey. They choose six of the foods listed and ask their classmates, *¿Te gustan los mariscos? ¿Te gusta el pescado?* etc. and note down their answers. Alternatively, give each person just one food item and ask them to survey half the class. (There are enough food items here for a class of 26 – add more for a larger group.) Students then feed back to the whole class e.g. T: *¿A cuántas personas le gustan las manzanas?* S: *diez* and compile a graph. (Students don't have the vocabulary to feed back in more detail here, though you might want to introduce *le gusta* to more able groups. They should be able to cope with it passively.) Limit or extend the list of food items depending on how long you want the survey to go on.

AT 1.2 PLTS 4 Escucha. Copia y completa.
Students listen and then complete the sentences. First, ask the students to look at the vocabulary box. Which words can they guess the meaning of? Which ones would they like to look up? Tell them to look up *sano*. So what does *malsano* mean? How can they guess at the meaning of *contiene*? (Looks a bit like the English word *contain*). This is a good opportunity to get the students to think for themselves and work out how to find meaning.

3A.2 Me gusta comer ...

CD 2, track 35 — página 91, actividad 4

1 El postre contiene mucho azúcar.
2 El helado es delicioso.
3 Los perritos calientes son sosos.
4 Las hamburguesas son muy malsanas.
5 Las patatas fritas contienen mucha grasa.
6 Los pasteles no son sanos.
7 Los bombones también contienen demasiado azúcar.

Answers:
1 azúcar; *2* delicioso; *3* sosos; *4* malsanas; *5* grasa; *6* sanos; *7* azúcar

Think!
Read through the Think! box as a class and elicit from students that they will need to use the 3rd person plural of the verb *contener*. Point out that *contener* contains the verb *tener* (or get the students to point it out for you) and therefore follows the same pattern.

Answer:
Los bombones contienen mucho azúcar.

Gramática
To check that students have fully understood the grammar explanation, read out similar sentences some of which are true, e.g. *Una hamburguesa contiene más grasa que una naranja.* and some of which are obviously false, e.g. *El pescado es menos sano que los bombones./ Una manzana contiene más grasa que las patatas fritas.* Students state whether each sentence is true or false.

AT 4.3
5 Compara la comida.
Students use the expressions from the grammar box and the prompts listed to write sentences comparing different foods. Less able students may need the activity written out in full with just the words *más* and *menos* to fill in.

Suggested answers:
1 Una hamburguesa contiene más grasa que una naranja.
2 El pescado es más sano que un perrito caliente.
3 Un melocotón contiene menos azúcar que los bombones.
4 El postre es más delicioso que una ensalada verde.
5 Las patatas fritas son más malsanas que las gambas.
6 El helado es menos soso que las verduras.

AT 2.3–4, 4.3–4
PLTS

Challenge
Work in a group to give a presentation, with illustrations, about the type of food you and your friends like. The other people in your class will decide how healthy you are.
This is an open-ended activity which can be extended as far as the students' ability will allow. Variations on this theme: give each class a hidden agenda – they have to be very healthy eaters, fast-food junkies, lovers of traditional Spanish food, etc. When all the presentations have been given the class decides which category each group represented. Or, the groups present the favourite food of one or two members only, and the rest of the class have to decide which people are being talked about. Students should also state which foods they DON'T like! More able students can include comparisons, e.g. *La hamburguesa es menos sana que las verduras, pero odio las verduras.*

3A.3 Me gusta comer ...

3A.3 ¡Tengo hambre!
páginas 92–93

Planner

Objectives
- ask for food in a café
- understand language used when ordering food
- use *tengo hambre* and *tengo sed*
- use *tú* and *usted*

Video
Video script, Unit 3A

Resources
Students' Book, pages 92–93
CD 2, tracks 33, 36–37
Foundation Workbook, page 50
Higher Workbook, page 50
Foundation Workbook audio, CD 3, track 68
Higher Workbook audio, CD 4, track 43
Interactive OxBox, Unit 3A
Copymasters 66–73
Assessment, Unit 3A

Key language
una coca-cola; una fanta naranja; un café solo; un café con leche; un vaso de vino tinto; un vaso de vino blanco; una cerveza; un agua mineral con gas; un agua mineral sin gas; tengo hambre; tengo sed; para comer; para beber

Grammar
- use *tú* and *usted*

Renewed Framework references
1.1, 1.4, 2.1, 2.4, 2.5, 3.1, 3.2, 4.2, 4.3, 4.5, 5.3, 5.4

PLTS
Activity 3: Team workers
Activity 5: Creative thinkers; Independent enquirers
Think!: Reflective learners; Independent enquirers
Activity 6: Team workers
Challenge: Creative thinkers; Independent enquirers

Starters
- Revise the use of *tú* and *usted*. Display the list of people featured in the Starter unit – friend's grandparents; a teacher; the head teacher; the young brother of a friend – and see if students can remember which form of 'you' they should use for each of them (friend's grandparents: *ustedes*; a teacher: *usted*; the head teacher: *usted*; the young brother of a friend: *tú*)
- Display the key language and give students a time limit to write down the English for all of the words. Or, you could also display the translations in jumbled order and ask students to match them up in a given time.

Plenaries
- If practical in the space available, turn the classroom into a restaurant with students sitting in pairs or small groups. Some students are customers; some are waiters. Students practise ordering food and drinks using the language they have learnt in the spread.

Homework/Self-study
Activity 1: Students find out more about the types of *tapas* or *pinchos* in Spain. They make notes to share with the class.
Challenge: Students research typical Spanish food and drink.

AT 1.4

1 Mira el video.
Students watch the final part of video and note down why Eva has to hurry home and what they decide to drink. Discuss the video with them – where are Eva and José? What are they doing, etc? They will be able to understand a lot from context. This would also be a good time to talk about the Spanish habit of *tapas* or *pinchos* with the class, explaining that there are hundreds of different types according to region.

Video script: Unit 3A (CD 2, track 33)

José: ¡Son ya las seis!
Eva: ¿De verdad? El tiempo vuela. Oye, tengo que volver a casa para cenar.
José: ¿Tan pronto?
Eva: Esta noche echan un documental de Dalí por la tele.
José: Nunca he oído hablar de ella. Bueno, ¿tienes claro lo que vas a pedir?
Eva: Sí. Creo que voy a pedir unas tapas. Aquí las hacen muy bien.
José: ¡Perfecto! Yo pediré una de olivas y una de patatas.
Eva: ¿No vas a probar los montaditos?
José: Bueno, vale.
Eva: Vale. Y, ¿para beber…? ¿Coca Cola?
José: Sí, me parece bien.
Eva: Vamos a pedir.
José: Vamos.

3A.3 Me gusta comer ...

Answers:
Eva has to get home to watch a documentary on Dali on TV.

AT 1.2 **2 Empareja. Luego escucha e identifica.**
Before starting the listening activity, students match the drinks to the words in the vocabulary box. This works well as a whole-class discussion, as there are lots of opportunities for students to explain their choices and to use previous knowledge. They then listen and note down which drink is mentioned each time.

🎧 **CD 2, track 36** página 92, actividad 2

1 - ¿Qué desea?
  - Un café solo, por favor.
  - Aquí tiene.
2 - ¿Qué desea?
  - Para mí, una cerveza.
  - Aquí tiene.
3 - ¿Qué desea?
  - Pues, un agua mineral con gas.
  - Aquí tiene.
4 - ¿Qué desea?
  - Una coca-cola, por favor.
  - Aquí tiene.
5 - ¡Oiga, camarero!
  - Sí, ¿qué desea?
  - Un vaso de vino tinto.
  - Vale, aquí tiene.
6 - ¡Oiga, camarero!
  - ¿Qué desea?
  - Pues, un agua mineral sin gas y un café solo.
  - En seguida. Aquí tiene.
7 - ¿Qué desea?
  - Para mí, un café con leche, y para él, una fanta naranja.
  - En seguida. Aquí tiene.

Answers: *1 f; 2 e; 3 i; 4 a; 5 d; 6 h, f; 7 g, b*

Gramática
Read through the grammar box as a class. Listen to the recording from Activity 2 again to illustrate the use of *¿Qué desea?* and *Aquí tiene.*

AT 2.2 **3 👥 Habla con tu compañero.**
PLTS Students work with a partner to practise ordering drinks. This activity works best if students playing the waiter have actual pieces of card with a picture of the drink or just the word on to hand over. It can also work as a team activity with the students having to touch the correct pictures on the board to get a point for their team. This is basic preparation for the restaurant scene activity on Spread 3A.4.

AT 1.4 **4 Escucha y lee.**
Students listen to and read the story and then note down what the customers order. This is an ideal opportunity to discuss café etiquette. *Oiga camarero* may sound rude to non-Spanish ears, but very often they speak more directly in Spain.

🎧 **CD 2, track 37** página 93, actividad 4

- Tengo hambre. ¡Oiga, camarero!
- ¿Sí? ¿Qué desea?
- Pues, para mí un café con leche.
- Y para mí un vaso de vino tinto.
- Vale. ¿Y para comer?
- Pues, para mí una ración de tortilla, y para élla...
- Para mí un bocadillo de chorizo, gracias.
- Muy bien, en seguida. Aquí tiene. ¡Qué aproveche!
- Gracias.

Answers:
customer 1: *coffee with milk, tortillas;* **customer 2:** *a glass of red wine, a chorizo (salami) sandwich*

AT 3.4 **5 ¿Cómo se dice ...?**
PLTS Students reread the story from Activity 4 and find the Spanish for the English words listed.

Answers:
1 Tengo hambre. 2 ¡Oiga, camarero! 3 pues; 4 para mí; 5 Vale. 6 ¿Y para comer? 7 para élla; 8 en seguida; 9 Aquí tiene.; 10 ¡Que aproveche!

PLTS **Think!**
Students think of other ways of they can use the verb *tener*.

AT 4.3–4 **6 👥 Escribe una escena. Practica con un compañero.**
PLTS Students use what they have learnt in the spread to write their own café scene. They choose what they would like to eat or drink and then practise it with a partner. Less able students can practise the scene in the picture story, possibly changing the food and drink ordered. The most able could add more people and extend the scene in other ways. This is designed to be further preparation for the restaurant role play on the next spread.

AT 4.2–4 **Challenge**
PLTS Using all the food and drink words you have learnt so far design a menu for a café or restaurant.
This can be used as a prop in the restaurant role play on the next spread. Students look back through the book for all food and drink, and research can be done to include typical Spanish dishes.

3A.4 Me gusta comer ...

3A.4 ¡Oiga, camarero!   páginas 94–95

Planner

Objectives
- invite someone to go out with you, order food and complain
- use *ir a*
- say who you are on the telephone, and complain politely

Resources
Students' Book, pages 94–95
CD 2, tracks 38–40
Foundation Workbook, page 51
Higher Workbook, page 51
Foundation Workbook audio, CD 3, track 69
Foundation Workbook audio, CD 4, track 44
Interactive OxBox, Unit 3A
Copymasters 66–73
Assessment, Unit 3A

Key language
una cuchara; un tenedor; un cuchillo; ¿Dónde está…? pedí; hay; una mosca; lo siento; lo traigo; en seguida; traigo otro

Grammar
- use *ir a*

Renewed Framework references
1.1, 1.4, 1.5, 2.1, 2.4, 2.5, 4.3, 4.5, 5.4

PLTS
Activity 4: Effective participators
Think!: Independent enquirers
Challenge: Team workers; Creative thinkers

Starters
- Quickly revise meeting times and days. Explain to students that you are arranging a meeting and will ask them when and at what time to meet. Then go round the class asking simply *¿Cuándo?* and then *¿A qué hora?*. You could either give students prompts to respond, or they should make up their own responses. Once they have responded, check that the rest of the class has understood what they have said. With less able students, you could display the days of the week and some times for support.
- Display the key vocabulary and give students a time limit to write the English for each item. Then check answers as a class. Less able students could match the Spanish to the English instead.

Plenaries
- Display the key vocabulary and challenge students to write five complaints incorporating this. With less able students, display an example sentence that they can adapt. Students could swap sentences with a partner and answer their partner's complaints.
- Students work in pairs to practise arranging to meet up. Encourage them to use the phrases from the Think! box and Grammar box.

Homework/Self-study
Gramática: Students find as many examples as possible in the spread of sentences including the phrases listed. More able students could try to use these phrases in sentences of their own, adapting sentences they have already met in the spread.

AT 1.3, 3.3

1 Escucha y lee.
Students listen to and read the photo story. They note down what Ángel and Rashida are talking about, and when, where and at what time they agree to meet. This photo story could be further exploited by giving students a copy of it with the speech bubbles, or selected words from the bubbles, blanked out, and doing a gap-fill exercise. Students could guess what time and day they arrange to meet, and see if they are right. Point out the use of *estar* (they did this in the last unit – ask students to explain why it is being used here.) Students could be given the speech bubbles only and asked to arrange them in the correct order before listening to the activity – another use of prediction.

CD 2, track 38   página 94, actividad 1

Ángel: Hola, soy Ángel. ¿Está Rashida?
Rashida: Hola, Ángel, soy yo.
Ángel: Oye, ¿quieres ir a la cafetería Dalí?
Rashida: Pues, sí. ¿Cuándo?
Ángel: Miércoles, por la tarde.
Rashida: ¿A qué hora?
Ángel: A las siete.
Rashida: Vale, hasta luego.
Ángel: Hasta luego.

Answers:
They are talking about meeting at a café.
They agree to meet on Wednesday at the Dalí café at 7pm.

3A.4 Me gusta comer ...

AT 1.3 **2 Escucha y escoge.**
Students listen and choose when, where and at what time the people are meeting.

🎧 **CD 2, track 39**   página 94, actividad 2

1
- Hola, Pilar, soy María. ¿Quieres ir al Restaurante San Miguel?
- Sí, quiero ir. ¿Cuándo vamos?
- El domingo, a las dos de la tarde.

2
- Soy Ramón. ¿Está Guillermo?
- Hola, Ramón, soy yo.
- Oye, Guille, vamos al Bar Marisco por la tarde. ¿Quieres ir?
- Sí, claro. ¿Hoy por la tarde?
- No, mañana, jueves, a las nueve.

3
- ¿Está Carlos?
- Sí, soy yo.
- Hola Carlos, soy Cristina. Vamos a la cafetería Lanzarote el domingo por la mañana. ¿Quieres ir?
- Pues, sí. ¿A qué hora?
- A las once y media.
- Vale.

Answers: *1* c, y; *2* a, x; *3* c, z

AT 3.3 **3 Lee. ¿Adónde van?**
Students read the text messages and note down where the people are going and when. Students can respond in English, Spanish, orally, or in writing as appropriate.

Answers:
a Bar Blanco, Thursday at 5.30pm after school;
b Lucía's birthday at the la Playa restaurant, Sunday at 2pm;
c Tapas, Saturday evening at 9pm

AT 4.3 **PLTS** **4 Escribe un mensaje.**
Students write a message to a friend inviting them to a café. Designate different areas of the classroom "Bar Madrid", "Restaurante del Elefante Rojo", etc. You or a student could be a speaking clock calling out times. At the correct time, students go to the designated place.

PLTS **Think!**
Read through the box as a class and ask students to think about what the Spanish phrases mean. They can practise these with a partner.

Gramática
Look at the phrases as a class. Ask students to give you examples of sentences they have already met in this spread using these phrases. Can more able students make up sentences of their own using these phrases?

Gramática
Look at the grammar explanation as a class and work through a couple of examples of *Pedí* used in sentences.

AT 1.3 **5 Escucha e identifica el problema.**
Students listen and choose the appropriate problem. To extend this activity for more able students, ask them to listen for what the waiter is going to do about each of the problems.

🎧 **CD 2, track 40**   página 95, actividad 5

1
- ¡Oiga, camarero!
- ¿Sí, señor?
- ¡No tengo tenedor!
- Lo siento, señor, lo traigo en seguida.

2
- ¡Camarera!
- ¿Sí, señor?
- ¿Dónde está mi vino tinto?
- Lo siento, señor, lo traigo en seguida.

3
- ¡Oiga, camarero!
- ¿Sí, señora?
- No tengo cuchara.
- Lo siento, señora, la traigo en seguida.

4
- ¡Camarera!
- ¿Sí, señor?
- No pedí un bocadillo de jamón. Pedí un bocadillo de queso.
- Lo siento, señor, lo traigo en seguida.

5
- ¡Oiga, camarera!
- Sí, señora.
- ¡Hay una mosca en mi café con leche!
- Ay, lo siento. Traigo otro.

Answers:
1 c; *2* f; *3* a; *4* e; *5* d

AT 2.2-3 **6 Habla con tu compañero.**
Students work with a partner. One person has a problem, the other identifies it. Students can point to the correct picture to identify it. More able students can also give the correct response to the problem.

3A.5 Me gusta comer ...

AT 2.3–4	**Challenge**
PLTS	Prepare and act a scene in a restaurant or café. Invite your friend by phone, text or email to join you. Order your food and drink. Complain to the waiter. Use the menu you made on page 93. Act out the scene to your class.

This completely open-ended activity can be made as complicated or kept as simple as you like; students can prepare props, give their restaurant a "theme" (superheros/rockstars/ghosts) and write up their script for publication on the school website with supporting pictures.

3A.5 Me encanta la comida

páginas 96–97

Planner

Objectives
- discuss different types of food
- practise using adjectives and *se come mucho*
- be aware of foods in different cultures

Video
Video script, Unit 3A

Resources
Students' Book, pages 96–97
CD 2, tracks 41–42
Foundation Workbook, page 52
Higher Workbook, page 52
Interactive OxBox, Unit 3A
Assessment, Unit 3A

Key language
el arroz; la pasta; las especias; es muy/es poco; contiene mucho; contiene poco; utiliza mucho; utiliza poco

Renewed Framework references
1.1, 1.4, 1.5, 2.4, 2.5, 4.3, 4.5, 3.2, 3.2, 5.5

PLTS
Activity 1: Independent enquirers
Activity 3: Effective participators
Activity 4: Self-managers
Activity 6: Independent enquirers
Challenge: Self-managers

Starters
- Display types of food, e.g. *la comida china, la comida del instituto, la comida catalana, la comida india, la comida italiana, la comida inglesa, la comida vegetariana, la comida rápida, la comida española* in one column and then, in a second column, display different foods and descriptions of foods, e.g. *la tortilla, la paella, los mariscos, el arroz, la pasta, las especias, es muy picante, contiene mucha grasa, utiliza mucho aceite, es muy soso, es muy variada, es muy sabroso*, etc. Ask students to match the foods and descriptions to the types of food. Compare answers as a class.
- Play a game as a class. Describe a food or a type of food and ask the class to try and guess what you are describing, e.g. T: *Es un desayuno típico catalán. Es una tostada de pan, con ajo y tomate untado por encima. Añades aceite de oliva y sal y ¡ya está!* S: *Pa amb tomàquet?* T: *Sí*

Plenaries
- Students chose their favourite type of food, e.g. Spanish, and write as much as they can about it, e.g. *Yo prefiero la tortilla, la paella, los mariscos y toda la comida típica española. La comida española utiliza mucho pescado.* etc.
- Display the key vocabulary and challenge students to write five sentences on the theme of the spread.

Homework/Self-study
Activity 1: Students think of as many British regional dishes as possible in order to start thinking about regional diversity. Can they also think of regional differences in any other countries they know well?
Gramática: Students write five sentences using the phrase *se come mucho*. Less able students find examples of this phrase in previous reading texts.

AT 1.4	**1 Mira el video otra vez.**
PLTS	Students watch the beginning of the video again. Eva describes what she had for breakfast – *Pa amb tomaquét*. Students explain what this is. This is a good opportunity to explain about Catalan being a different language to the Spanish the students are learning. Ask them to think about other regional languages or even strong dialects in Britain to get them thinking about regional diversity.

3A.5 Me gusta comer ...

> **Video script: Unit 3A (CD 2, track 33)**
>
> José: ¡Tengo hambre! Hoy no he comido nada.
> Eva: Yo he desayunado un montón. Pa amb tomàquet.
> José: ¿Pa amb qué?
> Eva: Pa amb tomàquet. Es un desayuno típico catalán. Es una tostada de pan, con tomate y ajo untados por encima. Añades un poco de aceite de oliva y sal y ¡ya está!
> José: Tiene que estar muy bueno.
> Eva: Lo está. En Madrid no se come eso, ¿eh?

Answer: Pa amb tomaquét is a typical Catalan breakfast of toasted bread with garlic and tomato on top.

Think!
Students look at the illustrations and captions and note down what the different types of food are and where they are from. Encourage students to use cognates as well as the illustrations to work out what each item of food is.

AT 1.3 **2 Escucha. ¿Qué prefieren?**
Students listen and decide which type of food each person likes best

> **CD 2, track 41** página 96, actividad 2
> 1 Pues, a mí me encanta la comida china. ¡Es deliciosa!
> 2 Todos los días como en la comedor del instituto con mis amigos, y, de verdad, me gusta mucho.
> 3 Vivo en Barcelona y a mí me encanta la comida típica catalana.
> 4 Yo prefiero la comida india. Me gustan mucho los currys.
> 5 Mi madre es italiana, así que me gusta mucho comer pasta.
> 6 Me gusta la carne con verduras. ¡Para mí la comida inglesa es perfecta!
> 7 ¿La carne? ¿Las hamburguesas? ¡Ni hablar! ¡Yo soy vegetariano!
> 8 Pues, no son muy sanas, pero me encantan las hamburguesas y las patatas fritas. ¡La comida rápida es mi favorita!
> 9 Yo prefiero la tortilla, la paella, los mariscos y toda la comida típica española.

Answers:
1 la comida china; 2 la comida del colegio; 3 la comida catalana; 4 la comida india; 5 la comida italiana; 6 la comida inglesa; 7 la comida vegetariana; 8 la comida rápida; 9 la comida española

AT 2.3 **PLTS** **3 Habla con tus compañeros. ¿Qué les gusta?**
Students find three other people who like the same foods as them. This works best if you or the students prepare small cards with the different types of food written on them. Each student picks one of the cards and must find others with the same card. Students should practise the example dialogue, though, rather than just show each other their cards. Students then swap cards and play again. As there are nine food types here, they could also be put into a noughts and crosses grid.

Gramática
Read the grammar exaplanation as a class. Give the class a couple of example sentences containing *se come mucho* to ensure that they understand how it is used.

AT 4.2–3 **PLTS** **4 Empareja.**
Students match the example foods to the food types. They should then write a sentence, similar to the example sentence, for each of the food types. This could be done orally first. More able students could use a dictionary to come up with additional types of food (e.g. *la comida mexicana*) and vital ingredients of these by using a dictionary.

Possible answers:
En la comida china se come mucho arroz.
En la la comida italiana se come mucha pasta.
En la comida inglesa se come muchas verduras.
En la comida vegetariana se come muchas patatas.
En la comida rápida se come muchas patatas fritas.
En la comida española se come mucho pescado.
En la comida inglesa se come mucha carne.
En la comida india se come muchas especias.

AT 1.2 **5 Escucha. Copia y completa.**
Students listen and complete the descriptions. Play the recording more than once, and encourage less able students to identify just one item each time.

> **CD 2, track 42** página 97, actividad 5
> 1 La comida india es muy picante.
> 2 La comida china es muy variada.
> 3 La comida inglesa utiliza menos aceite que la comida italiana.
> 4 La comida vegetariana no contiene carne.
> 5 La comida rápida contiene mucha grasa.
> 6 La comida del instituto es bastante sosa.
> 7 La comida española utiliza mucho pescado.

Answers:
1 ... muy picante; 2 ...muy variada; 3 ... utiliza menos

aceite…; **4** *… no contiene…;* **5** *…contiene mucha…;* **6** *…bastante sosa;* **7** *…utiliza mucho…*

AT 2.2-3
PLTS
6 ¿Qué contienen? ¿Se come frío o caliente?
Students look at the pictures of typical Spanish food and say what are they made of and whether you would you eat them hot or cold.

Answers:
paella – shellfish, chicken, rice (main ingredients) – eaten hot; tortilla – potatoes cooked in oil and eggs – eaten hot or cold; fabada – meat, beans (main ingredients) – eaten hot; gazpacho – tomatoes, onions (main ingredients) – eaten cold

AT 2.2-4
PLTS
Challenge
Make a poster. Ask different people (friends and/or family members) what types of food they like and why. Find pictures of the types of food and write about them – what do you eat a lot of in that type of food? Is it healthy or unhealthy? What are typical ingredients?
You could ask students to write about a certain number of food types, or to interview a certain number of people with more able students interviewing more people. The food types could be divided up between the class and students set the task of finding someone who likes that type, or someone who doesn't, and why.

3A.6 Labolengua
páginas 98–99

Planner

Objectives
- review language and grammar from the unit

Resources
Students' Book, pages 98–99
CD 2, tracks 43–44
Foundation Workbook, pages 53–54
Higher Workbook, pages 53–54
Foundation Workbook audio, CD 3, track 70
Higher Workbook audio, CD 4, track 45
Interactive OxBox, Unit 3A
Copymasters 74–75
Assessment, Unit 3A

Grammar
- *más … que; menos … que*
- *tú* and *usted*

Renewed Framework references
1.1, 1.4, 3.1, 3.2, 4.2, 4.3, 4.4, 5.1, 5.2, 5.4

PLTS
All activities: Reflective learners/Self-managers

Homework/Self-study
Activity 1: Students make up other similar sentences of their own using *más que* and *menos que*.

Comprender – comparing two things; using *tú* and *usted*

A Comparing – 'more than' and 'less than'

PLTS 1 Put *más que* or *menos que* in the correct places in these sentences.
Practice of using *más que* or *menos que*.

Answers:
1 El helado es **más/menos** delicioso **que** las manzanas.
2 El español es **más/menos** difícil **que** la geografía.
3 El profesor de ciencias es **más/menos** simpático **que** la profesora de inglés.
4 Los mariscos son **más** sanos **que** las patatas fritas.

B Using *tú* and *usted*

PLTS 2 Which one would you use to…?
Practice of using *tú* and *usted* correctly.

Answers:
1 usted; 2 ustedes; 3 tú; 4 vosotros

PLTS 3 How would you say…?
Further practice of using *tú* and *usted*.

Answers:
Oye, Carlos, ¿quieres ir a la cafetería?
¿Quiere una cerveza, señor López?

3A.6 Me gusta comer ...

Aprender – how to remember words

C Grouping words together

Students read through the examples listed and add to these when they come across similar examples

D Making up your own examples (memory joggers)

Students read the advice in the Students' Book on making up memory joggers and try to come up with some of their own. They could share these with the class so that students could note down any they think might be useful to them.

Hablar – having a conversation

E Talking on the telephone

PLTS 4 Listen to this conversation. Put the sentences in the right order.
Students practise telephone skills.

CD 2, track 43 página 99, actividad 4

Felipe: Diga.
Ana: Hola, ¿está Felipe?
Felipe: Soy yo.
Ana: Felipe, soy Ana. ¿Qué tal?
Felipe: Bien.
Ana: Oye, ¿quieres ir al bar?
Felipe: Mm, ¿cuándo?
Ana: El viernes por la tarde.
Felipe: ¿A qué hora?
Ana: Bueno, a eso de las nueve.
Felipe: Lo siento, ceno en casa con mi familia.
Ana: Ohhh, pues, hasta luego Felipe.
Felipe: Adiós.

Answers:
e, h, m, g, d, l, j, f, a, b, i, k, c
No. Sounds bored, uses abrupt words. Listen to how people say things. People say things differently in different countries – e.g. in the café, Oiga is not rude.

PLTS 5 Listen again. How is this conversation different?

CD 2, track 44 página 99, actividad 5

Felipe: ¡Diga!
Ana: Hola, ¿está Felipe?
Felipe: ¡Soy yo!
Ana: Felipe, soy Ana. ¿Qué tal?
Felipe: ¡Bien!
Ana: Oye, ¿quieres ir al bar?
Felipe: Mm, ¿cuándo?
Ana: El viernes por la tarde.
Felipe: ¿A qué hora?
Ana: Bueno, a eso de las nueve.
Felipe: Lo siento, ceno en casa con mi familia.
Ana: Ohhh, pues, hasta luego Felipe.
Felipe: Adiós.

Answers:
¡Diga!; Mm, ohhh, pues.
This time Ana is a little hesitant and nervous; Felipe is delighted to hear from her and sounds very regretful he can't go out.

PLTS 6 Make up a natural sounding conversation with a partner.
Students use what they have learnt from Activities 4 and 5 to make up their own conversation. They should pay particular attention to how they say things and their tone of voice.

3A.7 Me gusta comer ...

3A.7 Extra Star   página 100

Planner

Objectives
- understand problems you might have in a café
- practise asking for food and drinks in a café
- identify different meals

Resources
Students' Book, page 100
Copymaster 76

Renewed Framework references
2.1, 2.4, 3.1, 3.2

PLTS
Activity 2: Creative thinkers; Reflective learners
Activity 3: Reflective learners

AT 3.2   **1 Empareja los dibujos con los problemas.**
Students match the pictures to the problems.

Answers:
1 c, 2 d, 3 e, 4 b, 5 f, 6 a

AT 4.2–3 **PLTS**   **2 Escribe una conversación para cada dibujo.**
Students write short dialogues to go with the pictures. They then make up and illustrate some more of their own.

AT 3.2 **PLTS**   **3 Lee. ¿Es el desayuno, la comida, la merienda o la cena?**
Students read the lists and decide which meal each one refers to.

Answers:
1 la merienda; 2 la cena; 3 el desayuno; 4 la comida

3A.7 Extra Plus   página 101

Planner

Objectives
- solve problems in a café
- practise asking for food and drinks in a café
- describe different food

Resources
Students' Book, page 101
Interactive OxBox, Unit 3A

Copymaster 77
Assessment, Unit 3A

Renewed Framework references
2.1, 2.4, 2.5, 3.1, 3.2, 4.3

PLTS
Activity 2: Creative thinkers
Activity 3: Effective participators

AT 3.2   **1 Busca una solución para cada problema.**
Students find a solution for each of the problems listed.

Answers:
1 a; 2 b; 3 a; 4 b

AT 4.3–4 **PLTS**   **2 Escribe una conversación en un restaurante.**
Students use the prompts to create a written dialogue in a restaurant. They then go on to create their own dialogues. They could compare their dialogues to see who has ordered the largest meal.

AT 4.3–4 **PLTS**   **3 Describe las comidas. ¡No digas la verdad!**
Students write deliberate untruths about what food is like for another student to correct. This will stretch students considerably as they will need to consider agreements of adjectives, etc.

3A.8 Me gusta comer ...

3A.8 Prueba
página 102

Planner

Resources
Students' Book, page 102
CD 2, track 45

Renewed Framework references
1.1, 1.4, 2.1, 2.4, 2.5, 3.1, 3.2, 4.3, 4.4, 4.5

PLTS
All activities: Reflective learners

Escuchar

> **AT 1.2–3** Listen to the people talking. What food do they eat for which meal?
> This activity tests listening skills using the language covered in this unit.

> 🎧 **CD 2, track 45** — página 102, Escuchar
> 1 Para el desayuno tomo cereales y un café con leche.
> 2 Para la comida tomo una pizza y unas patatas fritas en la comedor del instituto.
> 3 Para la cena tomo carne y verduras y un postre con mi familia.
> 4 Para la merienda tomo un bocadillo de queso y un vaso de agua mineral.

Answers:
1 cereal and white coffee – breakfast; 2 pizza and chips – lunch; 3 meat and vegetables and dessert – evening meal; 4 cheese sandwich and mineral water – afternoon snack

Hablar

> **AT 2.3–4** How would you order the following items? How might the waiter reply?
> Students work in pairs. Partner A uses what he/she has learnt in this unit to order the items in the pictures and B responds as the waiter. They then swap roles.

Leer

> **AT 3.3** Which foods are healthy? Read the article and decide.
> This activity tests reading skills using the language covered in this unit.

Answers: fish, fruit, salad

Escribir

> **AT 4.3** Describe the foods shown in the pictures. What are they? Do you like them? Are they healthy? Give as much information as you can.
> This activity tests writing skills using the language covered in this unit.

Leer 3A
página 157

Planner

Resources
Students' Book, page 157

Renewed Framework references
2.1, 3.1, 3.2, 5.4

PLTS
Activity 1: Reflective learners
Activity 2: Independent enquirers, Effective participators

Homework/Self-study
Activity 1: This could be the basis for students to make up other true/false questions for their classmates to work out.

AT 3.4 / PLTS
1 **True or false? Use the text to help you.**
You could hold a class quiz based on this page e.g. *¿Qué se come mucho en Valencia? ¿Qué contiene mucha sal?*, etc.

Answers:
1 true; 2 false; 3 true; 4 true; 5 false; 6 false; 7 true

PLTS
2 **What other regions of Spain are there? Can you find out about the food that is typical there?**
Students carry out further research on the other regions of Spain and their most popular dishes. The end result could be a class collaboration on a *Menú De Las Especialidades De España*.

Me gusta comer ... 3A

Foundation Workbook

Página 48   3A.1 Es la hora de comer
- Use with Students' Book, pages 88–89

AT 3.1   **1 Label these pictures of things to eat in Spanish.**

Answers:
bread – pan; cheese – queso; chicken – pollo; potatoes – patatas; chocolate – chocolate; meat – carne

2 Think like a Spanish person. Fill in the grids.
Once they have filled in the grids, challenge students to think of more food items and to fit them into a similar grid.

Answers:
roast chicken; chicken roast; pollo asado
a cheese sandwich; a sandwich of cheese; un bocadillo de queso
chilli con carne; chilli with meat; chile con carne
crisps; potatoes fried; patatas fritas

AT 4.2   **3 Write the Spanish for the following.**
Students use what they have learnt from the grids to translate the foods into Spanish.

Answers:
un bocadillo de jamón; un pastel de chocolate

Página 49   3A.2 Comida sana
- Use with Students' Book, pages 90–91

AT 1.1, 2.1   **1 Listen. For each category of food mentioned, see how many different foods you can say. Use vocabulary page 55 to help (or page 103 of the Students' Book).**
Encourage some discussion over this.

> 🎧 **CD 3, track 67**   página 49, actividad 1
>
> Comida sana
> Fruta
> Comida deliciosa
> Comida italiana
> Comida malsana

AT 3.3   **2 Read the texts. Then answer the questions.**

Answers:
a Cristiano; **b** Lionel; **c** Lionel; **d** Magda; **e** Cristiano; **f** Magda

AT 4.2-3   **3 Underline the sentences in Activity 2 that could also apply to you. Use them to write about yourself.**
Students should use connectives and quantifiers and give opinions.

Página 50   3A.3 ¡Tengo hambre!
- Use with Students' Book, pages 92–93

AT 1.3   **1 Listen to the two people ordering food. Who do you think they are? Tick the ones you think they might be.**
Practice of restaurant vocabulary.

> 🎧 **CD 3, track 68**   página 50, actividad 1
>
> – ¿Qué desea?
> – Tengo mucha hambre. Para beber… un vaso de vino. Y para comer… un bocadillo de patatas fritas.
> – ¿Un bocadillo de patatas fritas?
> – Sí, con salsa de tomate.
>
> – ¿Qué desea?
> – Necesito proteínas, entonces, voy a comer pollo.
> – ¿Algo más?
> – Sí, necesito energía, entonces quiero pasta.
> – ¿Y para beber?
> – Agua, mucha agua.

Answers:
person 1: a British tourist (or could be the teacher);
person 2: an athlete

AT 4.2   **2 Create a special menu (in Spanish) for each of the three other people on the list.**
Students could make these menus look like real restaurant menus and they could be displayed in class.

AT 2.2-3   **3 Practise ordering from the menus.**
Confident volunteers could perform a restaurant scene in front of the class.

Página 51   3A.4 ¡Oiga, camarero!
- Use with Students' Book, pages 94–95

AT 3.3   **1 Read these four jokes and match them up with their English translations.**
Challenge students to find another Spanish joke that also works in English.

Answers:
1 c; **2** b; **3** d; **4** a

AT 3.3   **2 Find the Spanish for these words in the jokes.**

Answers:
a fly – una mosca; a spider – una araña; I'm sorry – lo siento; lifeguard – socorrista; today – hoy; soup – sopa; there is – hay; to eat – comer; I don't have any – no tengo; a mouse – un ratón

3A Me gusta comer ...

AT 1.3 **3 Listen to the jokes and underline any words you think are tricky to pronounce. Listen again and repeat these words.**
Students should look for some of the tricky vowel and consonant sounds they met in Unit 0. Can they remember how these are pronounced?

CD 3, track 69 página 51, actividad 3

1
- ¡Oiga, camarero! Hay una mosca en mi sopa.
- Lo siento, señor. ¿Es usted vegetariano?

2
- ¡Oiga, camarero! Hay una araña en mi sopa.
- ¿Una araña? Sí, le gusta comer las moscas.

3
- ¡Oiga, camarero! Hay un ratón en mi sopa.
- Lo siento. No tengo moscas hoy.

4
- ¡Oiga, camarero! Hay una mosca muerta en mi sopa.
- ¡Oiga, señor, soy camarero, no soy socorrista!

AT 2.3 **4 Practise telling one of the jokes until you can read it aloud perfectly, or you know it off by heart. Record it on your phone or mp3, or tell it to your teacher.**
Students could also perform their joke in front of the class in a 'comedy show'.

Página 52 3A.5 Me encanta la comida
- Use with Students' Book, pages 96–97

AT 3.3 **1 Read about the foods and identify what they are.**
Practice of food vocabulary.

Answers:
a pizza; **b** curry; **c** pancakes; **d** sushi

AT 4.2–3 **2 Explain the English dish Toad in the Hole to a Spanish person.**
Students may need to find out what the ingredients are in English first.

Página 53 3A.6A Labolengua
- Use with Students' Book, pages 98–99

1 Highlight the difference between the formal and informal forms.

Answers: the informal forms have an 's'

2 Join up the pairs that mean the same thing. Circle the ones that are in the formal form.
Students should be able to recognise which are informal and formal from what they have done in Activity 1.

Answers (formal forms in bold):
¿Tiene...? – ¿Tienes...?; **¿Quiere...?** – ¿Quieres...?; **¿Qué desea?** – ¿Qué deseas?; **Aquí tiene** – Aquí tienes.

AT 1.3 **3 Listen. Formal or informal? Circle the correct one.**

CD 3, track 70 página 53, actividad 3

1
- Buenos días, ¿qué deseas?
- ¿Tienes bocadillos?
- Sí. ¿Quieres de jamón o de queso?
- De queso.

2
- Hola. ¿Qué desea?
- Quiero un vaso de vino.
- Aquí tiene.

3
- ¿Tiene tapas?
- Sí, ¿qué desea?
- Quiero unas aceitunas y una ración de tortilla
- Aquí tiene.

Answers:
1 informal; **2** formal; **3** formal

Página 54 3A.6B Técnica
- Use with Students' Book, pages 98–99

1 Look at the vocabulary on page 55 (or page 103 in the Students' Book). Make yourself a memory jogging recipe by putting together ingredients that begin with the same letter of the alphabet.
This is a great way to remember vocabulary. You could display some of the recipes on the wall.

Me gusta comer ... 3A

Higher Workbook

Página 48   3A.1 Es la hora de comer
- Use with Students' Book, pages 88–89

AT 4.1–2   **1 Write the Spanish for these foods.**

Answers:
bread – pan; cheese – queso; chicken – pollo; potatoes – patatas; chocolate – chocolate; meat – carne

2 Think like a Spanish person. Fill in the grids.
Once they have filled in the grids, challenge students to think of more food items and to fit them into a similar grid.

Answers:
roast chicken; chicken roast; pollo asado
a cheese sandwich; a sandwich of cheese; un bocadillo de queso
crisps; potatoes fried; patatas fritas
chilli con carne; chilli with meat; chile con carne

AT 4.2   **3 Write the Spanish for the following.**
Students use what they have learnt from the grids to translate the foods into Spanish.

Answers:
un bocadillo de jamón; carne asada; un pastel de chocolate; un huevo frito

Página 49   3A.2 Comida sana
- Use with Students' Book, pages 90–91

AT 1.1, 2.1   **1 Listen. For each category of food mentioned, see how many different foods you can say. Use vocabulary page 55 to help (or page 103 of the Students' Book).**
Encourage some discussion over this.

> 🎧 **CD 4, track 42**   página 49, actividad 1
>
> Comida sana
> Fruta
> Comida deliciosa
> Mariscos
> Comida italiana
> Comida malsana
> Pescado

AT 3.3   **2 Read. Then answer the questions in English.**

Answers:
a Magda. She likes fruit and veg and is a vegetarian.
b Lionel. He knows he eats a lot of sugar, but he likes it.
c Cristiano. He thinks it's OK because he doesn't have puddings or sweets.

AT 4.3   **3 Write about what healthy and unhealthy foods you like to eat.**
Students should use connectives and quantifiers and give opinions.

Página 50   3A.3 ¡Tengo hambre!
- Use with Students' Book, pages 92–93

AT 1.3   **1 Listen to the two people ordering food. Who do you think they are? Tick the ones you think they might be.**
Practice of restaurant vocabulary.

> 🎧 **CD 4, track 43**   página 50, actividad 1
>
> – Buenos días ¿Qué desea?
> – Tengo mucha hambre. Para beber… un vaso de agua, sin gas.
> – ¿Y para comer?
> – Y para comer… voy a comer un bocadillo de queso, sin queso y sin pan.
>
> – ¿Qué desea?
> – Necesito proteínas, entonces, voy a comer pollo.
> – ¿Algo más?
> – Sí, necesito energía, así que quiero pasta.
> – ¿Y para beber?
> – Agua, mucha agua.

Answers:
person 1: *a super model;* **person 2:** *an athlete*

AT 4.2   **2 Create a special menu (in Spanish) for each of the three other people on the list.**
Students could make these menus look like real restaurant menus and they could be displayed in class.

AT 2.2–3   **3 Order for the three people in Activity 2 from the menus.**
Confident volunteers could perform a restaurant scene in front of the class.

Página 51   3A.4 ¡Oiga, camarero!
- Use with Students' Book, pages 94–95

AT 3.3   **1 Read the jokes and find these words in Spanish.**

Answers:
a fly – una mosca; a spider – una araña; I'm sorry – lo siento; lifeguard – socorrista; today – hoy; soup – sopa; there is – hay; to eat – comer; I don't have any – no tengo; a mouse – un ratón

3A Me gusta comer …

AT 3.3 **2 Translate each of the jokes in English.**
Challenge students to find another joke that works both in English and in Spanish.

Answers:
1 Waiter, waiter! There's a fly in my soup.
  I'm sorry, sir. Are you a vegetarian?
2 Waiter, waiter! There's a spider in my soup.
  A spider? Yes, he likes to eat the flies.
3 Waiter, waiter! There's a mouse in my soup.
  I'm sorry. I don't have any flies today.
4 Waiter, waiter!. There's a dead fly in my soup.
  Hey, sir. I'm a waiter, not a lifeguard.

AT 1.3 **3 Listen to the jokes and underline any words you think are tricky to pronounce. Listen again and repeat these tricky words.**
Students should look for some of the tricky vowel and consonant sounds they met in Unit 0. Can they remember how these are pronounced?

🎧 **CD 4, track 44**   página 51, actividad 3

1
– ¡Oiga, camarero! Hay una mosca en mi sopa.
– Lo siento, señor. ¿Es usted vegetariano?
2
– ¡Oiga, camarero! Hay una araña en mi sopa.
– ¿Una araña? Sí, le gusta comer las moscas.
3
– ¡Oiga, camarero! Hay un ratón en mi sopa.
– Lo siento. No tengo moscas hoy.
4
– ¡Oiga, camarero! Hay una mosca muerta en mi sopa.
– ¡Oiga, señor, soy camarero, no soy socorrista!

AT 2.3 **4 Practise telling the jokes until you can read them aloud perfectly and you know at least one off by heart. Record it on your phone or mp3, or tell it to your teacher.**
Students could perform one of their jokes in front of the class in a 'comedy show'.

Página 52   3A.5 Me encanta la comida
- Use with Students' Book, pages 96–97

AT 3.3 **1 Read about the foods and identify what they are.**
Practice of food vocabulary.

Answers:
a pizza; **b** curry; **c** pancakes; **d** sushi

AT 4.3 **2 Explain some English dishes to a Spanish person.**
Before students do this, ensure that they are familiar with the ingredients of these dishes in English.

Página 53   3A.6A Labolengua
- Use with Students' Book, pages 98–99

1 Change the informal form into the formal form.

Answers: tiene, desea

2 Join up the pairs that mean the same thing. Circle the ones that are in the formal form.

Answers (formal forms in bold):
Aquí tiene. – Aquí tienes.; ¿Y para ti? – **¿Y para usted?**; **¿Tiene…?** – ¿Tienes…?; **¿Qué va a tomar?** – ¿Qué vas a tomar?; **¿Quiere…?** – ¿Quieres…?; **¿Qué desea?** – ¿Qué deseas?

3 Listen. Formal or informal? Circle the correct one.

🎧 **CD 4, track 45**   página 53, actividad 3

1
– Buenos días. ¿Qué deseas?
– ¿Tienes bocadillos?
– Sí. ¿Quieres de jamón o de queso?
– De queso.
2
– Hola. ¿Qué va a beber?
– Quiero un vaso de vino tinto.
– Aquí tiene.
3
– Oiga. Me puede traer un vaso de agua por favor.
– Enseguida, señorita … Aquí tiene. ¿Desea alguna otra cosa?

Answers:
1 informal; **2** formal; **3** formal

Página 53   3A.6B Técnica
- Use with Students' Book, pages 98–99

1 Look at the vocabulary on page 55 (or page 103 in the Students' Book). Make yourself a memory jogging recipe by putting together ingredients that begin with the same letter of the alphabet.
This is a great way to remember vocabulary. You could display some of the recipes on the wall.

3B Las vacaciones

Unit Objectives

Contexts and cultural focus: holidays: locations, transport and accommodation

Grammar: the immediate future, comparisons (revise and extend), formal and informal language (*tú* and *usted*), adverbs

Language learning: creating a dialogue from a model, working out and comparing detail in information given, creating formal and informal dialogues, extending your writing by using a dictionary effectively

- *Aim:* To talk about holidays you are going on whilst incorporating the grammar and vocabulary covered in the spread.
- Each unit has an associated video which will feature throughout the unit. Below is the transcript of the video for this unit.
- As a starter activity to introduce the Unit and familiarise students with the language they will meet, you may find it useful for the class to view the video as a whole.

Video script (CD 2, track 47)

Marisa:	¡Esto es precioso!
Khalid:	Sí, ¡se puede ver toda la ciudad desde aquí! Incluso cuando sopla el viento en la dirección adecuada, también se puede oler la ciudad. Pero tienes razón. ¡Es increíble!
Marisa:	Creo que es maravilloso.

[Pause]

José:	¿Sabes ya lo que decir?
Khalid:	Sí.
José:	Entonces, ¿por qué no lo dices? Se nos acaba el tiempo. Si queremos que este plan salga bien, tenemos que comprar los billetes ahora.
Khalid:	Ya lo sé, ya lo sé pero… ¿por qué siempre tengo que soy yo que habla?
José:	Porque tú eres Khal y yo soy José. ¡Es así cómo funcionan las cosas!
Khalid:	¡Ejem!… Marisa, ¿sabes que otro sitio es también precioso? Figueres.
Marisa:	¿Qué tiene de especial Figueres?
Khalid:	El museo de Dalí. A José le encanta, ¿no es verdad, José?
José:	Sí, me encanta.
Marisa:	¿Desde cuándo te gustan a ti los museos, José?
Khalid:	A José le apasiona Dalí, ¿no es verdad, José?
José:	Sí. ¡Es una artista maravillosa!
Khalid:	Quiere decir, que es *un* artista increíble. *Salvador* Dalí es uno de los artistas más importantes del siglo XX.
Khalid:	Bueno, ¿entonces qué? ¿Te gustaría ir a Figueres?
Marisa:	Bueno, ¿por qué no?
Khalid:	¿Qué te parece el fin de semana que viene?
Marisa:	Vale.
Khalid:	Voy a mirar los horarios de los trenes en mi móvil ahora mismo.
Marisa:	Primero voy a pedirle permiso a mi padre. Probablemente quiera venir con nosotros.

[Pause]

Marisa:	A mi padre le parece bien. Me deja a ir.
Khalid:	¡Perfecto! Bien, hay un tren a Figueres cada hora. Podemos coger el tren de las 10.15. Tarda dos horas. El billete de ida y vuelta cuesta 18 euros. Es un poco más caro que el autobús pero el autobús tarda mucho más.
Marisa:	Entonces iremos en tren.
Khalid:	Oye José, ¿tu tía no tiene una pensión en Figueres?
Marisa:	¿De verdad? Me encantan las pensiones. Las prefiero a los hoteles, y normalmente, las habitaciones son mejores… y más baratas.
Khalid:	¡Estoy de acuerdo! Los hoteles son más caros y no necesariamente más lujosos.
Marisa:	¡Es verdad!
Khalid:	Entonces… llamo a Eva para confirmar si puede venir a las 10.15.
Marisa:	¿Cómo? ¿Eva también va a venir?
Khalid:	Oye José, ¿te quedan más bizcochos?

3B Las vacaciones

Unit 3B Vacaciones Overview grid

Page reference	Contexts and objectives	Language learning	Grammar	Key language	Framework	AT level
Pages 104–5 **El transporte**	• talk about means of transport	• create a dialogue from a model	• use the immediate future tense: *voy a viajar*	*en autobús; en metro; en barco; en bicicleta; en tren; en avión; en coche; en autocar; un viaje; viajar; cómodo/a; barato/a; corto/a; divertido/a; un billete; ida y vuelta; cada veinte minutes; tardar*	1.1, 1.4, 2.4, 2.5, 3.1, 3.2, 4.1, 4.2, 4.3, 4.4, 4.5, 5.3, 5.4	1.3, 2.2–3, 4.2–4
Pages 106–7 **Alojamiento**	• discuss different types of accommodation and facilities	• work out and compare detail in information given	• revise and extend comparisons	*alojarse; un albuergue juvenil; una pensión; un camping; quedarse; vale la pena; antiguo/a; tan … como; mejor; el/la mejor; peor; el/la peor; la sábana; el dormitorio; el ascensor*	1.1, 1.4, 2.1, 2.4, 2.5, 3.1, 4.3, 4.4, 4.5, 5.4	1.4, 2–3, 3.3–4, 4.4
Pages 108–9 **Quiero reservar …**	• make a reservation	• create formal and informal dialogues of your own	• use formal and informal language correctly (*tú* and *usted*)	*reservar; una reserva; confirmar; el precio; cerrar; cerrado/a; abrir; abierto/a; un plazo; una tienda; incluso; encampar*	1.1, 1.2, 1.4, 1.5, 2.1, 2.4, 2.5, 3.1, 4.1, 4.3, 5.4, 5.5	1.4, 2.3–4, 3.3, 4.2–3
Pages 110–1 **¿Adónde vamos?**	• talk about what you are going to do on holiday	• extend your writing by using a dictionary effectively	• form and use adverbs correctly	*precioso/a; maravilloso/a; cada; la media hora; apreciar; una parada; perderse; encontrarse; el dinero; tener suerte; menores de; la estación; nace; se casa con; un juguete; inolvidable*	1.1, 1.2, 1.4, 1.5, 2.1, 2.2, 2.4, 2.5, 3.1, 3.2, 4.2, 4.3, 4.4, 4.5, 5.1, 5.4, 5.5	1.3–4, 2.2–3, 3.4, 4.3–4
Pages 112–3 **Al extranjero**	• discuss holidays in a wider context • be aware of cultural differences in the Spanish-speaking world	• revise and extend language already covered		*divertido/a; genial; fatal; sensacional; guay; pasarlo bomba; un parque de atracciones; el mercado; antiguo/a; un guía; una guía; orientarse; guardar; vigilar; una torre; una tumba; las normas*	1.1, 1.4, 1.5, 2.4, 2.5, 4.3, 4.5, 3.2, 3.2, 5.5	1.4, 2.3, 3.3–4, 4.4–5
Pages 114–5 **Labolengua**	• review language and grammar from the unit				1.1, 2.4, 4.1, 4.2, 4.3, 4.4, 4.5, 5.1, 5.5, 5.8	
Pages 116–7 **Extra Star Extra Plus**	• differentiated extension/ homework material	• revise and consolidate all vocabulary and grammar covered in the unit	• revise and consolidate all vocabulary and grammar covered in the unit		1.1, 1.2, 1.4, 1.5, 2.1, 2.4, 2.5, 4.2, 4.3, 4.4, 4.5, 5.1, 5.8	1.3–4, 2.3–4, 3.2–4, 4.4–5

Las vacaciones 3B

Page 118 **Prueba**	• end-of-spread test				1.1, 1.2, 1.4, 1.5, 2.1, 2.2, 2.4, 2.5, 3.1, 4.2, 4.3, 4.4, 4.5, 5.1, 5.8	1.4, 2.3–4, 3.4, 4.4–5
Page 119 **Vocabulario**	• a summary of the key language covered in each spread of this unit					
Page 158 **Leer 3B**	• practice of longer reading texts based on the theme of the unit				2.1, 2.2, 3.1, 3.2, 5.3, 5.4, 5.5	3.4

Week-by-week overview
(Three-year KS3 Route: assuming six weeks' work or approximately 10–12.5 hours)
(Two-year KS3 Route: assuming four weeks' worth or approximately 6.5-8.5 hours)
*Please note that essential activities are highlighted.

About Unit 3B, *Las vacaciones:* Students work in the context of holidays. They talk about and give their opinion of different means of transport and different types of accommodation, as well as facilities. They learn to make reservations and to talk about what they are going to do on holiday. In doing this, students learn how to use the immediate future, continue to use comparisons and learn when to use formal and informal language. They also learn to form and use adverbs. The unit also provides tips on language learning techniques.

Three-Year KS3 Route			Two-Year KS3 Route		
Week	Resources	Objectives	Week	Resources	Objectives
1	**3B.1 El transporte** **3B.6 Lablolengua A** (p.114)	talk about means of transport create a dialogue from a model use the immediate future tense: *voy a viajar*	1	**3B.1 El transporte** omit activities 2, 5, Think!, 8, 9 & Challenge **3B.6 Lablolengua A** (p.114)	talk about means of transport create a dialogue from a model use the immediate future tense: *voy a viajar*
2	**3B.2 Alojamiento** **3B.6 Lablolengua C** (p.115)	discuss different types of accommodation and facilities work out and compare detail in information given revise and extend comparisons	2	**3B.2 Alojamiento** omit activities 5 & Challenge	discuss different types of accommodation and facilities work out and compare detail in information given revise and extend comparisons

3B Las vacaciones

3	**3B.3 Quiero reservar …** **3B.6 LabIolengua D** (p.115)	make a reservation create formal and informal dialogues of your own use formal and informal language correctly (*tú* and *usted*)	3	**3B.3 Quiero reservar…** **omit Think! activity**	make a reservation create formal and informal dialogues of your own use formal and informal language correctly (*tú* and *usted*)
4	**3B.4 ¿Adónde vamos?** **3B.6 LabIolengua B** (p.114)	talk about what you are going to do on holiday extend your writing by using a dictionary effectively form and use adverbs correctly	4	**3B.4 ¿Adónde vamos?** **omit activities 4, 7, Think!** **3B.6 LabIolengua B** (p.114) **3A.8 Prueba** (p.118) **Vocabulario** (p.119)	talk about what you are going to do on holiday extend your writing by using a dictionary effectively form and use adverbs correctly recapping on the vocabulary of the unit prepare and carry out assessment in all four skills
5	**3B.5 Al extranjero**	discuss holidays in a wider context be aware of and understand cultural differences in the Spanish-speaking world revise and extend language already covered			
6	**3B.7 Extra (Star)** (p.116) **3B.7 Extra (Plus)** (p.117) **3B.8 Prueba** (p.118) **Vocabulario** (p.119) **Leer** (p.158)	further reinforcement and extension of the language of the unit recapping on the vocabulary of the unit prepare and carry out assessment in all four skills further reading to explore the language of the unit and cultural themes			

3B.1 Las vacaciones

3B.1 El transporte
páginas 104–105

Planner

Objectives
- talk about means of transport
- use the immediate future tense: *voy a viajar*
- create a dialogue from a model

Video
Video script, Unit 3B

Resources
Students' Book, pages 104–105
CD 2, tracks 46–48
Foundation Workbook, page 56
Higher Workbook, page 56
Foundation Workbook audio, CD 3, track 71
Higher Workbook audio, CD 4, track 46
Interactive OxBox, Unit 3B
Copymasters 79–86
Assessment, Unit 3B

Key language
en autobús; en metro; en barco; en bicicleta; en tren; en avión; en coche; en autocar; un viaje; viajar; cómodo/a; barato/a; corto/a; divertido/a; un billete; ida y vuelta; cada veinte minutes; tardar

Grammar
- use the immediate future tense: *voy a viajar*

Renewed Framework references
1.1, 1.4, 2.4, 2.5, 3.1, 3.2, 4.1, 4.2, 4.3, 4.4, 4.5, 5.3, 5.4

PLTS
Activity 1: Reflective learners
Activity 5: Creative thinkers
Activity 6: Reflective learners
Activity 8: Creative thinkers; Reflective learners
Challenge: Effective participators; Reflective learners

Starters
- Play a class game. Slpit the class into small groups and give them a time limit to think of as many countries in Spanish as they can. Can they think of one for each letter of the alphabet? The group with the most countries at the end of the time wins.
- Display some sentences from the spread in jumbled order and give students a time limit to unjumble them. Include some sentences that use the immediate future. Once students have unjumbled the sentences, ask them to translate them into English.

Plenaries
- Display a variety of sentences from the spread including some using the immediate future. Students pick out any sentences in the immediate future and translate these into English. Challenge more able students to write three more sentences in the immediate future on the theme of the spread.
- Display the countries from Starter Activity 1 along with the key vocabulary. Challenge students to use these words to create sentences on the theme of the spread. Provide less able students with model sentences with blanks for them to fill in using this vocabulary.

Homework/Self-study
Gramática: Students write some sentences of their own in the immediate future. Less able students could adapt those in the Grammar box.
Students adapt the conversation from Activity 9 to create a new one. They then practise this with a partner. Encourge more able students to add more detail.

AT 1.3 | **PLTS**

1 Escucha y empareja.
Students listen and match the speakers with the forms of transport. First, they match the photos to the words in the vocabulary box. Check if they can pronounce the words correctly on sight. If not, practise pronunciation.

🎧 **CD 2, track 46** — página 104, actividad 1

1 Este verano voy a Cuba con mi familia. Vamos en tren hasta Madrid y luego cogemos el avión.
2 Bueno, nosotros vamos a Mallorca y vamos en barco porque es más divertido que el avión.
3 Creo que voy a Francia donde viven mis tíos. Voy en autocar porque voy sin mis padres. Ellos llegan más tarde y van a viajar en coche.
4 Voy a Londres, Inglaterra y voy en tren y en barco. Es un viaje largo pero voy con un grupo del instituto así que no está tan mal.
5 Vamos a Marruecos a visitar a mi familia que vive allí. Vamos en tren hasta Algeciras y luego vamos en ferri, un barco rápido, hasta Tanger y después no sé. Probablemente viajamos en tren o en coche.

Answers:
1 e, f; *2* c; *3* g, h; *4* e, c; *5* e, c, h

3B.1 Las vacaciones

AT 1.3 **2 Escucha y anota los países.**
Students listen again and note down the order of the countries mentioned.

Answers:
1 Cuba, Spain (Madrid); *2* Mallorca; *3* France; *4* England (London); *5* Morocco

AT 1.3 **3 Qué medios de transporte no se mencionan?**
Students listen once more and note down which forms of transport aren't mentioned.

Answers: bus; bicicleta; metro

AT 2.2–3 **4 Practica la conversación.**
Look at the dialogue as a class. Can they work out the meaning of any words they don't understand from the context? Once you are confident that students understand the dialogue, they work in pairs to act it out.

AT 2.3 / PLTS **5 Inventa otros diálogos.**
Students use the dialogue in Activity 4 as a model to invent further dialogues of their own. With less able students, display the dialogue from Activity 4 with the countries and the modes of transport blanked out.

Think!
This enables students to think about the different ways of translating Spanish prepositions into English.

Gramática
Read the grammar explanation. To check understanding, display some sentences in the immediate future tense and some in the present or preterite. Students pick out those that are in the immediate future tense.

AT 4.2–3 / PLTS **6 Escribe**
Students translate the sentences in the immediate future into Spanish. With less able students you could display the necessary vocabulary in jumbled order for support. Students go on to make up three more sentences of their own in English. They give them to a partner to write or say in Spanish. This is a good test of their knowledge of how to construct sentences in the immediate future.

Answers:
1 Voy a jugar al baloncesto. *2* Vamos a comer helado. *3* Van a vivir en Argentina.

AT 1.4 **7 Mira el video y contesta a las preguntas.**
Students watch the video and answer the questions.

Video script: Unit 3B (CD 2, track 47)

Marisa: A mi padre le parece bien. Me deja a ir.
Khalid: ¡Perfecto! Bien, hay un tren a Figueres cada hora. Podemos coger el tren de las 10.15. Tarda dos horas. El billete de ida y vuelta cuesta 18 euros. Es un poco más caro que el autobús pero el autobús tarda mucho más.
Marisa: Entonces iremos en tren.
Khalid: Oye José, ¿tu tía no tiene una pensión en Figueres?

Answers:
1 return ticket: 18 Euros; *2* the train is more expensive; *3* it takes much longer

AT 2.2–3 / PLTS **8 Inventa comparaciones ridículas.**
Students use their imagination to invent some silly comparisons using all the modes of transport mentioned in the spread and using countries or cities around the world.

AT 1.3 **9 Escucha y repite.**
Students listen and repeat the conversation.

CD 2, track 48 — página 105, actividad 9

Buenos días. Un billete de ida y vuelta a Sitges, por favor.
Vale; aquí tiene usted. ¿Algo más?
Sí. ¿A qué hora sale el tren, por favor?
Pues hay trenes cada veinte minutos. Tarda media hora.
Gracias. ¿Cuánto es?
El billete de ida y vuelta cuesta seis euros.

AT 4.3 **10 Inventa otros diálogos.**
Students make up more dialogues like the one in Activity 9.

AT 4.3–4 / PLTS **Challenge**
Say what form of transport you use to get to school. Ask a few friends what form of transport they use. Write a brief paragraph about what form of transport you prefer and why.
You could turn this into a game by giving all students a card upon which is a form of transport. Students must try to find classmates who have the same form of transport as them. The class could also produce a graph showing which is the most popular form of transport. Encourage students to be as inventive as possible when writing their paragraphs.

3B.2 Las vacaciones

3B.2 Alojamiento
páginas 106–107

Planner

Objectives
- discuss different types of accommodation and facilities
- revise and extend comparisons
- work out and compare detail in information given

Video
Video script, Unit 3B

Resources
Students' Book, pages 106–107
CD 2, tracks 47, 49
Foundation Workbook, page 57
Higher Workbook, page 57
Foundation Workbook audio, CD 3, track 72
Higher Workbook audio, CD 4, track 47
Interactive OxBox, Unit 3B
Copymasters 79–86
Assessment, Unit 3B

Key language
alojarse; un albuergue juvenil; una pensión; un camping; quedarse; vale la pena; antiguo/a; tan … como; mejor; el/la mejor; peor; el/la peor; la sábana; el dormitorio; el ascensor

Grammar
- revise and extend comparisons

Renewed Framework references
1.1, 1.4, 2.1, 2.4, 2.5, 3.1, 4.3, 4.4, 4.5, 5.4

PLTS
Activity 1: Independent enquirers
Gramática: Reflective learners
Think!: Independent enquirers
Challenge: Creative thinkers

Starters
- Display the different types of holiday accommodation in Spanish in one column with the English translations in a second column next to them. Give students a time limit to match the Spanish to the English. Check answers as a class.
- Describe a type of holiday accommodation to the class who must try to guess which one you are describing, e.g. *Es más divertido y, claro, más barato que una pension o un hotel. (Albergue Juvenil)*, etc.

Plenaries
- Display a list of different types of holiday accommodation and challenge students to write sentences comparing them. If necessary, display phrases used to compare things, e.g. *tan … como, mejor que, peor que, bueno, mejor, el/la/lo major, malo, peor, el/la/lo peor*.
- Following on from the Challenge Activity, students write a description of the worst holiday accommodation they can think of.

Homework/Self-study
Activity 1: Students do research to find out more about the geography of Spain and Peru.
Gramática: Students think up their own sentences using *tan … como, mejor que, peor que, bueno, mejor, el/la/lo mejor, malo, peor and el/la/lo peor*. Less able students could adapt the example sentences.

AT 1.4
PLTS

1 Escucha. Copia y completa la tabla.
Students listen to the five conversations and then copy and complete the table. This is an ideal opportunity to show students where the Pyrenees, Sierra Nevada and Picos are and to talk about the geography of Spain and Peru.

CD 2, track 49 — página 106, actividad 1

1
Vamos a visitar la ciudad de Sevilla en julio.
¿Vas a quedarte en un hotel o en una pensión?
Pues, creo que en una pensión porque es más barato.
Sí, de acuerdo y a veces una pensión es tan cómoda como un hotel.

2
¿Vas a ir a esquiar este invierno?
Claro que sí – no me lo pierdo.
¿Adónde vas a ir –a los Pirineos o a la Sierra Nevada?
Creo que es mejor ir a los Pirineos porque es más seguro.
Vale, siempre hay más nieve en los Pirineos que en la Sierra Nevada.
¿Dónde vas a alojarte?
Siempre nos vamos al Albergue Juvenil – es más divertido y, claro, más barato que una pension o un hotel.

3B.2 Las vacaciones

3
¿Vas a tu casa en el campo este verano?
Claro, como siempre vamos a pasar por lo menos un mes en los Picos, en casa de mis abuelos.
¿No vas a otra parte? Debe ser aburrido ir siempre al mismo lugar, ¿no?
Pues a mí me encanta y este año voy a hacer camping con mis primos. Vamos a un camping cerca de Gijón en la costa porque es más divertido y menos costoso.

4
Bueno, yo voy con mis padres a Perú. Vamos en un tour y vamos a visitar las ruinas de Machu Picchu. Nos quedamos en un hotel en Cuzco, una ciudad antigua y muy bonita. Me fascina la historia. Es un viaje caro pero vale la pena porque voy a aprender mucho.

5
Como somos una familia grande siempre nos quedamos en una pensión cuando viajamos. Este año vamos a Ibiza y vamos a ir a una pensión en el centro de la isla. Es una casa antigua pero es barata y cómoda.

Answers:
1 **Lugar:** Seville; **Alojamiento:** guest house; **Opinión:** cheaper than a hotel but just as comfortable
2 **Lugar:** Pyrenees; **Alojamiento:** youth hostel; **Opinión:** Pyrenees better than Sierra Nevada as it is safer and there is more snow; youth hostel is more fun and cheaper than a guest house or hotel
3 **Lugar:** Picos/Gijón; **Alojamiento:** grandparent's house/campsite with cousins; **Opinión:** likes it/more fun and cheap
4 **Lugar:** Peru (Cuzco); **Alojamiento:** hotel; **Opinión:** Cuzco is pretty, fascinated by history/an expensive journey but worth it as will learn a lot
5 **Lugar:** Ibiza; **Alojamiento:** guest house in the centre; **Opinión:** old but cheap and comfortable

PLTS Gramática
Read through the grammar explanation as a class. Ask students to provide examples of 'more than' and 'less than' – if necessary, remind them that they need to use *más ... que* (more than) *menos ... que* (less than). Students then translate the examples into English.

Answers:
It is a good idea – in fact it is the best idea of all.
It isn't a good idea; it is the worst idea of all.
It is the best hotel in the world.

PLTS Think!
Students think about agreement when comparing things. They should be able to work out that *cómoda* agrees with *pensión* which is feminine. If describing a hotel, they would need to use the masculine version, *cómodo*. Students then write their own sentence comparing a campsite to a guest house, using the same adjective. Remind students that it isn't always possible to translate literally. To illustrate this ask them to compare the Spanish and English for the last example. Which key word is used differently?

Answer: Spanish say of the world; English say in the world

AT 1.4 2 Mira el video y contesta a las preguntas.
Students watch the video and answer the questions.

Video script: Unit 3B (CD 2, track 47)
Marisa: ¿De verdad? Me encantan las pensiones. Las prefiero a los hoteles, y normalmente, las habitaciones son mejores… y más baratas.
Khalid: ¡Estoy de acuerdo! Los hoteles son más caros y no necesariamente más lujosos.
Marisa: ¡Es verdad!
Khalid: Entonces… llamo a Eva para confirmar si puede venir a las 10.15.

Answers:
1 guest houses; **2** he agrees with Marisa and prefers them to hotels which are more expensive and not necessarily more luxurious; **3** Eva

AT 3.3 3 Empareja las preguntas con las respuestas.
Students study the list of questions and match them to the answers given. Students could then practise asking and answering these questions in pairs.

Answers:
1 g; **2** h; **3** f; **4** b; **5** d; **6** c; **7** e; **8** a

AT 3.4 4 ¿Verdad o mentira?
Students decide whether the receptionist in Activity 3 is telling the truth by comparing what is said with the information given.

Answers:
No the receptionist isn't telling the truth:
*El hotel está a **varios** kilómetros de la playa. Hay una*

3B.3 Las vacaciones

*piscina **pequeña**. Hay **una sola ducha** detrás. Hay muchos restaurantes en la ciudad pero **aquí les ofrecemos un bar con bebidas frías nada más**. Los dormitorios están en el segundo piso. **Pueden subir por las escaleras a la derecha de la recepción**. Las **sábanas están encima de las camas**. El desayuno se sirve **desde las siete hasta las diez**. Para los deportistas hay muchas facilidades **en el polideportivo local**.*

AT 3.3 | **5 Da tu opinión.**
Students give their opinion about the hotel and its facilities.

AT 4.4 | **Challenge**
PLTS | **Write a brief paragraph about your ideal holiday accommodation – where it is, what it offers etc.**
More able students should incorporate some of the grammar points covered so far, e.g. adjectives and quantifiers, the immediate future and comparisons. Once students have completed their paragraph they should swap papers with a partner who asks questions based on the information written down. They should use the questions from Activity 3 to help them. How much can students remember about what they have written?

3B.3 Quiero reservar... páginas 108–109

Planner

Objectives
- make a reservation
- use formal and informal language correctly (*tú* and *usted*)
- create formal and informal dialogues of your own

Resources
Students' Book, pages 108–109
CD 2, tracks 50–52
Foundation Workbook, page 58
Higher Workbook, page 58
Interactive OxBox, Unit 3B
Copymasters 79–86
Assessment, Unit 3B

Key language
reservar; una reserve; confirmar; el precio; cerrar; cerrado/a; abrir; abierto/a; un plazo; una tienda; incluso; encampar

Grammar
- use formal and informal language correctly (*tú* and *usted*)

Renewed Framework references
1.1, 1.2, 1.4, 1.5, 2.1, 2.4, 2.5, 3.1, 4.1, 4.3, 5.4, 5.5

PLTS
Activity 3: Reflective learners
Think!: Self-managers; Independent enquirers
Challenge: Reflective learners

Starters
- Quickly revise dates and letters. Go round the class saying a date in English which students must translate into Spanish. Next go round the class asking each pupil to spell their surname (if a student has a particularly short surname, you may prefer to give them a word to spell). Explain to students that they will need to be confident with dates and spellings when reserving holiday accommodation.
- Go round the class asking questions based on the dialogues from the spread, e.g. *¿Para cuántas personas?* or *¿Para cuándo?*, etc. Students must respond appropriately, e.g. *Para cinco: dos adultos y tres chicos.* or *Desde el ocho hasta el veintiuno de julio.*

Plenaries
- Students make up a dialogue based on one of those in the spread. They then write it out with the lines in jumbled order on a piece of paper and give this to a partner to rewrite in the correct order. Each partner then reads out the unjumbled dialogue to see if they have unjumbled it correctly.
- Using the letter from the Challenge Activity as a template, students create their own prompts and give these to a partner who must complete the letter using these prompts.

Homework/Self-study
Students adapt the dialogue from Activity 5 inserting new details of their own. They practise their new dialogue with a partner.

AT 1.4 | **1 Escucha y lee la conversación.**
Students listen to and read the phone conversation. Ask them to listen for specific details to focus their minds.

CD 2, track 50 página 108, actividad 1
– Oiga, ¿es el albergue juvenil Mundojoven?
– Sí, dígame.

3B.3 Las vacaciones

- Quiero confirmar una reserva, por favor.
- El nombre, por favor.
- Rodríguez: R-O-D-R-I-G-U-E-Z.
- Vale. ¿Para cuántas personas?
- Para cinco: dos adultos y tres chicos.
- ¿Para cuándo?
- Desde el ocho hasta el veintiuno de julio.
- Gracias. Le confirmo: cinco personas del ocho al…

AT 2.3 **2 Practica la conversación.**
Students work in pairs to practise the conversation from Activity 1. Remind students to swap roles once they have practised playing one of the parts so that they have the chance to practise both parts.

AT 2.4 / PLTS **3 Inventa otros diálogos.**
Students create their own dialogues using the prompts. Depending on the level of the class, you could revise dates and letters before they begin. Encourage more able students to change the holiday accommodation as well, e.g. *pensión Mundojoven* or *hotel Mundojoven*.

AT 3.3 **4 Lee y anota.**
Students read the details about the Mundojoven youth hostel in order to answer their friend's questions about it. You could do this orally first and then ask students to write their answers.

Answers:
1 online, by email, telephone or fax; 2 singles or doubles; 3 breakfast from 8am–10am; 4 showers – free 24hrs a day; 5 yes, bring a duvet cover and pillow slips; 6 yes, free WiFi; 7 24 hr reception, entry until 12 o'clock, departure until 11 o'clock

AT 1.4 **5 Escucha y pon la conversación en orden.**
Students listen to the dialogue on a campsite, and put speech bubbles a–h into the correct order.

🎧 **CD 2, track 51** página 109, actividad 5

- Oye, ¿vais a hacer camping aquí?
- Sí, vamos a reservar una plaza.
- Bueno, dime cuántas personas sois.
- Pues somos cinco personas.
- ¿Cuántas tiendas tenéis entre los cinco?
- Tenemos tres: una para las dos chicas; otra para mis dos hermanos y una individual para mí.
- Vale. ¿Y cuántas noches vais a pasar en el camping?
- Vamos a pasar cuatro noches, del seis al nueve inclusive.
- Está bien; podéis acampar allá al lado de las duchas.

Answers:
e, b, d, a, f, g, h, c

AT 2.3 **6 Escribe el diálogo y practícalo.**
Students write the dialogue and practise it with a partner.

PLTS **Think!**
Students use a bilingual dictionary to find the two meanings of *una tienda*.

Answer: a shop or a tent/awning

PLTS **Think!**
This illustrates how Spanish differs from English in what is considered polite and what isn't. Point out to students that Spanish is more direct; what they may consider impolite is acceptable in Spanish.

Answer: Oiga/Oye; Hey you!/Excuse me!/Please would you…/I would like…/I want…, etc.

AT 1.4 **7 Escucha la información y contesta a las preguntas.**
Students listen to the information and answer the questions.

🎧 **CD 2, track 52** página 109, actividad 7

El nuevo chiringuito El Gulo a orillas del mar anuncia que está abierto todo el año desde las 11 de la mañana hasta las 22 horas de la noche. Ofrece tapas y platos fuertes para todos los gustos. Todos pueden comer allí porque hay facilidades para discapacitados.

Answers:
1 11am; 2 No, it is open all year round; 3 tapas, dishes for all tastes; 4 on the seashore; 5 facilities for the disabled

AT 4.3–4 / PLTS **Challenge**
Write a letter, fax or email to book a holiday for your family in Sitges.
Elicit from the class that this will be a formal letter. Remind them to include the number of people, dates of the stay, rooms required and facilities. They should also use the appropriate beginning and ending.

3B.4 Las vacaciones

3B.4 ¿Adónde vamos?
páginas 110–111

Planner

Objectives
- talk about what you are going to do on holiday
- form and use adverbs correctly
- extend your writing by using a dictionary effectively

Video
Video-blog, Unit 3B
Video script, Unit 3B

Resources
Students' Book, pages 110–111
CD 2, tracks 47, 53–55
Foundation Workbook, page 59
Higher Workbook, page 59
Foundation Workbook audio, CD 3, track 73
Higher Workbook audio, CD 4, track 48
Interactive OxBox, Unit 3B
Copymasters 79–86
Assessment, Unit 3B

Key language
precioso/a; maravilloso/a; cada; la media hora; apreciar; una parada; perderse; encontrarse; el dinero; tener suerte; menores de; la estación; nace; se casa con; un juguete; inolvidable

Grammar
- form and use adverbs correctly

Renewed Framework references
1.1, 1.2, 1.4, 1.5, 2.1, 2.2, 2.4, 2.5, 3.1, 3.2, 4.2, 4.3, 4.4, 4.5, 5.1, 5.4, 5.5

PLTS
Activity 4: Reflective learners
Activity 5: Creative thinkers; Reflective learners
Activity 7: Independent enquirers
Think!: Reflective learners
Challenge: Independent enquirers; Creative thinkers; Reflective learners; Self-managers

Starters
- Display the adjectives: *frecuente, lento/a, rápido/a, probable, normal, fácil.* Ask students to change these into adverbs. They can add adverbs to the list, including some that don't follow the rule of adding *–mente* to the end of the adjective, e.g. *siempre, mucho, poco, bien, mal, bastante, demasiado*
- Play a quick game around the class. Ask each student, *Oye, X, ¿tú qué vas a hacer durante las vacaciones de verano?* Students make up an answer which can be very simple or more complicated, e.g. *Sí, voy a X.* or *Sí, voy a X a visitar a X. Voy a viajar...*, etc.

Plenaries
- Display the key language and ask students to translate each word/phrase by looking it up in a dictionary. They should note down what they find under each word, e.g. *precioso/a: adj. precious; (de mucho valor) valuable; (fam) lovely, beautiful,* and which is the correct translation in this context. Can students see the possible pitfalls of using a dictionary?
- Challenge students to write five sentences on the theme of the spread using some of the adverbs they listed in Starter Activity 1. Compare sentences as a class.

Homework/Self-study
Gramática: Students start a list of Spanish adverbs, adding any new ones each time they come across them.
Activity 7: Students find out more about Figueres or another Spanish town of their choice. They share their findings with the class. Students could use their findings to produce posters.

AT 1.3–4

1 Escucha y lee el diálogo.
Students listen and read the dialogue. This could be further exploited by giving students a copy of the dialogue with selected words, e.g. adverbs, blanked out, and doing a gap-fill exercise. They could fill in the words, either whilst listening to the recording again or by guessing and then listening to check their answers.

CD 2, track 53   página 110, actividad 1

- Vamos a dar una vuelta en bus turístico. Pasan frecuentemente, cada media hora.
- No me gusta porque va muy **lentamente** – prefiero ir **rápidamente**.
- Así no aprecias nada. Podemos bajarnos en varias paradas y subir a otro autobús más tarde.
- Bueno, en autobús **probablemente** no nos perdemos.
- **Normalmente** comenzamos en la Plaza Catalunya.
- Vale, así nos encontramos **fácilmente**.

3B.4 Las vacaciones

Gramática
Read the grammar explanation as a class. Students think about how adverbs are ususally formed in English (by adding –**ly** to the end of an adjective). This may help them to understand that adding –**mente** to a Spanish adjective changes it into an adverb. Encourage students to make a note of and learn the Spanish adverbs that don't follow this rule.

AT 1.4 | 2 Mira el video-blog.
Students watch the video and note down the answers to the questions. They can answer in Spanish, but encourage them to use full sentences and remind them to use the third person singular.

Video-blog: Unit 3B (CD 2, track 54)
¿Qué te gusta hacer durante las vacaciones?
Eva: Me gusta hacer actividades culturales como ir al teatro, dibujar, visitar museos.
José: Durante las vacaciones me gusta ir a la playa con mis amigos, a jugar a fútbol, nadar.
Khalid: Me gusta viajar: conocerme más culturas y gente diferente.
Marisa: Durante las vacaciones me gusta descansar, viajar y conocer a gente.

¿Adónde vas durante las vacaciones?
Eva: Normalmente vamos a ciudades donde haya muchos museos como Madrid o París, Londres, Francia. Me gusta mucho Italia porque es el centro de la cultura.
José: Voy a visitar a mi familia a Madrid.
Khalid: No tengo un destino fijo. Viajo en diferentes partes cada año.
Marisa: Durante las vacaciones voy a la playa al sur de España si no voy a Argentina.

¿Cómo viajas?
Eva: Normalmente viajamos en avión que es más rápido.
José: Normalmente viajo en tren.
Khalid: Viajo en avión, en tren o en barco: depende del destino.
Marisa: Viajo en avión porque es más rápido.

Answers:
Eva: Se gusta hacer actividades culturales como ir al teatro, dibujar, visitar museos. Normalmente va a ciudades donde hay muchos museos como Madrid o París, Londres, Francia y se gusta Italia. Normalmente viaja en avión
José: Se gusta ir a la playa con mis amigos, a jugar al fútbol, nadar. Va a visitar a su familia a Madrid. Normalmente viaja en tren.
Khalid: Se gusta viajar: conocer más culturas y gente diferente. Viaja en diferentes partes cada año. Viaja en avión, en tren o en barco: depende del destino.
Marisa: Se gusta descansar, viajar y conocer a gente. Va a la playa al sur de España si no va a Argentina. Viaja en avión.

AT 1.4 | 3 Escucha y contesta.
Students listen and answer the questions. To further exploit the dialogue, give students a copy of it with Ana's questions missing. Can students remember what the questions are?

🎧 CD 2, track 55   página 110, actividad 3
Ana: Oye, Javier, ¿tú qué vas a hacer durante las vacaciones de verano?
Javier: Pues no voy a hacer mucho, Ana, porque tengo que ayudar a mis padres en su tienda; es muy aburrido pero por lo menos voy a tener dinero para comprarme una guitarra nueva.
Ana: ¡Guay! ¿Y tú, Elena, ¿vas a viajar?
Elena: Sí, Ana, tengo mucha suerte porque voy a California a visitar a mis primos que viven allí. Voy a viajar en jumbo desde el aeropuerto de Barajas en Madrid hasta Los Angeles. Va a ser fenomenal, ¿no crees?
Ana: Claro, ¡y nosotros aquí en casa, en Barcelona, con el calor que hace en verano! ¿Verdad, Roberto?
Roberto: No me importa el calor porque voy a hacer camping; vamos a la Sierra Nevada y en las montañas hace menos calor que en la costa.

Answers:
1 *Elena;* **2** *Roberto;* **3** *Javier;* **4** *Roberto;* **5** *Javier*

AT 2.3 | PLTS | 4 Contesta a las preguntas sobre ti.
Students answer the questions in Activity 2 for themselves.

AT 4.3–4 | PLTS | 5 Escribe un párrafo.
Students write a brief paragraph about what they are going to do during the holidays. They should mention the place they are going to, the accommodation, who they are going with, transport and activities. Provide less able students with a template to fill in.

3B.4 Las vacaciones

AT 1.4 · 6 Mira el video.
Students watch the video and decide whether Marisa likes the idea of Eva joining them on their trip to Figueres. They then note down what they think the two boys are plotting. Guide students by asking questions to help them understand.

Video script: Unit 3B (CD 2, track 47)

Khalid: ¡Ejem!… Marisa, ¿sabes que otro sitio es también precioso? Figueres.
Marisa: ¿Qué tiene de especial Figueres?
Khalid: El museo de Dalí. A José le encanta, ¿no es verdad, José?
José: Sí, me encanta.
Marisa: ¿Desde cuándo te gustan a ti los museos, José?
Khalid: A José le apasiona Dalí, ¿no es verdad, José?
José: Sí. ¡Es una artista maravillosa!
Khalid: Quiere decir que es *un* artista increíble. *Salvador Dalí es uno de los artistas más importantes del siglo 20.*
Khalid: Bueno, ¿entonces qué? ¿Te gustaría ir a Figueres?
Marisa: Bueno, ¿por qué no?
Khalid: ¿Qué te parece el fin de semana que viene?
Marisa: Vale.
Khalid: Voy a mirar los horarios de los trenes en mi móvil ahora mismo.
Marisa: Primero voy a pedirle permiso a mi padre. Probablemente quiera venir con nosotros.
[Pause]
Marisa: A mi padre le parece bien. Me deja a ir.
Khalid: ¡Perfecto! Bien, hay un tren a Figueres cada hora. Podemos coger el tren de las 10.15. Tarda dos horas. El billete de ida y vuelta cuesta 18 euros. Es un poco más caro que el autobús pero el autobús tarda mucho más.
Marisa: Entonces iremos en tren.
Khalid: Oye José, ¿tu tía no tiene una pensión en Figueres?
Marisa: ¿De verdad? Me encantan las pensiones. Las prefiero a los hoteles, y normalmente, las habitaciones son mejores… y más baratas.
Khalid: ¡Estoy de acuerdo! Los hoteles son más caros y no necesariamente más lujosos.
Marisa: ¡Es verdad!
Khalid: Entonces… llamo a Eva para confirmar si puede venir a las 10.15.
Marisa: ¿Cómo? ¿Eva también va a venir?
Khalid: Oye José, ¿te quedan más bizcochos?

Suggested answers:
By the way she exclaims ¿Cómo?, it seems that Marisa isn't happy that Eva is coming but rather surprised. The boys seem to be plotting to get Marisa and Eva to go to Figueres so that they will become friends.

AT 3.4 · PLTS · 7 ¿Qué tiene de especial Figueres?
Students study the information and answer the questions. Ask them to summarise the information in English or give one piece of information they have understood first. If any of the students have ever visited Figueres they could tell the class about it, either in English or in Spanish.

Answers:
1 b; **2a** Niños menores de nueve años; **2b** El resto del año; **2c** el viaje dura una hora y media; **2d** hasta nuestros días; **3a** norte; **3b** todos; **3c** tren; **3d** museos

PLTS · Think!
Students reflect upon how they were able to understand the last reading passage using their exisiting knowledge of Spanish, the images and the headings. Explain that they don't need to look up every word in a dictionary but should try to use what they already know and find connections, e.g. between nouns and verbs, to work out the meaning of texts. They may, however, need to look up some things in a dictionary and need to know the best way to use one. They can find advice on this on page 115.

AT 4.4 · PLTS · Challenge
Prepare a web page about a place of interest near your home or about what there is to do in your home area. If you need to, read page 115 to help you use your dictionary.
Explain to students that although, at first, this may sound a daunting task, they have all of the necessary basic vocabulary and may just need to look up a few specific words. Speak about the surrounding area as a class and make a list of local tourist attractions or places of interest. Students can refer to the reading passage from Activity 7 for ideas.

3B.5 Las vacaciones

3B.5 Al extranjero
páginas 112–113

Planner

Objectives
- discuss holidays in a wider context
- revise and extend language already covered
- be aware of cultural differences in the Spanish-speaking world

Resources
Students' Book, pages 112–113
CD 2, track 56
Foundation Workbook, page 60
Higher Workbook, page 60
Foundation Workbook audio, tracks 74–75
Higher Workbook audio, tracks 49–50
Interactive OxBox, Unit 3B
Assessment, Unit 3B

Key language
divertido/a; genial; fatal; sensacional; guay; pasarlo bomba; un parque de atracciones; el mercado; antiguo/a; un guía; una guía; orientarse; guardar; vigilar; una torre; una tumba; las normas

Renewed Framework references
1.1, 1.2, 1.4, 1.5, 2.1, 2.2, 2.4, 2.5, 3.1, 3.2, 4.2, 4.4, 4.5, 4.6, 5.5

PLTS
Think!: Reflective learners
Activity 3: Team workers
Activity 6: Reflective learners; Creative thinkers
Activity 7: Independent enquirers; Self-managers
Think!: Reflective learners
Challenge: Creative thinkers; Reflective learners; Self-managers

Starters
- Display question words in Spanish in one column and the English translations in jumbled order in a second column. Give students a time limit to match these up. Check answers as a class.
- Go round the class asking each student to use one of the question words from Starter Activity 1 in a sentence. With less able classes, display model sentences or go through some examples orally first.

Plenaries
- Challenge students to write five sentences on the theme of the spread using some of the question words listed.
- Students pretend to be a famous person and write about a trip they are going to make. Encourage them to be as creative as possible – where is this famous person likely to go, who with, what will they do? Volunteers could read their work to the class. Can the class guess who they are pretending to be?

Homework/Self-study
Students use each of the words in their list from Activity 1 in a sentence. Less able students could use at least five of them in a sentence or you could give them sentences with question words missing for them to fill in.
Activity 7: Students find out more about Buenos Aires or Argentina in general. They could make an oral presentation with a few notes written under headings. You could provide a list of headings if necessary for support, e.g. *habitants; capital; idiomas; situación; comida; monumentos; historia*, etc. Useful websites: http://www.ohbuenosaires.com; www.bue.gov.ar

---

PLTS **Think!**
Students unjumble the question words. What do they notice about these words? Elicit from students that they all have accents. Remind students also that Spanish question marks differ from English ones. Students then note down the English for the words.

Answers:
¿cómo? – how? **dónde** – where? **¿cuándo?** – when? **¿quién?** – who? **¿qué?** – what? **¿cuántos?** – how many? **¿cuál?** – which? **¿adónde?** – where to? **¿por qué?** – why?

AT 4.1 **1 ¿Cuántas preguntas puedes hacer?**
Students show how many Spanish question words they know. Turn this into a game: who can make the longest list the fastest? Give students a time limit of your choosing and when this is up, check answers as a class. Ask more able classes to use one of their question words in a sentence.

AT 3.4 **2 Copia y completa el diálogo.**
Students use the question words from Activities 1 and 2 to complete the dialogue.

Answers:
1 adónde; 2 cuándo; 3 cuánto; 4 cómo; 5 qué; 6 qué

AT 2.3 **3 Practica el diálogo.**
PLTS Students practise the dialogue from Activity 2. They should try to sound as Spanish as possible. Encourage more able students to try and change certain details, e.g. places, transport, etc.

3B.5 Las vacaciones

AT 3.3–4

4 Lee la carta y busca las palabras.
Students read Marisa's aunt's letter and find the Spanish for the words listed. You could exploit the letter further by asking true and false questions. You could also test how much students can remember about family members, clothing, food, weather, etc. by having a class quiz.

Answers:
1 acuérdate de; *2* para la lluvia; *3* los gemelos; *4* en el campo; *5* escríbeme pronto

AT 3.4

5 ¿ Analiza el texto.
Students analyse the letter in Activity 5 in more detail.

Answers:
1 vas a visitarnos, vas a necesitar, vamos a celebrar, vas a comer, vamos a hacer, vas a ir; *2* primos, abuelos, mamá; *3* un impermeable, un chándal, un jersey grueso; *4* (any three of) contentos, adecuada, grueso, argentinos, favoritos, grande

AT 4.4 / PLTS

6 Escribe una carta de respuesta.
Students write a letter of reply from Marisa to her aunt. You may need to discuss this orally as a class first with students offering ideas as to what they could include in their reply, e.g. questions to ask and suggestions about what they would like to do there. Some students may need a template for support.

AT 3.3 / PLTS

7 Lee y empareja.
Students read Marisa's Facebook entry and match the photos and descriptions.

Answers:
1 c; *2* b; *3* f; *4* a; *5* h; *6* g; *7* d; *8* e

AT 1.4

8 Escucha el guía. ¿Qué fotos describe?
Students listen and note down which photos the guide is describing.

🎧 **CD 2, track 56**   página 113, actividad 8

1. Aquí llegan muchos equipos de todas partes del mundo para participar en lo que se llama 'el juego bello'. Es la sede del famoso equipo Boca Juniors y tiene capacidad para 49.000 personas; fanáticos del fútbol, todos. Se llama la Bonbonera porque se parece a una caja de chocolates.
2. Durante el mes de agosto muchos porteños – gente de la capital, Buenos Aires – salen de la ciudad para ir a gozar de la nieve y el paisaje tan espectacular de las montañas alrededor de Bariloche. Parece una escena navideña de Austria o Suiza, ¿verdad?
3. Argentina también es famosa por la carne que produce en las enormes estancias en el interior del país en las pampas. Aquí en el campo viven los gauchos, los hombres que cuidan los animales.

Answers:
a, e, g

PLTS Think!
Students practise their dictionary skills. Turn this into a class competition. Call out words from the spread. Students write down what they mean in English. Check answers as a class. Who has remembered the most words?

AT 4.4–5 / PLTS Challenge
Write some real or imaginary details about a trip you are going to make.
Students should be as creative as possible. Explain that they can embellish in order to make their writng more sophisticated.

3B.6 Labolengua   páginas 114–115

Planner

Objectives
- review language and grammar from the unit

Resources
Students' Book, pages 114–115
CD 2, tracks 57–58
Foundation Workbook, pages 7, 61–62
Higher Workbook, pages 7, 61–62
Foundation Workbook audio, track 76
Higher Workbook audio, track 51
Interactive OxBox, Unit 3B
Copymasters 87–88
Assessment, Unit 3B

Grammar
- tenses
- reflexive verbs
- adverbs

Renewed Framework references
1.1, 2.4, 4.1, 4.2, 4.3, 4.4, 4.5, 5.1, 5.5, 5.8

PLTS
All activities: Reflective learners/Self-managers

Homework/Self-study
Students write three sentences in the immediate future tense.

3B.6 Las vacaciones

Comprender – verb tenses and adverbs

A Tenses

> **PLTS** **1 Translate these sentences into English.**
> Practice of the immediate future.

Answers:
1 I am going to eat at one o'clock. **2** You are going to swim in the swimming pool. **3** He/She/You is/are going to go out with his/her/your friends. **4** We are going to go on holiday. **5** You are going to travel to Colombia. **6** They/You are going to play basketball.

> **PLTS** **2 Write out these sentences correctly.**
> Practice of using reflexive verbs in the immediate future.

Answers:
1 despertarnos; **2** acostarme; **3** ponerte; **4** bañaros; **5** lavarse

B Adverbs

> **PLTS** **3 There are some useful adverbs which do not end like this. Unscramble these other adverbs. Make up a sentence for each to show you know what they mean.**
> Practice of recognising and using adverbs which do not follow the -mente ending rule.

Answers:
siempre – always, still; **mucho** – a lot of, much; **poco** – little, not much; **bien** – well; **mal** – badly, wrongly; **bastante** – quite, rather; **demasiado** – too

Aprender – extending sentences

C Connectives, reasons, and using your dictionary

> **PLTS** **4 How well do you know your way around your dictionary? What do these symbols mean?** *n, m, f, adj, vb.* **Find five more symbols in your dictionary and learn what they mean.**
> Practice of dictionary skills.
>
> *Answers:*
> noun, masculine, feminine, adjective, verb

> **PLTS** **5 Don't forget that words often have more than one meaning! How many meanings does the word 'pool' have in English? Can you think of two meanings for the word café in Spanish?**
> Further practice of using a dictionary correctly.

Answers: coffee, café

> **PLTS** **6 Now look up the verb** *hacer* **and find out all the meanings and examples of the way this verb can be used.**
> This provides students with more practice of using a dictionary.

Hablar – pronunciation

D Speaking fluently and sounding really Spanish

> **PLTS** **7 Listen and practise.**
> Students practise sliding two words together, or *sinalefa*.

> 🎧 **CD 2, track 57**   página 115, actividad 7
>
> Anita y Amalia_aprenden a_hablar italiano.
> José_e_Inés van a_escribir una carta_a_Alberto.

> **PLTS** **8 Listen and work out which words slide into each other.**
> Practice of *sinalefa* and of *entrelazamiento* (when consonants also slide into the next word).

> 🎧 **CD 2, track 58**   página 115, actividad 8
>
> Los otros amigos van a alojarse en los hoteles más baratos.
> Vamos a Buenos Aires en un avión de Iberia.

3B.7 Las vacaciones

3B.7 Extra Star
página 116

Planner

Objectives
- discuss and write about holidays
- use the immediate future and adverbs correctly
- write longer sentences

Resources
Students' Book, page 116
CD 2 track 59
Copymaster 89

Renewed Framework references
1.1, 1.2, 1.4, 1.5, 2.1, 2.4, 2.5, 4.2, 4.3, 4.4, 4.5, 5.1, 5.8

PLTS
Activity 3: Reflective learners; Creative thinkers; Self-managers

---

1 Escucha. Copia y completa la tabla.
Students listen to the people describing their holiday plans and then copy and complete the table.

CD 2, track 59 — página 116, actividad 1

- José, ¿adónde vas de vacaciones este año?
- Pues, vamos a Sitges como siempre. Me encanta pasar el mes de agosto en la playa. Nos quedamos en el hotel Santa María y normalmente vamos en coche porque es más cómodo. Siempre lo pasamos bomba.

- Y tú, María, ¿vas de vacaciones este año?
- Pues no lo sé; normalmente vamos al campo, a casa de mis abuelos cerca de Barcelona. Vamos en autocar porque es más barato pero el viaje dura horas y es muy lento. Es bastante aburrido.

- ¿Tú, qué vas a hacer, Roberto?
- Bueno, voy con un grupo del instituto a Tarifa, en el sur. Vamos en tren hasta Algeciras y luego en autocar. Vamos a alojarnos en un camping en la Costa de la Luz. Lo vamos a pasar bomba. Seguro que va a ser genial.

- Y Raquel, ¿tú adónde vas?
- Voy a hacer un intercambio en Inglaterra con una chica de mi misma edad. Se llama Fiona y voy a quedarme en su casa. Voy en avión hasta Manchester y luego en coche hasta su casa. Estoy un poco nerviosa porque algunos de mi amigos dicen que puede ser fatal alojarse en una casa donde no conoces a la familia, pero otros dicen que puede ser divertido. Vamos a ver.

Answers:
José: Sitges; en coche (porque es más cómodo); el hotel Santa María; Siempre lo pasama bomba.
María: normalmente, al campo; en autocar (porque es más barato); casa de sus abuelos; Es bastante aburrido.
Roberto: Tarifa, en el sur; en tren hasta Algeciras y luego en autocar; un camping; Lo va a pasar bomba. Seguro que va a ser genial.
Raquel: un intercambio en Inglaterra; casa de Fiona; en avión hasta Manchester y luego en coche hasta su casa; un poco nerviosa (puede ser fatal alojarse en una casa donde no conoces a la familia, pero puede ser divertido)

2 Lee y empareja.
Students read the texts and match them with the photos. Explain that there is an extra photo so they must read the texts carefully.

Answers:
1 b; **2** e; **3** a; **4** d

3 Prepara una presentación oral sobre un viaje.
Students prepare an oral presentation about a journey they are going to make based on the prompts in the Students' Book. They should use the illustrations and the questions listed as a guide to structure their presentation. They could add opinions, adjectives, adverbs, etc.

3B.7 Las vacaciones

3B.7 Extra Plus
página 117

Planner

Objectives
- read and understand tourist information
- convert commands to infinitives
- listen for detailed information

Resources
Students' Book, page 117
CD 2, track 60
Copymaster 90

Renewed Framework references
1.1, 1.2, 1.4, 1.5, 2.1, 2.4, 2.5, 4.2, 4.3, 4.4, 4.5, 5.1, 5.8

PLTS
Activity 4: Reflective learners; Creative thinkers; Self-managers; Independent enquirers

---

AT 1.4 **1 Escucha y anota. Copia y completa la tabla.**
Students listen and take notes. Allow them to listen a second time in order to check what they have written or add any details they missed the first time. They then copy and complete the table.

CD 2, track 60 — página 117, actividad 1

- Bueno, Sebas, ¿vas como siempre a Málaga de vacaciones?
- Pues no, este año voy un mes a Sevilla. Voy con mis padres y vamos a visitar a mis abuelos. Vamos en coche porque queremos conocer la región de Andalucía un poco; visitar Córdoba y Granada, por ejemplo.
- Me alegro. Vas a pasarlo bien. ¿Y tú, Anita?
- Bueno, yo quiero ir al campo y a las montañas pero mi familia quiere ir a la playa como siempre. Vamos a Moraira, no muy lejos de Valencia, y vamos a alojarnos en una pensión a orillas del mar. Vamos en tren porque es bastante cómodo y rápido. Quiero visitar Tierra Mítica, el parque de atracciones.
- Fantástico – me dicen que vale la pena. Maripacha, ¿tú, qué vas a hacer?
- Tengo mucha suerte porque voy a Méjico con un grupo de jóvenes. Vamos a pasar quince días explorando las ruinas aztecas. Vamos en avión desde Madrid y en Méjico cogemos el autocar. Creo que nos alojamos en hoteles pequeños. Va a ser una aventura fenomenal.
- Obviamente. Bueno, y tú Julián, ¿te quedas en casa?
- No, por supuesto que no. Voy a hacer algo que hace años quiero hacer; caminar el Camino de Santiago. Es una ruta famosa que hacen a pie los peregrinos y que acaba en la Catedral de Santiago de Compostela. Voy a dormir por el camino en albergues y hostales o en una tienda de campaña.
- Vale. ¡Qué valor tienes!

Answers:
Sebas: *Sevilla; un mes; en coche; sus abuelos; quiere conocer la región de Andalucía un poco; visitar Córdoba y Granada, por ejemplo*
Anita: *Moraira; en tren; en una pensión a orillas del mar; visitar Tierra Mítica, el parque de atracciones*
Maripacha: *México; quince días; en avión desde Madrid, en México: el autocar; en hoteles pequeños; explorar las ruinas aztecas*
Julián: *Camino de Santiago/Santiago de Compostela; a pie; en albergues y hostales o en una tienda de campaña; conocer la Catedral de Santiago de Compostela*

AT 1.4 **2 Escucha otra vez y corrige los errores. ¡Cuidado! Tres frases son correctas.**
Students listen to the recording from Activity 1 again and read the sentences in the Students' Book. They correct any mistakes in the sentences. Point out that three of the sentences are already correct and so they must listen carefully. As students have already heard the recording, you could ask them to read and correct the sentences before listening again.

Answers:
*1 Sebas va a ir a Sevilla. 2 Va a quedarse en casa de **sus abuelos**. 3 Anita quiere ir **al campo y a las montañas**. 4 Quiere **visitar Tierra Mítica, el parque de atracciones**. 5 Maripacha va **con un grupo de jóvenes a Méjico**. 6 Van a pasar **quince días** allí. 7 Julián va a ir a pie a Santiago de Compostela. 8 Va a quedarse en albergues juveniles.*

AT 2.3–4 **AT 3.4** **3 Lee el informe turístico. Explica lo que tienes que hacer.**
Students read the tourist information leaflet and explain what you have to do. This practises using the infinitive. More able students could also convert the commands into the *tú* form.

## 3B.8 Las vacaciones

Answers:
Tienes que…
seguir las recomendaciones.
reservar su entrada.
comprar una guía para orientarse mejor.
guardar su pasaporte y su dinero en un lugar seguro.
vigilar sus objetos de valor como cámaras de fotos o relojes.
subir a la torre con mucho cuidado.
visitar la tumba de Gaudí en la cripta.
seguir la ruta indicada.
observar las normas, por favor.

4 Planea una visita a Isla Mágica. Escribe un texto sobre lo que vas a hacer. Usa las preguntas de la Actividad 4 (página 116) para ayudarte.
Students plan a visit to *Isla Mágica*, a theme park in Seville. They write about what they are going to do using the questions from Activity 4 on page 116 to guide them. Talk about the theme park as a class first; have any students visited it? What adjectives could be used to describe it? Students write as extensively as possible, including opinions, adverbs and adjectives.

3B.8 Prueba   página 118

Planner

Resources
Students' Book, page 118
CD 2, track 61

Renewed Framework references
1.1, 1.2, 1.4, 1.5, 2.1, 2.2, 2.4, 2.5, 3.1, 4.2, 4.3, 4.4, 4.5, 5.1, 5.8

PLTS
All activities: Reflective learners
Hablar: Creative thinkers
Escribir: Creative thinkers; Independent enquirers

Escuchar

AT 1.4 — Listen and write down the most appropriate answer.
This activity tests listening skills using the language covered in this unit.

🎧 **CD 2, track 61**   página 118, Escuchar

Tomás: Oye, Pepe, voy a ir de viaje con mi hermano mayor. Vamos a Bilbao en tren y vamos a quedarnos en un albergue cerca del puerto de Santurce. Mi hermano dice que allí se come mucho pescado pero yo quiero comer las famosas tapas. Son más deliciosas que el pescado. También voy a comprarte un regalo – algo típico de la región.
Pepe: Gracias, Tomás. Una boina típica me parece genial. ¿Qué más vas a hacer?
Tomás: Bueno, mi hermano quiere hacer surf pero yo prefiero montar a caballo. Vamos a pasarlo bomba. Van a ser las mejores vacaciones de mi vida – ¡sin mis padres, claro!

Answers:
1 Tomás va a visitar Bilbao. 2 Va a viajar en tren. 3 Va a alojarse en un albergue juvenil. 4 Va a quedarse cerca del puerto. 5 Quiere comprar regalos. 6 Va a comer tapas. 7 Va a montar a caballo. 8 Las vacaciones van a ser las mejores.

Hablar

AT 2.3–4 — Describe an imaginary trip to Figueres or Barcelona. Give the information listed.
Encourage students to include opinions and to use adjectives, adverbs and quantifiers to make their description more interesting. This activity will also require students to remember what there is to do in Figueres and Barcelona.

Leer

AT 3.4 — Read the information and answer these questions in English.
This activity tests reading skills using the language covered in this unit.

Answers:
1 Valencia; 2 four: Museo de Ciencias Príncipe Felipe, L'Oceanografic, L'Hemisferic, El Palacio de las Artes; 3 you are forbidden not to touch the exhibits; 4 go on a journey under the sea to discover the magic and secrets of the seas and oceans; 5 shops, car parks, rest areas, children's areas, cafeterias and restaurants. 6 a La Ciutat entry card; 7 children under 12, pensioners, senior citizens, disabled people, students

3B Las vacaciones

Escribir

AT 4.4–5 Write an account of an imaginary day trip to the *Ciudad de las Artes y las Ciencias* in Valencia. Think about what you are going to do there, how you are going to get there, etc.

This activity tests writing skills using the language covered in this unit. Students should make their account as interesting as possible and include opinions about transport, etc. as well as adjectives and adverbs. They may find it useful to find out more about Valencia before they begin.

Leer 3B   página 158

Planner

Resources
Students' Book, page 158

Renewed Framework references
2.1, 2.2, 3.1, 3.2, 5.3, 5.4, 5.5

PLTS
Activity 1: Reflective learners; Creative thinkers; Self-managers
Activity 2: Creative thinkers; Independent enquirers

Homework/Self-study
Students find out as much as they can about *paradors* in Spain.

AT 3.4 / PLTS **1** Read the text. Using all the reading strategies you have developed, try your best to work out the meanings of new words. Look up words you don't know in a bilingual dictionary. Remind yourself about how to use a dictionary on page 115 first.
You could discuss the different strategies as a class before students begin. Remind students of the importance of using a dictionary correctly.

AT 3.4 / PLTS **2** What does the word *parador* mean? Do we have anything similar in the UK?
Students should try to find out what this means themselves. Do any students already know? They could try to guess what it means before researching it and then check to see if they were correct.

Answer: a parador is a luxury hotel, e.g. monasteries, castles, stately homes, etc.; paradors are state run and owned which means cheaper tourism

AT 3.4 **3** When were the *paradores* established, by whom and for what reason?

Answer:
King Alfonso 13th established them in 1928 to entice foreign tourists to get to know Spain.

AT 3.4 **4** Name three different types of parador.
Students should be able to work these out by recognising cognates and drawing upon the vocabulary they have learnt in this unit.

Answers:
Any three of: medieval castles, ancient monasteries or convents, fortresses, old country houses/stately homes, historical places, first-rate modern hotels

Foundation Workbook

Página 56   **3B.1 El transporte**
- Use with Students' Book, pages 104–105

AT 4.1 **1** Write the correct word(s) under each picture

Answers:
a coche; **b** bicicleta; **c** avión; **d** metro; **e** autobús; **f** autocar; **g** a pie; **h** tren; **i** barco

AT 1.2 **2** Listen for the correct form of transport for each person.
Students should think about how each of the forms of transport from Activity 1 is pronounced in Spanish.

Las vacaciones 3B

CD 3, track 71 — página 56, actividad 2

1. Voy al instituto en bicicleta.
2. Voy a Orlando en Florida en avión.
3. Voy al centro de la ciudad en metro.
4. Voy a Londres en tren.
5. Voy a Madrid en coche.
6. Voy a mi dormitorio a pie.

Answers:
1 b; 2 c; 3 d; 4 h; 5 a; 6 g

AT 3.2 **3 Draw lines to link up the parts of the sentences so they all make sense.**
Point out to students that there could be a couple of options for some of the sentences.

Possible answers:
a Voy al instituto en coche porque es más barato.
b Voy a Orlando en avión porque es más divertido.
c Voy a Londres en tren porque es más cómodo.
d Voy a mi dormitorio a pie porque es más corto.

Página 57 — 3B.2 Alojamiento
- Use with Students' Book, pages 106–107

AT 1.1 **1 Listen. Find the right word and say it as soon as you can.**
Pupils keep score of how many they get before the CD says the next one.

CD 3, track 72 — página 57, actividad 1

Listen to some words in Spanish. Try to say the English before you hear the next word. Keep your score!

un hotel
un albergue juvenil
un hotel
un camping
una habitación
una pensión
un albergue juvenil
un camping
una habitación
sábanas

Now you say the Spanish:
a hotel
a campsite
a hotel
a youth hostel
a campsite
a youth hostel
a room

AT 3.3 **2 Read the adverts and underline the Spanish for the words. Decide what is being described in each (a–f).**

Answers:
playa, duchas, balcón, básico, restaurante, jóvenes, cama doble, barato, piscina, habitaciones
1 b; 2 a; 3 d; 4 c

AT 4.2–3 **3 Write a sentence about where you are going to stay on holiday.**
Encourage students to draw upon the vocabulary and structures from the previous activities.

Página 58 — 3B.3 Quiero reservar...
- Use with Students' Book, pages 108–109

AT 3.3–4 **1 Read the letter and fill in the details.**

Answers:
Dates: 8-11 August
Number of rooms: 2
Number of people: 4
Bathroom: one bath, one shower
Room facilities: TV and WiFi
Important note: vegetarians

AT 4.3–4 **2 Write a similar letter for this family.**
Practice of writing a reservation letter. Students can refer back to the text in Activity 1 for support, but must use the details given.

Página 59 — 3B.4 ¿Adónde vamos?
- Use with Students' Book, pages 110–111

AT 3.2 **1 Try to match up the sentence halves.**

Answers:
1 e; 2 a; 3 c; 4 b; 5 d

AT 1.2 **2 Listen and check.**
Students should pay attention to how the different places are pronounced.

CD 3, track 73 — página 59, actividad 2

1. Voy a ir a España.
2. Voy a trabajar en una tienda.
3. Voy a alojarme en un hotel.
4. Voy a nadar en la piscina.
5. Voy a visitar museos.

3B Las vacaciones

AT 3.3 **3 Read the information below. Which sentence tells you…**
This practises tourist information vocabulary.

Answers:
when it is open in the summer: c (every day from 9am–8pm); when it is open the rest of the year: d (Tuesday–Sunday, from 10.30am–6pm); what days it is shut: e (25th December, 1st January); who gets free entry/discounts: f (children under 9 free and students/retired people discount); how long it takes to walk from the station: i (15 minutes); who Dalí was: a (a famous Spanish painter); how far it is from Barcelona: g (100 km); how to get there from Barcelona and how long it takes: h (train or car, an hour and a half)

Página 60   3B.5 Al extranjero
• Use with Students' Book, pages 112–113

AT 3.2 **1 Draw lines to match up the Spanish and the English.**
Practice of recognising different question words in Spanish.

Answers:
a Where are you going on holiday? b When are you leaving? c How long are you going to be there? d How are you going to travel? e What is the weather like in August? f What are you going to do?

AT 3.2 **2 Find these question words in Activity 1.**
Students who finish quickly could try to use each question word in simple sentences of their own.

Answers:
a adónde; b cuándo; c cómo; d qué; e cuánto tiempo

AT 1.2 **3 Listen and note the answer to each question in Spanish.**
Further practice of understanding question words in Spanish.

🎧 CD 3, track 74   página 60, actividad 3

1
– ¿Adónde vas de vacaciones?
– Voy a Barcelona.
2
– ¿Cuándo vas a ir?
– Voy en agosto.
3
– ¿Cuánto tiempo vas a estar allí?
– Un fin de semana.
4
– ¿Cómo vas a viajar?
– En avión.
5
– ¿Qué tiempo hace en agosto?
– Hace sol.
6
– ¿Qué vas a hacer?
– Voy a visitar museos.

Answers:
1 a Barcelona; 2 en agosto; 3 un fin de semana; 4 en avión; 5 hace sol; 6 visitar museos

AT 1.2, 2.2 **4 Listen to the questions. Use your answers to Activity 3 to reply in Spanish. Then listen again and give your own answers.**
Students could also practise asking and answering these questions in pairs.

🎧 CD 3, track 75   página 60, actividad 4

¿Adónde vas de vacaciones?
[Pause]
¿Cuándo vas a ir?
[Pause]
¿Cuánto tiempo vas a estar allí?
[Pause]
¿Cómo vas a viajar?
[Pause]
¿Qué tiempo hace en agosto?
[Pause]
¿Qué vas a hacer?

Página 61   3B.6A Labolengua
• Use with Students' Book, pages 114–115

1 Write the correct person from this list next to each verb in the examples above.
Practice of forming the immediate future tense in Spanish.

Answers:
I; you; he/she/it; we; you (plural); they

2 Translate the examples in the Grammar box into English.

Answers:
I'm going to swim in the pool. You are going to go out with your friends. He/She is going on holiday. We are going to have lunch at one o'clock. You are going to travel to Colombia. They are going to play basketball.

3 Translate into Spanish.
Students draw upon what they have done in Activities 1 and 2 to translate the sentences.

Las vacaciones 3B

Answers:
a Voy a comer en un restaurante. b Va a visitar un museo.
c Vamos a viajar en avión. d Van a trabajar en un café.

Página 62   3B.6B Técnica

- Use with Students' Book, pages 114–115

1 Listen and tick off any words in the boxes that you hear.

> 🎧 **CD 3, track 76**   página 62, actividad 1
>
> Voy a ir a España
> porque
> me gusta
> ir a la playa

> con mi familia
> pero
> también me gusta
> ir con mis amigos
> ir con mis amigos
> por ejemplo
> me encanta
> ir de compras
> con mis amigos
> sin embargo
> puedo
> comer
> en un restaurante
> con mi familia

2 Now it's your turn. Start with *Voy a ir a España…* then roll a dice for a connective. Carry on for as long as you can.
This is a fun way to practise using extended sentences which will lead to better marks.

Higher Workbook

Página 56   3B.1 El transporte

- Use with Students' Book, pages 104–105

[AT 4.1-2] 1 Write the correct words under each picture.

Answers:
a en coche; b en bicicleta; c en avión; d en metro; e en autobús;
f en autocar; g a pie; h en tren; i en barco

[AT 1.2] 2 Listen and select a suitable form of transport for each person.
Remind students to think about how each of the forms of transport from Activity 1 is pronounced in Spanish. Students' answers may vary for this activity; encourage some discussion.

> 🎧 **CD 4, track 46**   página 56, actividad 2
>
> 1 Voy al instituto.
> 2 Voy a Orlando en Florida.
> 3 Voy al centro de la ciudad.
> 4 Voy a Londres.
> 5 Voy a Madrid.
> 6 Voy a mi dormitorio.

Answers:
1 b; 2 c; 3 d; 4 h; 5 a; 6 g

[AT 4.2-3] 3 Write up your answers to Activity 2 in sentences, explaining why.
Students explain why they answered how they did in Activity 2 using the words in the box for support.

Página 57   3B.2 Alojamiento

- Use with Students' Book, pages 106–107

[AT 1.1] 1 Listen. Find the right word and say it as soon as you can.
Pupils keep score of how many they get before the CD says the next one.

> 🎧 **CD 4, track 47**   página 57, actividad 1
>
> You are going to hear some words in Spanish. Try to say the English before you hear the next word. Keep your score!
> un hotel
> un albergue juvenil
> un camping
> una habitación
> una pensión
> un albergue juvenil
> una habitació
> sábanas
>
> Now you say the Spanish:
> a hotel   a room
> a campsite   a guest house
> a hotel   a youth hostel
> a youth hostel   a hotel
> a campsite   a campsite
> a youth hostel   sheets
> a room   a room

3B Las vacaciones

AT 3.3   **2**   **Read and decide what is being described (a–f) in each advert.**

Answers:
1 b; 2 a; 3 d; 4 c

AT 4.2–3   **3**   **Write a sentence about each place in Activity 2.**
Students should try to use connectives and adjectives, and give opinions.

Página 58   3B.3 Quiero reservar...
- Use with Students' Book, pages 108–109

AT 3.4   **1**   **Read and note all the details in English.**
Students read the letter of reservation of note down the information given.

Answers:
Dates: 8–11 August; Number of rooms: 2; Number of people: 4; 2 children 6 and 8; Bathroom: one bath in children's room, one shower; Room facilities: TV and WiFi; Important note: vegetarians

AT 4.3–4   **2**   **Write a similar letter for this family.**
Practice of writing a reservation letter. Students can refer back to the text in Activity 1 for support, but must use the details given.

Página 59   3B.4 ¿Adónde vamos?
- Use with Students' Book, pages 110–111

AT 3.2   **1**   **Try to match up the sentence halves.**

Answers:
1 e; 2 a; 3 c; 4 b; 5 d

AT 1.2–3   **2**   **Listen and check.**
Students should pay attention to how the different places are pronounced.

> 🎧 **CD 4, track 48**   página 59, actividad 2
>
> Voy a ir a España de vacaciones y voy a alojarme en un hotel de lujo. Voy a nadar en la piscina todos los días. Me encanta explorar, y voy a visitar museos. ¿Y para pagar el viaje? Pues voy a trabajar en una tienda.

AT 3.4   **3**   **Read the information. Traffic light the sentences.**

4   **Translate your green sentences. Give one piece of information for each orange sentence. Make an intelligent guess as to what each red sentence is about.**
You may find it useful for students to discuss this as groups as some may understand sentences that others don't and vice versa.

Answer:
Dalí was a very famous Spanish painter. Museum is in Figueres, north of Barcelona. June–Sept open 9am to 8pm seven days a week. Oct–May from 10.30am to 6pm, Tues to Sun. Not open 25th Dec or 1st Jan. Children under 9 get in free. Discounts for students or retired people. Figueres 100 km from Barcelona. Train or car an hour and a half journey. If go by train, museum 15 mins walk from Figueres station.

Página 60   3B.5 Al extranjero
- Use with Students' Book, pages 112–113

AT 3.3   **1**   **Read and fill in the missing question words.**
Practice of forming questions.

Answers:
a Adónde; b Cuándo; c Cuánto; d Cómo; e Qué; f Qué

AT 3.2   **2**   **Find these question words in Activity 1.**
Further practice of question words.

Answers:
a adónde; b cuándo; c cómo; d qué; e cuánto tiempo

AT 1.2   **3**   **Listen and note the answer to each question in Spanish.**
Further practice of understanding question words in Spanish.

> 🎧 **CD 4, track 49**   página 60, actividad 3
>
> 1
> – ¿Adónde vas de vacaciones?
> – Voy a Barcelona.
> 2
> – ¿Cuándo vas a ir?
> – Voy en agosto.
> 3
> – ¿Cuánto tiempo vas a estar allí?
> – Voy a estar allí un fin de semana.
> 4.
> – ¿Cómo vas a viajar?
> – Voy a viajar en avión.
> 5
> – ¿Qué tiempo hace en agosto?
> – En agosto hace sol.
> 6
> – ¿Qué vas a hacer?
> – Voy a visitar museos.

Answers:
1 a Barcelona; 2 en agosto; 3 un fin de semana; 4 en avión; 5 hace sol; 6 visitar museos

Las vacaciones 3B

AT 1.2/ 2.2–3

4 Listen to the questions. Use your answers to Activity 3 to reply in Spanish in full sentences. Then listen again and give your own answers.
Students could also practise asking and answering these questions in pairs.

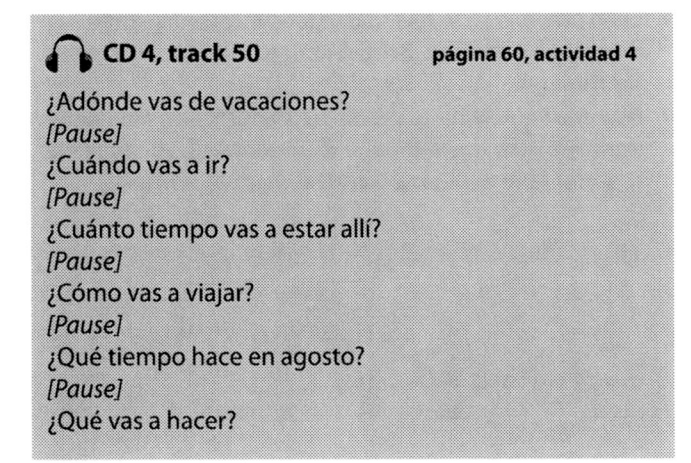

🎧 **CD 4, track 50** página 60, actividad 4

¿Adónde vas de vacaciones?
[Pause]
¿Cuándo vas a ir?
[Pause]
¿Cuánto tiempo vas a estar allí?
[Pause]
¿Cómo vas a viajar?
[Pause]
¿Qué tiempo hace en agosto?
[Pause]
¿Qué vas a hacer?

Página 61   3B.6A Labolengua
- Use with Students' Book, pages 114–115

1 Write the correct person next to the verb in the examples above.
Practice of forming the immediate future tense in Spanish.

Answers:
I; you; he/she/it; we; you (plural); they

2 Translate the examples into English.

Answers:
I'm going to swim in the pool. You are going to go out with your friends. He/She is going on holiday. We are going to have lunch at one o'clock. You are going to travel to Colombia. They are going to play basketball.

3 Translate the following into Spanish.
Students translate the sentences.

Answers:
a Voy a comer en un restaurante. **b** Va a visitar un museo.
c Vamos a viajar en avión. **d** Van a trabajar en un café.
e Va a quedarse en un hotel. **f** Vas/Vais a ir de compras.

Página 62   3B.6B Técnica
- Use with Students' Book, pages 114–115

1 Listen and tick off any words on this page that you hear.

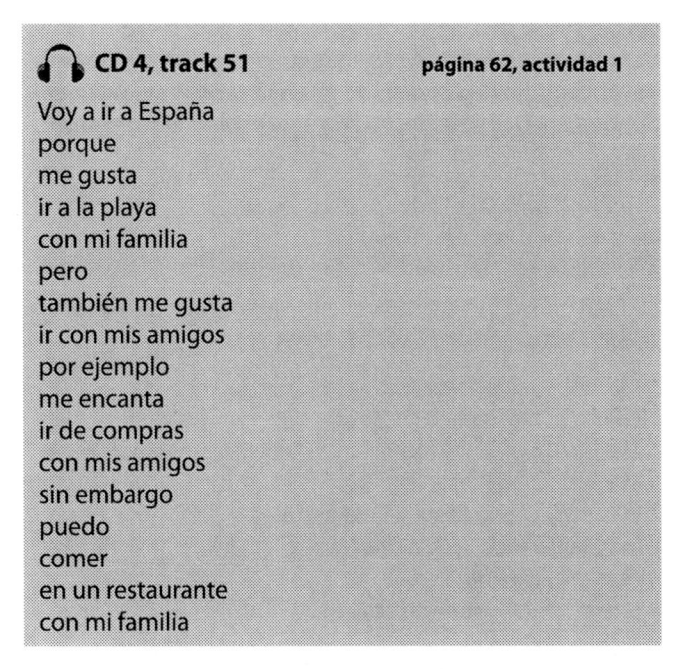

🎧 **CD 4, track 51** página 62, actividad 1

Voy a ir a España
porque
me gusta
ir a la playa
con mi familia
pero
también me gusta
ir con mis amigos
por ejemplo
me encanta
ir de compras
con mis amigos
sin embargo
puedo
comer
en un restaurante
con mi familia

2 Your turn. Start with 'Voy a ir a España…' then roll a dice for a connective. Carry on for as long as you can.
This is a fun way to practise using extended sentences which will lead to better marks.

4A ¿Lo pasaste bien?

Unit Objectives

Contexts and cultural focus: what to do on holiday, weather, activities, past holidays, Spanish festivals
Grammar: the expression *(no) se puede*, the past tense, the verb *ir* in the past tense, opinions in the past tense
Language learning: avoiding repetition of conventional vocabulary, linking sentences to avoid repetition, writing about someone else, improving spoken and written work

- *Aim:* to talk about what you can do/did on holiday whilst incorporating the grammar and vocabulary covered in the spread.
- Each unit has an associated video which will feature throughout the unit. Below is the transcript of the video for this unit.
- As a starter activity to introduce the Unit and familiarise students with the language they will meet, you may find it useful for the class to view the video as a whole.

Video script (CD 3, track 3)

Marisa: ¿Dónde están?
Eva: No lo sé.
Marisa: Son las diez y cinco. El tren sale en diez minutos.
Marisa: ¿Qué hora es?
Eva: Son las diez y siete minutos.
Marisa: Pero… ¿Dónde están?
Marisa: ¡Oh, no!
Eva: ¿Oh, no? ¿Qué?
Marisa: ¡No me lo puedo creer! No van a venir.
Eva: ¿Qué quieres decir?
Marisa: Quiero decir que no van a venir y nunca tuvieron la intención de venir.
Eva: No entiendo.
Marisa: Creo que lo único que querían es que… bueno, ya sabes… nos conociéramos mejor.
Eva: ¡Qué retorcidos!
[Pause]
Marisa: Bueno, entonces, ¿qué hacemos ahora?
Eva: No sé.
Marisa: Tenemos los billetes…
Eva: Sí, y Figueres está muy bien.
Marisa: Sí…y…y… no conozco a nadie mejor que tú, Eva, que me podría enseñar Figueres.
Eva: Bueno pues, ¡vamos!
[Pause]
Marisa: Mi padre y yo nos fuimos a Machu Picchu el año pasado.
Eva: Seguro que fue un viaje alucinante.
Marisa: Sí, lo fue. Fuimos de excursión por el camino del Inca. Nos llevó 6 días. Dormimos en tiendas de campaña y anduvimos entre 10 y 15 kilómetros de media por día. ¡Vimos las plantas y las flores más increíbles que te puedas imaginar!

Eva: Y ¿visteis algún cóndor?
Marisa: ¡Sí! Vimos bastantes. Son fabulosos. ¿Y tú? ¿Dónde estuviste la última vez que te fuiste de vacaciones?
Eva: También fue genial. Estuvimos en Méjico. Fuimos al Museo de Frida Kahlo en Ciudad de Méjico. Y después, alquilamos un coche y fuimos a su casa en Coyoacán.
Marisa: Tiene pinta de haber sido muy…
Eva: …aburrido, ya lo sé, pero en realidad fue muy interesante. Incluso conocí a un chico.
Marisa: ¡Cuenta, cuenta!
Eva: No hay nada que contar. Nos conocimos, charlamos, nos caímos bien, paseamos juntos, y… al final, el último día… nos besamos. Eso es todo lo que hay que contar.
Marisa: Yo también tenía novio en Argentina.
Eva: ¿*Tenías* novio? ¿En pasado?
Marisa: Sí. Conoció a otra chica.
Eva: ¡Ah!
Marisa: Sí. De todas maneras me considero muy joven para tener novio. A decir verdad, sólo quiero tener buenos amigos, amigos de verdad.
Eva: Sí, yo también.
Marisa: ¿Sabes?, creo que es lo único que tenemos en común.
Eva: Creo que tienes razón.

¿Lo pasaste bien? 4A

Unit 4A, ¿Lo pasaste bien? Overview grid

Page reference	Contexts and objectives	Language learning	Grammar	Key language	Framework	AT level
Pages 120–1 ¿Qué se puede hacer?	• say what can/can't be done in your region and why	• avoid repetition of common vocabulary	• use (no) se puede correctly	se puede; no se puede; se puede visitar; se puede ir; se puede ver; se puede pasear; se puede pescar; se puede comprar; se puede jugar; se puede hacer; el río; al aire libre; lamentablemente	1.1, 1.2, 1.4, 2.4, 2.5, 3.1, 4.2, 4.3, 4.4, 4.5, 4.6, 5.1, 5.8	1.4, 2.3, 3.3, 4.3–4
Pages 122–3 ¿Adónde fuiste?	• talk about the weather in the past tense	• link sentences to avoid repetition	• use the verb *ir* correctly in the preterite	el verano pasado; el invierno pasado; el año pasado; hace dos años; el pasado junio; las Navidades pasadas; hizo sol; hizo calor; hizo frío; hizo viento; hizo buen tiempo; hizo mal tiempo; estuvo nublado; hubo tormenta; hubo niebla; llovió	1.1, 1.2, 2.1, 2.4, 2.5, 3.1, 3.2, 4.2, 4.3, 4.4, 4.5, 5.1, 5.8	1.3–5, 2.3, 3.2–5, 4.4–5
Pages 124–5 ¿Qué hiciste?	• talk about free time activities in the past tense	• write about someone else	• use the preterite of regular verbs correctly	alojarse / nos alojamos; hacer / hice vela; tomar / tomé el sol; bañarse / me bañé en el mar; comer / comimos comida típica; relajarse / nos relajamos; pasear / paseamos; sacar / saqué muchas fotos; salir / salí de compras; comprar / compré recuerdos; escribir / escribí unas postales; la mayoría de las tardes; volver / volví a casa	1.1, 1.2, 1.4, 1.5, 2.1, 2.2, 2.4, 4.2, 4.3, 4.4, 4.5, 4.6, 5.1	1.5, 2.5, 3.5, 4.5
Pages 126–7 ¿Lo pasaste bien?	• give your views on a past holiday	• turn Level 4 spoken or written work into Level 5	• use opinions in the preterite tense	¡Lo pasé / pasamos fenomenal!; ¡Lo pasé / pasamos bomba!; ¡Qué aburrido!; ¡Qué desastre!; fue / fueron regular; fue / fueron muy emocionante(s); fue / fueron increíbles; no estuvo / estuvieron mal; me / nos encantó; me / nos gustó	1.1, 1.2, 1.4, 1.5, 2.1, 3.1, 3.2, 4.2, 4.3, 4.4, 4.5, 4.6, 5.3, 5.4, 5.8	1.4–5, 2.4–5, 3.5 4.5–6
Pages 128–9 ¿Qué compraste?	• practise language for buying souvenirs in a Spanish-speaking country			un imán; unas castañuelas; un abanico; una camiseta; un vestido de flamenco; una guitarra española; una muñeca; un sombrero; un llavero; unas gafas de sol; el / la dependiente; el / la cliente; ¿Qué deseas?; ¿Cuánto cuesta?; muy caro; algo más barato;¡Mira!; Me lo quedo; ¿Algo más?	1.1, 1.2, 1.4, 1.5, 2.1, 3.1, 3.2, 4.1, 4.2, 5.3	1.3, 2.4, 3.2–4

4A ¿Lo pasaste bien?

Pages 130–1 **Labolengua**	• review language and grammar from the unit				1.1, 1.4, 2.1, 2.4, 4.1, 4.2, 4.3, 4.4, 4.5, 5.1, 5.6	
Pages 132–3 **Extra Star** **Extra Plus**	• differentiated extension/ homework material	• revise and consolidate all vocabulary and grammar covered in the unit	• revise and consolidate all vocabulary and grammar covered in the unit		2.1, 2.2, 2.4, 2.5, 3.1, 3.2, 4.2, 4.3, 4.4, 4.5, 4.6, 5.1, 5.8	3.3–5, 4.3–5
Page 134 **Prueba**	• end-of-spread test				1.1, 1.4, 1.5, 2.1, 2.2, 2.4, 2.5, 4.2, 4.3, 4.4, 4.5, 4.6, 5.4	1.5, 2.5, 3.5, 4.5–6
Page 135 **Vocabulario**	• a summary of the key language covered in each spread of this unit					
Page 159 **Leer 2A**	• practice of longer reading texts based on the theme of the unit				1.5, 2.1, 2.4, 2.5, 4.2, 4.3, 4.4, 4.5, 5.4	3.3–5, 4.5–6

¿Lo pasaste bien? 4A

Week-by-week overview
(Three-year KS3 Route: assuming six weeks' work or approximately 10–12.5 hours)
(Two-year KS3 Route: assuming four weeks' worth or approxmately 6.5-8.5 hours)
*Please note that essential activities are highlighted.

About Unit 4A, ¿Lo pasaste bien?: Students work in the context of what you can do on holiday. They talk about what can/can't be done in the region and why. They also talk about the weather and free time activities in the past tense. They give their opinion of a past holiday and practise language to buy souvenirs in a Spanish-speaking country. Students learn how to use *(no) se puede* correctly and how to use *ir* correctly in the preterite. They also learn how to use regular verbs and give opinions in the preterite tense. The unit also provides tips on language learning techniques.

	Three-Year KS3 Route			Two-Year KS3 Route	
Week	**Resources**	**Objectives**	**Week**	**Resources**	**Objectives**
1	4A.1 ¿Qué se puede hacer?	say what can/can't be done in your region and why avoid repetition of common vocabulary use *(no) se puede* correctly	1	4A.1 ¿Qué se puede hacer? omit activities Think! & 4	say what can/can't be done in your region and why avoid repetition of common vocabulary use *(no) se puede* correctly
2	4A.2 ¿Adónde fuiste? 4A.6 LabIolengua B (p.130) 4A.6 LabIolengua C (p.131)	talk about the weather in the past tense link sentences to avoid repetition use the verb *ir* correctly in the preterite	2	4A.2 ¿Adónde fuiste? omit activities Think!, Gramática & Challenge 4A.6 LabIolengua B (p.130) omit activities 3 & 5 4A.6 LabIolengua C (p.131) Omit activity 7	talk about the weather in the past tense link sentences to avoid repetition use the verb *ir* correctly in the preterite
3	4A.3 ¿Qué hiciste? 4A.6 LabIolengua A (p.130)	talk about free time activities in the past tense write about someone else use the preterite of regular verbs correctly	3	4A.3 ¿Qué hiciste? omit activities Think! & 5 4A.6 LabIolengua A (p.130)	talk about free time activities in the past tense write about someone else use the preterite of regular verbs correctly
4	4A.4 ¿Lo pasaste bien? 4A.6 LabIolengua D (p.131)	give your views on a past holiday turn Level 4 spoken or written work into Level 5 use opinions in the preterite tense	4	4A.4 ¿Lo pasaste bien? omit activities Think! 4A.8 Prueba (p.134) Vocabulario (p.135)	give your views on a past holiday turn Level 4 spoken or written work into Level 5 use opinions in the preterite tense recapping on the vocabulary of the unit prepare and carry out assessment in all four skills
5	4A.5 ¿Qué compraste?	practise language for buying souvenirs in a Spanish-speaking country			
6	4A.7 Extra (Star) (p.132) 4A.7 Extra (Plus) (p.133) 4A.8 Prueba (p.134) Vocabulario (p.135) Leer (p.159)	further reinforcement and extension of the language of the unit recapping on the vocabulary of the unit prepare and carry out assessment in all four skills further reading to explore the language of the unit and cultural themes			

4A.1 ¿Lo pasaste bien?

4A.1 ¿Qué se puede hacer? — páginas 120–121

Planner

Objectives
- say what can/can't be done in your region and why
- use *(no) se puede* correctly
- avoid repetition of common vocabulary

Resources
Students' Book, pages 120–121
CD 3, track 2
Foundation Workbook, page 64
Higher Workbook, page 64
Foundation Workbook audio, CD 3, track 77
Higher Workbook audio, CD 4, track 52
Interactive OxBox, Unit 4A
Copymasters 92–99
Assessment, Unit 4A

Key language
se puede; no se puede; se puede visitar; se puede ir; se puede ver; se puede pasear; se puede pescar; se puede comprar; se puede jugar; se puede hacer; el río; al aire libre; lamentablemente

Grammar
- use *(no) se puede* correctly

Renewed Framework references
1.1, 1.2, 1.4, 2.4, 2.5, 3.1, 4.2, 4.3, 4.4, 4.5, 4.6, 5.1, 5.8

PLTS
Think!: Reflective learners
Think!: Self-managers; Reflective learners
Activity 4: Reflective learners; Team workers; Creative thinkers
Challenge: Reflective learners; Creative thinkers

Starters
- Play a class game using the key language. Ask a student, *¿Qué se puede hacer en...?* The student mimes one of the activities and the rest of the class says what it is you can do, e.g. *Se puede comprar....* Some of items of key language will be difficult to mime so you may need to add a few activities with which the students are familiar. *Se puede jugar...* can be used with a variety of games, e.g. football, rugby, tennis, hockey, basketball, etc. in order to add more variety.
- Go round the class asking each student *¿Qué se puede hacer en...?* Each student must say something you can do, using the expression *se puede....* With more able classes, extend the activity by asking students to say why you can/can't do certain activities, using as many different words for because as possible.

Plenaries
- Students work in pairs to have a conversation about an imaginary town where there is nothing to do. Partner A asks if you can do certain activities, e.g. *¿Se puede comer bien?*; partner B answers saying no and explaining why. They then swap roles, but this time, they talk about a town where there is lots to do.
- Students use the information from the spread to write a paragraph about Zaragoza. What is it like? What is there to do there? Remind them to use *(no) se puede*. Students could present it as a tourist brochure with pictures to illustrate the different places and activities.

Homework/Self-study
Think!/Gramática: Students write a couple of sentences incorporating the verb *se puede*.
Think!: Students write sentences saying what you can/can't do in their town/village and why. They should try and use all of the different words for 'because'.

AT 1.4 **1 Escucha. ¿Qué se puede hacer en Zaragoza?**
Students listen and match the photos to the places. They then listen again and list the photos in the order they are mentioned.

🎧 **CD 3, track 2** — página 120, actividad 1

¿Qué se puede hacer en Zaragoza? Uy… ¡mucho! Zaragoza es una ciudad muy histórica y ofrece mucho. Por ejemplo, entre otros lugares se puede visitar la Catedral de la Seo o se puede ir al Palacio de la Aljafería, mi lugar preferido porque me encantan los edificios árabes.

Si te gustan los toros, se puede ver una corrida en la Plaza de Toros de la Misericordia o si prefieres el fútbol, se puede ver un partido en el Estadio de la Romareda. Si buscas relajarte, se puede pasear por el Parque Grande o incluso se puede pescar en el Río Ebro aunque creo que para eso es mejor alejarse un poco de la ciudad. Para comprar hay el Mercado Central donde se puede comprar de todo y más.

¡Ah! Me olvidaba… otro lugar impresionante es el Parque Metropolitano del Agua donde se puede jugar al golf o incluso se puede hacer rafting.

4A.1 ¿Lo pasaste bien?

Answers:
1 b, la Seo; 2 g, el Palacio de la Aljafería; 3 f, la Plaza de Toros de la Misericordia; 4 c, el Estadio de la Romareda; 5 h, el Parque Grande; 6 a, el río Ebro; 7 d, el Mercado Central; 8 e, el Parque Metropolitano del Agua

PLTS | Think!
Elicit from students that verbs following *se puede* are all in the infinitive. Can they use this verb in a sentence of their own?

AT 3.3 | 2 Une las dos partes de las frases. En Zaragoza …
Students match the two halves of the sentences about Zaragoza to complete them.

Answers:
1 c; 2 d; 3 a; 4 e; 5 f; 6 b

PLTS | Think!
Students note down the various ways of saying 'because' in Activity 2. Check answers as a class. Exploit this further by asking students to say what you can/can't do in their town and why, using the different words for 'because'.

PLTS | Gramática
Read the explanation as a class. Students should already have noted that *se puede* is followed by a verb in the infinitive.

AT 4.3 | 3 Escribe las frases de la Actividad 2 en su sentido contrario.
Students put in to practice what they have learnt about *se puede* and rewrite the sentences from Activity 2 so that they mean the opposite.

Answer:
*1 **No** se puede comer bien porque **no** hay mucha variedad de restaurantes. 2 Se puede ir a la playa ya que afortunadamente hay mar. 3 **No** se puede continuar estudiando pues **no** hay una universidad. 4 **No** se puede ir de compras porque **no** hay muchas tiendas o centros comerciales. 5 **No** se puede visitar la ciudad sin necesidad de un coche puesto que el transporte público **no** es muy bueno. 6 **No** se puede hacer deporte al aire libre porque no hay parques o polideportivos con espacio exterior.*

AT 2.3 | PLTS | 4 Hablar. En dos equipos debéis llegar a la meta.

Split the class into two teams. Students must go from left to right saying grammatically correct sentences that make sense, using the pictures as prompts. They can choose their starting hexagon but must then only choose a hexagon that touches the previous one. They can use a small piece of paper or similar to place on the last box correctly answered. The team that gets from one end to the other first wins.

AT 4.3–4 | PLTS | Challenge
Write a paragraph about what you can/can't do in your city and why.
Students should try to vary their writing by using different ways of saying 'because'.

4A.2 ¿Lo pasaste bien?

4A.2 ¿Adónde fuiste?
páginas 122–123

Planner

Objectives
- talk about the weather in the past tense
- use the verb *ir* correctly in the preterite
- link sentences to avoid repetition

Video
Video script, Unit 4A

Resources
Students' Book, pages 122–123
CD 3, tracks 3–4
Foundation Workbook, page 65
Higher Workbook, page 65
Foundation Workbook audio, CD 3, track 78
Higher Workbook audio, CD 4, track 53
Interactive OxBox, Unit 4A
Copymasters 92–99
Assessment, Unit 4A

Key language
el verano pasado; el invierno pasado; el año pasado; hace dos años; el pasado junio; las Navidades pasadas; hizo sol; hizo calor; hizo frío; hizo viento; hizo buen tiempo; hizo mal tiempo; estuvo nublado; hubo tormenta; hubo niebla; llovió

Grammar
- use the verb *ir* correctly in the preterite

Renewed Framework references
1.1, 1.2, 2.1, 2.4, 2.5, 3.1, 3.2, 4.2, 4.3, 4.4, 4.5, 5.1, 5.8

PLTS
Think!: Creative thinkers; Reflective learners
Activity 4: Reflective learners
Challenge: Reflective learners

Starters
- Play a class game to practise using weather expressions in the preterite. Divide the class into small groups. Say a place, e.g. *Méjico*. Students raise their hand to give an appropriate weather phrase in the preterite, e.g. *Hizo sol y mucho calor*. The group that gives the most answers wins. Encourage more able students to extend their answers, e.g. *Fui a Méjico y hizo sol y mucho calor*. They could even add when they went, e.g. *El verano pasado…*
- Go round the class and give each student in turn one of the phrases from Activity 2 to complete, e.g. *El verano pasado…* Students complete the phrase with something feasible, e.g. *El verano pasado fui a Barcelona*.

Plenaries
- Challenge students to write five sentences on the theme of the spread using the preterite of *ir*. More able students should try to use a different person for each of the five sentences.
- Students write about their best ever holiday using the language they have learnt in the spread. They mention where they went, who with, what the weather was like and any places they visted while they were there.

Homework/Self-study
Students add the phrases from Activity 2 to their vocabulary list and learn them so that they can use them when writing or speaking about past events.
Think!: Students try to create more sentences along the lines of those in Activity 3, i.e. using different months, seasons, days of the week, etc.
Gramática: Students learn the preterite of *ir* off by heart.
Gramática: Students learn the possessive pronouns and use each of these in a sentence, or, for less able students, in a phrase.

AT 1.5 **1 Mira el video. ¿Adónde fueron Eva y Marisa de vacaciones? ¿Con quién fueron?**
Students watch the video and note down where Eva and Marisa went on holiday and who with. Students won't yet be familiar with *ir* in the preterite so you could brainstorm the type of vocabulary to listen out for, e.g. place names, references to the past (*el año pasado*), vacaciones, family members (*mis padres*, etc.).

Video script: Unit 4A (CD 3, track 3)

Marisa: Mi padre y yo nos fuimos a Machu Picchu el año pasado.
Eva: Seguro que fue un viaje alucinante.
Marisa: Sí, lo fue. Fuimos de excursión por el camino del Inca. Nos llevó 6 días. Dormimos en tiendas de campaña y anduvimos entre 10 y 15 kilómetros de media por día. ¡Vimos las plantas y las flores más increíbles que te puedas imaginar!

4A.2 ¿Lo pasaste bien?

Eva: Y ¿visteis algún cóndor?
Marisa: ¡Sí! Vimos bastantes. Son fabulosos. ¿Y tú? ¿Dónde estuviste la última vez que te fuiste de vacaciones?
Eva: También fue genial. Estuvimos en Méjico. Fuimos al Museo de Frida Kahlo en Ciudad de Méjico. Y después, alquilamos un coche y fuimos a su casa en Coyoacán.
Marisa: Tiene pinta de haber sido muy…
Eva: …aburrido, ya lo sé, pero en realidad fue muy interesante. Incluso conocí a un chico.
Marisa: ¡Cuenta, cuenta!
Eva: No hay nada que contar. Nos conocimos, charlamos, nos caímos bien, paseamos juntos, y… al final, el último día… nos besamos. Eso es todo lo que hay que contar.

Answers:
Marisa: went to Machu Picchu last year with her father
Eva: went to Mexico, doesn't mention who with, but use of *fuimes* suggests with her parents

AT 3.2 — 2 ¿Cuándo? Empareja estas expresiones con su significado.
Students match the Spanish phrases to the correct English translation.

Answers:
1 b; 2 d; 3 f; 4 a; 5 e; 6 c

PLTS — Think!
Students use what they have learnt from Activity 2 to write other, similar sentences.

Gramática
Explain to students that this is an irregular preterite and elicit from them that it has no accents. Using the example in the past as a model, can students create their own sentence using the preterite of *ir*? More able classes can change the person to practise using all forms of this verb.

AT 3.4–5 — 3 Lee. ¿Verdadero o falso? Corrige las frases falsas.
Students read the text and state whether the sentences are true or false. They correct incorrect sentences.

Answers:
1 falso – Generalemente Eva y su familia van a Italia de vacaciones. *2 falso* – El año pasado Eva fue a Méjico con sus padres. *3 falso* – Viajaron a Méjico en avión. *4 verdadero*; *5 falso* – Durante sus vacaciones hizo sol y mucho calor. *6 falso* – Un día estuvo nublado, llovió y por la noche hubo tormenta.

AT 3.4–5 / PLTS — 4 Copia y completa la tabla.
Students use the weather expressions in Activity 3 to work out the past tense of the expressions listed.

Answers:
Hizo calor; Hizo viento; Hizo buen tiempo; Estuvo nublado; Hubo tormenta; Hubo niebla; Llovió

AT 1.3–4 — 5 Escucha y decide si es en pasado o en presente.
Students listen and decide if it's in the past or present..

CD 3, track 4 — página 123, actividad 5
1 Hoy hace buen tiempo pero ayer hizo frío.
2 Hace viento.
3 Hubo tormenta.
4 Estuvo nublado.
5 Llueve bastante.

Answers:
1 present, past; *2* present; *3* past; *4* past; *5* present

Gramática
Read through the grammar explanation as a class. Work through a few examples of possessive adjectives, e.g. *mis padres*, etc. Can students give you any examples of their own? They have come across possessive pronouns in previous reading passages. You could test students' knowledge of possessive pronouns by displaying the personal pronouns and asking students to give you the corresponding possessive pronouns.

AT 4.5 / PLTS — Challenge
Throw a dice six times and note the sequence (e.g. 322464). Don't let your partner see! Write the sentence in Spanish: work your way from A to F using the number sequence to choose from 1 to 6 in each line. Then read the complete sentence to your partner who must work out your sequence.

4A.3 ¿Lo pasaste bien?

4A.3 ¿Qué hiciste?   páginas 124–125

Planner

Objectives
- talk about free time activities in the past tense
- use the preterite of regular verbs correctly
- write about someone else

Resources
Students' Book, pages 124–125
CD 3, track 5
Foundation Workbook, page 66
Higher Workbook, page 66
Interactive OxBox, Unit 4A
Copymasters 92–99
Assessment, Unit 4A

Key language
alojarse/nos alojamos; hacer/hice vela; tomar/tomé el sol; bañarse/me bañé en el mar; comer/comimos comida típica; relajarse/nos relajamos; pasear/paseamos; sacar/saqué muchas fotos; salir/salí de compras; comprar/compré recuerdos; escribir/escribí unas postales; la mayoría de las tardes; volver/volví a casa

Grammar
- use the preterite of regular verbs correctly

Renewed Framework references
1.1, 1.2, 1.4, 1.5, 2.1, 2.2, 2.4, 4.2, 4.3, 4.4, 4.5, 4.6, 5.1

PLTS
Gramática: Reflective learners
Think!: Reflective learners; Self-managers
Activity 5: Effective participators
Challenge: Reflective learners; Self-managers

Starters
- Display some holiday activities in the present tense. Give students a time limit to rewrite these in the past tense. Check answers as a class. Less able students, can match activities in the preterite to the corresponding activity in the present tense. With more able students, include a variety of forms, rather than just the first person singular.
- Play a class game to practise using preterites. Start by saying *Fui a Barcelona* (or another town or country of your choice) *y...*. Go round the class asking each student to add an activity. They should also repeat what you have said, i.e.
Student 1: *Fui a Barcelona y compré unas postales.*
Student 2: *Fui a Barcelona y compré unas postales y visité un museo.* etc.

Plenaries
- Challenge students to write about a dream holiday they have been on (made up or true) using as many different verbs in the preterite as possible. They read their account to the class. Who has used the greatest variety of verbs in the preterite? Encourage more able students to try and use these verbs in the 2nd or 3rd person or in the plural using the verb table for support.
- Students choose what they consider to be the best holiday from their interviews in Activity 5. They then write a paragraph about it in the third person, reporting what the interviewee did, where they went, what the weather was like, etc. Volunteers could read their report to the class who tries to guess who they are talking about.

Homework/Self-study
Activity 2: Students use each of these verbs in the preterite in a sentence of their own in order to help them remember them.
Think!: Students think of and note down any examples of words where the addition of an accent changes the meaning.

AT 3.5 1 Lee lo que dicen Ana María y Charo. Escribe las letras.
Students read what Ana María and Charo say and note down the letters of the activities that each one mentions. Students should think about which of the activities might go together and where/on what type of holiday people are likely to do the activities.

Answers:
Ana María: a, e, d, f, i, l
Charo: j, b, c, k, g, h

PLTS 2 Pon las palabras en la sección correspondiente del diagrama.
Students copy the spider diagram and place the words in the box in the appropriate section. This activity introduces students to regular forms of the preterite.

Answers:
me alojé en: un hotel; un albergue juvenil; un camping; casa de mis abuelos; castillo
fui a: Dinamarca; Canadá; la piscina
hice: surf; vela; ciclismo; los deberes
compré: unas postales; recuerdos; unos CDs; una revista
visité: un museo; las ruinas romanas; una exposición de arte;

4A.3 ¿Lo pasaste bien?

un centro comercial
comí: fruta; comida típica; paella; muchas ensaladas
fui en: avión; barco; moto; bicicleta
hizo: calor; buen tiempo; sol; viento

> **PLTS** **Gramática**
> Read through the explanation as a class and work through a few example sentences using the verbs listed. You could give students some phrases to translate using the verb table for support.

> **PLTS** **Think!**
> Explain the importance of accents and look at the example given. Can students think of any similar examples of their own?

> **AT 3.5** **3 Identifica los verbos en pretérito. ¿Qué significan?**
> Students identify verbs in the preterite for themselves and say what they mean.

Answers:
Ana María: fui – I went; fuimos – we went; nos alojamos – we stayed; tomé el sol – I sunbathed; me bañé – I bathed; comimos – we ate; hice vela – I went sailing; hice surf – I went surfing
Charo: fui – I went; hizo frío – it was cold; hizo sol – it was sunny; nos relajamos – we relaxed; visitamos – we visited; paseamos – we walked; saqué – I took; me quedé – I stayed; leí – I read; salí – I went out; compré – I bought; escribí – I wrote

> **AT 1.5** **4 Escucha. ¿Qué contestaron los chicos?**
> Students listen and note down the young people's responses to the reporter's questions. They should listen for the forms of the preterite they have just seen. Students should also look at the questions listed and think about the type of reply and vocabulary they are likely to hear.

🎧 CD 3, track 5   página 125, actividad 4

1
Fui de vacaciones a Alemania con mi novio. Fuimos en autocar... ¡Qué pesado! En Alemania nos alojamos en casa de los padres de mi novio y tuvimos suerte porque hizo sol todos los días. En Berlín visitamos museos y comimos mucho.

2
Yo fui de vacaciones a Andalucía con mi madre. Fuimos en el AVE, que es el tren de alta velocidad. Allí nos alojamos en un apartamento de alquiler cerca de la playa. Hizo mucho calor así que nadamos en el mar y tomamos el sol en la playa.

3
Fui de vacaciones a Buenos Aires, en Argentina. Fui con mis padres y evidentemente fuimos en avión. Nos alojamos en un hotel pequeño cerca del centro. Generalmente hizo buen tiempo así que hicimos turismo y saqué muchas fotos.

4
Yo fui de vacaciones a Ibiza con mis amigos. Fuimos en avión y nos alojamos en un albergue juvenil. No hizo muy buen tiempo porque era invierno pero lo pasamos bien: comimos en restaurantes diferentes todos los días y bailamos en las discotecas por las noches.

Answers:
1 Alemania; su novio; en autocar; en casa de los padres de su novio; hizo sol; En Berlín vistó museos y comió mucho.
2 Andalucía; su madre; en el AVE; en un apartamento de alquiler; hizo mucho calor; nadó en el mar y tomó el sol en la playa
3 Buenos Aires, en Argentina; sus padres; en avión; en un hotel pequeño; generalmente hizo bueno tiempo; hizo turismo y saqué muchas fotos
4 Ibiza; sus amigos; en avión; en un albergue juvenil; no hizo muy buen tiempo; comió en restaurantes diferentes todos los días y bailó en las discotecas por las noches

> **AT 2.5** **5 Hablar. Utiliza las preguntas del reportero**
> **PLTS** **para hacer un sondeo en la clase.**
> Students use the reporter's questions in Activity 4 to interview their classmates about their last holiday. They can embellish to make their answers as varied and interesting as possible. More able students could choose the most interesting holiday and write up their findings using the third person.

Think!
Read through the box as a class. Have a quick recap of possessive adjectives. Explain to students that they will need to know these in order to complete the Challenge Activity.

> **AT 4.5** **Challenge**
> **PLTS** **Choose either Ana Maria's or Charo's paragraph and rewrite it in the third person.**
> Depending on the ability of the class, you may decide to go through the beginning of the texts together before students continue on their own. Remind students to pay attention to verb conjugations as well as possessive adjectives. Encourage them to read and reread their work to check that it all makes sense.

Answers:
Ana María: El invierno pasado **fue** de vacaciones a Chile con sus tíos. **Fueron** en avión y **se alojaron** en un camping porque es más barato. En Chile era verano así que la mayoría de las tardes **tomó** el sol y **se baño** en la playa con **su** primo. Después, por la noche, **comieron** comidas típicas en

4A.4 ¿Lo pasaste bien?

restaurantes de la zona. El lunes **hizo** vela con el club náutico y el miércoles **hizo** surf. ¡Uff! ¡**Fue** muy difícil!
Charo: El año pasado **fue** con **su** familia a Dublín donde hizo frío todos los días menos el jueves que hizo sol, así que **se relajaron** al lado de la piscina. El lunes visitaron los museos y **pasearon** por las calles. **Saqué** muchas fotos. El martes **se quedó** en el hotel y **leyó** una revista puesto que llovía y el miércoles **salió** de compras y **compró** unos recuerdos. El viernes, antes de volver a casa, **escribió** unas postales a **sus** amigos.

4A.4 ¿Lo pasaste bien?   páginas 126–127

Planner

Objectives
- give your views on a past holiday
- use opinions in the preterite tense
- turn Level 4 spoken or written work into Level 5

Video
Video-blog, Unit 4A

Resources
Students' Book, pages 126–127
CD 3, tracks 6–7
Foundation Workbook, page 67
Higher Workbook, page 67
Interactive OxBox, Unit 4A
Copymasters 92–99
Assessment, Unit 4A

Key language
¡Lo pasé/pasamos fenomenal!; ¡Lo pasé/pasamos bomba!; ¡Qué aburrido!; ¡Qué desastre!; fue/fueron regular; fue/fueron muy emocionante(s); fue/fueron increíbles; no estuvo/estuvieron mal; me/nos encantó; me/nos gustó

Grammar
- use opinions in the preterite tense

Renewed Framework references
1.1, 1.2, 1.4, 1.5, 2.1, 3.1, 3.2, 4.2, 4.3, 4.4, 4.5, 4.6, 5.3, 5.4, 5.8

PLTS
Think!: Reflective learners
Challenge: Creative thinkers; Reflective learners

Starters
- Display the headings: connectives, quantifiers, adjectives, opinions. Split the class into small groups and give them a time limit to write as many words as they can under each heading. Check answers as a class. Groups score a point for each correct word and two points if no other group has thought of it. The group with the most points wins.
- Go round the class asking each student to give their opinion of whatever activity you say, e.g.
  Teacher: *El esquí acuático*
  Student 1: *Me encantó*, etc.

Plenaries
- Challenge students to write a paragraph on the theme of the spread incorporating as much of the key language as possible. They should try to use different time frames and to add connectives, quantifiers, adjectives and opinions.
- Students work in pairs. Each partner describes a holiday they may or may not have been on. The other partner guesses if they have been on the holiday or if they have made it up.

Homework/Self-study
Activity 5: Students make up further extended sentences of their own using different countries, activities, etc.
Think!: Students use the suggestions given and try to improve a previous piece of written work. Alternatively, they could repeat a speaking activity, this time using more time frames, quantifiers, adjectives, etc.

AT 3.5 | **1 Lee y empareja.**
Students read the text and match the expressions in bold with the English ones. Before they begin, elicit from students that the phrases in bold are all opinions. Are there any that look a bit like English words that they can guess easily?

Answers:
1 me gustó; **2** fueron increíbles; **3** ¡Lo pasé bomba!; **4** no estuvo mal; **5** lo pasé fenomenal; **6** fue muy emocionante; **7** fue regular; **8** ¡Qué desastre!; **9** me encantó; **10** ¡Qué aburrido!

PLTS | **Think!**
Students begin to think about what they can do to improve their writing and speaking. Guide them by suggesting they look at time frames, adjectives, quantifiers, connectives and the number of opinions included.

AT 3.5 | **2 Lee de nuevo. Contesta a las preguntas en inglés.**
Students reread the text and answer the questions in English.

4A.4 ¿Lo pasaste bien?

Answers:
1 two years ago; **2** it lasted 10 hours; **3** the large avenue running along the sea front; **4** there was salsa music in all of the bars and restaurants and she danced at the disco almost every night; **5** sunbathed, rested, practised water sports such as water skiing and diving; **6** went horse riding and visited a tobacco plantation; **7** a Che Guevara T-shirt for her brother, a box of Havana cigars for her father and rum for her grandfather; **8** she left the rum behind in the bus; **9** she saw a baseball game; **10** it was incredible

> **AT 1.5**   **3 Mira el video-blog. ¿Qué contestan los chicos a estas preguntas?**
> Students watch the video blog and note down how the young people answer the questions. Students can make notes in English or in Spanish making sure they change the verb to the third person singular if they do this.

Video-blog: Unit 4A (CD 3, track 6)

¿Adónde fuiste durante las vacaciones pasadas?
Eva: Durante las vacaciones pasadas fui a Méjico con mi familia.
José: Fui a Figueres que está en el norte de Cataluña y a Madrid que es la capital de España.
Khalid: Fui a Italia.
Marisa: Fui a Perú, a Machu Picchu.

¿Qué hiciste?
Eva: Allí, visitamos el museo de Frida Kahlo.
José: En Figueres, visité a mi tía qui tiene una finca y en Madrid visité a mis abuelos.
Khalid: Visité la capital y sus monumentos más importantes.
Marisa: Visité las ruinas, tomé muchas fotos y viajé con mi padre.

¿Cómo viajaste?
Eva: Viajamos en avión.
José: A Figueres, fui en autobús y a Madrid, como siempre, en tren.
Khalid: Viajé en barco y luego allí alquilamos un coche.
Marisa: Viajé en avión.

¿Lo pasaste bien?
Eva: Muy bien. Conocí a mucha gente. Conocí a la pintura de Frida Kahlo y me encantó.
José: Por supuesto que lo pasé bien. Genial.
Khalid: Bueno, lo pasamos bastante bien pero no fue el viaje de mi vida.
Marisa: Lo pasé muy bien, muy bien.

Answers:
Eva: Fui a Méjico con su familia. Visitó el museo de Frida Kahlo. Viajó en avión. Muy bien. Conoció a mucha gente. Conoció a la pintura de Frida Kahlo y se encantó.
José: Fue a Figueres que está en el norte de Cataluña y a Madrid que es la capital de España. Visitó a su tía qui tiene una finca y en Madrid visitó a sus abuelos. A Figueres, fue en autobús y a Madrid, como siempre, en tren. Por supuesto que lo pasó bien.
Khalid: Fue a Italia. Visitó la capital y sus monumentos más importantes. Viajó en barco y luego allí alquiló un coche. Bueno, lo pasó bastante bien pero no fue el viaje de su vida.
Marisa: Fue a Perú, a Machu Picchu. Viajó en avión. Lo pasó muy bien, muy bien.

Gramática
Students have already met these two verbs and this is an ideal time to revise them.

> **AT 1.4–5**   **4 Escucha y decide qué dibujo se describe: a, b, o, c.**
> Students listen and note down which holiday is being described.

CD 3, track 7   *página 127, actividad 4*
Generalmente para mis vacaciones voy a Irlanda pero el verano pasado fui a Francia. Fui con mi amigo Jean-Pierre. Fuimos en tren y nos quedamos en la casa de su abuela. Hizo buen tiempo y sol todos los días. Lo pasamos bomba en París, la capital de Francia. Subimos a la Torre Eiffel y comimos en un buen restaurante.

Answer: c

> **AT 2.4–5**   **5 Elabora frases sobre las vacaciones. Utiliza los otros dibujos.**
> Students use the prompts to make extended sentences of their own. Check that they know what all of the symbols mean and can remember how to say each of the countries included.

> **PLTS**   **Think!**
> Students reflect upon how they write at the moment and on ways in which they can improve their work. They could look back at their last piece of written work and try to improve it by using the suggestions given.

> **AT 4.5–6**   **Challenge**
> **PLTS**   **Write a detailed description of a past holiday.**
> Students draw upon what they have learnt in the spread in order to produce a higher-level piece of work. Remind them that they don't have to tell the truth, but can make up details to make their writing more interesting and to use a good variety of vocabulary and structures.

4A.5 ¿Lo pasaste bien?

4A.5 ¿Qué compraste?

páginas 128–129

Planner

Objectives
- practise language for buying souvenirs in a Spanish-speaking country

Resources
Students' Book, pages 128–129
CD 3, track 8
Foundation Workbook, page 68
Higher Workbook, page 68
Foundation Workbook audio, CD 3, track 79
Higher Workbook audio, CD 4, track 54
Interactive OxBox, Unit 4A
Assessment, Unit 4A

Key language
un imán; unas castañuelas; un abanico; una camiseta; un vestido de flamenco; una guitarra española; una muñeca; un sombrero; un llavero; unas gafas de sol; el/la dependiente; el/la cliente; ¿Qué deseas?; ¿Cuánto cuesta?; muy caro; algo más barato; ¡Mira!; Me lo quedo; ¿Algo más?

Renewed Framework references
1.1, 1.2, 1.4, 1.5, 2.1, 3.1, 3.2, 4.1, 4.2, 5.3

PLTS
Activity 1: Independent enquirers
Think!: Reflective learners
Challenge: Team workers; Reflective learners

Starters
- Quickly revise numbers in Spanish as these will be needed to understand or tell somebody the price of an item. You could do this by playing 'buzz'. Go round the class with students counting in ones, but saying buzz (or a Spanish word of your choice) whenever they reach a multiple of three, e.g. *uno, dos, buzz, cuatro, cinco, buzz...*
- Play a memory game as a class. You start by saying what you bought and for whom, e.g. *Compré un llavero de Sevilla para mi hermana.* Go round the class with each student repeating what has already been said and adding their own sentence, e.g.
Student 1: *Compré un llavero de Sevilla para mi hermana y me compré un vestido de flamenco.*
Student 2: *Compré un llavero de Sevilla para mi hermana, me compré un vestido de flamenco y compré un imán para mis padres.*

Plenaries
- Following on from Activity 3, students practise the conversation in pairs. Encourage more able students to adapt the conversation to make it their own, asking for different items and using different prices, etc. Remind students to watch out for pronunciation, especially when Spanish words look like English ones.
- Display the key language and challenge students to write five sentences on the theme of the spread. They could do this in the form of a dialogue.

Homework/Self-study
Activity 1: Students find out about typically Spanish souvenirs. If they have been to Spain and have a typically Spanish souvenir, e.g. castanets, a flamenco dress, etc. they could bring it in.
Think!: Students practise pronouncing any Spanish words they know that look like English words.
Students use the conversation in Activity 3 as a model to create their own conversation. They should include different items, change the prices, etc. They could practise their conversation in class.

AT1.3 **1 Escucha. ¿Qué compraron? ¿Para quién?**
PLTS Students listen and note down what the people buy and who for. First, brainstorm possible gifts and people they are likely to buy gifts for. This could lead to a discussion about typically Spanish souvenirs. Can the class think of any gifts that are typically Spanish?

🎧 **CD 3, track 8** página 128, actividad 1

1 Compré un llavero de Sevilla para mi hermana.
2 Compré una guitarra española para mi novio porque está aprendiendo a tocar la guitarra.
3 Yo compré un sombrero de matador para mi abuelo.
4 Me compré un vestido de flamenco.
5 Compré unas castañuelas para mi hermana pequeña y un abanico muy bonito para mi madre.
6 Mi amiga Silvia colecciona muñecas, así que le compré una muñeca.
7 Me compré unas gafas de sol pero a mis hermanos no les compré nada.
8 Compré un imán para mis padres y una camiseta del Real Madrid para mi hermano menor.

Answer:
1 un llavero, hermana; *2* una guitarra, novio; *3* un sombrero de matador, abuelo; *4* un vestido de flamenco, ella misma; *5* unas castañuelas, hermana pequeña/un abanico, madre; *6* una muñeca, amiga (Silvia); *7* unas gafas de sol, ella misma/él mismo/nada, hermanos; *8* un imán, padres/una camiseta del Real Madrid, hermano menor

4A.6 ¿Lo pasaste bien?

AT 3.2 — **2 ¿Recuerdas los números? Empareja estos precios con su etiqueta.**
Students match the prices with their price tag. This is good revision of numbers in Spanish.

Answers:
1 c; **2** g; **3** h; **4** e; **5** d; **6** f; **7** b; **8** a

PLTS — **Think!**
Students to practise pronouncing the word *euro* in Spanish. Brainstorm other Spanish words they know that look like English words. Can they remember how to pronounce these correctly? They could practise in pairs or as a class.

AT 3.3–4 — **3 Completa la conversación.**
Students complete the conversation by putting the customer's part in the correct order.

Answers:
- Buenos días. ¿Qué deseas?
- **Quiero un regalo para mi abuela.**
- Hay este abanico rojo. Es muy bonito. ¿Te gusta?
- **Sí, es bonito. ¿Cuánto cuesta?**
- Cuesta 25,99€.
- **¡Uy! ¡Es muy caro! No tengo suficiente dinero. ¿Tiene algo más barato?**
- Hmmm … Tenemos imanes y llaveros.
- **Un llavero, por favor. ¿Cuánto cuesta?**
- 3,50€. ¡Mira! ¿Te gusta?
- **Sí, me gusta. Me lo quedo.**
- ¿Algo más?
- **No, nada más, gracias. 3,50€ … aquí tiene.**
- Gracias, adiós.
- **Adiós.**

AT 3.3–4 — **4 Busca el español.**
Students reread the conversation from Activity 3 and note down the Spanish for the English phrases listed.

Answers:
1 ¿Qué deseas?; **2** quiero; **3** para mi abuela; **4** ¿Cuánto cuesta?; **5** ¡Es muy caro!; **6** ¿Tiene algo más barato?; **7** ¡Mira! ¿Te gusta?; **8** Me lo quedo. **9** ¿Algo más? **10** No, nada más.

AT 2.4 — **Challenge**
PLTS — **Practise the conversation with a partner.**
Students use the prompts to practise the conversation with a partner. Go through the shopkeeper's lines first to ensure that students understand them. With less able students, display a list of souvenirs in Spanish for support.

4A.6 Labolengua
páginas 130–131

Planner

Objectives
- review language and grammar from the unit

Resources
Students' Book, pages 130–131
CD 3, track 9
Foundation Workbook, pages 69–70
Higher Workbook, pages 69–70
Interactive OxBox, Unit 4A
Copymasters 100–101
Assessment, Unit 4A

Grammar
- regular verbs
- irregular verbs

Renewed Framework references
1.1, 1.4, 2.1, 2.4, 4.1, 4.2, 4.3, 4.4, 4.5, 5.1, 5.6

PLTS
All activities: Reflective learners/Self-managers

Homework/Self-study
Students use one of the verbs in the preterite from Activity 2 in a sentence of their own.
Students use two of the irregular verbs in the preterite from Activity 3 in sentences of their own.

Comprender – the multiple kingdoms of verbs (preterite)

A Regular verbs

PLTS — **1 How do you say the following in Spanish?**
Practice of using the infinitive of regular verbs with the correct ending, *-ar*, *-er*, or *-ir*.

Answers:
1 visitar; **2** cocinar; **3** comer; **4** beber; **5** ver; **6** pasear; **7** tomar el sol; **8** sacar fotos; **9** comprar; **10** alojarse

PLTS — **2 Translate.**
Practice of forming the preterite of regular verbs.

4A.7 ¿Lo pasaste bien?

Answers:
1 visité; 2 cocinamos; 3 comiste; 4 bebió; 5 vimos; 6 pasearon; 7 tomé el sol; 8 sacasteis fotos; 9 compró; 10 nos alojamos

B Irregular verbs

PLTS **3 Complete the sentences with the preterite of the verb in brackets.**
Practice of using irregular verbs in the preterite.
Point out that the preterite of *ser* and *ir* are identical.

Answers: 1 fuimos; 2 fue; 3 hizo; 4 estuvo

PLTS **4 Rewrite this paragraph in the preterite. Remember to change the time markers where necessary.**
Remind students of phrases they could use with the preterite, e.g. *el verano pasado, el invierno pasado, el año pasado, hace dos años, el pasado junio, las Navidades pasadas.*

Possible answer:
El año pasado fui de vacaciones a Mijas, cerca de Málaga. **Fui** con mis abuelos en avión y **nos alojamos** en un apartamento de alquiler. En Mijas **hizo** buen tiempo y **hizo** mucho calor. Durante las vacaciones **fuimos** a la playa, **nos bañamos** en el mar y **nos relajamos** al lado de la piscina. También **comimos** comida típica en restaurantes del pueblo. ¡Lo **pasé** fenomenal!

Aprender – writing or talking about past events

C Time markers

PLTS **5 Place these time phrases in three categories depending on whether they refer to past, present or future. Be careful: some may apply to more than one time frame.**
Practice of using time markers correctly.

Answers:
past: *ahora; el verano pasado; el viernes pasado; ayer; la semana pasada; los sábados; anteayer; el martes*
present: *ahora; hoy; en estos momentos; los sábados*
future: *ahora; los sábados; el martes; mañana por la mañana; el próximo año*

PLTS **6 Complete these sentences with the 1st person present, past or future of the verb *ir* accordingly.**
Practice of using the correct tense.

Answers:
1 voy, fui; 2 fui, voy a ir, voy a ir; 3 voy a ir, fui; 4 fui, voy; 5 voy, voy a ir

Hablar – pronunciation

D Accents

7 Say the words out loud. Check the recording.
Practice of pronouncing accents correctly.

🎧 **CD 3, track 9**   página 131, actividad 7
compro – compró; si – sí; bebe – bebé

PLTS **8 Read the sentences out loud.**
Further practice of pronouncing accents.

4A.7 Extra Star   página 132

Planner

Objectives
- find out about Spanish festivals

Resources
Students' Book, page 132
Copymaster 102

Renewed Framework references
2.1, 2.4, 2.5, 3.1, 3.2, 4.2, 4.3, 4.4, 4.5, 4.6, 5.1

PLTS
Activity 2: Independent enquirers
Activity 3: Independent enquirers; Creative thinkers; Self-managers

4A.7 ¿Lo pasaste bien?

AT 4.3 **1 ¿Qué se puede y no se puede hacer?**
Students use the illustrations as prompts in order to write down what you can and can't do. More able students write these as extended sentences, rather than six short sentences.

Answers:
1 Se puede jugar al fútbol. 2 No se puede sacar fotos.
3 Se puede visitar el castillo. 4 No se puede comer.
5 Se puede ir al cine. 6 No se puede pescar.

AT 3.3–4 PLTS **2 Lee y busca el español.**
Students read the text find the Spanish for the English phrases listed. First, discuss the illustrations and captions. Have students heard of any of these terms before? Have any students been to a Spanish festival?

Answers:
1 voy de vacaciones a…; 2 fui a la fiesta de los Sanfermines; 3 con mis amigos; 4 durante la fiesta; 5 vi un encierro; 6 una corrida; 7 me gustaron mucho…; 8 no me gustó…; 9 en mi opinión; 10 El año próximo no voy a volver a…; 11 porque voy a visitar a…

AT 4.3–4 PLTS **3 Investigación cultural. Busca información sobre los Sanfermines.**
Students use the Internet to find out about the San Fermín festival and make a display poster with the key information. They should make their writing as interesting as possible by adding opinions, adjectives, quantifiers, etc.

4A.7 Extra Plus   página 133

Planner

Objectives
- find out about Spanish festivals

Resources
Students' Book, page 133
Interactive OxBox, Unit 4A
Copymaster 103
Assessment, Unit 4A

Renewed Framework references
2.1, 2.2, 2.4, 2.5, 3.1, 3.2, 4.2, 4.3, 4.4, 4.5, 4.6, 5.8

PLTS
Activity 3: Independent enquirers; Self-managers
Activity 4: Independent enquirers; Self-managers; Creative thinkers

AT 3.5 **1 ¿Qué significan las frases en negrita?**
Students read the text and then note down the meaning of the emboldened text. They should use the context to help them.

Answers:
a finales de agosto – at the end of August; *el verano pasado* – last summer; *durante la semana* – during the week; *durante las vacaciones* – all holiday long; *el último miércoles de agosto* – the last Wednesday in August; *este verano* – this summer

AT 3.5 **2 Lee el texto y contesta a las preguntas en español. Da respuestas completas.**
Students reread the text and answer the questions in Spanish, using full sentences.

Answers:
1 Martin fue de vacaciones a Buñol. 2 Fue con sus amigos. 3 Viajó desde Barcelona en coche. 4 Allí se alojó en un hotel cerca del centro. 5 Hizo muchísimo calor. 6 Durante la semana visitó el pueblo, comió en los restaurantes locales, viajó a Valencia para ver la ciudad y, participó en la Tomatina.

AT 3.5 PLTS **3 ¿Verdadero o falso? Corrige las frases falsas.**
Students read the text once more and decide if the sentences are true or false. They correct any false statements. First, discuss *La Tomatina* festival as a class. Have students heard of *La Tomatina* festival before? Students could find out more about this for themselves and bring their findings into class.

Answers:
1 verdadero; 2 falso – La Tomatina es en agosto. 3 verdadero; 4 falso – Se tiran 100 toneladas de tomates. 5 falso – La fiesta dura dos horas. 6 verdadero

AT 4.4–5 PLTS **4 Investigación cultural. Busca información sobre otra fiesta española o latinoamericana y diseña un póster en inglés con la información clave.**
Students use the Internet to find out about another Spanish or Latin American festival. They then make a display poster with the key information. They should try to make their writing as interesting as possible by adding opinions, adjectives, quantifiers, etc.

4A.8 ¿Lo pasaste bien?

4A.8 Prueba
página 134

Planner

Resources
Students' Book, page 134
CD 3, track 10

Renewed Framework references
1.1, 1.4, 1.5, 2.1, 2.2, 2.4, 2.5, 4.2, 4.3, 4.4, 4.5, 4.6, 5.4

PLTS
All activities: Reflective learners
Escribir: Creative thinkers; Reflective learners

Escuchar

AT 1.5 / PLTS — **Listen, and copy and fill in the table.**
This activity tests listening skills using the language covered in this unit.

CD 3, track 10 — página 134, Escuchar

1. Fui de vacaciones a Irlanda con mi hermana. Fuimos en coche y nos alojamos en la casa de una amiga. Hizo viento, pero visitamos los museos y nos relajamos. No estuvo mal.
2. Fui de vacaciones a Argentina con mi familia. Fuimos en avión y en Buenos Aires nos alojamos en un hotel bastante céntrico. Hizo buen tiempo y fuimos a la playa dos veces y sacamos muchas fotos. ¡Lo pasamos fenomenal!
3. Fui en tren a París con mis amigos. Nos alojamos en un albergue juvenil. Llovió e hizo frío así que fue regular. En París comimos comida típica y paseamos por la ciudad.
4. Fui de vacaciones a Mallorca en barco. Fui con mis abuelos y nos alojamos en la casa de mis tíos. Hizo mucho sol y tomé el sol todos los días y me bañé en el mar. ¡Lo pasé fenomenal!

Answers:
1 Ireland; sister; car; friend's house; windy; visited museums, relaxed; it wasn't bad
2 Argentina; family; aeroplane; hotel quite near the centre; good weather; went to the beach twice, took lots of photos; had a great time
3 Paris; friends; train; youth hostel; it rained and was cold; ate typical French food, walked around the city; it was average
4 Majorca; grandparents; boat; uncle's house; very sunny; sunbathed every day and swam in the sea; had a great time

Hablar

AT 2.5 / PLTS — **Choose one of these cards and answer the questions.**
Students use the prompts on the card they have chosen to answer the questions. They should enhance sentences with opinions, adjectives, adverbs and quantifiers.

Leer

AT 3.5 / PLTS — **Read the text and answer the questions in English.**
This activity tests reading skills using the language covered in this unit.

Answers:
1 they are boring; 2 he went to Ibiza with this friends; 3 (any three of) go to the disco every day, go to the beach, visit famous monuments, play volleyball, go sailing;
4 (any four of) played volleyball, went sailing, ate dishes typical to the region, drank sangria, danced at discos;
5 good; 6 it was exciting and fun and much different from his holidays in Andalucia with his parents

Escribir

AT 4.5–6 / PLTS — **Write an account of a real or imaginary holiday to a Spanish destination. Aim to achieve a Level 5 or above.**
This activity tests writing skills using the language covered in this unit. Remind students thet they must try to include a variety of opinions, adjectives, adverbs, connectives and quantifiers, as well as two or three time frames.

¿Lo pasaste bien? **4A**

Leer 4A   página 159

Planner

Resources
Students' Book, page 159

Renewed Framework references
1.5, 2.1, 2.4, 2.5, 4.2, 4.3, 4.4, 4.5, 5.4

PLTS
Activity 2: Reflective learners; Self-managers
Activity 3: Creative thinkers; Reflective learners; Self-managers

Homework/Self-study
Students write out the sentences from Activity 1 again, but this time adding their own endings.

AT 3.3 **1 Before looking at the text below, read these sentences and choose the option that makes most sense for each one.**
This will help students in their understanding of the main text.

Answers:
1 b; 2 c; 3 a; 4 c; 5 b; 6 a; 7 c; 8 c; 9 b

AT 3.4–5 **PLTS** **2 Read the email and complete it with the appropriate verbs from the box.**
This requires students to fully understand the text. Remind them to pay attention to verb tenses and time markers and also to use the context.

Answers:
1 voy; 2 tenemos; 3 fui; 4 nos alojamos; 5 hizo; 6 se pueden; 7 comer; 8 hicimos; 9 comimos; 10 fue; 11 nos relajamos; 12 nos contaron; 13 me encantaron; 14 pasé; 15 fuiste

AT 4.5–6 **PLTS** **3 Respond to Pepe's e-mail.**
Students write an answer to Pepe's email. They should make their response as full as possible and include opinions, different tenses, adjectives, etc.

Foundation Workbook

Página 64   4A.1 ¿Qué se puede hacer?
- Use with Students' Book, pages 120–121

AT 3.1 **1 Write the correct Spanish word or phrase under each picture.**
This reinforces the 'freetime' vocabulary that students have learnt.

Answers:
a nadar; b comer; c jugar; d ver el fútbol; e pasear; f ir de compras; g ver una película

AT 1.4 **2 Listen to what you can and can't do in the town. Tick or cross each picture.**
Encourage students to try to predict what they might hear, e.g. *piscina* with verb *nadar*, a sport with the verb *jugar*, etc.

🎧 **CD 3, track 77**   página 64, actividad 2

En mi pueblo no se puede nadar porque no hay piscina.
Se puede comer bien porque hay muchos restaurantes.
Se puede jugar al tenis en el parque.
No se puede ver un partido de fútbol, porque no hay estadio.
Se puede pasear porque el centro es muy bonito.
Se puede ir de compras, pero no hay muchas tiendas.
Se puede ver una película en el cine.

Answers:
✗: *swimming (a) and watch football match (d)*
✓: *all other activities*

AT 2.3 **3 Use your answers to Activity 2 to talk in short sentences about the town.**
Students work in pairs and take it in turns to say something about the town. They could extend this by asking each other questions about the town, e.g. *Se puede ver una película en el cine?*

AT 4.2–3 **4 Write about what you can and can't do in your own town.**
Students can embellish to make their writing more interesting and to use a wider variety of vocabulary. They should also give opinions and use connectives and quantifiers.

4A ¿Lo pasaste bien?

Página 65   4A.2 ¿Adónde fuiste?
- Use with Students' Book, pages 122–123

AT 2.1   **1 Listen and repeat.**

> **CD 3, track 78**   página 65, actividad 1
> fui, fuiste, fue, fuimos, fuisteis, fueron
> fui, fuiste, fue, fuimos, fuisteis, fueron

AT 3.2   **2 Translate into English.**
This practises recognising the various forms of the verb *ir* in the preterite.

Answers:
a Marisa went to Argentina. She went in August. She went by plane. She went to visit her family.
b We went to Spain. We went in July. We went to the beach. We went by car.
c My friends went to France. They went by boat. They went in April. They went to Paris. They went shopping.

3 Translate into Spanish.
This practises forming the various forms of the verb *ir* in the preterite.

Answers:
a Fui a España. **b** Fui en avión. **c** Fui en julio. **d** Fui a la playa.

Página 66   4A.3 ¿Qué hiciste?
- Use with Students' Book, pages 124–125

AT 3.3–4   **1 Read the text and underline the six preterite endings.**

Answers:
fui; decidí; visité; comí; hablé; me alojé

2 Complete the table.
Students differentiate between verbs in present and the past.

Answers:

Normally	Last year
goes to Málaga	went to Madrid
goes to the beach	went to art galleries
doesn't like Spanish food	ate in fantastic restaurants
speaks English	spoke Spanish
camps	stayed in a five-star hotel

AT 4.3–4   **3 Write about your own holidays.**
Students use the template as a guide for writing about their own holiday. Using two tenses in this way in their own writing will lead to better marks.

Página 67   4A.4 ¿Lo pasaste bien?
- Use with Students' Book, pages 126–127

1 Put the expressions below into the correct column in the table.

Answers:

Me gustó	¡Qué…!	Fue…	_____é
me gustó ☺ – I liked it (it pleased me); me encantó ☺ – I loved it; no me gustó ☹ – I didn't like it	qué desastre ☹ – what a disaster; qué aburrido ☹ – how boring	fue emocionante ☺ – it was exciting; fue increíble ☺ – it was incredible; fue regular ☺ – it was OK	lo pasé muy mal ☹ – I had an awful time; disfruté ☺ – I enjoyed; lo pasé bomba ☺ – I had a great time

2 Colour the positive opinions in red. Colour the negative opinions in green.

Answers:
positive opinions: me gustó, me encantó, fue emocionante, fue increíble, disfruté, lo pasé bomba
negative opinions: no me gustó, qué desastre, qué aburrido, fue regular, lo pasé muy mal

AT 3.2–3   **3 Read this text aloud, adding an opinion in Spanish each time you see ☺ or ☹.**
Students use the grid from Activity 1 for support. They use a different opinion each time.

Página 68   4A.5 ¿Qué compraste?
- Use with Students' Book, pages 128–129

AT 4.2–3   **1 Roll a dice to see what you are going to buy and for whom.**
Students write sentences according to the numbers they get when they roll the die, e.g. 2, 3, 6: *Quiero comprar una camiseta… es para mi padre… no tengo dinero.* Remind students to pay attention to adjective endings.

AT 1.2, 2.2–3   **2 Listen to the questions and use your answers from Activity 1 to take part in the conversation.**
Students should watch out for any tricky sounds in Spanish.

¿Lo pasaste bien? 4A

CD 3, track 79 página 68, actividad 2

– Buenos días. ¿Qué deseas?
 [Pause]
– ¿Es para ti?
 [Pause]
– Cuesta veinte euros. ¿Te gusta?

3 Repeat Activities 1 and 2 until you get to '*no gracias, adiós*'.

Página 69   4A.6A Labolengua
- Use with Students' Book, pages 130–131

1 Draw lines to match up each verb with its infinitive. You must not cross any lines once you have drawn them!
This activity practises recognising preterite endings.

Answers:
jugar – jugué; bailar – bailé; visitar – visité; comer – comí; beber – bebí

2 Find the Spanish for the following.
Practice of forming the preterite.

Answers:
a jugué; **b** bailé; **c** visité; **d** comí; **e** bebí

3 Put these sentences into the first person of the past tense.
Further practice of conjugating the past tense.

Answers:
a Tomé el sol en la playa. **b** Comí en un restaurante. **c** Nadé en el mar. **d** Viajé en avión.

Página 70   4A.6 Técnica
- Use with Students' Book, pages 130–131

1 Colour in these time expressions. Use blue for past, green for present, red for future.
These are useful to know as they will help in understanding texts.

Answers:
el año pasado – past; hoy – present; mañana – future; ayer – past; el próximo año – future; hace dos años – past; ahora – present

2 Do the same for these sentences.
Students should look at the tense used as well as time markers.

Answers: past: a, e; present: c; future: b, d

3 Write a postcard home. Include two things you did yesterday and three things you are going to do tomorrow.
Students use their knowledge of the immediate future and preterite tenses to write a postcard. They can also include the present tense to say what they usually do and time markers.

Higher Workbook

Página 64   4A.1 ¿Qué se puede hacer?
- Use with Students' Book, pages 120–121

AT 1.4 1 Listen to what you can and can't do in the town. Tick or cross each picture.
Encourage students to try to predict what they might hear, e.g. *piscina* with verb *nadar*, a sport with the verb *jugar*, etc.

CD 4, track 52 página 64, actividad 1

En mi pueblo no se puede nadar porque no hay piscina.
Se puede comer bien porque hay muchos restaurantes.
Se puede jugar al tenis en el parque.
No se puede ver un partido de fútbol, porque no hay estadio.
Se puede pasear porque el centro es muy bonito.
Se puede ir de compras, pero no hay muchas tiendas.
Se puede ver una película en el cine.

Answers:
X: swimming (a) and watch football match (d)
✓: all other activities

AT 2.2–3 2 Use your answers to Activity 1 to talk in sentences about the town.
Students work in pairs and take it in turns to say something about the town. They could extend this by asking each other questions about the town, e.g. *Se puede ver una película en el cine?*.

AT 4.3–4 3 Write a paragraph about what you can and can't do in your own town and why.
Students can embellish to make their writing more interesting and to use a wider variety of vocabulary. They should also give opinions and use connectives and quantifiers.

4A ¿Lo pasaste bien?

Página 65   34A.2 ¿Adónde fuiste?
- Use with Students' Book, pages 122–123

1 Put the parts of the verb into the correct order. Then listen and check.
This practises forming the verb *ir* in the preterite tense.

> **CD 4, track 53**   página 65, actividad 1
> fui; fuiste; fue; fuimos; fuisteis; fueron

Answers:
I went – fui; you went – fuiste; he/she/it went – fue; we went – fuimos; you (plural) went – fuisteis; they went – fueron

AT 3.3   **2 Translate into English.**
Practice of recognising the verb *ir* in the preterite tense.

Answers:
a Marisa went to Argentina. She went in August. She went by plane. She went to visit her family. **b** We went to Spain. We went in July. We went to the beach. We went by car. **c** My friends went to France. They went by boat. They went in April. They went to Paris. They went shopping.

AT 4.3–4   **3 Now write five short sentences about your own holiday. Where? When? Where exactly? Who with? What did you go to do?**
Students practise using the verb *ir* in the preterite tense.

Página 66   4A.3 ¿Qué hiciste?
- Use with Students' Book, pages 124–125

AT 4.3–4   **1 Read and underline the six preterite endings.**

Answers:
fui; decidí; visité; comí; hablé; me alojo

2 Complete the table.
Students differentiate between verbs in the present and the past.

Answers:

Normally	Last year
goes to Málaga	went to Madrid
goes to the beach	went to art galleries
doesn't like Spanish food	ate in fantastic restaurants
speaks English	spoke Spanish
camps	stayed in a five-star hotel

AT 4.5   **3 Write about your own holidays.**
Students use the template as a guide for writing about their own holiday. Using two tenses in this way in their own writing will lead to better marks.

Página 67   4A.4 ¿Lo pasaste bien?
- Use with Students' Book, pages 126–127

1 Put these expressions into the correct column and add the English.

Answers:

Me gustó	¡Qué…!	Fue…	_____ é
me gustó ☺ – I liked it (it pleased me); me encantó ☺ – I loved it; no me gustó ☹ – I didn't like it	qué desastre ☹ – what a disaster; qué aburrido ☹ – how boring	fue emocionante ☺ – it was exciting; fue increíble ☺ – it was incredible; fue regular 😐 – it was OK	lo pasé muy mal ☹ – I had an awful time; disfruté ☺ – I enjoyed; lo pasé bomba ☺ – I had a great time

2 Colour the positive opinions in red. Colour the negative opinions in green.

Answers:
positive opinions: me gustó, me encantó, fue emocionante, fue increíble, disfruté, lo pasé bomba
negative opinions: no me gustó, qué desastre, qué aburrido, fue regular, lo pasé muy mal

AT 2.3   **3 Read this text aloud, adding an opinion in Spanish each time you see ☺ or ☹.**
Students use the grid from Activity 1 for support. They use a different opinion each time.

AT 4.4–5   **4 Write about your own holiday in Spain, giving details of what you liked and what you didn't.**
Students show what they have learnt. They should include opinions, adjectives, connectives and quantifiers.

¿Lo pasaste bien? 4A

Página 68   4A.5 ¿Qué compraste?
- Use with Students' Book, pages 128–129

AT 4.2–3 **1 Roll a dice to see what you are going to buy and for whom.**
Students write sentences according to the numbers they get when they roll the die, e.g. 2, 3, 6: Q*uiero comprar una camiseta… es para mi padre… no tengo dinero.* Remind students to pay attention to adjective endings.

AT 1.2, 2.2–3 **2 Listen to the questions and use your answers from Activity 1 to take part in the conversation.**
Students should watch out for any tricky sounds in Spanish.

> 🎧 **CD 4, track 54**   página 68, actividad 2
> - Buenos días. ¿Qué deseas?
>   [Pause]
> - ¿Es para ti?
>   [Pause]
> - Cuesta veinte euros. ¿Te gusta?

3 Repeat Activities 1 and 2 until you get to *no gracias, adiós*.

AT 4.2–3 **4 Write out one of your conversations, complete with the shopkeeper's part.**
When students have written out a conversation, they could act it out with a partner.

Página 69   4A.6A Labolengua
- Use with Students' Book, pages 130–131

1 Draw lines to match each verb with its infinitive. You must not cross any lines once you have drawn them!
This activity practises recognising preterite endings.

Answers:
jugar – jugué; bailar – bailamos; visitar – visitaron; comer – comimos; beber – bebieron

2 Find the Spanish for the following.
Practice of forming the preterite.

Answers:
a jugué; **b** bailamos; **c** visitaron; **d** comimos; **e** bebieron

3 Put these sentences into the past tense.
Further practice of conjugating the past tense.

Answers:
a *Tomamos el sol en la playa.* **b** *Comió en un restaurante.* **c** *Nadaron en el mar.* **d** *Viajaron en avión.*

Página 70   4A.6B Técnica
- Use with Students' Book, pages 130–131

1 Colour in these sentences. Use blue for past, green for present and red for future.
Students will need to recognise tenses and time markers in order to do this sucessfully.

Answers:
past: a, e, f, h, j; **present:** c; **future:** b, d, g, i

2 Write these sentences with the first person verb in the correct time frame: past, or future.
This practises the preterite and the immediate future.

Answers:
a *El año pasado* **tomé** *el sol en la playa.* **b** *Mañana* **voy a ir** *a la playa.* **c** *Ayer* **comí** *en un restaurante.* **d** *El próximo martes* **voy a visitar** *un museo.*

3 Write a postcard home. Include three things you did yesterday and three things you are going to do tomorrow.
Students use their knowledge of the immediate future and preterite tenses to write a postcard. They can also include the present tense to say what they usually do as well as time markers.

4B La vida tecno

Unit Objectives

Contexts and cultural focus: media-based activities
Grammar: words of frequency, *gustar* to say what other people like; the preterite tense; questions, *lo bueno* and *lo malo*
Language learning: practising questions and answers, carrying out surveys; looking up verbs in a dictionary; presenting and defending a point of view

- *Aim:* to talk about what you like to watch on the television and what type of films you like; to describe what happened in a film; to describe advantages and disadvantages of different types of media
- Each unit has an associated video which will feature throughout the unit. Below is the transcript of the video for this unit.
- As a starter activity to introduce the Unit and familiarise students with the language they will meet, you may find it useful for the class to view the video as a whole.

Video script (CD 3, track 15)

Eva:	No, hablando en serio… puede que esa sea una de las peores películas que haya visto en mi vida.
Marisa:	Lo que pasa es que a ti no te gustan las películas de ciencia ficción.
Eva:	Eso no es verdad. Me gustan todo tipo de películas.
Marisa:	Claro, siempre y cuando no sean películas de terror, de vaqueros, comedias, o películas de misterio.
Eva:	¡No es verdad! La última película que vi, fue una de terror; ¡La Venganza de las Momias! Trataba de… unas momias… que se vengaban.
Marisa:	Ya pero, ¿te gustó?
Eva:	No. Era una película estúpida. Pero, yo no tengo nada en contra del género.
Khalid:	¿Quiénes son estas chicas y qué les han hecho a Eva y a Marisa?
Eva:	Ha salido la película nueva de Almodóvar. Me encanta Pedro Almodóvar.
Marisa:	Lo que quiere decir es que a mí no me gustará.
Eva:	No, pero aun así deberías ir a verla, Mar. Almodóvar es uno de los directores de cine más importantes de España.
Marisa:	Vale, vale… pero entonces tú tienes que ir al partido de fútbol del sábado porque el FC Barcelona es uno de los clubs de fútbol más importantes de España.
José:	¡Tiene razón, Eva!
Eva:	¿Y no puedo ver un documental sobre el club en vez de ir al partido? ¿Podría ver algunos videos en Youtube?
Marisa:	Ver una obra de teatro en la tele no es lo mismo que ir al teatro, ¿no es así? Bueno, pues con el fútbol ocurre lo mismo. ¡Tienes que verlo en vivo!
Marisa:	¿Por qué no te vienes a mi casa esta noche también? Podríamos navegar… quiero decir, hablar sobre nuestros libros favoritos.
Eva:	Sí, vale. Puedo traerte esas novelas de misterio de las que hablamos el otro día.
Khalid:	Pero, ¿tú lees novelas de misterio?
Marisa:	Sí, Khal, sé leer, ¿sabes?
Khalid:	Sí, ya, las páginas de deportes.
[Pause]	
Marisa:	¿Les decimos de qué trataba la telenovela que vimos el otro día?
Eva:	¿Qué telenovela?
Marisa:	Ya sabes… la telenovela – la de los tres amigos que se llaman Jesús, Carlos y Elena. Pues, eso… trata de tres amigos… que se llaman… Jesús, Carlos y Elena y viven en Barcelona. Han sido amigos desde hace muchos años pero de repente, llega una chica muy guapa de Argen… de Perú que se llama… eh… se llama… eh…
Eva:	¡María!
Marisa:	Eso, se llama María. A Elena, María le cae mal desde el principio porque cree que le puede quitar a sus amigos.
Eva:	Bueno, en realidad se odian mutuamente, ¿no es cierto?
Marisa:	Sí, pero eso porque no se conocen lo suficiente bien, ¿verdad?
Eva:	¡Verdad! Verdad.
Marisa:	Sea como sea, todo cambia porque Elena y María se hacen amigas.
Eva:	A pesar de no tener nada en común.
Marisa:	¡Nada en absoluto!
Eva:	Pero, esa es la mejor parte de su amistad… el hecho de ser tan diferentes.
Marisa:	Si, esa es la mejor parte.
[Pause]	
Khalid:	Pero, ¿es una telenovela, no? Así que las cosas podrían cambiar…
Eva y Marisa:	No, ¡eso no va a cambiar nunca!

La vida tecno 4B

Unit 4B La vida tecno Overview grid						
Page reference	Contexts and objectives	Language learning	Grammar	Key language	Framework	AT level
Pages 136–7 **Los medios y la televisión**	• talk about different media-based activities, say what you like to watch on TV and why	• practise questions and answers with a partner	• words of frequency	hablo por teléfono; navego por internet; veo la televisión; escucho la radio; juego con videojuegos; utilizo el correo electrónico; leo los periódicos; leo revistas; participo en los chats; de vez en cuando; todos los días; una vez/tres veces a la semana; nunca; a menudo; divertido/a; gracioso/a; tonto/a; emocionante; informativo/a; las noticias; las series; las telenovelas; los anuncios; los concursos; los dibujos animados; los documentales; los programas deportivos; los programas musicales	1.1, 1.2, 1.4, 2.4, 2.5, 4.2, 4.4, 4.5, 4.6, 5.1	1.3, 2.3, 3.3, 4.3–4
Pages 138–9 **El cine y los libros**	• talk about the type of films you like and why	• carry out a survey	• practise using gustar to say what other people like	una película romántica; de terror; de ciencia-ficción; de vaqueros; de acción; de misterio; de guerra; una comedia; la fantasía	1.1, 1.4, 2.4, 2.5, 3.1, 3.2, 4.2, 4.3, 4.4, 4.5, 4.6, 5.1, 5.3, 5.4, 5.8	1.3–5, 2.4–5, 3.2, 4.3–5
Pages 140–1 **¿De qué trató? ¿Qué pasó?**	• describe what a film is about and what happened	• look up verbs in a dictionary	• practise using the preterite tense	un asesinato; un atentado; un robo; un secuestro; un timo; un viaje; una amistad; una guerra; una historia de amor; una lucha entre el bien y el mal; una misión secreta; vampiros; buscar; batallar; robar; descubrir; solucionar; enamorarse de	1.1, 1.2, 1.4, 1.5, 2.1, 2.2, 2.4, 2.5, 3.1, 3.2, 4.3, 4.4, 4.5, 5.1, 5.4, 5.5	1.2–6, 2.2–3, 3.3, 4.4–5
Pages 142–3 **Repaso**	• revise what you have learnt so far	• independent learning	• ask and answer questions		1.1, 1.4, 1.5, 2.1, 2.4, 2.5, 4.2, 4.3, 4.4, 4.5, 4.6, 5.1	1.5, 2.4–5, 3.4, 4.4–5
Pages 144–5 **En mi opinión…**	• describe the advantages and disadvantages of different types of media	• present and defend a point of view	• use lo bueno and lo malo	es muy…; puede ser…; útil; rápido/a; personal; educativo/a; entretenido/a; fácil; peligroso/a; una ventaja/desventaja es…; lo malo/bueno es que…; es una pérdida de tiempo; se puede hacer…; con amigos/solo/en casa/donde quieras; se puede llevar consigo/adonde quieras; (no) necesitas tecnología especial; (no) es caro; es antisocial	1.1, 1.2, 1.4, 1.5, 3.2, 4.2, 4.3, 4.4, 4.5, 4.6, 5.1	1.4, 2.4–5

4B La vida tecno

Pages 146–7 **Labolengua**	• review language and grammar from the unit				1.1, 1.4, 2.1, 2.4, 4.1, 4.2, 4.3, 4.4, 4.5, 4.6, 5.1, 5.2	
Pages 148–9 **Extra Star Extra Plus**	• differentiated extension/ homework material	• revise and consolidate all vocabulary and grammar covered in the unit	• revise and consolidate all vocabulary and grammar covered in the unit		1.1, 1.2, 1.4, 1.5, 2.1, 2.4, 2.5, 4.2, 4.3, 4.4, 4.5, 5.1, 5.8	1.3–4, 2.4–5, 3.3–5, 4.4–6
Page 150 **Prueba**	• end-of-spread test				1.1, 1.2, 1.4, 1.5, 2.1, 2.4, 2.5, 4.2, 4.3, 4.4, 4.5, 4.6, 5.1, 5.4	1.3–4, 2.3–4, 3.4–5, 4.4–6
Page 151 **Vocabulario**	• a summary of the key language covered in each spread of this unit					
Page 160 **Leer 3B**	• practice of longer reading texts based on the theme of the unit				2.1, 2.2, 4.3, 4.4, 4.5, 4.6, 5.3, 5.4	3.4

Week-by-week overview
(Three-year KS3 Route: assuming six weeks' work or approximately 10–12.5 hours)
(Two-year KS3 Route: assuming four weeks' worth or approxmately 6.5–8.5 hours)
*Please note that essential activities are highlighted.

About Unit 4B, *La vida tecno*: Students work in the context of media-based activities. They talk about what they like to watch on TV and why. They also talk about the type of films they like and describe what happened in a film. They describe the advantages and disadvantages of different types of media. Students practise using words of frequency and using *gustar* to say what other people like. They continue to work with the preterite tense, practise asking questions and learn how to use the phrases *lo bueno* and *lo malo* correctly. The unit also provides tips on language learning techniques.

Three-Year KS3 Route			Two-Year KS3 Route		
Week	Resources	Objectives	Week	Resources	Objectives
1	**4B.1 Los medios y la televisión** **4B.6 LabIolengua B** (p.146)	talk about different media-based activities, say what you like to watch on TV and why practise questions and answers with a partner words of frequency	1	**4B.1 Los medios y la televisión** **omit activities 5 & Challenge** **4B.6 LaBIolengua B** (p.146)	talk about different media-based activities, say what you like to watch on TV and why practise questions and answers with a partner words of frequency

La vida tecno 4B

2	4B.2 El cine y los libros 4B.6 LaIoLengua A (p.146)	talk about the type of films you like and why carry out a survey practise using *gustar* to say what other people like	2	4B.2 El cine y los libros omit activities Gramàtica & Challenge 4A.6 LaIoLengua A (p.146) Omit activity 2	talk about the type of films you like and why carry out a survey practise using *gustar* to say what other people like
3	4B.3 ¿De qué trató? ¿Qué pasó? 4B.6 LaIoLengua C (p.147)	describe what a film is about and what happened look up verbs in a dictionary practise using the preterite tense	3	4B.3 ¿De qué trató? ¿Qué pasó? omit activities 3 & Gramàtica 4B.6 LaIoLengua C (p.147)	describe what a film is about and what happened look up verbs in a dictionary practise using the preterite tense
4	4B.3 ¿De qué trató? ¿Qué pasó? 4B.6 LaIoLengua C (p.147)	revise what you have learnt so far independent learning questions	4	B.4 Repaso omit activity 2 4B.6 LaIoLengua D (p.147) omit activities 6, 7 & 8 4A.8 Prueba (p.150) Vocabulario (p.151)	revise what you have learnt so far independent learning questions recapping on the vocabulary of the unit prepare and carry out assessment in all four skills
5	4B.5 En mi opinión…	describe the advantages and disadvantages of different types of media present and defend a point of view use *lo bueno* and *lo malo*			
6	4B.7 Extra (Star) (p.148) 4B.7 Extra (Plus) (p.149) 4B.8 Prueba (p.150) Vocabulario (p.151) Leer (p.160)	further reinforcement and extension of the language of the unit recapping on the vocabulary of the unit prepare and carry out assessment in all four skills further reading to explore the language of the unit and cultural themes			

4B.1 La vida tecno

4B.1 Los medios y la televisión
páginas 136–137

Planner

Objectives
- talk about different media-based activities, say what you like to watch on TV and why
- words of frequency
- practise questions and answers with a partner

Resources
Students' Book, pages 136–137
CD 3, tracks 11–13
Foundation Workbook, page 72
Higher Workbook, page 72
Interactive OxBox, Unit 4B
Copymasters 105–112
Assessment, Unit 4B

Key language
hablo por teléfono; navego por internet; veo la televisión; escucho la radio; juego con videojuegos; utilizo el correo electrónico; leo los periódicos; leo revistas; participo en los chats; de vez en cuando; todos los días; una vez / tres veces a la semana; nunca; a menudo; divertido/a; gracioso/a; tonto/a; emocionante; informativo/a; las noticias; las series; las telenovelas; los anuncios; los concursos; los dibujos animados; los documentales; los programas deportivos; los programas musicales

Grammar
- words of frequency

Renewed Framework references
1.1, 1.2, 1.4, 2.4, 2.5, 4.2, 4.4, 4.5, 4.6, 5.1

PLTS
Gramática: Reflective learners
Activity 2: Independent enquirers
Activity 3: Team workers
Gramática: Independent enquirers

Think!: Independent enquirers
Activity 5: Effective participators
Activity 7: Creative thinkers
Challenge: Creative thinkers

Starters
- Play a quick class game. Display the following: *hablo por teléfono; navego por internet; veo la televisión; escucho la radio; juego con videojuegos; utilizo el correo electrónico; leo los periódicos; leo revistas; participo en los chats*. Ask a volunteer to come to the front of the class and mime one of these activities. The rest of the class must guess which activity they are miming. Whoever guesses correctly then gets to have a go at miming, and so on.
- Call out one of the activities. Students write down on a piece of paper how often they do this activity, e.g. *de vez en cuando*. Compare answers as a class. How often do most students do each activity? If necessary, display the words of frequency.

Plenaries
- Students speak with a partner about their favourite television programmes, e.g. *Me gusta ver los dibujos animados; son bastante graciosos.* They note down their partner's views and write sentences comparing these with their own views, e.g. *Se gusta ver los dibujos animados. Estoy de acuerdo; los dibujos animados son graciosos.* Less able students just note down what their partner says.
- Challenge students to write at least five extended sentences on the theme of the spread incorporating the key language. Compare sentences as a class.

Homework/Self-study
Students make a note of the activities mentioned in Activity 1 and add them to their vocabulary list.
Think!: Students make a note of any feminine words that end in 'o' and any masculine words that end in 'a' whenever they come across them.

AT 1.3 **1 Escucha. ¿Les gustan o no les gustan?**
Students listen and decide if the people like the activities or not. They write the appropriate activity or activity letter with either a tick or a cross.

🎧 **CD 3, track 11**　　　　página 136, actividad 1

Sara: Hablo por teléfono mucho con mis amigos. ¡Me encanta! Pero no leo los periódicos – son aburridos.
Miguel: Navego por internet – me gusta mucho. Pero no utilizo mucho el correo electrónico.
Jaime: Pues, a mí me encanta ver la televisión, pero no me interesa leer revistas.
Maite: Es muy divertido participar en los chats, pero no juego con videojuegos.

Answers:
Sara: talking on the phone (a) ✓, reading newspapers (g) ✗; **Miguel:** Internet (b) ✓, correo electrónico (f) ✗; **Jaime:** televisión (c) ✓, revistas (h) ✗; **Maite:** los chats (i) ✓, videojuegos (e) ✗

4B.1 La vida tecno

Gramática
Students can adapt the other activities e.g. *Me gusta navegar por internet*. Ask them how they could find out what type of verb each is.

AT 3.3 **PLTS**
2 Lee el correo electrónico de Javi.
Students read Javi's email and then copy and complete the sentences. First, make sure that students understand the phrases of frequency. Display the days of the week and tick them all saying *Hablo por teléfono los lunes, hablo por teléfono los martes*, etc. and then say *hablo por teléfono todos los días* to give the idea of *every day*. Use variations on this then to explain the other phrases of frequency.

Answers:
1 ... uses email. 2 ... watches television. 3 ... reads newspapers.
4 ... talks to his friends on the phone every day.

AT 2.3 **PLTS**
3 Juega a las 20 preguntas.
Students play 20 questions with a partner to try to guess what they like doing and how often. First, quickly revise how to change *navego* to *navegas* and the same for the other verbs in order to form the questions. Use the grammar box as a starting point.

PLTS
Gramática
Read through the examples given as a class. Ask students to categorise the verbs from the vocabulary box into *–ar* and *–er* verbs and then to change them into the 2nd person singular.

PLTS
Think!
Students should be able to find *el día* and *la radio* on this spread. They can look further for other examples if you wish.

AT 1.3
4 Escucha. ¿Quién gana?
Students listen carefully to the girl and boy playing the game of noughts and crosses and note down who wins. Students could have a copy of the grid to mark the Os and Xs as they listen; or they could place small card Os and Xs on the page.

🎧 **CD 3, track 12**   página 137, actividad 4
- Me gusta ver los dibujos animados.
- Me gustan mucho las telenovelas.
- No me gusta ver las noticias.
- No me gustan los anuncios.
- Me gusta ver los programas musicales.
- No me gustan los programas deportivos.
- No me gustan los documentales.

Answer: the boy wins

AT 2.3 **PLTS**
5 Juega con tu compañero.
Students play the game from Activity 4 with a partner. They say they like or dislike the type of programme to make their move. Check they understand the difference between *Me gusta ver los dibujos animados* and *Me gustan los dibujos animados*.

AT 1.3
6 Escucha. ¿Qué opinan?
Students listen and note down the opinion they hear each time. They can do this in note form, in Spanish or in English. Feedback should include the piecing together of the whole sentences in order to be able to do Activity 7.

🎧 **CD 3, track 13**   página 137, actividad 6
1. Las telenovelas son tontas pero graciosas.
2. Los documentales son informativos y divertidos.
3. Los dibujos animados son bastante graciosos.
4. Las noticias son aburridas pero útiles.
5. Los programas deportivos son muy, muy emocionantes.
6. Las series son informativas y divertidas.
7. Los concursos son divertidos y emocionantes.
8. Los programas musicales son tontos y aburridos.
9. Los anuncios son divertidos y graciosos.

Answers: see audioscript

AT 4.3 **PLTS**
7 Escribe. ¿Estás de acuerdo con los otros?
Students write their opinion of the types of television programme mentioned in Activity 6. They should include phrases like *para mí, en mi opinión*, etc. They can compare some of the sentences in class. One student reads out a sentence and others say *Sí, estoy de acuerdo* or *Yo también* or put their hand up if they agree.

AT 4.4 **PLTS**
Challenge
Write about the activities you do. Which ones do you do? How often do you do them? Which TV programmes do you like to watch? Which ones don't you like? Why? Include as much information as you can and word-process your statement. Can your friends guess who you are?
Students can write anonymously, as a famous person, as a character from a TV programme, etc. Would Batman read the newspapers or spend time in chat rooms? Develop a character in class first to give them the idea.

4B.2 La vida tecno

4B.2 El cine y los libros
páginas 138–139

Planner

Objectives
- talk about the type of films you like and why
- practise using *gustar* to say what other people like
- carry out a survey

Video
Video script, Unit 4B

Resources
Students' Book, pages 138–139
CD 3, tracks 14–16
Foundation Workbook, page 73
Higher Workbook, page 73
Foundation Workbook audio, CD 3, track 80
Higher Workbook audio, CD 4, track 55
Interactive OxBox, Unit 4B
Copymasters 105–112
Assessment, Unit 4B

Key language
una película romántica; una película de terror; una película de ciencia-ficción; una película de vaqueros; una película de acción; una película de misterio; una película de guerra; una comedia; la fantasía

Grammar
- practise using *gustar* to say what other people like

Renewed Framework references
1.1, 1.4, 2.4, 2.5, 3.1, 3.2, 4.2, 4.3, 4.4, 4.5, 4.6, 5.1, 5.3, 5.4, 5.8

PLTS
Activity 1: Team workers
Activity 3: Reflective learners
Activity 7: Effective participators
Activity 8: Reflective learners

Challenge: Self-managers; Creative thinkers

Starters
- Display a list of the different types of films. Give students a time limit to write down one or more adjectives for each film type. With less able students, display a list of adjectives for them to allocate accordingly. Compare answers as a class. More able students can produce sentences using the film types and adjectives listed, e.g. *Las comedias son divertidas*.
- Carry out a class survey. Students ask a partner what is their favourite type of film and note down the answer. They then report back, using a full sentence in the 3rd person. Collate all of the results and keep them for students to use later.

Plenaries
- Students use the collated results from Starter Activity 2 to produce a graph or to write a short report describing the class results, e.g. *A 20 personas les gustan las películas de acción.* or *10 personas piensan que las películas de guerra son aburridas.*
- Students write a sentence for each type of film saying why they like/dislike it. They should use phrases such as, *en mi opinion, para mí* as well as adjectives. They could also mention how often they watch particular types of film. Follow this up with a class discussion.

Homework/Self-study
Students adapt the sentences in the recording from Activity 3 so that they are true for them, e.g. *En mi opinión, las películas de guerra son **emocionantes**. Me gustan*.
Students write out their own answers to the questions in Activity 5.
Gramática: Students write a sentence for each person in the singular and plural using the phrase, *A X me/te/le/nos/os/les gusta …*.

AT 3.2 | **PLTS** — **1** 👥 **Habla con tu compañero.**
Students discuss with a partner what the different types of films are. They should look for cognates, familiar words, and use visual clues. Encourage them to pick apart *vaqueros* and *guerra* (like *guerrilla*) to arrive at understanding.

AT 1.3 — **2 Escucha y lee. ¡No es correcto!**
Students listen and read and note down any errors in the sentences. Students just need to pinpoint the error in this activity, and go on to correct the sentences in Activity 3.

Answers:
a a romance; **b** a horror film; **c** a science fiction film; **d** a western; **e** an action film; **f** a thriller; **g** a war film; **h** a comedy

4B.2 La vida tecno

CD 2, track 14 — página 138, actividades 2 y 3

1 Me encantan las películas de **acción** – ¡son emocionantes!
2 En mi opinión, las películas de guerra son **aburridas**. No me gustan.
3 Las comedias son **divertidas**. Son mi tipo de películas preferidas.
4 Para mí, las películas de ciencia-ficción son **divertidas**. Las veo a menudo.
5 **Me gustan mucho** las películas románticas. Son graciosas.
6 Las películas de vaqueros son **tontas**. Pero me gustan mucho.

Answers:
1 terror ✗, acción ✓; *2* tontas ✗, aburridas ✓; *3* interesantes ✗, divertidas ✓; *4* aburridas ✗, divertidas ✓; *5* No me gustan nada ✗, me gustan mucho ✓; *6* divertidas ✗, tontas ✓

AT 1.3, 4.3 / PLTS

3 Escucha otra vez. Escribe las frases correctamente.
Students listen to the recording again if necessary and write the sentences out correctly.

Answers:
1 Me encantan las películas de <u>acción</u> – ¡son emocionantes!
2 En mi opinión, las películas de guerra son <u>aburridas</u>. No me gustan. *3* Las comedias son <u>divertidas</u>. Son mi tipo de películas preferidas. *4* Para mí, las películas de ciencia-ficción son <u>divertidas</u>. Las veo a menudo. *5* <u>Me gustan mucho</u> las películas románticas. Son graciosas. *6* Las películas de vaqueros son <u>tontas</u>. Pero me gustan mucho.

4 Habla con tu compañero. ¿Qué tipo de películas no le gustan a Eva?
Students discuss with a partner what type of films they think Eva does *not* like. Collect the students' guesses and put them on the board. After watching the video you can circle the ones Eva doesn't like – how many guessed correctly?

Answer: According to Marisa in the video, Eva doesn't like sci-fi films, horror films, westerns, comedies or mysteries.

AT 1.5

5 Mira el video.
Students watch the video as many times as you think necessary. They note down what they are talking about, what Eva wants Marisa to do and what Marisa wants Eva to do.

Video script: Unit 4B (CD 3, track 15)

Eva: No, hablando en serio… puede que esa sea una de las peores películas que haya visto en mi vida.
Marisa: Lo que pasa es que a ti no te gustan las películas de ciencia ficción.
Eva: Eso no es verdad. Me gustan todo tipo de películas.
Marisa: Claro, siempre y cuando no sean películas de terror, de vaqueros, comedias, o películas de misterio.
Eva: ¡No es verdad! La última película que vi, fue una de terror; ¡La Venganza de las Momias! Trataba de… unas momias… que se vengaban.
Marisa: Ya pero, ¿te gustó?
Eva: No. Era una película estúpida. Pero, yo no tengo nada en contra del género.
Khalid: ¿Quiénes son estas chicas y qué les han hecho a Eva y a Marisa?
Eva: Ha salido la película nueva de Almodóvar. Me encanta Pedro Almodóvar.
Marisa: Lo que quiere decir es que a mí no me gustará.
Eva: No, pero aun así deberías ir a verla, Mar. Almodóvar es uno de los directores de cine más importantes de España.
Marisa: Vale, vale… pero entonces tú tienes que ir al partido de fútbol del sábado porque el FC Barcelona es uno de los clubs de fútbol más importantes de España.
José: ¡Tiene razón, Eva!
Eva: ¿No puedo ver un documental sobre el club en vez de ir al partido? ¿Podría ver algunos videos en Youtube?
Marisa: Ver una obra de teatro en la tele no es lo mismo que ir al teatro, ¿no es así? Bueno, pues con el fútbol ocurre lo mismo. ¡Tienes que verlo en vivo!

Answers:
They are talking about different types of films. Eva wants Marisa to see a film by Almodóvar "one of the most important directors in Spain", and Marisa wants Eva to watch a Barcelona FC match "one of the most important football clubs in Spain".

AT 1.5

6 Escucha a Tomás. ¿Cómo responde a las preguntas?
Students listen to Tomás and note down how he answers the questions.

CD 3, track 16 — página 139, actividad 6

Interviewer: ¿Te gusta leer libros?
Tomás: Bueno, leo solamente de vez en cuando.
Interviewer: ¿Por qué?
Tomás: Porque me parece bastante aburrido.
Interviewer: ¿Leíste un libro la semana pasada?

4B.2 La vida tecno

Tomás:	Pues, no.
Interviewer:	¿Leíste un libro el mes pasado?
Tomás:	La verdad es que no.
Interviewer:	¿Leíste un libro el año pasado?
Tomás:	¡Eso sí!
Interviewer:	¿Qué prefieres hacer? ¿Por qué?
Tomás:	Prefiero ver la televisión o navegar por internet. Es más fácil.
Interviewer:	Da el título de un libro que conoces.
Tomás:	*El color de la magia* de Terry Pratchett.
Interviewer:	¿Qué tipo de libro es?
Tomás:	Es un libro de fantasía, y ¡es muy, muy bueno!

Answers: as per audioscript

7 Habla con tus compañeros. ¿Qué dicen?
Students ask their classmates the questions from Activity 6 and write down their responses in note form. Compare their findings as a class to decide if the class likes reading and if there is a particular type of book that is popular.

Gramática
Read the grammar explanation as a class. Work through a few examples using as many forms as possible to ensure that all students fully understand how to say 'X likes ...'. To check understanding, ask students to give you some examples of their own.

8 Escribe sus respuestas.
Students now write out in full their findings from Activity 7, giving reasons why their classmates like/dislike certain activities.

Challenge
Advertise your favourite film for the local Spanish film club.
This is meant to be a brief poster-style advert with the type of film and some opinions. It will lead into the longer Challenge on the next spread. If you have particularly literary students, get them to do the same thing for books.

4B.3 La vida tecno

4B.3 ¿De qué trató? ¿Qué pasó?

páginas 140–141

Planner

Objectives
- describe what a film is about and what happened
- practise using the preterite tense
- look up verbs in a dictionary

Video
Video script, Unit 4B

Resources
Students' Book, pages 140–141
CD 3, tracks 15, 17–18
Foundation Workbook, page 74
Higher Workbook, page 74
Foundation Workbook audio, CD 3, track 81
Higher Workbook audio, CD 4, track 56
Interactive OxBox, Unit 4B
Copymasters 105–112
Assessment , Unit 4B

Key language
un asesinato; un atentado; un robo; un secuestro; un timo; un viaje; una amistad; una guerra; una historia de amor; una lucha entre el bien y el mal; una misión secreta; vampiros; buscar; batallar; robar; descubrir; solucionar; enamorarse de

Grammar
- practise using the preterite tense

Renewed Framework references
1.1, 1.2, 1.4, 1.5, 2.1, 2.2, 2.4, 2.5, 3.1, 3.2, 4.3, 4.4, 4.5, 5.1, 5.4, 5.5

PLTS
Activity 1: Team workers
Activity 3: Effective participants
Activity 4: Effective participants
Challenge: Creative thinkers

Starters
- Display the key language and also the English for this in jumbled order. Give students a time limit to match the Spanish and the English. Check answers as a class. How did students work out which Spanish phrase went with which English one?
- Display the film descriptions and give students a time limit to see if they can think of a film title for each one of them. The film titles can be in English, although you could give students the Spanish title if there is one. Alternatively, you could display a list of film titles and ask students to categorise them according the the subject matter.

Plenaries
- Students choose three of the film titles from Starter Activity 1 and write a sentence about each of them saying what they were about and giving their opinion of them. If they haven't seen any of the films, they can make up an opinion.
- Choose a film that the majority of the class will have seen, e.g. *Shrek*, and have a class 'discussion show'. Students say what the film was about (remind them that there may be more than one theme in any given film) and then give their opinion of it.

Homework/Self-study
Activity 2: Students think of three films they have seen recently and note down what each one was about, using the phrase *Trató de* ….

AT 3.1 | PLTS

1 Empareja los dibujos y las palabras.
Students work with a partner to match the pictures of the films to the descriptions in the vocabulary box.

Answers:
a un atentado; **b** una amistad; **c** un viaje; **d** un secuestro; **e** una historia de amor; **f** un asesinato; **g** un robo; **h** un timo; **i** una misión secreta; **j** una lucha entre el bien y el mal; **k** una guerra; **l** vampiros

AT 1.2

2 Escucha. ¿De qué trató la película?
Students listen and note down what the film was about. They can answer in Spanish or English or just by giving the letter of the correct picture.

CD 3, track 17 — página 140, actividad 2

1 Era una película vieja. Trató de una guerra.
2 Era una película bastante estúpida. Trató de un timo.
3 Era muy emocionante. Trató de un secuestro.
4 Era una película de acción. Trató de un atentado.
5 ¡Era muy romántica! Trató de una historia de amor.
6 Era bastante violenta pero divertida. Trató de vampiros.
7 Trató de un viaje a la próxima galaxia.
8 Era muy bonita. Trató de una amistad.
9 Era una película de terror – trató de un asesinato.
10 No me gustó nada. Trató de un robo.
11 ¡Era una película fantástica! Trató de una misión secreta.
12 Trató de una lucha entre el bien y el mal, pero era muy aburrida.

4B.3 La vida tecno

Answers:
1 Trató de una guerra – k; **2** Trató de un timo – h; **3** Trató de un secuestro – d; **4** Trató de un atentado – a; **5** Trató de una historia de amor – e; **6** Trató de vampiros – l; **7** Trató de un viaje – c; **8** Trató de una amistad – b; **9** Trató de un asesinato – f; **10** Trató de un robo – g; **11** Trató de una misión secreta – i; **12** Trató de una lucha entre el bien y el mal – j

3 Habla con tu compañero.
Students work in pairs to play a guessing game. One of them thinks of a film from Activity 2. The other tries to guess which one they are thinking of, using the phrase *¿Trató de …?*. They then swap roles.

Gramática
Look up verbs with students. Provide them with the infinitive of a couple of the verbs, and then ask them to work out the rest. Give them some other examples using *–ar, -er, -ir* verbs and ask them what clues they can use to help them e.g. *batallaron* has to be an *–ar* verb because 3rd person plural preterite of *–er* and *–ir* verbs end *–ieron*.

4 ¿Qué pasó? Haz frases correctas.
Students work with a partner, or individually if you prefer, and use the grid to find the correct descriptions. They feed back their attempts to the class. You could set a time limit, and see how many they get right in that time. The grid can be copied onto paper and cut up like a jigsaw to be placed into the right order. Remind students that when *se enamoró de* is followed by *el*, it becomes *se enamoró del*.

Answers:
1 Un astronauta descubrió un planeta nuevo. **2** Un policía solucionó un asesinato misterioso. **3** Unos ladrones robaron a un casino. **4** Un espía buscó una bomba atómica. **5** Una estudiante se enamoró del novio de su amiga. **6** Unos vampiros batallaron contra los ángeles.

5 Escucha. ¿Tienes razón?
Students listen to check their answers to Activity 4. Highlight the singular and plural endings of the different verbs. Get the students to make the singular verbs plural, etc. to practise changing verb endings. Point out *un policía* and *un espía* and ask them what is unusual about these nouns (masculine, ending in a.) They use the grid to make up more sentences in groups or pairs. Other students have to decide if their sentence is *posible* or *ridícula* e.g. *Un policía robó una bomba atómica* is *ridícula*, but *Un espía solucionó un asesinato misterioso* is *posible*. Make sure they change the verb ending if necessary.

CD 3, track 18 — página 141, actividad 5
1. Un astronauta descubrió un planeta nuevo.
2. Un policía solucionó un asesinato misterioso.
3. Unos ladrones robaron un casino.
4. Un espía buscó una bomba atómica.
5. Una estudiante se enamoró del novio de su amiga.
6. Unos vampiros batallaron contra los ángeles.

6 Mira el video.
Students watch the video and note down what Eva and Marisa are talking about and what happens in their story. Get students to think back about what has happened in the video story so far, and how the two girls have related up until this point. A transcript of the video may be helpful either before or after watching. Once students understand what is happening, they can watch again. Ask them to listen for specific details, or to note down verbs in the preterite.

Video script: Unit 4B (CD 3, track 15)

Marisa: ¿Por qué no te vienes a mi casa esta noche también? Podríamos navegar… quiero decir, hablar sobre nuestros libros favoritos.
Eva: Sí, vale. Puedo traerte esas novelas de misterio de las que hablamos el otro día.
Khalid: Pero, ¿tú lees novelas de misterio?
Marisa: Sí, Khal, sé leer, ¿sabes?
Khalid: Sí, ya, las páginas de deportes.
[Pause]
Marisa: ¿Les decimos de qué trataba la telenovela que vimos el otro día?
Eva: ¿Qué telenovela?
Marisa: Ya sabes… la telenovela – la de los tres amigos que se llaman Jesús, Carlos y Elena. Pues, eso… trata de tres amigos… que se llaman… Jesús, Carlos y Elena y viven en Barcelona. Han sido amigos desde hace muchos años pero de repente, llega una chica muy guapa de Argen… de Perú que se llama… eh… que se llama… eh…
Eva: ¡María!
Marisa: Eso, se llama María. A Elena, María le cae mal desde el principio porque cree que le puede quitar a sus amigos.
Eva: Bueno, en realidad se odian mutuamente, ¿no es cierto?
Marisa: Sí, pero eso porque no se conocen lo suficiente bien, ¿verdad?
Eva: ¡Verdad! Verdad.
Marisa: Sea como sea, todo cambia porque Elena y María se hacen amigas.
Eva: A pesar de no tener nada en común.
Marisa: ¡Nada en absoluto!

4B.4 La vida tecno

Eva:	Pero, esa es la mejor parte de su amistad… el hecho de ser tan diferentes.
Marisa:	Si, esa es la mejor parte.
[Pause]	
Khalid:	Pero, ¿es una telenovela, no? Así que las cosas podrían cambiar…
Eva y Marisa:	No, ¡eso no va a cambiar nunca!

Answers:
They are talking about books which Marisa and Eva are going to read and then about a soap opera about three friends and another girl who comes from Peru. The storyline of the soap opera reflects the situation with Eva and Marisa who dislike each other because they don't know each other well enough and Eva feels that Marisa is going to take her friends away from her. The girls in the soap opera get to know each other and slowly become friends despite their differences. Eva and Marisa are doing the same.

Challenge
AT 4.4–6 / PLTS

Write a brief film review and present it to the class. Remember to include the title, the type of film, what it was about, what happened and what your opinion was.

Students could also do this without naming the film, and see if the others can guess which film they are describing.

4B.4 Repaso   páginas 142–143

Planner

Objectives
- revise what you have learnt so far
- ask and answer questions
- independent learning

Resources
Students' Book, pages 142–143
CD 3, track 19
Foundation Workbook, page 75
Higher Workbook, page 75
Foundation Workbook audio, track 82
Higher Workbook audio, track 57
Interactive OxBox, Unit 4B
Copymasters 105–112
Assessment, Unit 4B

Grammar
- asking questions

Renewed Framework references
1.1, 1.4, 1.5, 2.1, 2.4, 2.5, 4.2, 4.3, 4.4, 4.5, 4.6, 5.1

PLTS
Activity 1: Self-managers; Team workers
Activity 2: Independent enquirers
Activity 4: Reflective learners; Self-managers

Starters
- Go round the class giving each student in turn a type of television programme, e.g. *las telenovelas, los anuncios*, etc. Students give an appropriate adjective to describe that particular type of programme. More able students can give a full sentence, e.g. *Me gusta los programas deportivos. Son emocionantes.*
- Ask students to note down in Spanish two things about them that are true and one that is false, e.g. *Prefiero ver la televisión o navegar por internet. Me llamo X. Tengo catorce años. Me gusta un poco la historia.* etc. Their partner must guess which of the statements are true and which is false. You could also do this as a whole class.

Plenaries
- Students pretend to be a famous person and describe themselves to the rest of the class using some of the questions from Activity 1 to help them. The rest of the class tries to guess who they are pretending to be.

Homework/Self-study
Students write out their answers to the questions, or their presentation from Activity 1.
Activity 4: For Part 3, students can also be asked to write about Zaragoza which relates more closely to the Students' Book.

1 Entrevista a tu compañero.
AT 2.4–5 / PLTS

Students interview a friend and then answer the questions themselves. They then act out their interview in front of the class. To add interest, rather than answering as themselves, they could answer in character as a famous person or character from a film or TV programme. More able students could use the questions to give a presentation about themselves to the class.

4B.4 La vida tecno

AT 4.4–5
PLTS

2 Describe una persona.
Students write a description of one of the people, using the questions listed to help them. They can look back through the book for any information they need. Weaker students may need a 'crib sheet' of details about the characters from the video to help them. Alternatively, turn it into a quiz – how old is Marisa? How many people are there in José's family? This is an ideal opportunity to re-use parts of the video. Students can write in the the 3rd person for the description, or they can pretend to be one of the people and write in the 1st person.

AT 1.4

3 Escuchar
Students listen and choose the correct answer each time. For part 4, give less able students a copy of the list to number.

🎧 **CD 3, track 19** página 143, actividad 3

1 Hola, me llamo Antonio. Tengo catorce años. Tengo el pelo marrón y los ojos azules.
2 Soy Melisa y vivo en Granada. Me encanta vivir aquí. Granada es una ciudad grande y antigua cerca de las montañas en Andalucía. La región de Andalucía está en el sur de España.
3 Pues, el inglés es bastante aburrido, y no me gusta mucho, pero el profe es simpático. Me gusta un poco la historia – es bastante divertida, pero no es muy útil. Sin embargo, la tecnología sí que es muy interesante y me gusta mucho.
4 Pues, los días de colegio por la mañana me despierto a las siete. Me levanto a las siete y cuarto, más o menos, y voy a la cocina en pijama. Desayuno unas tostadas y un café grande, y luego voy al cuarto de baño donde me ducho y me peino. Finalmente me pongo el uniforme y voy al instituto.

Answers:
1 b; *2* b; *3* c, e; *4* me despierto, me levanto, desayuno, me ducho, me peino, me pongo el uniforme

AT 3.4; 4.4–5
PLTS

4 Leer y Escribir
Students complete the questions. This is a good opportunity for students to revise what they have learnt.

Answers:
1 students' own answers; *2* vamos a ir; vamos a nos alojar; voy a hacer; va a tomar el sol; van a comer; vas a hacer;
3 students' own answers; *4a* No me **gustan** las telenovelas – son tontas. *4b* Me **encanta** ver **los** anuncios – normalmente son graciosos. *4c* Me **gustan** los programas deportivos. **Son** emocionantes. *4d* No me **gustan** nada **los** documentales – **son** aburrido**s**.

4B.5 La vida tecno

4B.5 En mi opinión...
páginas 144–145

Planner

Objectives
- describe the advantages and disadvantages of different types of media
- use *lo bueno* and *lo malo*
- present and defend a point of view

Resources
Students' Book, pages 144–145
CD 3, tracks 20–21
Foundation Workbook, page 76
Higher Workbook, page 76
Foundation Workbook audio, CD 3, track 83
Higher Workbook audio, CD 4, track 58
Interactive OxBox, Unit 4B
Assessment, Unit 4B

Key language
es muy…; puede ser…; divertido/a; útil; rápido/a; personal; emocionante; tonto/a; gracioso/a; educativo/a; entretenido/a; fácil; peligroso/a; una ventaja es…; una desventaja es…; lo malo es que…; lo bueno es que…; es una pérdida de tiempo; se puede hacer…; con amigos/ solo/en casa/donde quieras; se puede llevar consigo/ adonde quieras; (no) necesitas tecnología especial; (no) es caro; es antisocial

Renewed Framework references
1.1, 1.2, 1.4, 1.5, 3.2, 4.2, 4.3, 4.4, 4.5, 4.6, 5.1

PLTS
Activity 1: Independent enquirers
Activity 2: Reflective learners
Gramática: Independent enquirers
Activity 4: Effective participants
Think!: Independent enquirers; Self-managers
Activity 6: Effective participators
Challenge: Effective participators

Starters
- Play a class game of noughts and crosses. Display a large noughts and crosses grid with a symbol representing one of the activities mentioned in the spread in each box. Split the class into two teams. The 'noughts' team picks a box and must make a statement about the activity represented in that box, e.g. *Creemos que navegar por internet es antisocial.* in order to win it. The 'crosses' team then has a go, and so on until one of the teams gets a row of three and wins.
- Play a quick-fire class game. Call out an opinion about one of the activities from the spread. Either individually, or in groups, students respond with an opposing opinion, e.g. *Leer periódicos me parece muy útil y bastante educativo. ¿Leer periódicos? ¡Ni hablar! Es muy aburrido.* etc.

Plenaries
- Challenge students to write two sentences about the activities from the spread using *Lo bueno...*, and two using *Lo malo....* Compare sentences as a class.
- Following the Challenge Activity, ask students to write up their debate in the form of a short article, e.g. *Navegar por internet es antisocial, pero lo bueno es que se se puede hacer solo.* With less able students, display model sentences for them to use and adapt as necessary.

Homework/Self-study
Gramática: Students write sentences using *Lo malo....*
Think!: Students use the phrase *donde quieras* in a sentence of their own.

AT 2.2–3

1 ¿Qué opinas?

PLTS

Students match the adjectives to the types of activity. This can be done as a whole class starter activity, checking for comprehension as you go. Most students should be able to guess at any adjectives they have not met before. Alternatively, students could work individually or in small groups and feed back their ideas to the rest of the class. You could keep a tally to see how many people agree.

AT 2.3

2 ¡Al contrario!

PLTS

Students make negative statements about the activities. This could be done as a quick-fire group game. Call out an activity and an adjective. The first group to come up with the negative sentence wins. Extend this by calling out an activity OR an adjective.

AT 1.4–5

3 Escucha. ¿Qué opinan?

Students listen and copy and complete the table. Remind them to keep in mind the activities and adjectives from Activities 1 and 2.

CD 3, track 20 — página 144, actividad 3

Beatriz: Dime, Alfonso, ¿te gusta leer periódicos?
Alfonso: ¿Cómo? ¿Leer periódicos? ¡Ni hablar! Es muy aburrido.
Beatriz: No estoy de acuerdo. Me parece muy útil y bastante educativo.

4B.5 La vida tecno

Alfonso: Pues, navegar por internet también es útil, y mucho más interesante y divertido.
Beatriz: ¿Divertido? No lo sé. Navegar por internet es bastante rápido, pero no es muy personal.
Alfonso: A mí me gusta hablar por teléfono con mis amigos. Eso sí que es personal y rápido y divertido.
Beatriz: Para mí es demasiado rápido. Prefiero utilizar el correo electrónico. Es más fácil, ¿sabes?
Alfonso: Sí, estoy de acuerdo, pero participar en los chats es más divertido.
Beatriz: ¡Qué va! Eso es bastante tonto y además puede ser peligroso.
Alfonso: Ay, Bea, qué aburrida eres …

Answers:

Actividad	Beatriz	Alfonso
leer periódicos	útil, bastante educativo	aburrido
navegar por internet	bastante rápido, no muy personal	útil, interesante, divertido
hablar por teléfono	demasiado rápido	personal, rápido, divertido
correo electrónico	fácil	fácil
participar en los chats	bastante tonto, peligroso	divertido

PLTS **Gramática**
Look at the two structures and give a few example sentences using each of them. More able classes can also think of some examples of their own. Ask students how they could change this phrase to talk about bad things. Elicit from them that *Lo bueno…* could be changed to *Lo malo….*

AT 2.3–4 **4 ¿Una ventaja o una desventaja?**
PLTS Students describe each of the phrases as an advantage or disadvantage? This can be done as a class discussion or in pairs or small groups. There can be disagreement as to whether e.g. doing something alone is a positive or a negative. Encourage students to use the negative also, thus *no es caro* becomes an advantage.

Suggested answers:
Ventajas: se puede hacer con amigos, se puede hacer solo, se puede hacer en casa, se puede llevar adonde quieras
Desventajas: es una pérdida de tiempo, necesitas tecnología especial, es caro, es antisocial

PLTS **Think!**
Read the sentence as a class and give students some time to work out what *donde quieras* means. Can any of them work out the correct answer (wherever you want)?

AT 1.5 **5 Escucha. Nota las ventajas y las desventajas.**
Students listen and note the advantages and disadvantages of the activities.

CD 3, track 21 — página 145, actividad 5

1
A Pues, para mí, la ventaja de ver la televisión es que se puede hacer en casa.
B Sí, pero la desventaja es que es una pérdida de tiempo.
2
A ¿Sabes? Me encanta leer libros. Lo malo es que es muy antisocial.
B Pero lo bueno es que se puede llevar adonde quieras.
3
A Para mí hay muchas ventajas en ir al cine. Es divertido, es sociable, se puede hacer con amigos y es emocionante.
B Pero es muy caro y necesitas tecnología especial – son desventajas, ¿no?
4
A Lo bueno de navegar por internet es que se puede hacer en casa y no es caro. También es muy interesante.
B Pero lo malo es que es muy antisocial, no siempre se puede llevar adonde quieras, y puede ser peligroso.

Answers:
1 TV – advantage: can do it at home; disadvantage: waste of time; **2** reading books – disadvantage: anti-social; advantage: can take it anywhere; **3** cinema – advantages: fun, sociable, can do it with friends, exciting; disadvantages – very expensive and you need special technology; **4** surfing the net – advantages: can do it at home, cheap, interesting; disadvantages: antisocial, can't take it with you, can be dangerous

AT 2.3–4 **6 Encuentra un compañero.**
PLTS Students note down their opinion of one of the activities from the spread. They go round the class until they find someone else who thinks the same thing. You could share out opinions or activities to avoid everyone ending up in a huge group saying that TV is fun…

AT 2.4–5 **Challenge**
PLTS **Hold a debate. Work with a group to present an argument for or against a particular activity.**
Nominate a subject e.g. TV, and divide the class into 'for' and 'against' groups, who prepare statements in line with their argument. They should use the structures and vocabulary they have learnt here. You could have several mini-debates. The class can vote either for the argument they liked the best, or for those who argued with most conviction. This is also a useful exercise in getting students to look at different points of view other than their own.

4B.6 La vida tecno

4B.6 Labolengua

páginas 146–147

Planner

Objectives
- review language and grammar from the unit

Resources
Students' Book, pages 146–147
CD 3, tracks 22–23
Foundation Workbook, pages 77–78
Higher Workbook, pages 77–78
Interactive OxBox, Unit 4B
Copymasters 113–114
Assessment, Unit 4B

Grammar
- verbs
- irregular verbs
- asking questions

Renewed Framework references
1.1, 1.4, 2.1, 2.4, 4.1, 4.2, 4.3, 4.4, 4.5, 4.6, 5.1, 5.2

PLTS
All activities: Reflective learners/Self-managers

Homework/Self-study
Activity 4: Students write another couple of sentences saying what is good and what is bad about an activity of their choice.
Section C: Students try to find examples of other irregular verbs. More able students could also write out the preterite tense of these verbs.

Comprender – verbs and opinions

A Ayer, hoy y mañana

PLTS 1 Copy and complete these sentences. Use the words in the box.
Practice of using the correct tense in the correct form.

Answers:
1 voy; **2** fui; **3** voy a ir; **4** como; **5** comí; **6** voy a comer

PLTS 2 Write sentences about what you normally do, did yesterday and are going to do tomorrow using activities from this unit.
If necessary, give students a list of activities to write about. More able students can look up and adapt new activities.

B *Lo bueno y lo malo* – expressing opinions

PLTS 3 Complete these sentences. Use the words below.
Practice of using *lo bueno es que…* and *lo malo es que…* correctly.

Answers:
1 internet; educativo; antisocial; **2** libros; aburrido; llevar

PLTS 4 What is the good thing or the bad thing about…?
Further practice of the phrases *lo bueno de… es que…* and *lo malo de… es que…*. Students feed back their ideas to the class, or compare them in groups.

Aprender – irregular verbs

C Remembering irregular verbs

PLTS Where are the endings different? How many different endings do you actually have to learn? How would you say 'you put the newspaper on the TV yesterday'?
Practice of forming irregular verbs.

Answers:
1st and 3rd person only; you have to learn 2 different endings; Pusiste la revista en la televisión ayer.

PLTS How would you say: 'He couldn't go to school yesterday' and 'We couldn't go to school yesterday'?
Recognising patterns with irregular verbs.

Answers: No pudo ir al instituto ayer. No pudimos ir al instituto ayer.

4B.7 La vida tecno

Hablar – asking questions

D Communicating with questions

> **PLTS** **5 Listen to these people. Are they asking a question or making a statement?**
> Practice of recognising when people are asking questions.

🎧 **CD 3, track 22** página 147, actividad 5

1 ¿Te gustan los documentales?
2 Te gusta ver las telenovelas.
3 No te gusta navegar por internet.
4 ¿Prefieres los dibujos animados?
5 ¿Juegas con videojuegos a menudo?
6 Escuchas la radio cada día.

Answers:
1 question; 2 statement; 3 statement; 4 question; 5 question; 6 statement

PLTS **6 Make up questions that go with these statements; look back through the book to help you.**
This could be a mini-group competition; set a time limit, and then ask groups to feed back their questions. They get a point for each one they get right.

Answers: see audioscript below

PLTS **7 Now listen – were you right?**
Students mark their answers from Activity 6.

🎧 **CD 3, track 23** página 147, actividad 7

– ¿Cómo te llamas?
– ¿Cuántos años tienes?
– ¿Cuántas personas hay en tu familia?
– ¿Dónde vives?
– ¿Qué te gusta ver en la televisión?

PLTS **8 Practise the questions from Activity 6 with a partner – they read out the statement; you say the correct question. Does it sound like a question when you say it?**
Practice of making questions sound like questions. As an extension activity, more able students can make up five statements about themselves (preferably practising language from this unit) and their partner has to make up questions to match them.

3B.7 Extra Star página 148

Planner

Objectives
- understand which TV programmes other people like
- practise using *me gusta* and *me gusta ver*
- personalise a template

Video
Video-blog, Unit 4B

Resources
Students' Book, page 148
CD 3, track 24, Copymaster 115

Renewed Framework references
2.1, 2.4, 2.5, 3.1, 3.2, 4.3, 4.4, 4.5, 5.1

PLTS
Activity 3: Creative thinkers
Gramática: Reflective learners

AT 3.3–4 **1 ¿Verdad o mentira?**
Students read the texts and decide if the statements are true or false.

Answers:
1 verdad; 2 mentira; 3 verdad; 4 mentira; 5 verdad; 6 verdad

AT 1.3 **2 Mira el video-blog.**
Students watch the video-blog and note down which films they like, what they like watching on TV and why.

4B.7 La vida tecno

Video-blog: Unit 4B (CD 3, track 24)

¿Qué películas te gustan y por qué?
Eva: Me gustan todo tipo de películas. Me gustan las comedias, las de terror, las dramáticas. Pero mis favoritas son las de Almodóvar.
José: Me gustan las películas de terror y las de ciencia-ficción porque me lo paso genial viéndolas.

¿Qué programas te gustan ver en la tele y por qué?
Eva: En la tele me gusta ver documentales y noticias.
José: Me gustan los programas de deportes y los reality-shows porque son muy divertidos.

Habla de una película que viste.
Eva: La última película que vi fue la de Harry Potter – la última – y me gustó mucho porque había muchas escenas de fantasía, de ficción, había mucha magia y fue muy emocionante.
José: El otro día vi *Alicia en el País de las Maravillas* – una película genial y además sale uno de mis actores preferidos que se llama Johnny Depp.

¿Utilizas las redes sociales?
Eva: Las utilizo pero poco. Prefiero buscar cosas de cultura, exposiciones que hagan en Barcelona antes que chatear por Internet.
José: Utlizo mucho Facebook y Twenty para restar en contacto con mis familiares de Madrid, con mis amigos para jugar al fútbol. Todo eso.

Answers:
Eva likes all types of film: comedies, horror films, plays, but her favourites are Almodóvar films. On TV she likes documentaries and the news. The last film she saw was Harry Potter. She really liked it due to the many fantasy scenes and because there was a lot of magic and it was very exciting. She does use social networking sites, but not often. She prefers to look for cultural things such as exhibitions taking place in Barcelona.

José likes horror films and sci-fi films. On TV he likes sports programmes and reality shows as they are very entertaining. He saw Alice in Wonderland *which he thought was brilliant and also starred one of his favourite actors, Johnny Depp. He uses Facebook and Twenty a lot to keep in touch with his family in Madrid and with his friends to play football.*

3 Describe lo que te gusta ver en la televisión. [AT 4.2–3] [PLTS]
Students use the template provided to describe what they like watching on television. They write it out in full and personalise it. More able students can add extra details, e.g. what their brother/friend/Mum likes to watch, or what they watched yesterday/will watch tomorrow.

Gramática [PLTS]
Ask students to come up with their own sentences using *gustar* in the singular, plural and with another verb.

4B.7 Extra Plus   página 149

Planner

Objectives
- talk about films
- practise recognising and using verbs
- write a description

Resources
Students' Book, page 149
CD 3, track 25
Copymaster 116

Renewed Framework references
1.1, 1.2, 1.4, 1.5, 2.1, 2.2, 2.4, 2.5, 4.3, 4.4, 4.5, 5.1

PLTS
Activity 1: Self-managers
Activity 2: Reflective learners
Activity 4: Independent enquirers
Activity 5: Creative thinkers

1 Completa la historia. Usa las palabras de la casilla de vocabulario. [AT 3.4–5] [PLTS]
Students complete the story using the words from the vocabulary box. Remind students to read the text carefully, paying attention to time markers, gender and number.

Answers:
1 *semana;* **2** *cine;* **3** *película;* **4** *famoso;* **5** *fantasía;* **6** *gustan;* **7** *tontas;* **8** *muy;* **9** *aventuras;* **10** *trata*

2 Escucha. ¿Tienes razón? [AT 1.4] [PLTS]
Students listen to check their answers. If you prefer students to work independently on this page, and don't have the facilities for pupils to listen on their own, give students a copy of the script to check their work.

4B.8 La vida tecno

CD 3, track 25 página 149, actividad 2

– ¿Qué hiciste el fin de **semana**?
– Fui al cine. Vi la nueva película de Harry Potter.
– ¿Harry Potter? ¿Qué tipo de **película** es?
– ¿Cómo? ¿No conoces a Harry Potter? ¡Es muy **famoso**! Es una película de **fantasía**.
– Pues, no me **gustan** las películas de fantasía. Son **tontas**.
– No, no – ¡es **muy** emocionante! Trata de un chico, Harry, que es mago, y de todas sus **aventuras** en el colegio de magos.
– Mm, no sé… Una película que **trata** de un colegio…
– Tienes que verla. ¡Es genial!

3 **Explica lo que pasó. ¿Qué hizo el chico? ¿Qué piensa? ¿Qué piensa la chica? ¿De qué trató la película?**
AT 2.4–5
Students demonstrate that they have understood the listening passage from Activity 2 by describing what happens.

4 Busca los verbos. ¿Son en presente o pasado? Escribe los infinitivos.
AT 3.4–5 PLTS
Students find the verbs in the cartoon story and note down if they are in the present or past tense. They then write them in the infinitive form. Remind students of the different groups –ar, –er, –ir. Check answers as a class. Students use the verbs they have listed in example sentences of their own to help them remember them.

5 Describe una película. ¿Qué tipo de película es? ¿De qué trata? ¿Qué piensas?
AT 4.4–6 PLTS
Students write their own description of a film. It doesn't have to be a film they like, or even have seen. Permit them to lie fluently in Spanish! First, read through the Think! box with them as these phrases will come in useful.

4B.8 Prueba página 150

Planner

Resources
Students' Book, page 150
CD 3, track 26

Renewed Framework references
1.1, 1.2, 1.4, 1.5, 2.1, 2.4, 2.5, 4.2, 4.3, 4.4, 4.5, 4.6, 5.1, 5.4

PLTS
All activities: Reflective learners
Escribir: Reflective learners; Creative thinkers

Escuchar

Which TV programmes are they talking about? What do they think of them?
AT 1.3–4 PLTS
This activity tests listening skills using the language covered in this unit. Students can answer in English or Spanish, as you prefer.

CD 3, track 26 página 150, Escuchar

1 Me gusta mucho ver los documentales. En mi opinión son interesantes e informativos.
2 Pues, a mí me encantan los programas deportivos porque son emocionantes y divertidos.
3 Las noticias son útiles, pero ¡a veces son bastante aburridas!
4 Los concursos son muy divertidos, pero un poco tontos.
5 Me gusta mucho ver las telenovelas. En mi opinión son graciosas y entretenidas.
6 Los dibujos animados son para niños. Son aburridos y tontos.

Answers:
1 c – interesting and informative; **2** e – exciting and entertaining; **3** d – useful but at times quite boring; **4** f – entertaining but a bit silly; **5** b – funny and entertaining; **6** a – boring and silly.

Hablar

Describe what you do in your free time and how often you do it.
AT 2.3–4 PLTS
Students can use the stimulus pictures to describe what the people illustrated do, or they can talk about their own personal experiences. They should give opinions and use different tenses, as this will lead to higher marks.

La vida tecno 4B

Leer

Match the reviews to the pictures.
AT 3.4–5
PLTS
This activity tests reading skills using the language covered in this unit.

Answers:
1 b; **2** c; **3** a

Escribir

Describe a film. Include what type of film it is, what it was about, and what happened. What do you think of it?
AT 4.4–6
PLTS
This activity tests writing skills using the language covered in this unit. Students can describe a film of their choice but should include the elements set out in the question. They should include a variety of opinions, adjectives, adverbs connectives and quantifiers.

Leer 4B   página 160

Planner

Resources
Students' Book, page 160

Renewed Framework references
2.1, 2.2, 4.3, 4.4, 4.5, 4.6, 5.3, 5.4

PLTS
Activity 2: Effective participators

Homework/Self-study
After completing Activity 2, students write their own reply to Tele-chica. More able students could say whether they agree or disagree and why, giving an opinion using the phrases they have learnt in this unit. Less able students could simply say how much television they watch each day.

AT 3.4 **1 Read and decide.**
Students read the text and decide to which person numbers 1–7 refer.

Answers:
1 Marta la rosa; **2** Juan jo 23; **3** Tele-chica; **4** Marta la rosa; **5** Madrileño; **6** Juan jo 23; **7** Madrileño

AT 3.4–5
PLTS
2 What do you think of what Madrileño said to Marta la rosa? Was he rude or truthful? What would you do if someone said something you didn't like when you were on the Internet?
Use these questions as an opportunity for a bit of cross-curricular PSHE discussion. Very able students could be encouraged to write opinions about the pros and cons of watching too much TV or using chatrooms – *El internet es peligroso a veces porque la gente no es siempre simpática.*

Foundation Workbook

Página 72   4B.1 Los medios y la televisión
• Use with Students' Book, pages 136–137

AT 3.3–4 **1 Read and underline the activities and the frequency words. Then write the correct name under each bar chart.**
Practice of time phrases and media vocabulary.

Answers:
a Ofelia; **b** David; **c** Felipe

AT 3.3–4 **2 Draw the bar chart for the person who is left.**

Answer:
Ana: TV often, Internet never, radio sometimes, magazine often

Página 73   4B.2 El cine y los libros
• Use with Students' Book, pages 138–139

AT 4.1 **1 Write out these types of film in order of personal preference. Start with your favourite.**
Practice of different types of film. Students could discuss this with a partner to see to what extent they agree.

AT 2.2–3 **2 Use your list to talk about what films you do and don't like.**
Students include opinion words and the names of specific films if they want to as examples. If they do, encourage them to try to find out what the Spanish name is.

4B La vida tecno

AT 1.3 **3 Listen to Alvina and think of a film you would recommend she sees.**
If students can't think of a specific film, they can just note down what she says she likes.

> 🎧 **CD 3, track 80** — *página 73, actividad 3*
>
> Pues, me gustan las películas románticas, pero no me gustan las comedias. Me encantan las películas de vaqueros, pero no me gustan las películas de acción.

Página 74 4B.3 ¿De qué trató? ¿Qué pasó?
- Use with Students' Book, pages 140–141

AT 1.4–5 **1 Read the film titles. Then listen. Who saw which film?**
Students think about what type of film each one title listed is likely to be before they start.

> 🎧 **CD 3, track 81** — *página 74, actividad 1*
>
> 1 Vi una película muy triste. Era una película romántica – la historia de un amor imposible entre un chico y una chica de dos familias que se odian.
> 2 Vi una película muy emocionante sobre la película de ciencia-ficción y de acción sobre la lucha entre el bien y el mal. Al final el emperador es derrotado, pero escapa para luchar otra vez...
> 3 Vi una comedia que trata de un espía que tiene una misión secreta. El planeta está en peligro de destrucción total y sólo él puede evitarla.
> 4 Es una película romántica y de misterio. Trata sobre unos vampiros que estudian en un instituto y que se reúnen en un bosque por las noches cuando sale la luna llena...
> 5 Es una película que relata un viaje a África en busca de civilizaciones perdidas en el desierto.

Answers: **1** d; **2** e; **3** a; **4** c; **5** b

AT 3.4 **2 Read the text and underline these words in Spanish.**
This will help students complete Activity 3.

Answers: vi; era; se enamoró de; novio; robó; descubrió

AT 3.4–5 **3 Now translate the whole description into English.**
Students' answers from Activity 2 should help them with this activity.

Answer:
I saw a romantic science-fiction film. It was a comedy. An astronaut fell in love with a student. The student's boyfriend was a vampire and he stole a nuclear bomb. The astronaut solved the problem when he discovered a new planet.

Página 75 4B.4 Repaso
- Use with Students' Book, pages 142–143

1 Traffic light the questions: Green = I can answer it. Orange = I understand the question. Red = I need to revise this.
This will give students an idea of what they need to focus on and revise.

AT 1.4 **2 Listen. Which question is each person answering?**

> 🎧 **CD 3, track 82** — *página 75, actividad 2*
>
> 1 En mis ratos libres, me gusta escuchar música, ir a la piscina a nadar y jugar al tenis en el parque con mis amigos.
> 2 Vi una película que se titula 'Monsty' y es una comedia. Trató de un monstruo que quiere jugar, pero los niños no le dejan jugar con ellos.
> 3 Tengo el pelo largo y negro. Tengo los ojos verdes y soy bastante alto.
> 4 En las vacaciones, normalmente voy a la costa, tomo el sol o juego en la playa.
> 5 Con mis amigos, prefiero hablar por teléfono. No utilizo mucho el internet.
> 6 Todos los días, me levanto a las siete, luego me ducho y desayuno.

Answers:
1 Bi; **2** Diii; **3** Aiii; **4** Cii; **5** Di; **6** Bii

AT 2.4 **3 Interview yourself in Spanish using the questions above.**
Students can use the listening text for support, especially for questions that they highlighted as red.

Página 76 4B.5 En mi opinión...
- Use with Students' Book, pages 144–145

AT 1.2 **1 Listen and follow the sentences on the grid. Sensible (S) or nonsense (N)?**

> 🎧 **CD 3, track 83** — *página 75, actividad 1*
>
> 1 Prefiero hacer los deberes porque es educativo.
> 2 Me gusta comer los deberes porque es divertido.
> 3 Prefiero leer la radio porque es emocionante.

Answers: **1** S; **2** N; **3** N

La vida tecno 4B

AT 4.2 **2 Roll a dice and write out the sentence you make. Sensible or nonsense?**
Students roll the die four times and use the numbers to make a sentence from the grid. They write it down and state whether it is sensible or nonsense.

AT 2.2–3 **3 How many sensible sentences can you say in one minute using the grid?**
This would work well as a class competition. Students work individually or in groups to write down as many sensible sentences as thay can in a given time. The student/group with the most sensible sentences wins.

Página 77   4B.6A Labolengua
- Use with Students' Book, pages 146–147

1 Think like a Spanish person. Complete the grids.
Students who finish this quickly can make up similar grids for different people, i.e. 'you', 'us', or for a different verb, e.g. *me encantar*.

Answers: They please me; He/She likes it; It pleased me

2 Decide which grid to use as a model for these sentences. Then translate them into Spanish.

Answers:
a Me gusta ver la televisión. b No me gusta la música.
c Le gusta ver la televisión. d Le gusta hablar por teléfono.
e Me gustan las películas. f Me gustó la película.

Página 78   4B.6B Técnica
- Use with Students' Book, pages 146–147

1 Complete the grid.
Practice of verb endings and infinitives.

Answers:

Verb	Infinitive	Ending	Meaning
come	comer	present – he/she/it	he eats
bebí	beber	past – I	I drank
habla	hablar	present – he/she/it	he talks
jugué	jugar	past – I	I played
fuimos	ir	past – we	we went
escucho	escuchar	present – I	I listen

2 Find the infinitives of these verbs. Look up the meaning of the infinitives in your dictionary.
Practice of dictionary skills.

Answers:
salvamos – salvar – to save; secuestró – secuestrar – to kidnap; perdieron – perder – to lose; rescatan – rescatar – to rescue; se casan – casarse – to get married

3 Work out what the underlined verbs mean.
Further practice of dictionary skills. Students should be aware that they need to look up the infinitive to get the meaning but must remember to use the correct person when translating the verbs in context.

Answers:
helps; they look for; they travel; they complete; they are reunited

Higher Workbook

Página 72   4B.1 Los medios y la televisión
- Use with Students' Book, pages 136–137

AT 3.3–4 **1 Read the texts and write the correct name under each bar chart.**
Practice of time phrases and media vocabulary.

Answers:
a Ofelia; b David; c Felipe; e Ana

AT 4.4 **2 Write a similar text for the bar chart which is left.**
Students use the other texts for support, changing the details accordingly.

Suggested answer:
Veo la televisión todos los días, y juego a menudo a los videojuegos. A veces escucho la radio. No leo nunca una revista.

Página 73   4B.2 El cine y los libros
- Use with Students' Book, pages 138–139

AT 4.2 **1 Missing vowels! Write out these types of film in full.**
Practice of film vocabulary.

Answers:
a una película romántica; b una película de terror; c una película de ciencia-ficción; d una película de vaqueros; e una película de acción; f una película de misterio; g una película de guerra; h una comedia

4B La vida tecno

2 Talk about whether you like each type of film. [AT 2.2-3]
Students include opinion words and the names of specific films if they want to as examples. If they do, encourage them to try to find out what the Spanish name is.

3 Listen to Alvina and think of a film you would recommend she sees. [AT 1.3]
If students can't think of a specific film, they can just note down what she says she likes.

CD 4, track 55 — página 73, actividad 3

Pues, yo soy muy rara porque me gustan las películas románticas, pero no me gustan las comedias. ¿Sabes qué? Me encantan las películas de vaqueros, pero no me gustan las películas de acción.

Página 74   4B.3 ¿De qué trató? ¿Qué pasó?
- Use with Students' Book, pages 139–140

1 Read the film titles. Listen – who saw which film? [AT 1.4-5]
Students think about what type of film each title listed is likely to be before they start.

CD 4, track 56 — página 74, actividad 1

1 Vi una película muy triste. Era una película romántica – la historia de un amor imposible entre un chico y una chica de dos familias que se odian.
2 Vi una película muy emocionante. Es una película de ciencia-ficción y de acción sobre la lucha entre el bien y el mal. Al final el emperador es derrotado, pero escapa para luchar otra vez…
3 Vi una comedia que trata de un espía que tiene una misión secreta. El planeta está en peligro de destrucción total y sólo él puede evitarla.
4 Es una película romántica y de misterio. Trata sobre unos vampiros que estudian en un instituto y que se reúnen en un bosque por las noches cuando sale la luna llena…
5 Es una película que relata un viaje a África en busca de civilizaciones perdidas en el desierto.

Answers:
1 d; 2 e; 3 a; 4 c; 5 b

2 Translate into English. [AT 3.4-5]

Answer:
I saw a romantic science-fiction film. It was a comedy. An astronaut fell in love with a student. The student's boyfriend was a vampire and he stole a nuclear bomb. The astronaut solved the problem when he discovered a new planet.

Página 75   4B.4 Repaso
- Use with Students' Book, pages 141–142

1 Read through the questions. Listen. Which question is each person answering? [AT 1.4-5]

CD 4, track 57 — página 75, actividad 1

1 Me gusta escuchar música, ir a la piscina a nadar y jugar al tenis en el parque con mis amigos.
2 Se titula 'Monsty' y es una comedia. Trató de un monstruo que quiere jugar, pero los niños no le dejan jugar.
3 Tengo el pelo largo y negro. Tengo los ojos verdes y soy bastante con ellos.
4 Normalmente voy a la costa alto, tomo el sol o juego en la playa.
5 Prefiero hablar por teléfono. No utilizo mucho el internet.
6 Me levanto a las siete, luego me ducho y desayuno.

Answers:
1 Bi; 2 Diii; 3 Aiii; 4 Cii; 5 Di; 6 Bii

2 Interview yourself in Spanish using the questions above. [AT 2.4]

Página 76   4B.5 En mi opinión…
- Use with Students' Book, pages 143–144

1 Listen and follow the three sentences on the grid. Sensible (S) or nonsense (N)? [AT 1.2]

CD 4, track 58 — página 76, actividad 1

1 Prefiero hacer los deberes porque es educativo.
2 Me gusta comer los deberes porque es divertido.
3 Prefiero leer la radio porque es emocionante.

Answers: 1 S; 2 N; 3 N

2 Roll a dice and write out the sentence you make. Sensible or nonsense? [AT 4.2]
Students roll the die and use the numbers to make a sentence from the grid. They write it down and state whether it is sensible or nonsense.

3 Use the grid to keep talking for one minute. [AT 2.3-4]
How many sensible sentences can students say in one minute? A few confident volunteers could have a competition. Each one in turn speaks to the class for one minute using the grid for support. The student who produces the most sensible sentences is the winner.

La vida tecno 4B

Página 77   4B.6A Labolengua
- Use with Students' Book, pages 145–146

1 Think like a Spanish person. Complete the grids.
Students who finish this quickly can make up similar grids for a different verb, e.g. *me encantar*.

Answers:
I like them, They please me; He/She likes it, It pleases him/her; Does it please you?, Te gusta; It pleases us, Nos gusta; It pleased me

2 Translate into Spanish.
Students use the grids from Activity 1 for support.

Answers:
a *Me gusta ver la televisión.* **b** *¿Te gusta la música?* **c** *Le gusta ver la televisión.* **d** *Le gusta hablar por teléfono.* **e** *Me gustan las películas.* **f** *Me gustó la película.* **g** *Nos gusta ir al cine.*

Página 78   4B.6B Técnica
- Use with Students' Book, pages 145–146

1 Complete the grid.
Practice of verb endings and infinitives.

Answers:

Verb	Infinitive	Ending	Meaning
come	comer	present – he/she/it	he eats
bebí	beber	past – I	I drank
habla	hablar	present – he/she/it	he talks
jugué	jugar	past – I	I played
fuimos	ir	past – we	we went
escucho	escuchar	present – I	I listen

2 Use a dictionary to find the meaning of these verbs.
Practice of dictionary skills. Students will need to remember to look up the verb in the infinitive form to find the meaning and must then look at the ending to see which person it is in.

Answers:
salvamos – we save; *secuestró* – he/she kidnapped; *perdieron* – they lost; *rescatan* – they rescue; *se casan* – they get married

3 Work out what the underlined verbs mean. Then translate the whole text into English.
Further practice of dictionary skills. Students look up the infinitive to get the meaning but must remember to use the correct person when translating the verbs in context.

Answers:
helps; they look for; they travel; they complete; they are reunited

In the film a magic cat helps a girl. They look for her parents. They travel across the world. They complete a series of dangerous adventures. They are reunited with her parents.